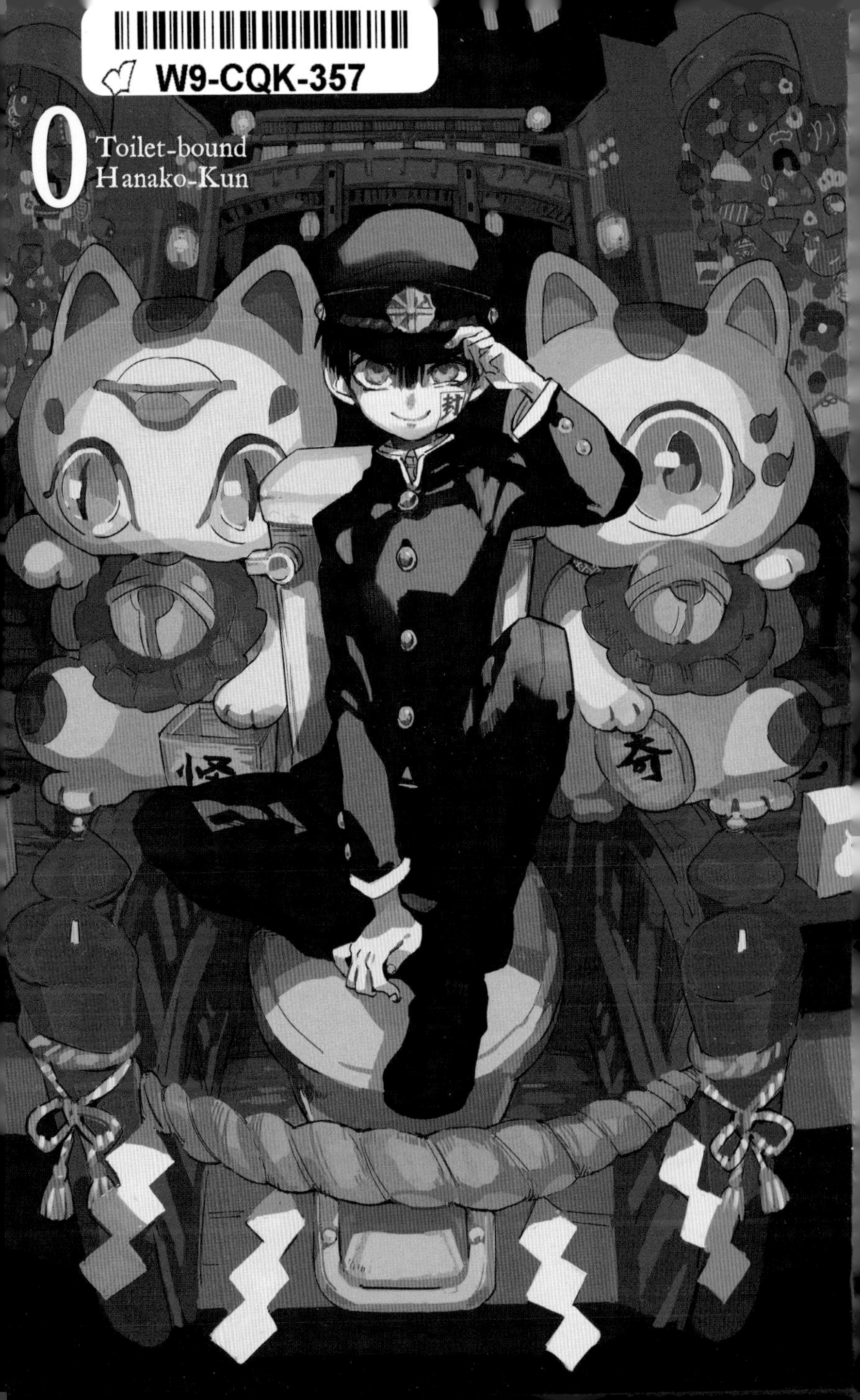
W9-CQK-357
0 Toilet-bound Hanako-Kun
封
怪
奇

Contents

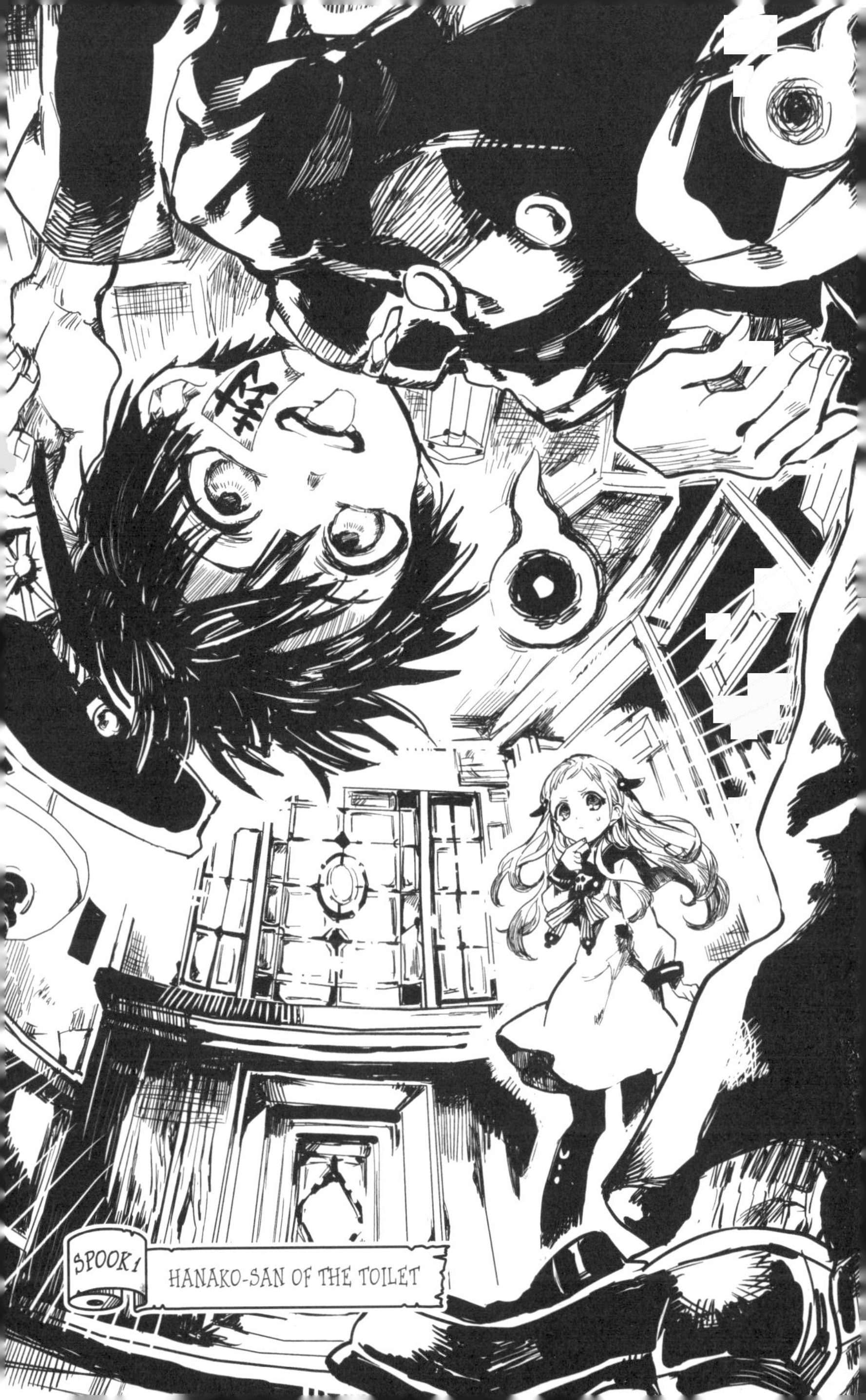
SPOOK 1
HANAKO-SAN OF THE TOILET

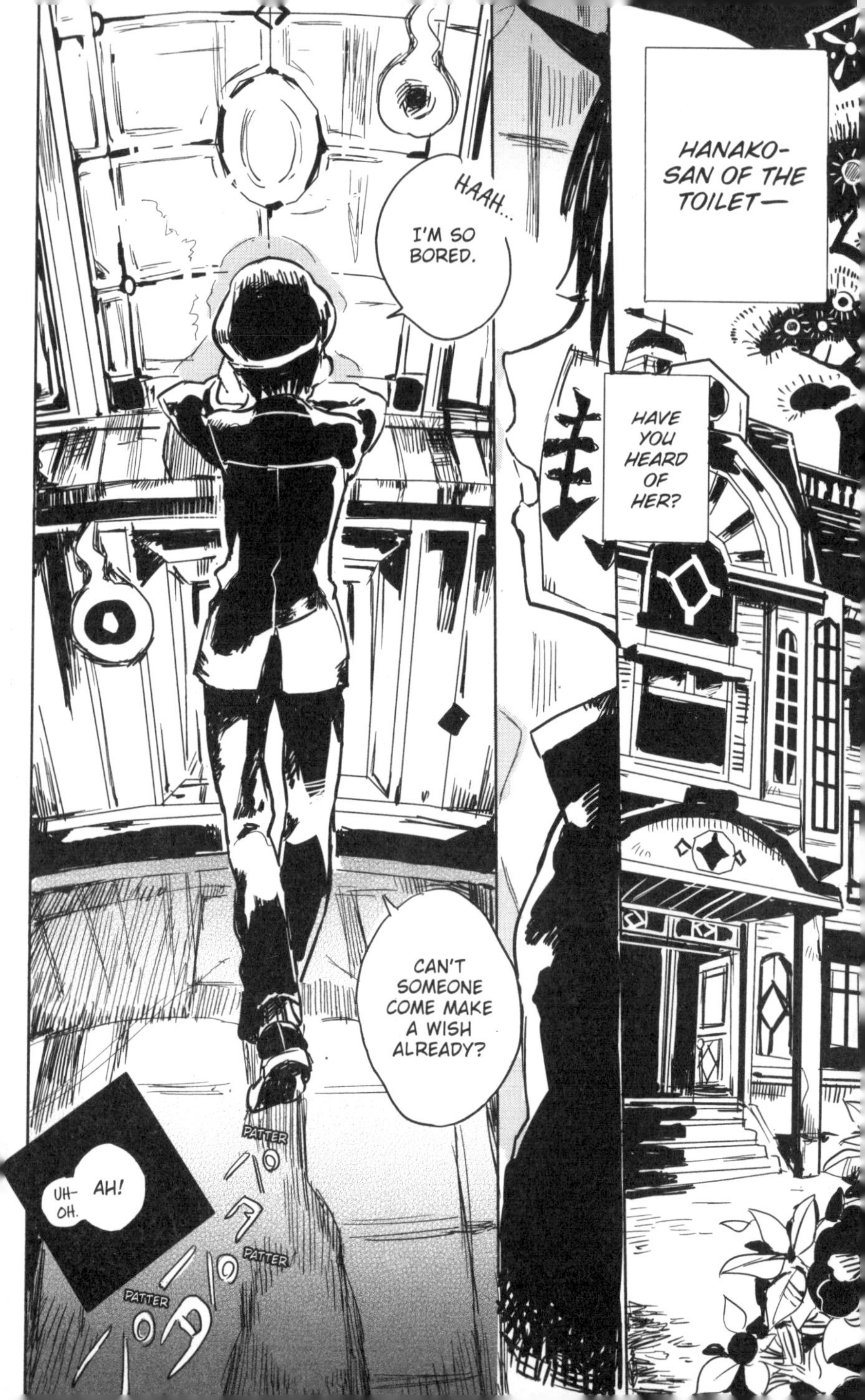
HANAKO-SAN OF THE TOILET—
HAVE YOU HEARD OF HER?
HAAH...
I'M SO BORED.
CAN'T SOMEONE COME MAKE A WISH ALREADY?
PATTER
PATTER
PATTER
AH!
UH-OH.

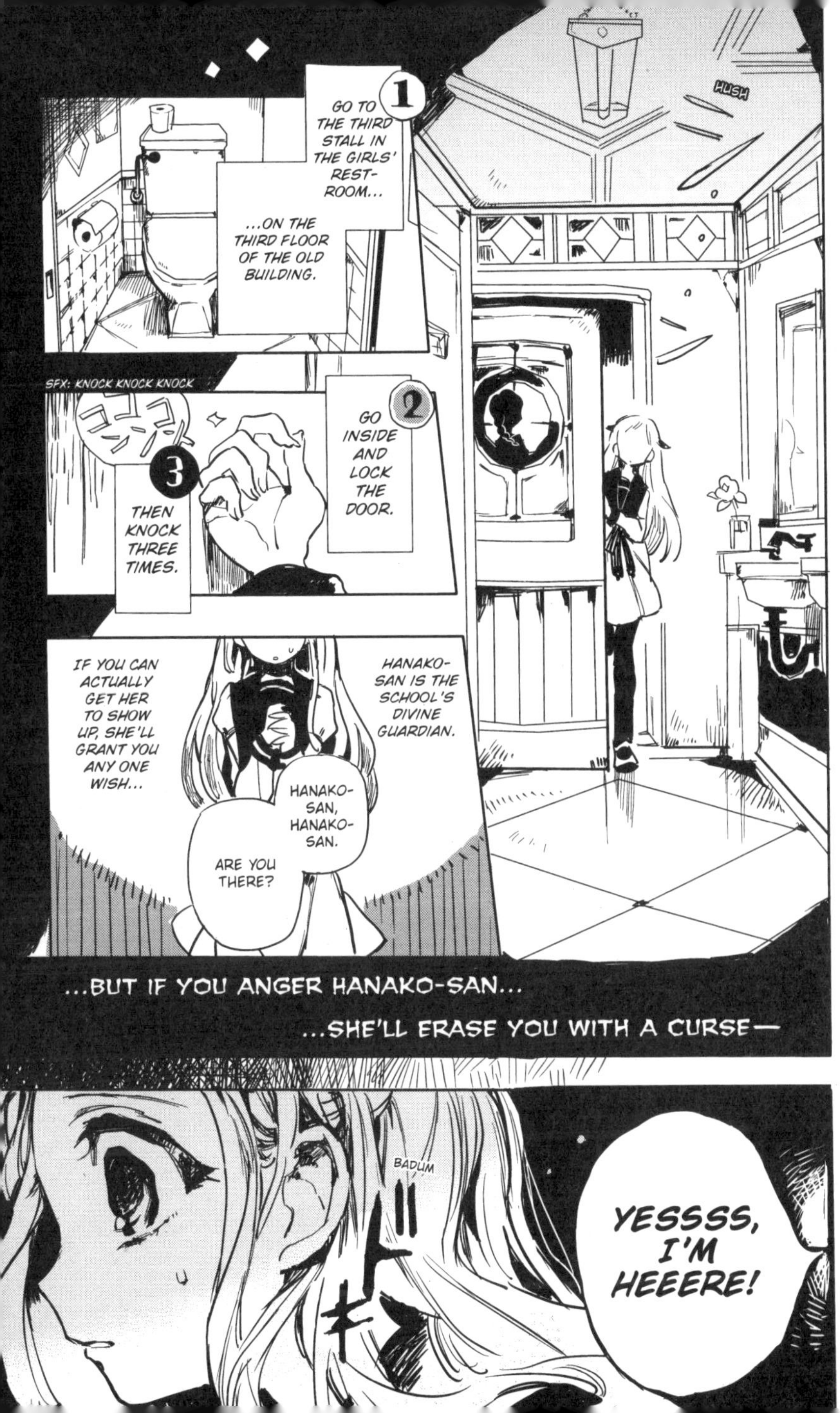
HUSH
GO TO THE THIRD STALL IN THE GIRLS' REST-ROOM...
...ON THE THIRD FLOOR OF THE OLD BUILDING.
GO INSIDE AND LOCK THE DOOR.
SFX: KNOCK KNOCK KNOCK
THEN KNOCK THREE TIMES.
HANAKO-SAN IS THE SCHOOL'S DIVINE GUARDIAN.
IF YOU CAN ACTUALLY GET HER TO SHOW UP, SHE'LL GRANT YOU ANY ONE WISH...
HANAKO-SAN, HANAKO-SAN.
ARE YOU THERE?
...BUT IF YOU ANGER HANAKO-SAN...
...SHE'LL ERASE YOU WITH A CURSE—
YESSSS, I'M HEEEERE!
BADUM

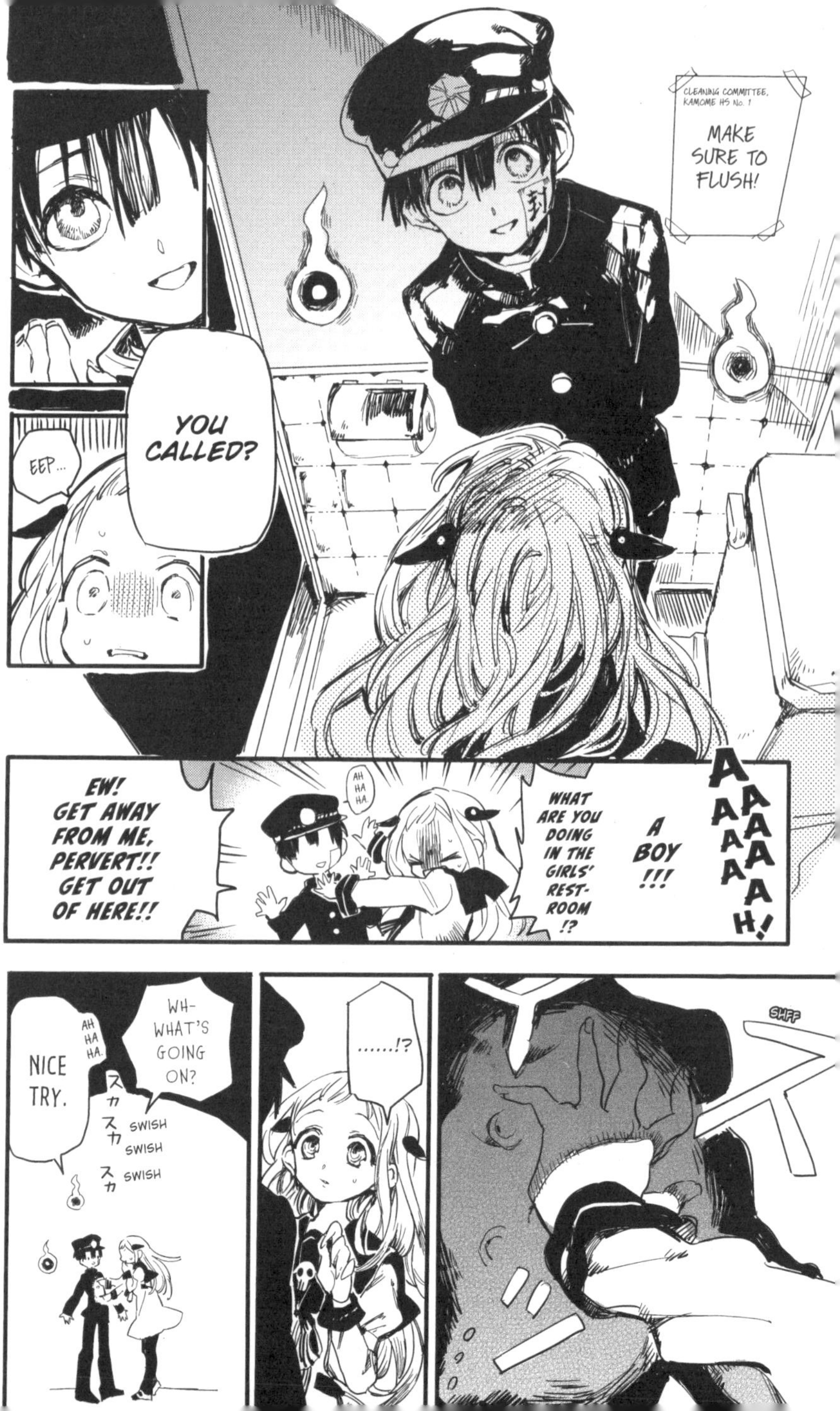

CLEANING COMMITTEE, KAMOME HS No. 1
MAKE SURE TO FLUSH!
YOU CALLED?
EEP...
AAAAAAAAH!
A BOY!!!
WHAT ARE YOU DOING IN THE GIRLS' REST-ROOM!?
AH HA HA.
EW! GET AWAY FROM ME, PERVERT!! GET OUT OF HERE!!
SHFF
......!?
WH-WHAT'S GOING ON?
AH HA HA.
NICE TRY.
スカ SWISH
スカ SWISH
スカ SWISH

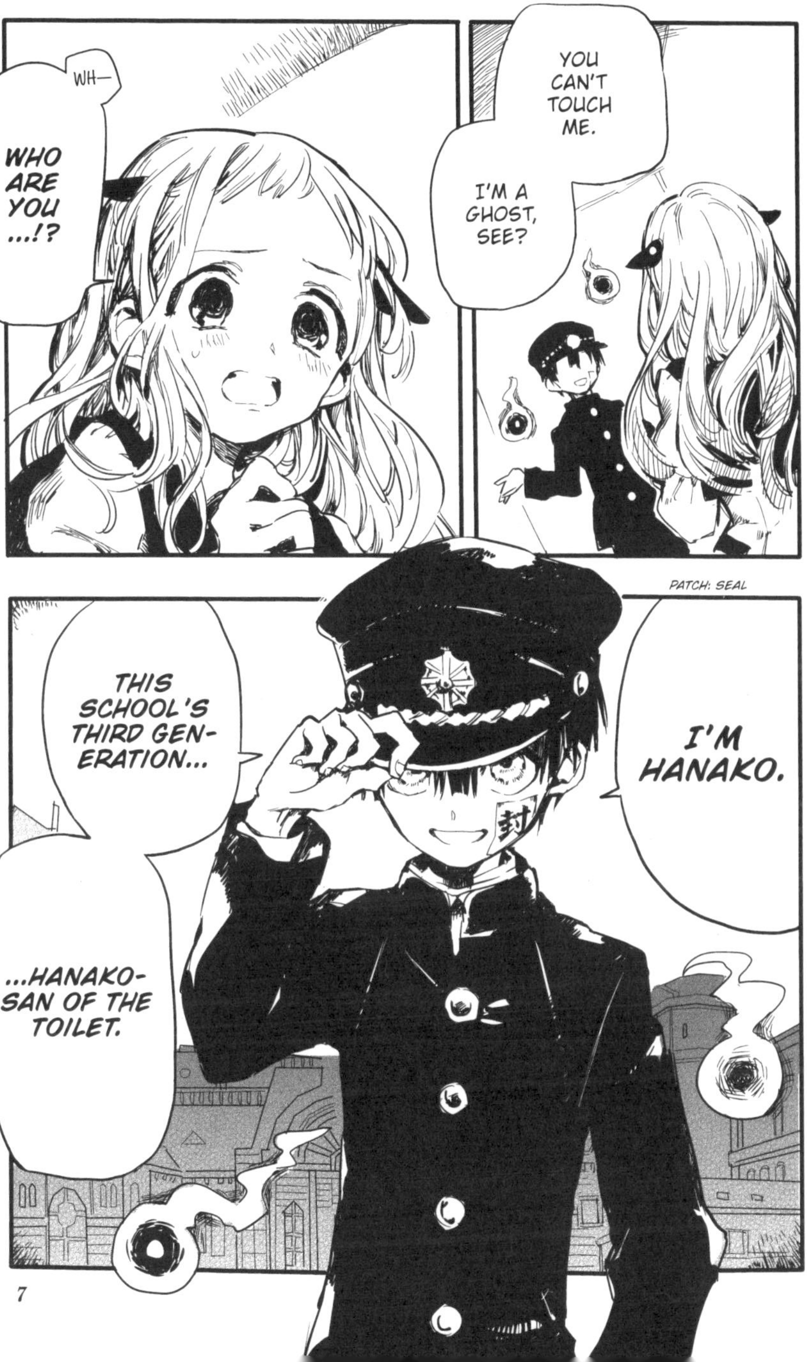
YOU CAN'T TOUCH ME.
I'M A GHOST, SEE?
WH—
WHO ARE YOU ...!?
PATCH: SEAL
I'M HANAKO.
THIS SCHOOL'S THIRD GENERATION...
...HANAKO-SAN OF THE TOILET.

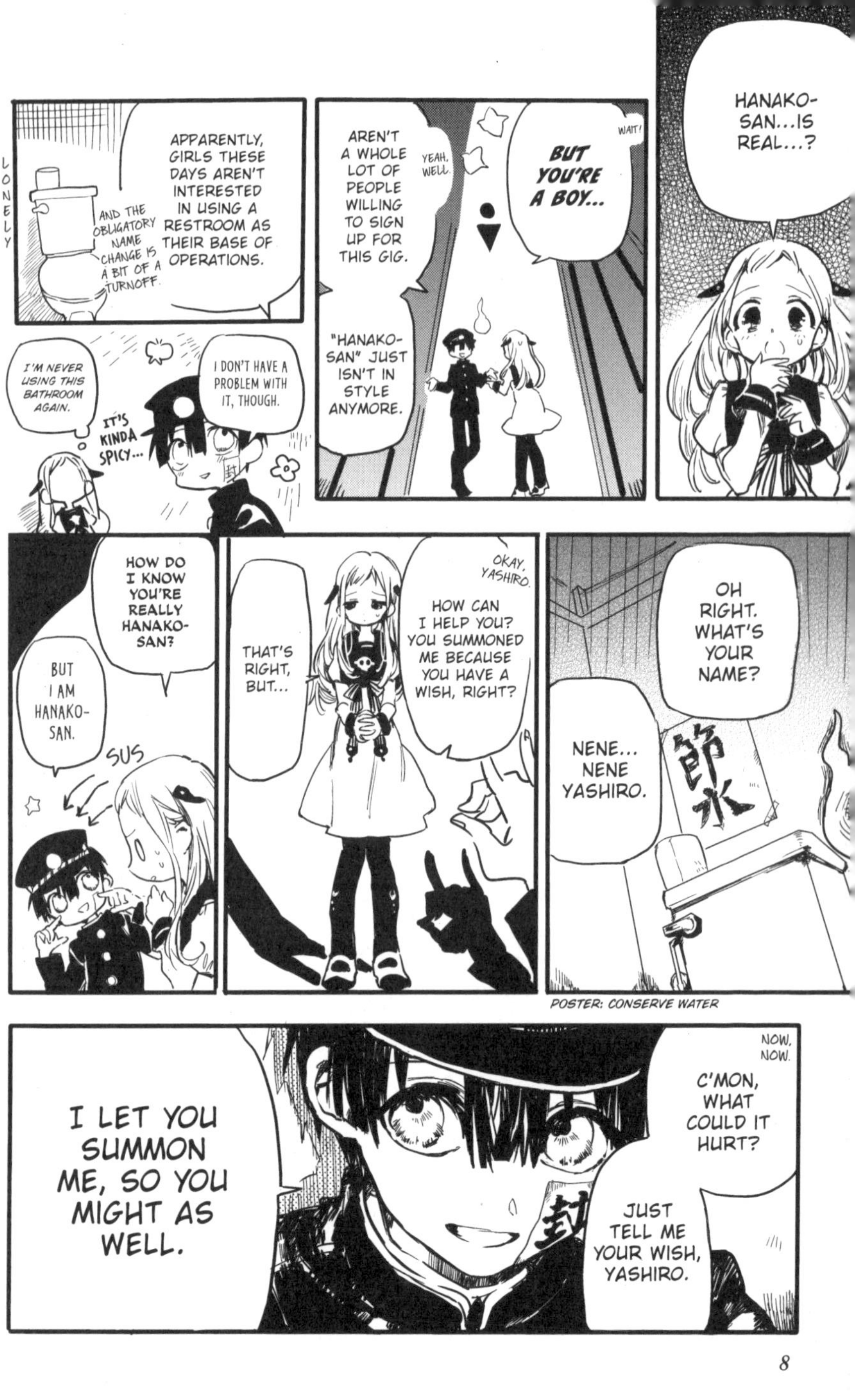
HANAKO-SAN...IS REAL...?
WAIT!
BUT YOU'RE A BOY...
YEAH, WELL.
AREN'T A WHOLE LOT OF PEOPLE WILLING TO SIGN UP FOR THIS GIG.
"HANAKO-SAN" JUST ISN'T IN STYLE ANYMORE.
APPARENTLY, GIRLS THESE DAYS AREN'T INTERESTED IN USING A RESTROOM AS THEIR BASE OF OPERATIONS.
AND THE OBLIGATORY NAME CHANGE IS A BIT OF A TURNOFF.
LONELY
I DON'T HAVE A PROBLEM WITH IT, THOUGH.
IT'S KINDA SPICY...
I'M NEVER USING THIS BATHROOM AGAIN.
OH RIGHT. WHAT'S YOUR NAME?
NENE... NENE YASHIRO.
POSTER: CONSERVE WATER
OKAY, YASHIRO.
HOW CAN I HELP YOU? YOU SUMMONED ME BECAUSE YOU HAVE A WISH, RIGHT?
THAT'S RIGHT, BUT...
HOW DO I KNOW YOU'RE REALLY HANAKO-SAN?
BUT I AM HANAKO-SAN.
SUS
NOW, NOW.
C'MON, WHAT COULD IT HURT?
JUST TELL ME YOUR WISH, YASHIRO.
I LET YOU SUMMON ME, SO YOU MIGHT AS WELL.

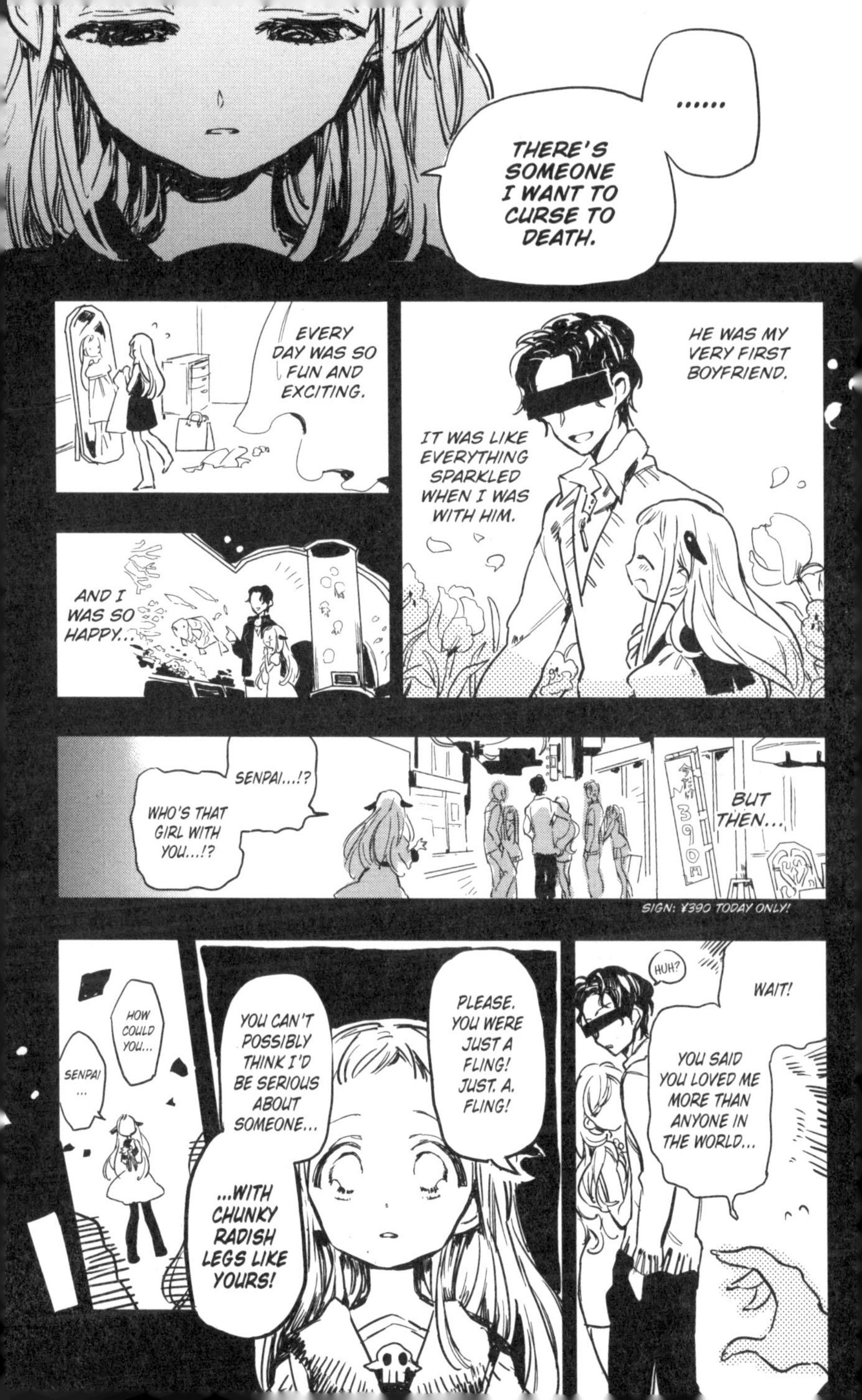
......
THERE'S SOMEONE I WANT TO CURSE TO DEATH.
HE WAS MY VERY FIRST BOYFRIEND.
IT WAS LIKE EVERYTHING SPARKLED WHEN I WAS WITH HIM.
EVERY DAY WAS SO FUN AND EXCITING.
AND I WAS SO HAPPY...
BUT THEN...
SENPAI...!?
WHO'S THAT GIRL WITH YOU...!?
SIGN: ¥390 TODAY ONLY!
HUH?
WAIT!
YOU SAID YOU LOVED ME MORE THAN ANYONE IN THE WORLD...
PLEASE. YOU WERE JUST A FLING! JUST. A. FLING!
YOU CAN'T POSSIBLY THINK I'D BE SERIOUS ABOUT SOMEONE...
...WITH CHUNKY RADISH LEGS LIKE YOURS!
HOW COULD YOU...
SENPAI...

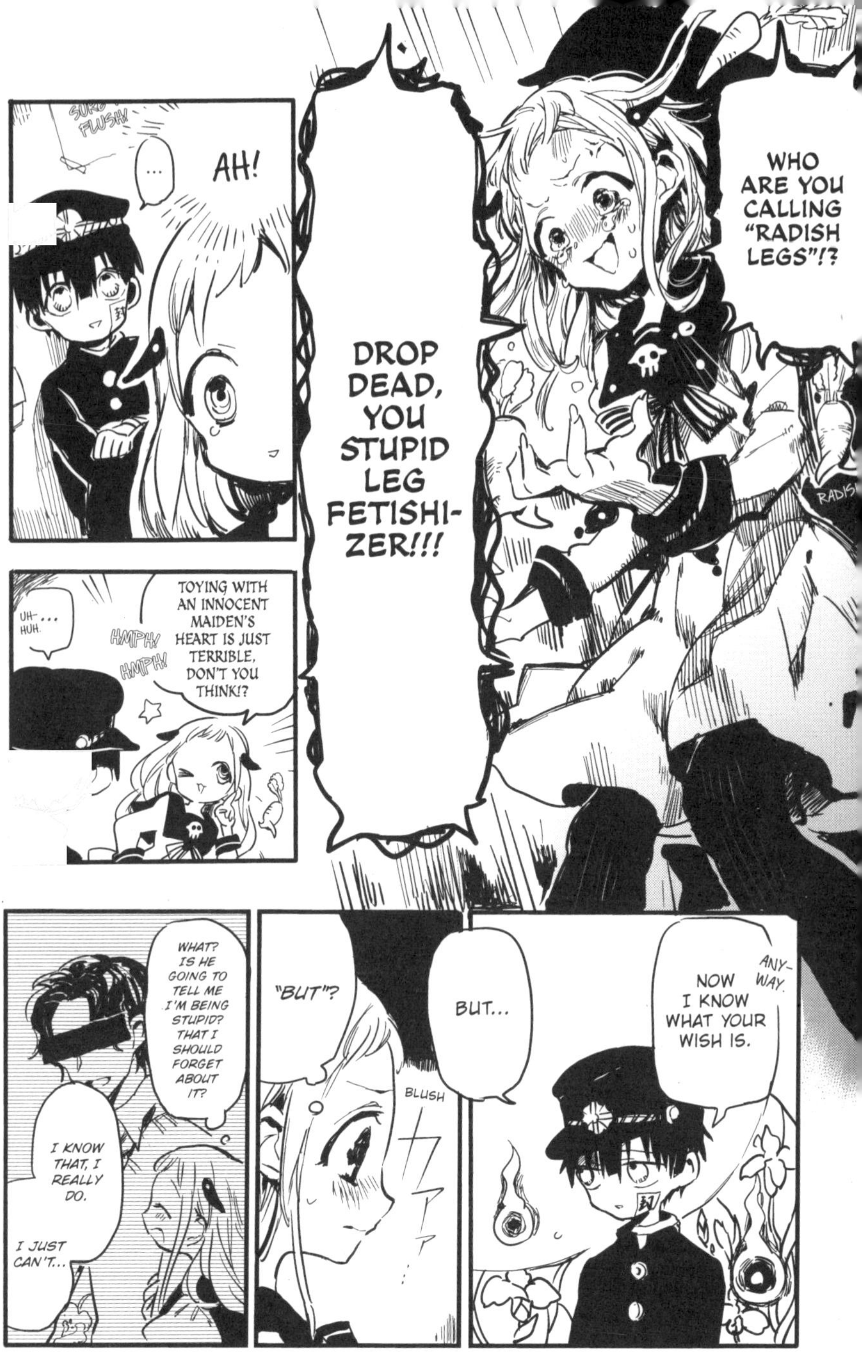
WHO ARE YOU CALLING "RADISH LEGS"!?
DROP DEAD, YOU STUPID LEG FETISHIZER!!!
FLUSH!
...
AH!
TOYING WITH AN INNOCENT MAIDEN'S HEART IS JUST TERRIBLE, DON'T YOU THINK!?
HMPH! HMPH!
UH-HUH...
ANYWAY.
NOW I KNOW WHAT YOUR WISH IS.
BUT...
"BUT"?
BLUSH
WHAT? IS HE GOING TO TELL ME I'M BEING STUPID? THAT I SHOULD FORGET ABOUT IT?
I KNOW THAT, I REALLY DO.
I JUST CAN'T...

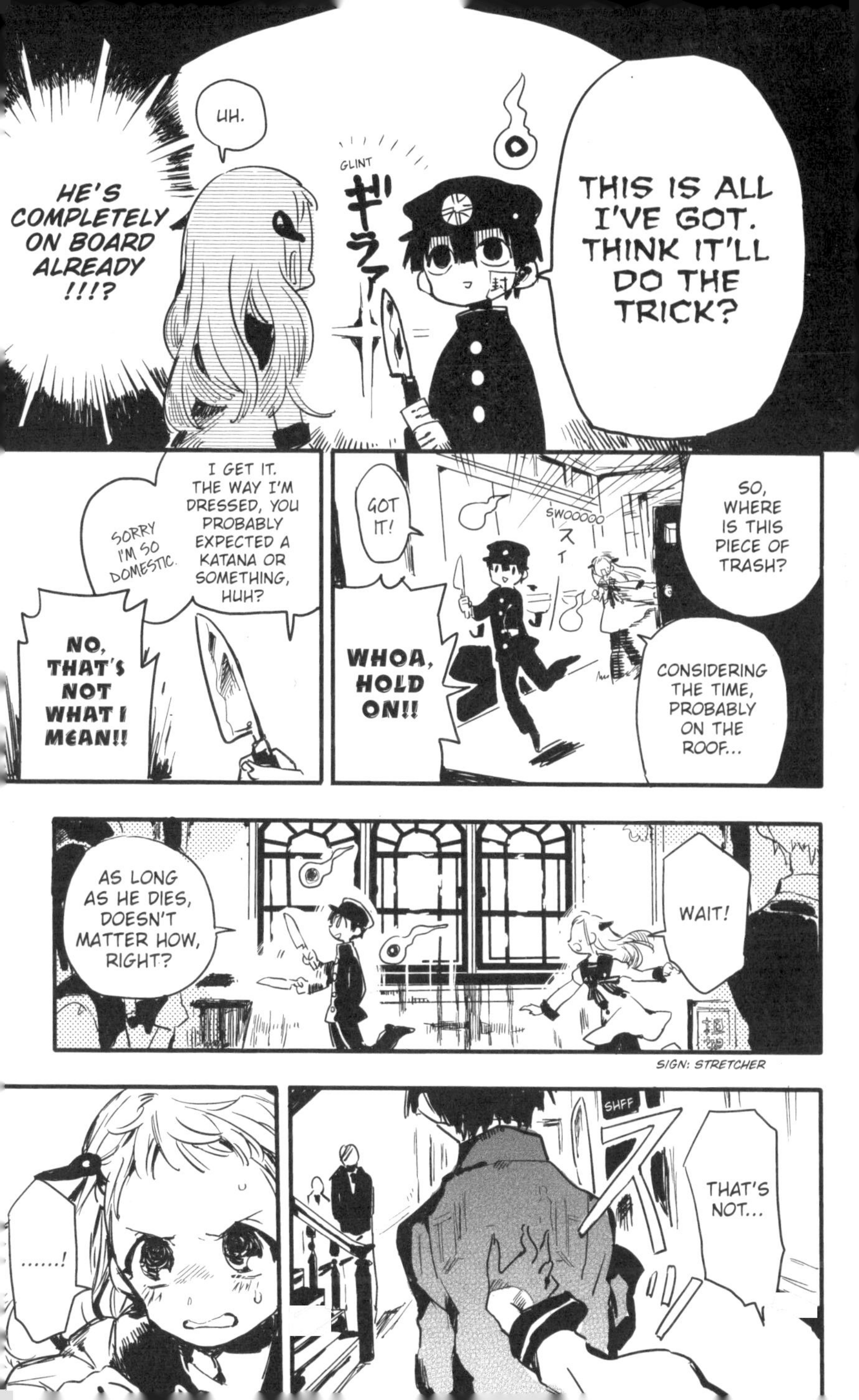
THIS IS ALL I'VE GOT. THINK IT'LL DO THE TRICK?
GLINT
UH.
HE'S COMPLETELY ON BOARD ALREADY!!!?
SO, WHERE IS THIS PIECE OF TRASH?
CONSIDERING THE TIME, PROBABLY ON THE ROOF...
SWOOOOO
GOT IT!
WHOA, HOLD ON!!
I GET IT. THE WAY I'M DRESSED, YOU PROBABLY EXPECTED A KATANA OR SOMETHING, HUH?
SORRY I'M SO DOMESTIC.
NO, THAT'S NOT WHAT I MEAN!!
WAIT!
AS LONG AS HE DIES, DOESN'T MATTER HOW, RIGHT?
SIGN: STRETCHER
SHFF
THAT'S NOT...
......!

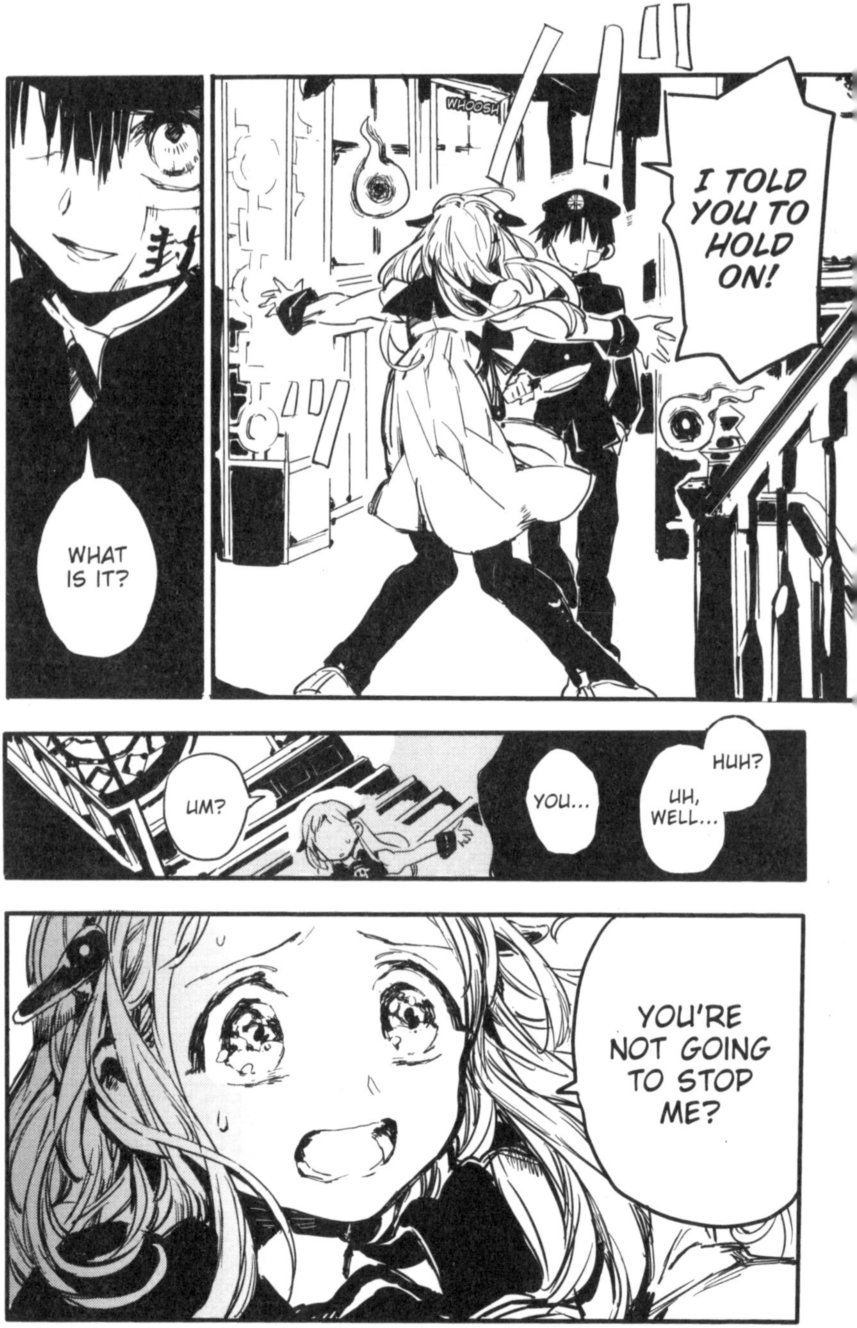
WHOOSH
I TOLD YOU TO HOLD ON!
WHAT IS IT?
HUH?
UH, WELL...
YOU...
UM?
YOU'RE NOT GOING TO STOP ME?

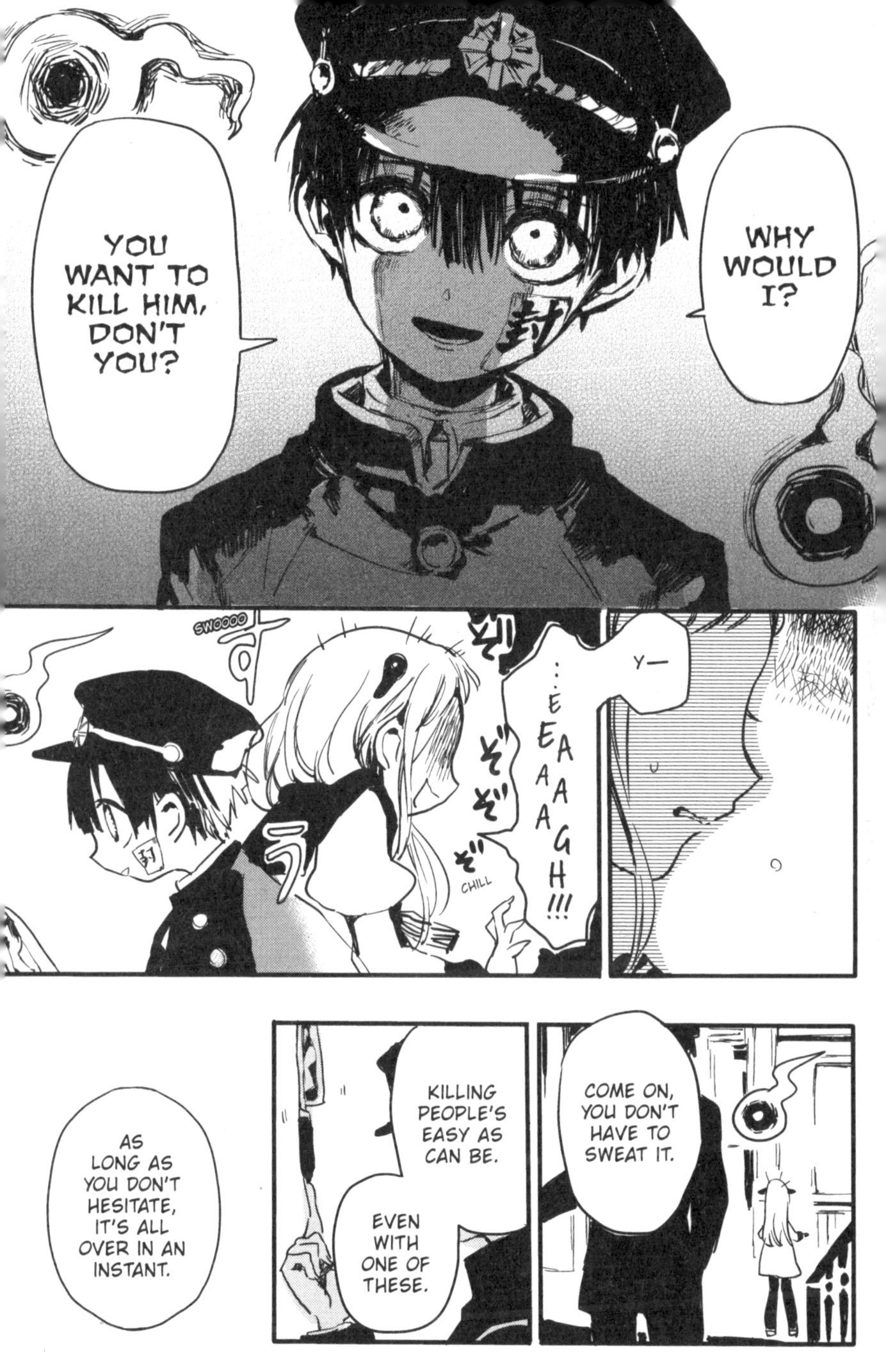
WHY WOULD I?
YOU WANT TO KILL HIM, DON'T YOU?
Y—
...EEAAAAAGH!!!
CHILL
SWOOOO
COME ON, YOU DON'T HAVE TO SWEAT IT.
KILLING PEOPLE'S EASY AS CAN BE.
EVEN WITH ONE OF THESE.
AS LONG AS YOU DON'T HESITATE, IT'S ALL OVER IN AN INSTANT.

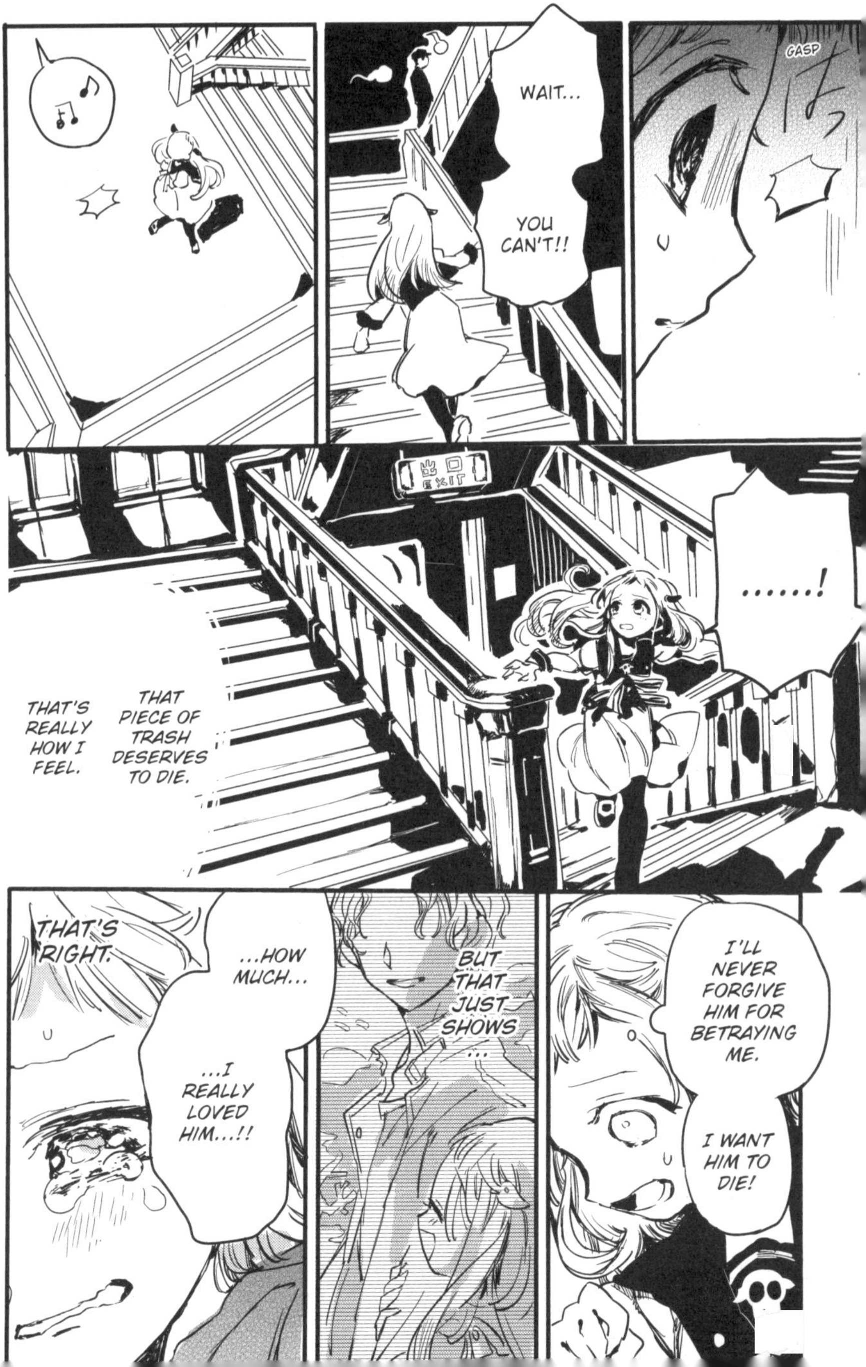
GASP
WAIT...
YOU CAN'T!!
......!
THAT PIECE OF TRASH DESERVES TO DIE.
THAT'S REALLY HOW I FEEL.
出口 EXIT
I'LL NEVER FORGIVE HIM FOR BETRAYING ME.
I WANT HIM TO DIE!
BUT THAT JUST SHOWS...
...HOW MUCH...
...I REALLY LOVED HIM...!!
THAT'S RIGHT.

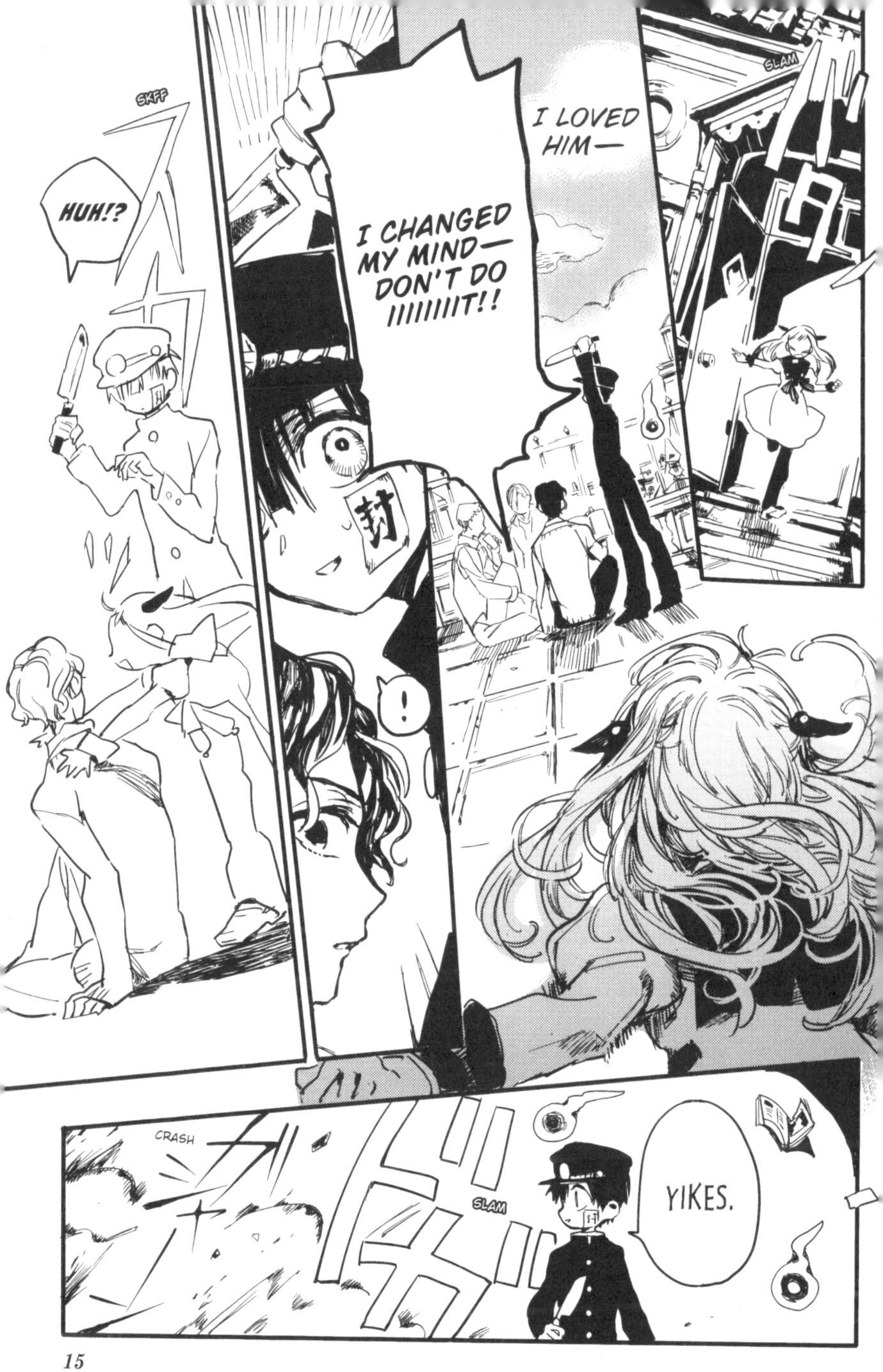
SLAM
I LOVED HIM—
I CHANGED MY MIND— DON'T DO IIIIIIIIT!!
!
SKFF
HUH!?
YIKES.
SLAM
CRASH

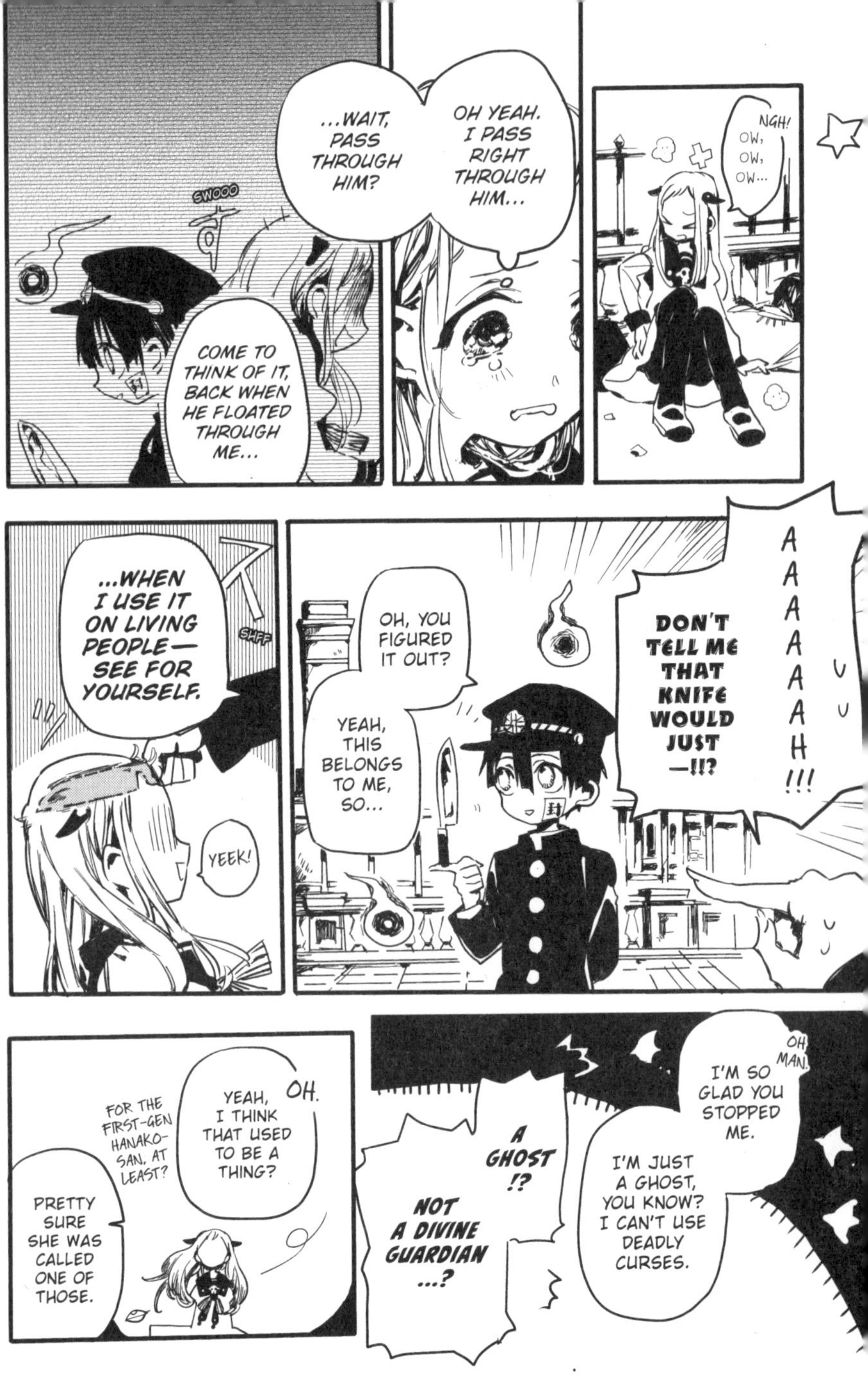
NGH! OW, OW, OW...
OH YEAH. I PASS RIGHT THROUGH HIM...
...WAIT, PASS THROUGH HIM?
SWOOO
COME TO THINK OF IT, BACK WHEN HE FLOATED THROUGH ME...
AAAAAAAH!!!
DON'T TELL ME THAT KNIFE WOULD JUST—!!?
OH, YOU FIGURED IT OUT?
YEAH, THIS BELONGS TO ME, SO...
SHFF
...WHEN I USE IT ON LIVING PEOPLE—SEE FOR YOURSELF.
YEEK!
OH MAN.
I'M SO GLAD YOU STOPPED ME.
I'M JUST A GHOST, YOU KNOW? I CAN'T USE DEADLY CURSES.
A GHOST!?
NOT A DIVINE GUARDIAN...?
OH.
YEAH, I THINK THAT USED TO BE A THING?
FOR THE FIRST-GEN HANAKO-SAN, AT LEAST?
PRETTY SURE SHE WAS CALLED ONE OF THOSE.

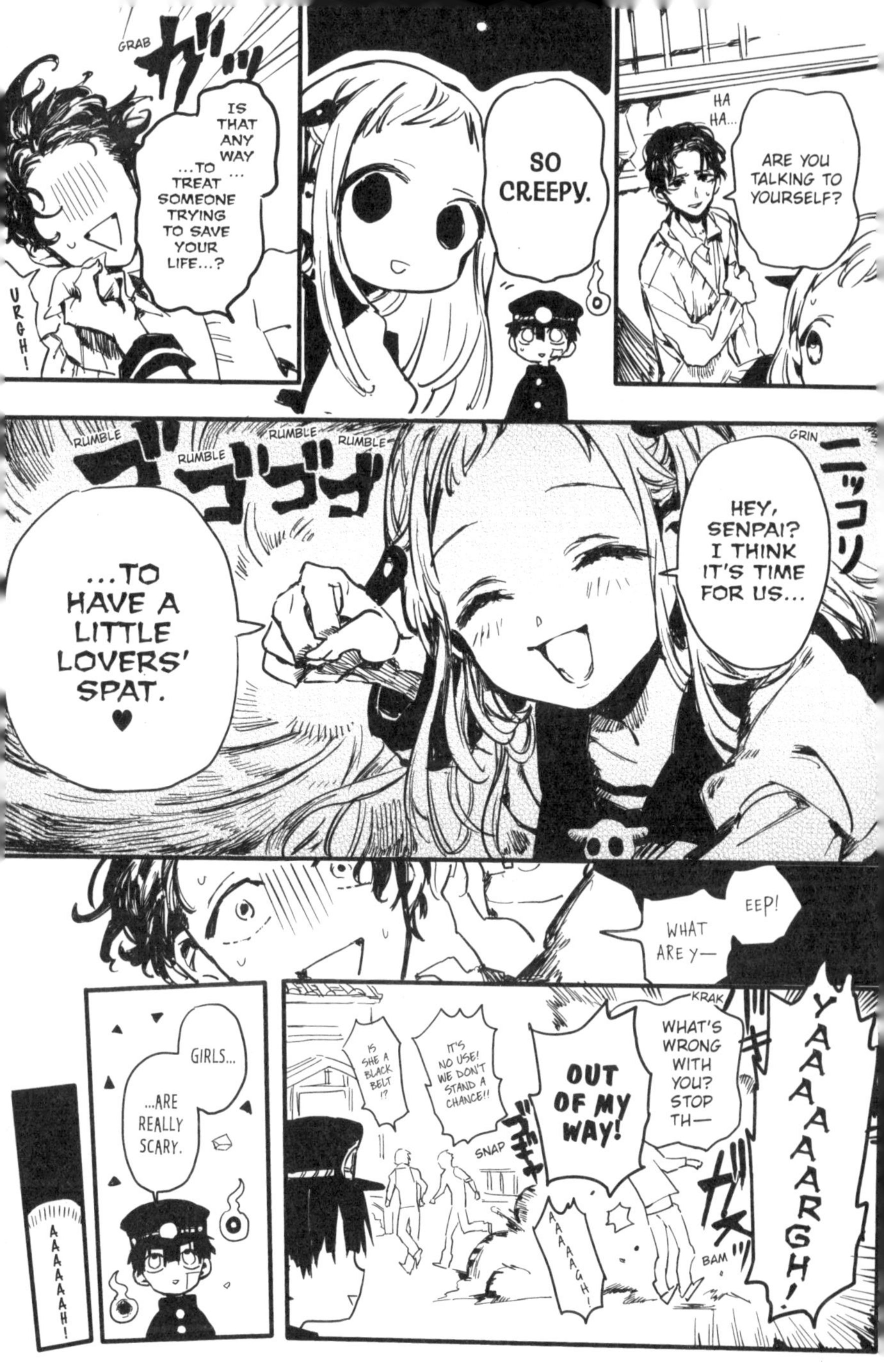
HA HA...
ARE YOU TALKING TO YOURSELF?
SO CREEPY.
GRAB
IS THAT ANY WAY... ...TO TREAT SOMEONE TRYING TO SAVE YOUR LIFE...?
URGH!
GRIN
HEY, SENPAI? I THINK IT'S TIME FOR US...
RUMBLE
RUMBLE
RUMBLE
RUMBLE
...TO HAVE A LITTLE LOVERS' SPAT. ♥
EEP!
WHAT ARE Y—
YAAAAAARGH!
KRAK
WHAT'S WRONG WITH YOU? STOP TH—
BAM
OUT OF MY WAY!
AAAAAGH!
SNAP
IT'S NO USE! WE DON'T STAND A CHANCE!!
IS SHE A BLACK BELT!?
GIRLS...
...ARE REALLY SCARY.
AAAAAAAH!

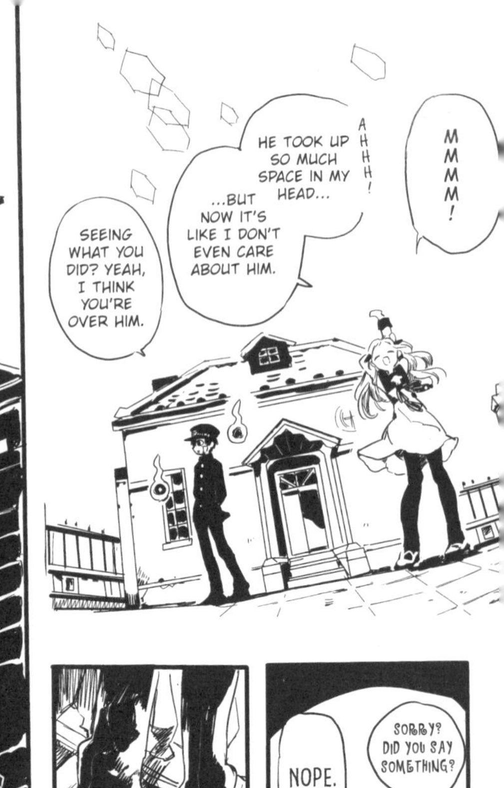
MMMM!
AHHHH!
HE TOOK UP SO MUCH SPACE IN MY HEAD...
...BUT NOW IT'S LIKE I DON'T EVEN CARE ABOUT HIM.
SEEING WHAT YOU DID? YEAH, I THINK YOU'RE OVER HIM.
SORRY? DID YOU SAY SOMETHING?
NOPE.
TWIRL
ANYWAY.
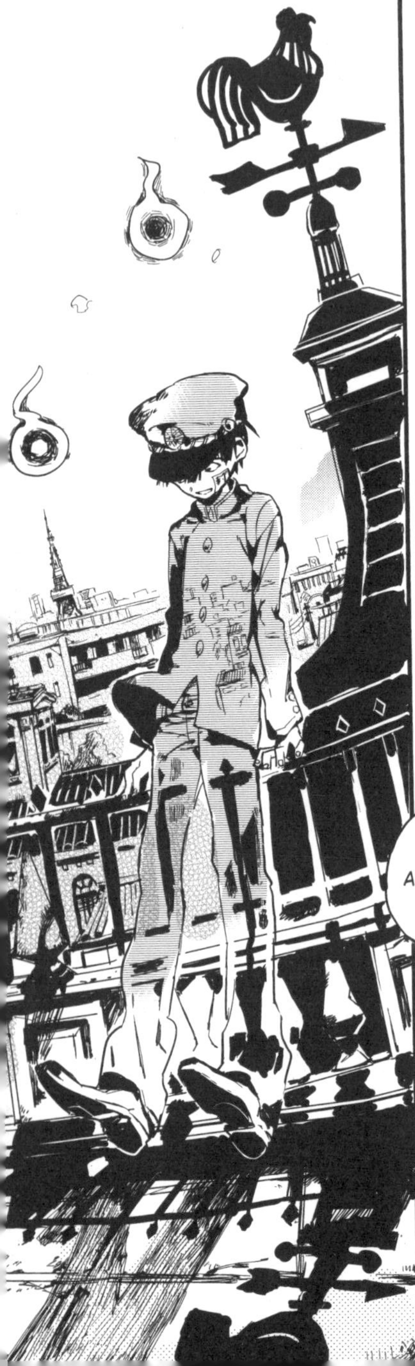

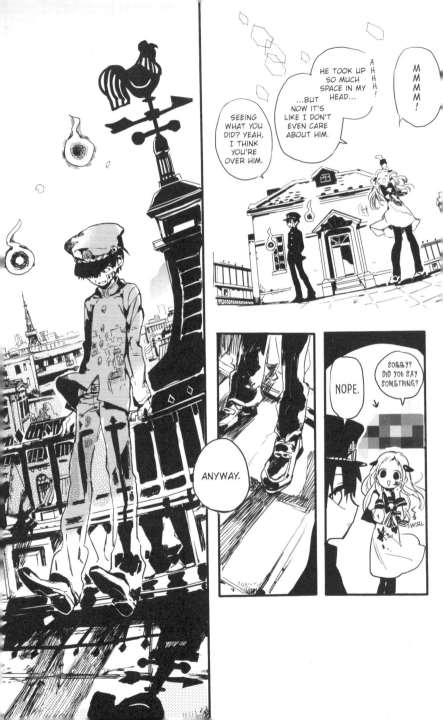

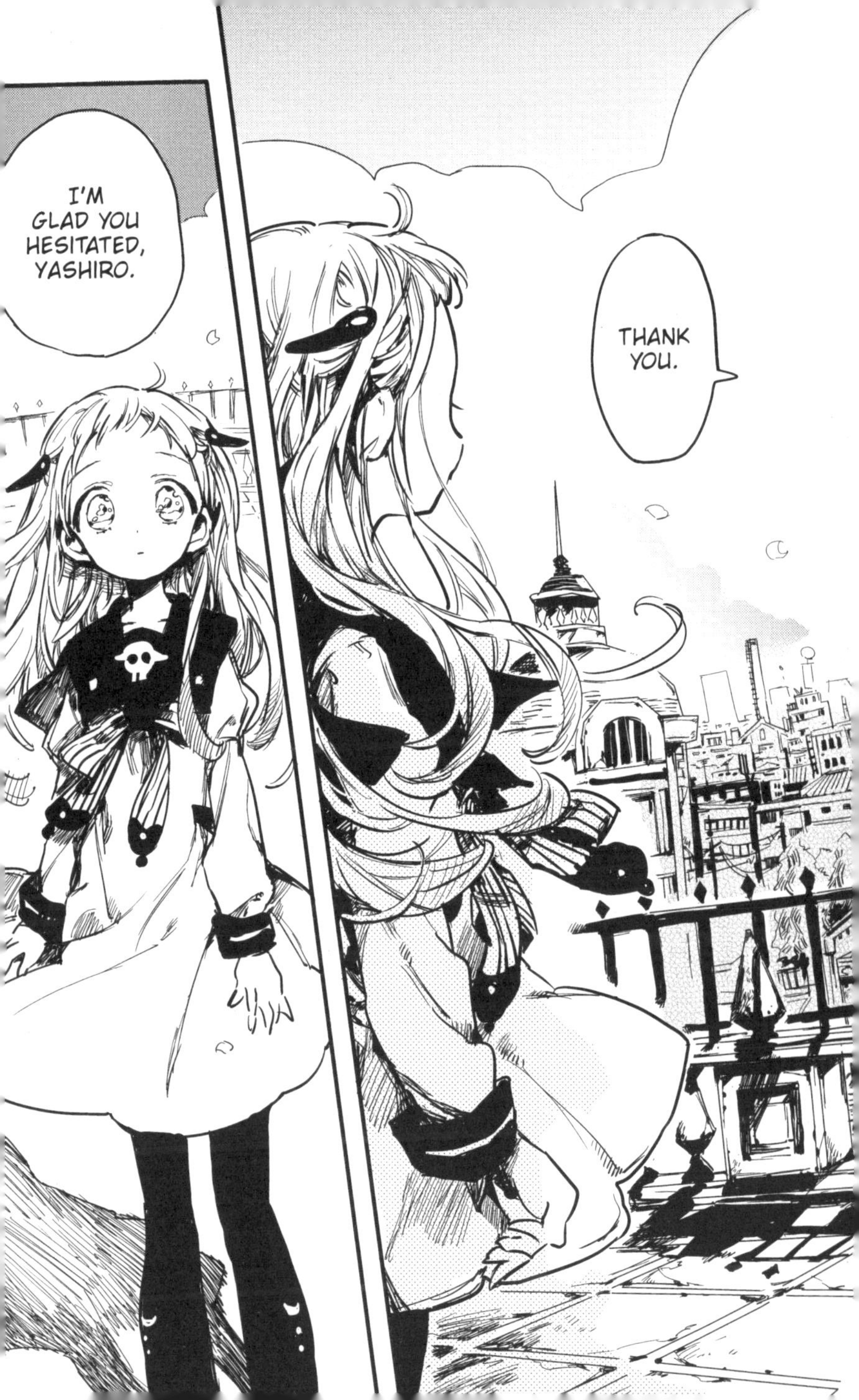
THANK YOU.
I'M GLAD YOU HESITATED, YASHIRO.

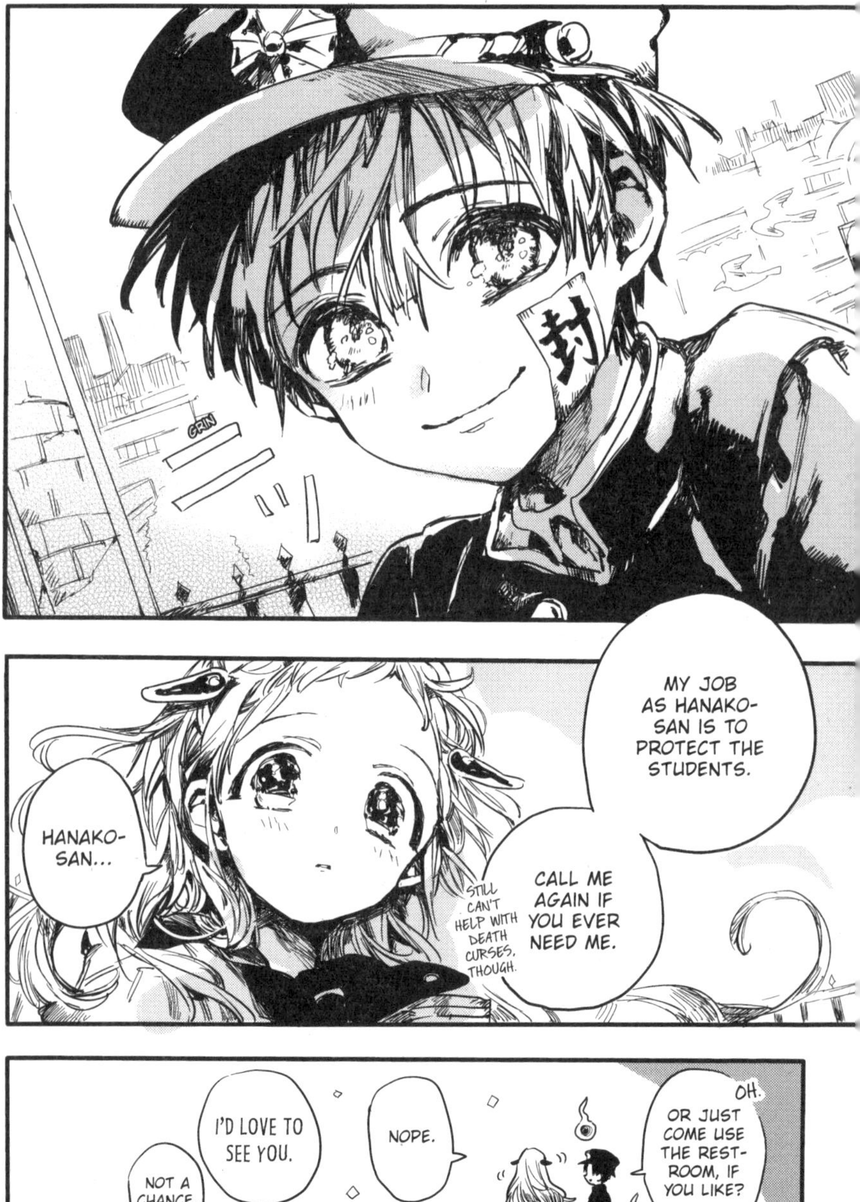
GRIN
MY JOB AS HANAKO-SAN IS TO PROTECT THE STUDENTS.
CALL ME AGAIN IF YOU EVER NEED ME.
STILL CAN'T HELP WITH DEATH CURSES, THOUGH.
HANAKO-SAN...
OH.
OR JUST COME USE THE REST-ROOM, IF YOU LIKE?
NOPE.
I'D LOVE TO SEE YOU.
NOT A CHANCE.

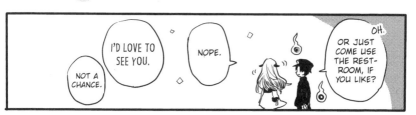

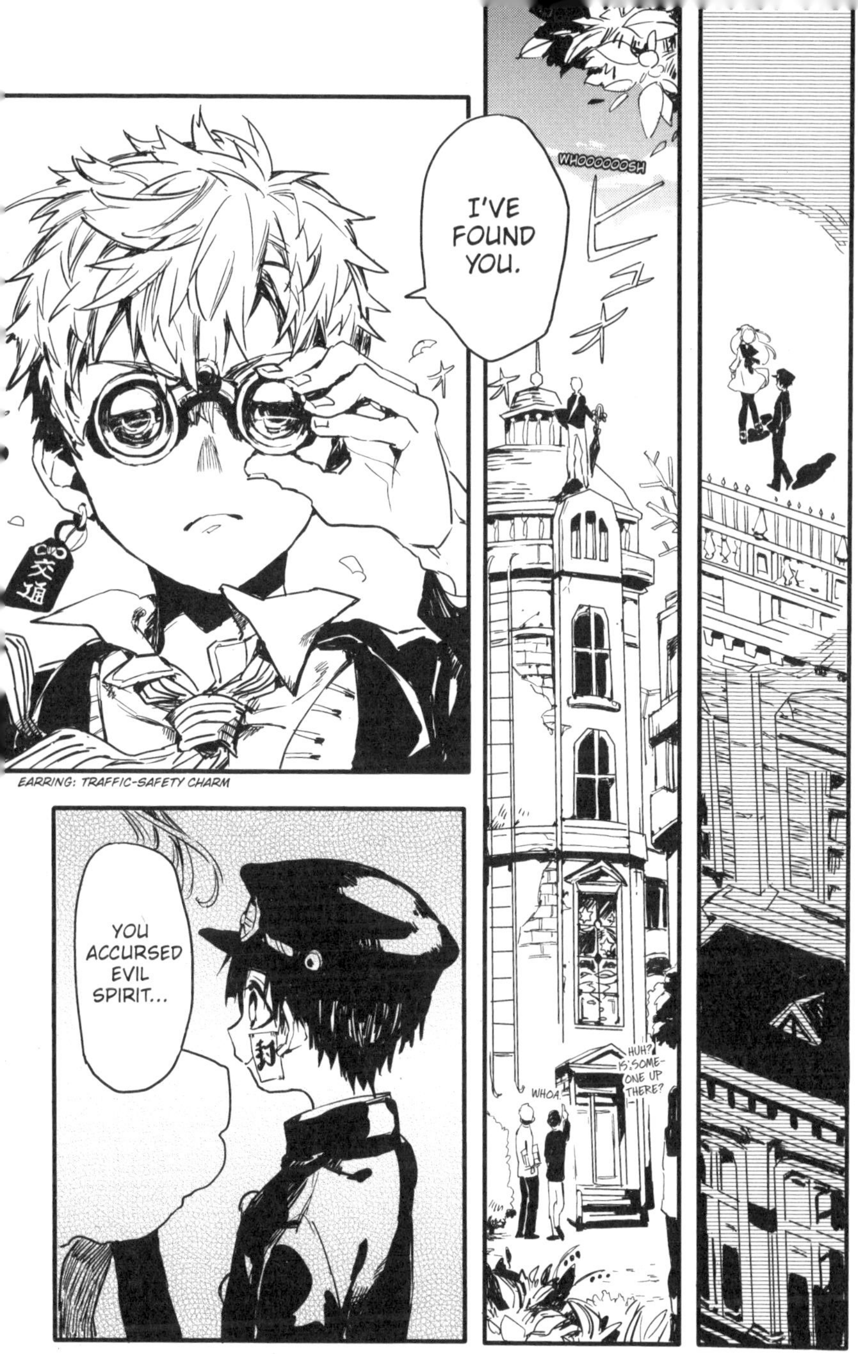
WHOOOOOOSH
HUH? IS SOME-ONE UP THERE?
WHOA.
I'VE FOUND YOU.
EARRING: TRAFFIC-SAFETY CHARM
YOU ACCURSED EVIL SPIRIT...

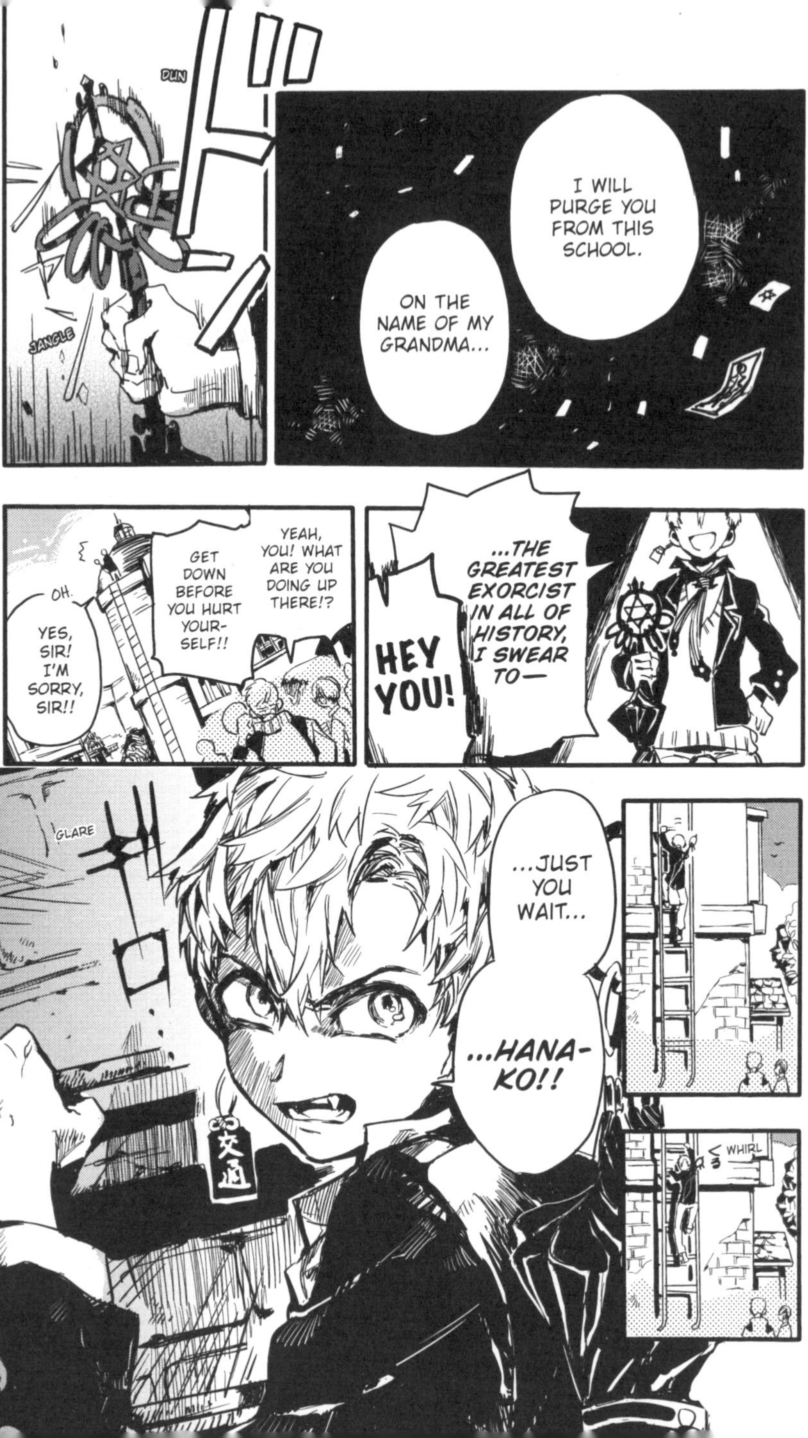
I WILL PURGE YOU FROM THIS SCHOOL.
ON THE NAME OF MY GRANDMA...
DUN
JANGLE
...THE GREATEST EXORCIST IN ALL OF HISTORY, I SWEAR TO—
HEY YOU!
YEAH, YOU! WHAT ARE YOU DOING UP THERE!?
GET DOWN BEFORE YOU HURT YOUR-SELF!!
OH.
YES, SIR! I'M SORRY, SIR!!
WHIRL
...JUST YOU WAIT...
...HANA-KO!!
GLARE

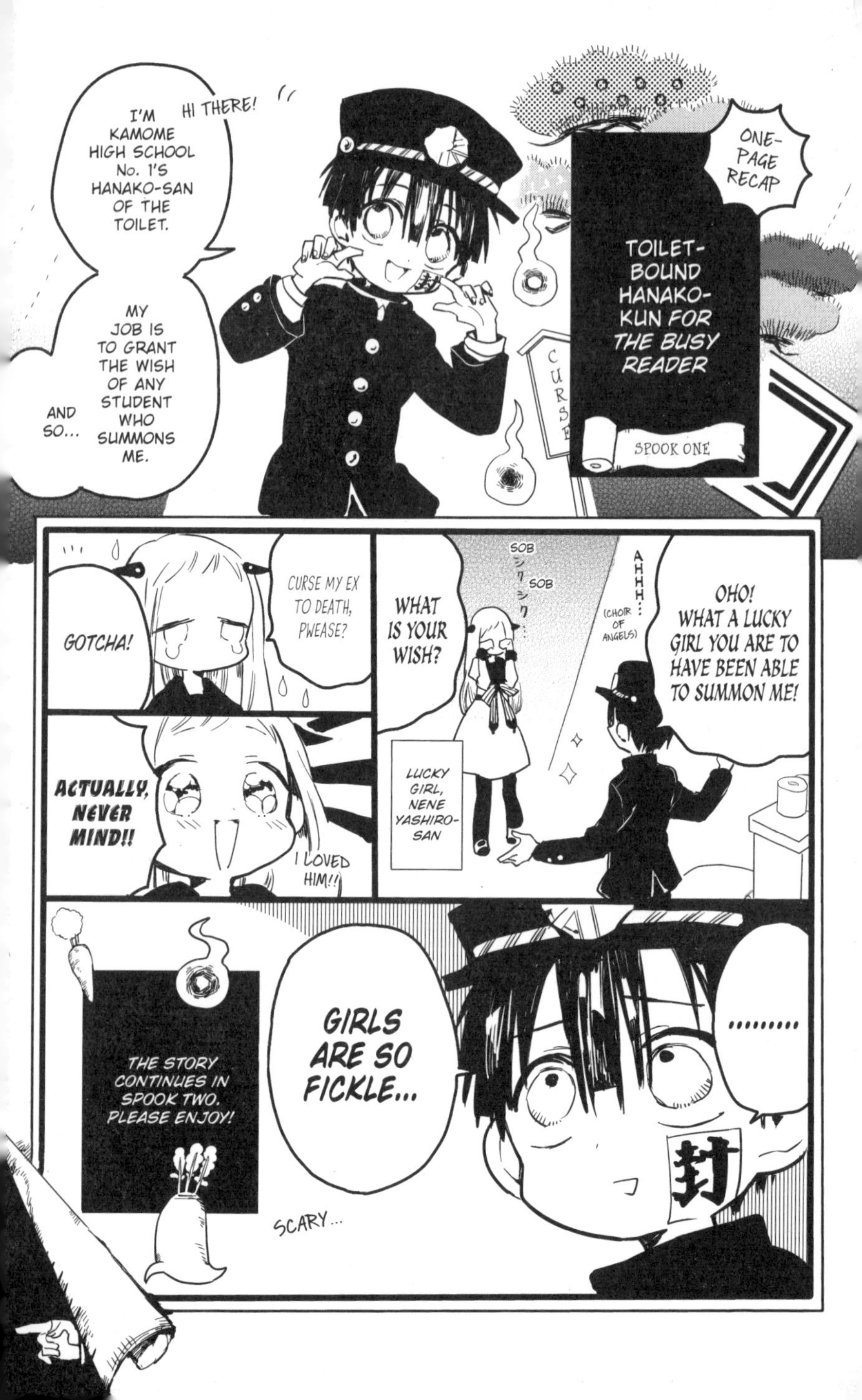
ONE-PAGE RECAP
TOILET-BOUND HANAKO-KUN FOR THE BUSY READER
SPOOK ONE
CURSE
HI THERE!
I'M KAMOME HIGH SCHOOL No. 1'S HANAKO-SAN OF THE TOILET.
MY JOB IS TO GRANT THE WISH OF ANY STUDENT WHO SUMMONS ME.
AND SO...
AHHH...
(CHOIR OF ANGELS)
OHO! WHAT A LUCKY GIRL YOU ARE TO HAVE BEEN ABLE TO SUMMON ME!
SOB
シクシク
SOB
WHAT IS YOUR WISH?
LUCKY GIRL, NENE YASHIRO-SAN
CURSE MY EX TO DEATH, PWEASE?
GOTCHA!
ACTUALLY, NEVER MIND!!
I LOVED HIM!!
....
GIRLS ARE SO FICKLE...
SCARY...
THE STORY CONTINUES IN SPOOK TWO. PLEASE ENJOY!

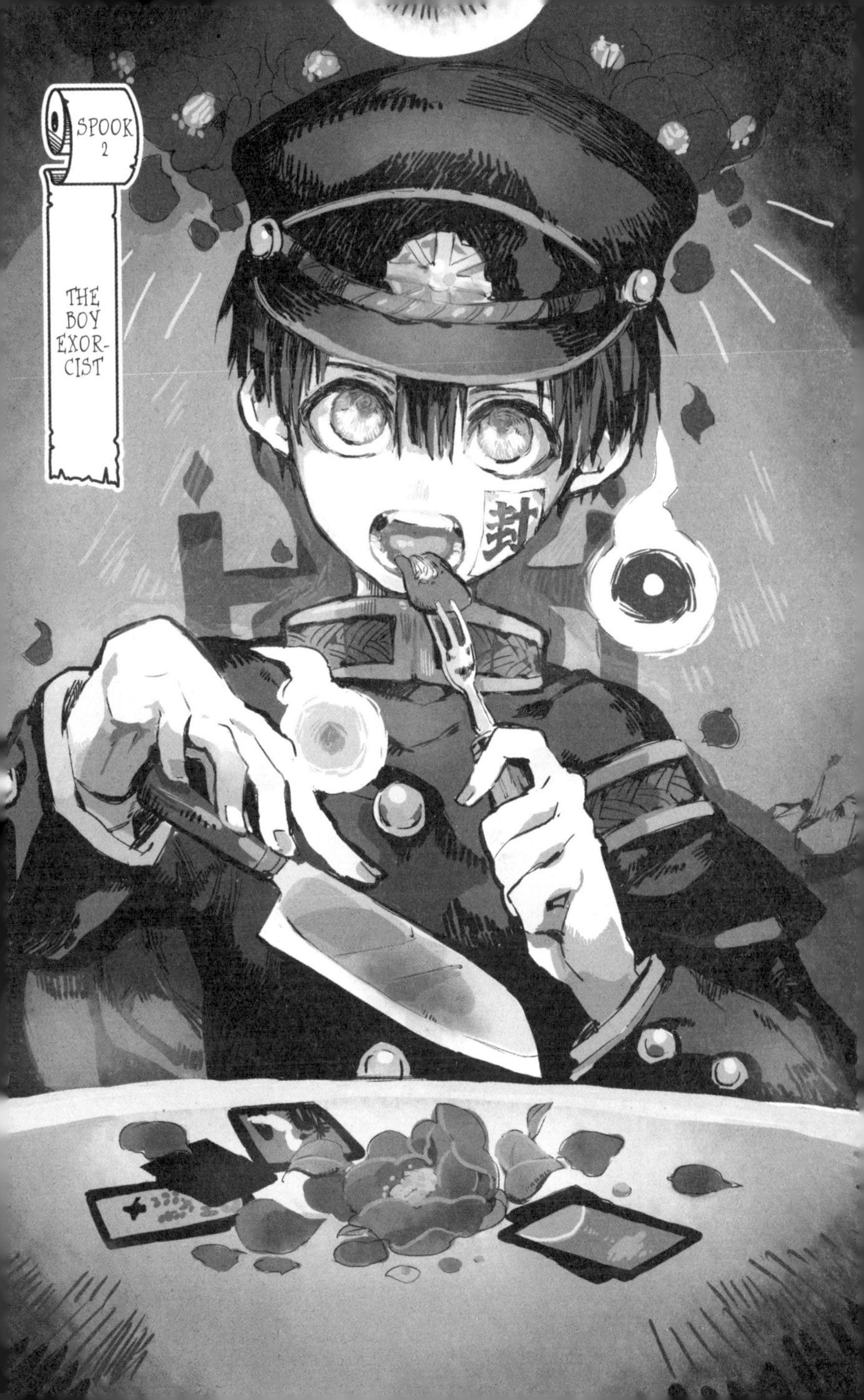
SPOOK 2
THE BOY EXOR-CIST
封

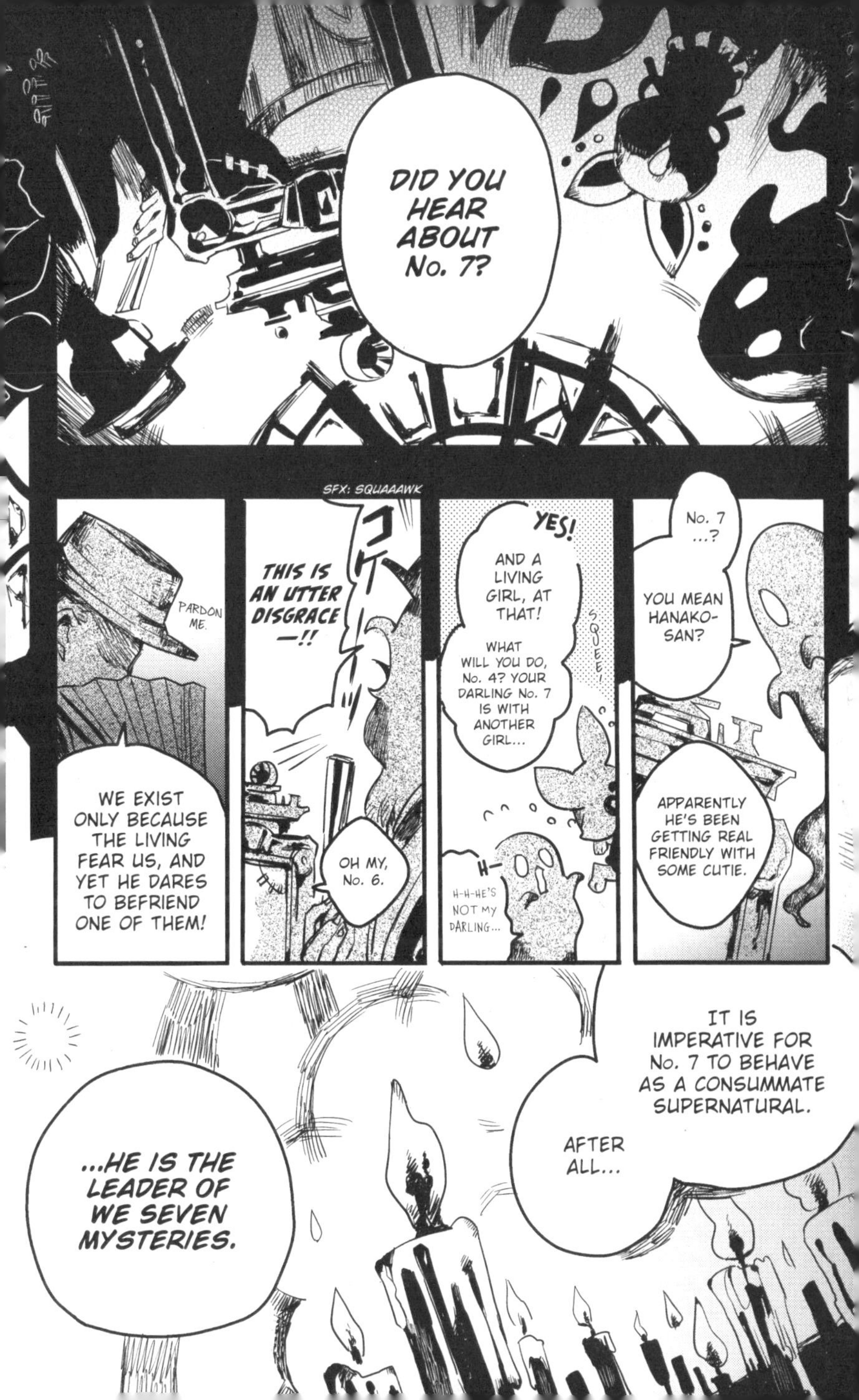
DID YOU HEAR ABOUT No. 7?
No. 7 ...?
YOU MEAN HANAKO-SAN?
APPARENTLY HE'S BEEN GETTING REAL FRIENDLY WITH SOME CUTIE.
YES!
AND A LIVING GIRL, AT THAT!
WHAT WILL YOU DO, No. 4? YOUR DARLING No. 7 IS WITH ANOTHER GIRL...
SQUEE!
H-
H-H-HE'S NOT MY DARLING...
SFX: SQUAAAWK
THIS IS AN UTTER DISGRACE—!!
OH MY, No. 6.
PARDON ME.
WE EXIST ONLY BECAUSE THE LIVING FEAR US, AND YET HE DARES TO BEFRIEND ONE OF THEM!
IT IS IMPERATIVE FOR No. 7 TO BEHAVE AS A CONSUMMATE SUPERNATURAL.
AFTER ALL...
...HE IS THE LEADER OF WE SEVEN MYSTERIES.

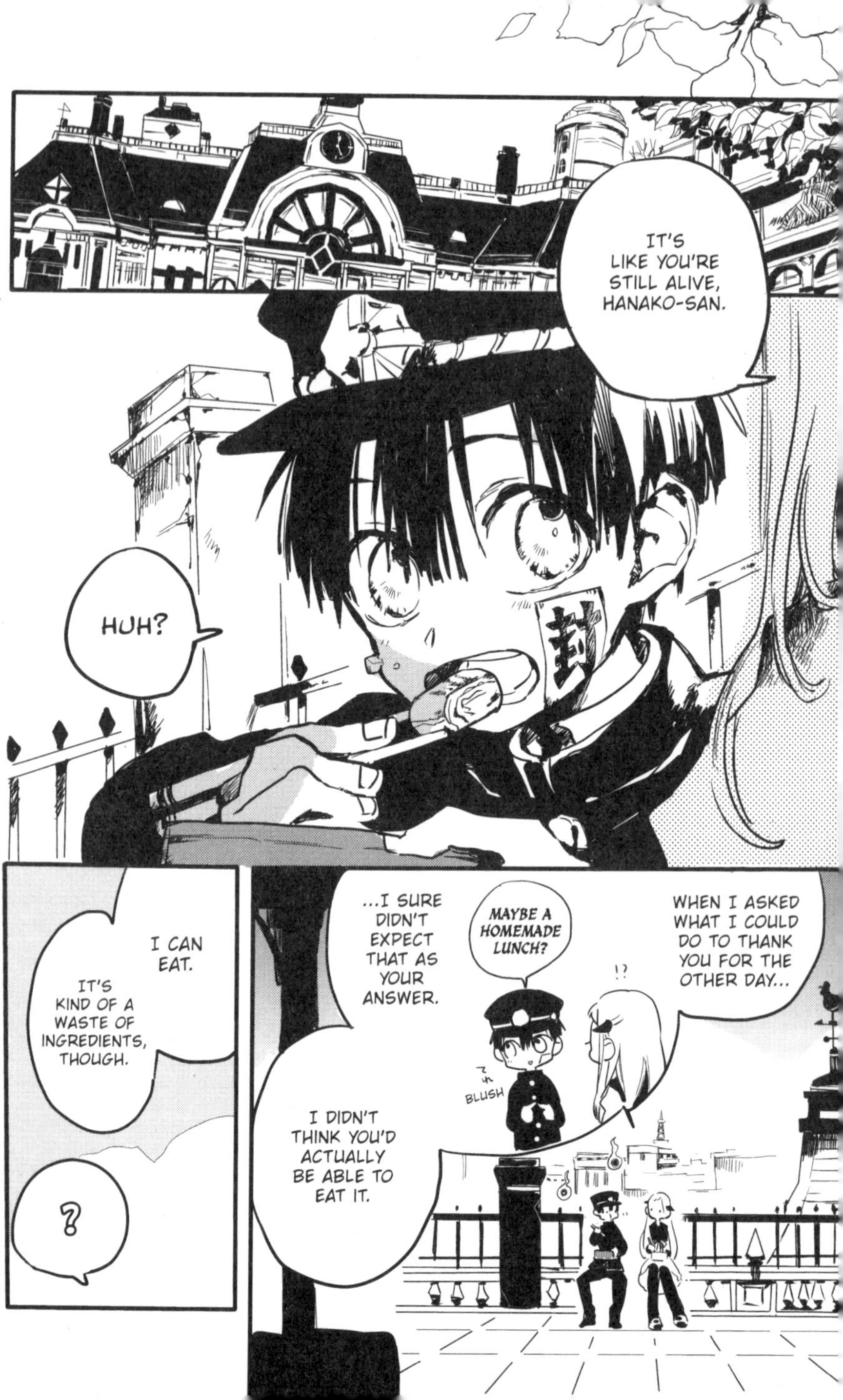
IT'S LIKE YOU'RE STILL ALIVE, HANAKO-SAN.
HUH?
WHEN I ASKED WHAT I COULD DO TO THANK YOU FOR THE OTHER DAY...
!?
MAYBE A HOMEMADE LUNCH?
BLUSH
...I SURE DIDN'T EXPECT THAT AS YOUR ANSWER.
I DIDN'T THINK YOU'D ACTUALLY BE ABLE TO EAT IT.
I CAN EAT.
IT'S KIND OF A WASTE OF INGREDIENTS, THOUGH.
?

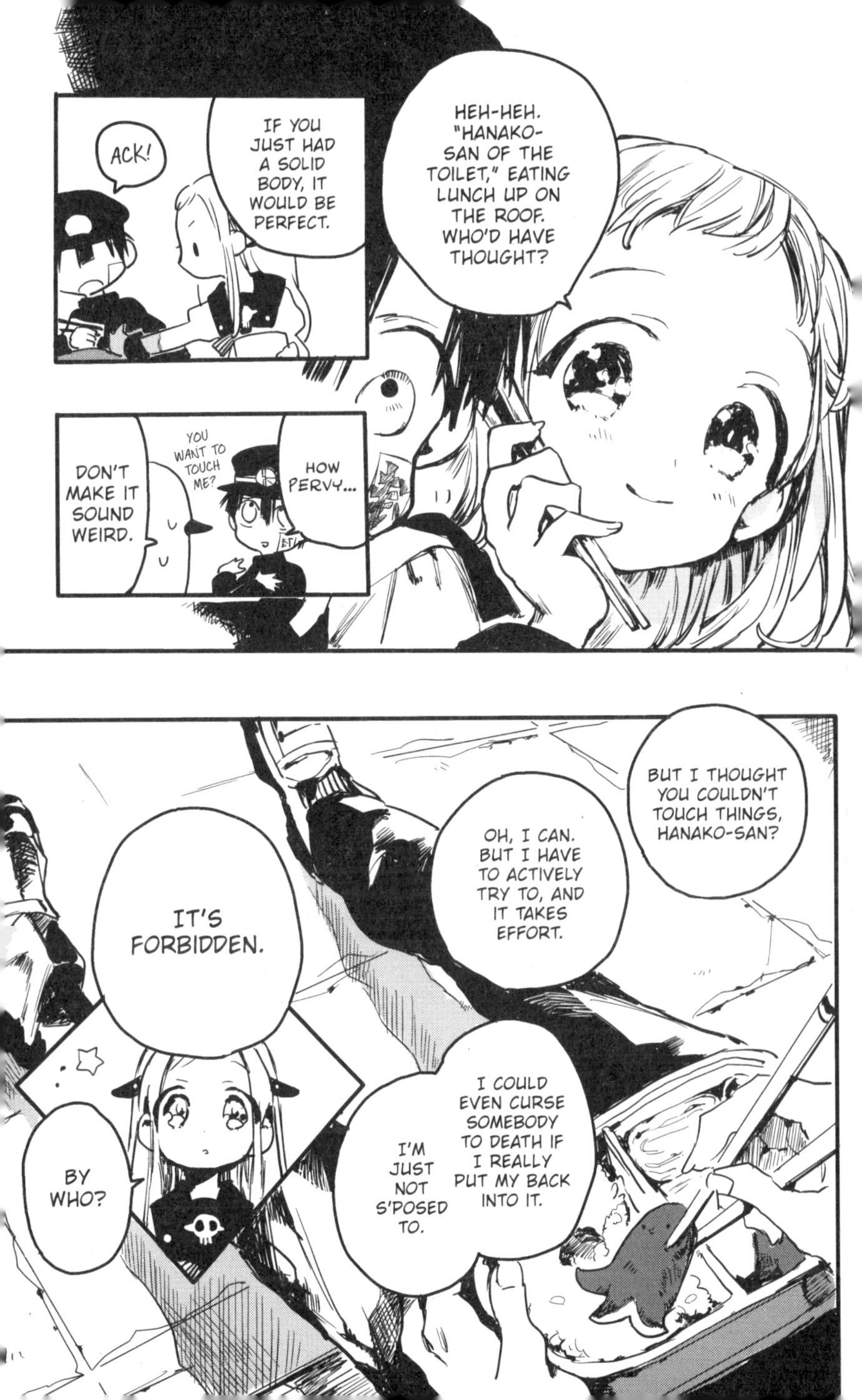
HEH-HEH. "HANAKO-SAN OF THE TOILET," EATING LUNCH UP ON THE ROOF. WHO'D HAVE THOUGHT?
IF YOU JUST HAD A SOLID BODY, IT WOULD BE PERFECT.
ACK!
HOW PERVY...
YOU WANT TO TOUCH ME?
DON'T MAKE IT SOUND WEIRD.
BUT I THOUGHT YOU COULDN'T TOUCH THINGS, HANAKO-SAN?
OH, I CAN. BUT I HAVE TO ACTIVELY TRY TO, AND IT TAKES EFFORT.
I COULD EVEN CURSE SOMEBODY TO DEATH IF I REALLY PUT MY BACK INTO IT.
I'M JUST NOT S'POSED TO.
IT'S FORBIDDEN.
BY WHO?

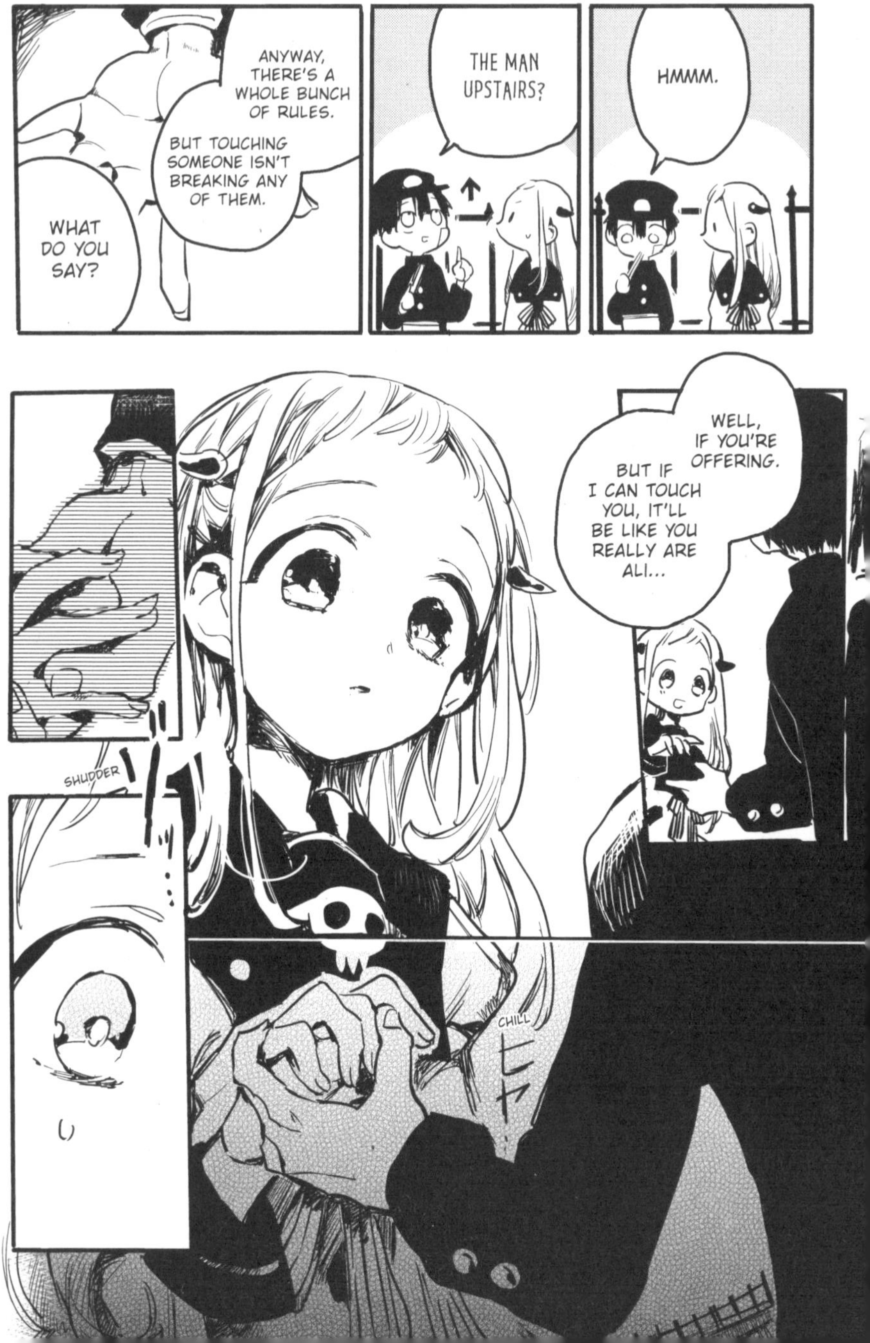
HMMM.
THE MAN UPSTAIRS?
ANYWAY, THERE'S A WHOLE BUNCH OF RULES.
BUT TOUCHING SOMEONE ISN'T BREAKING ANY OF THEM.
WHAT DO YOU SAY?
WELL, IF YOU'RE OFFERING.
BUT IF I CAN TOUCH YOU, IT'LL BE LIKE YOU REALLY ARE ALI...
SHUDDER
CHILL

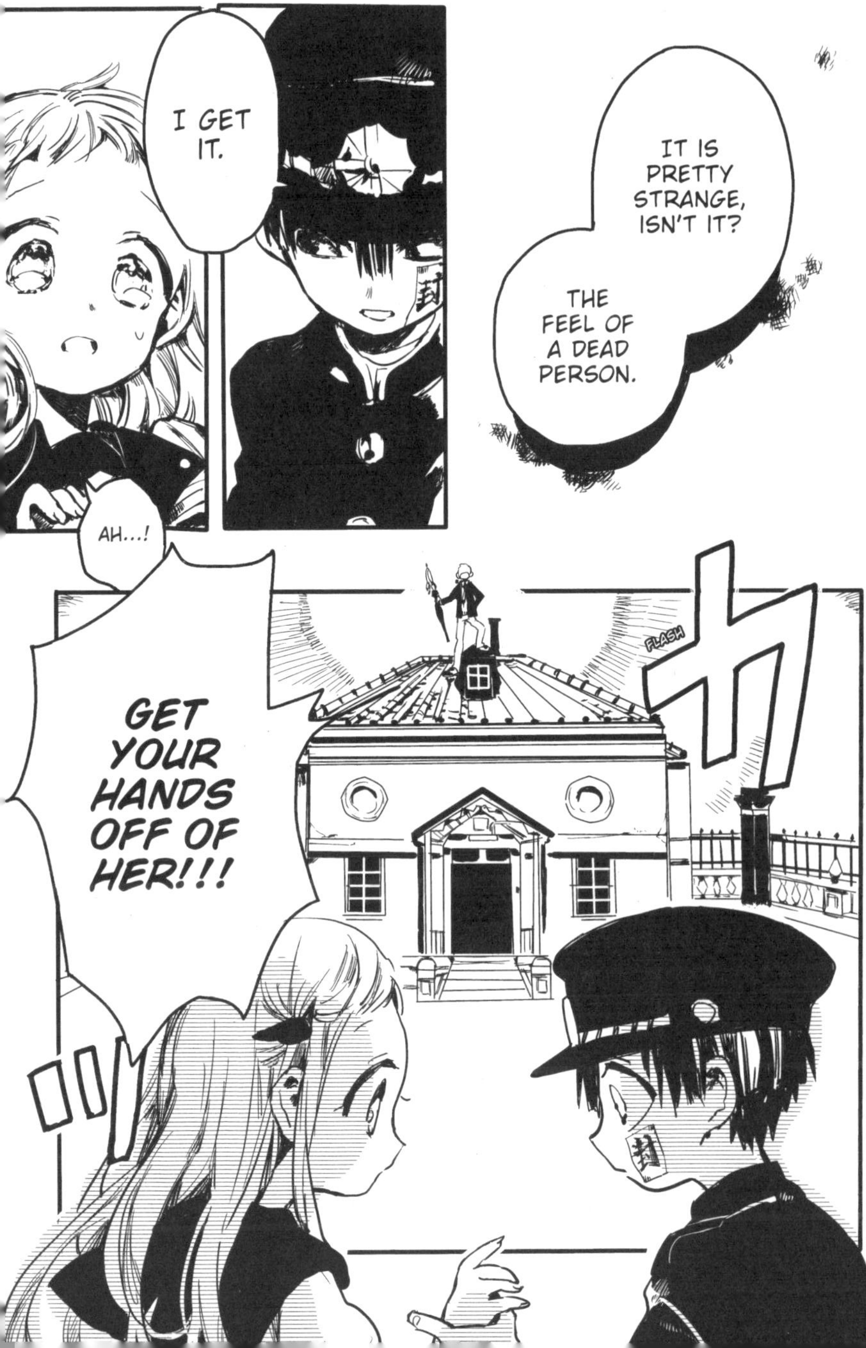
IT IS PRETTY STRANGE, ISN'T IT?
THE FEEL OF A DEAD PERSON.
I GET IT.
AH...!
FLASH
GET YOUR HANDS OFF OF HER!!!

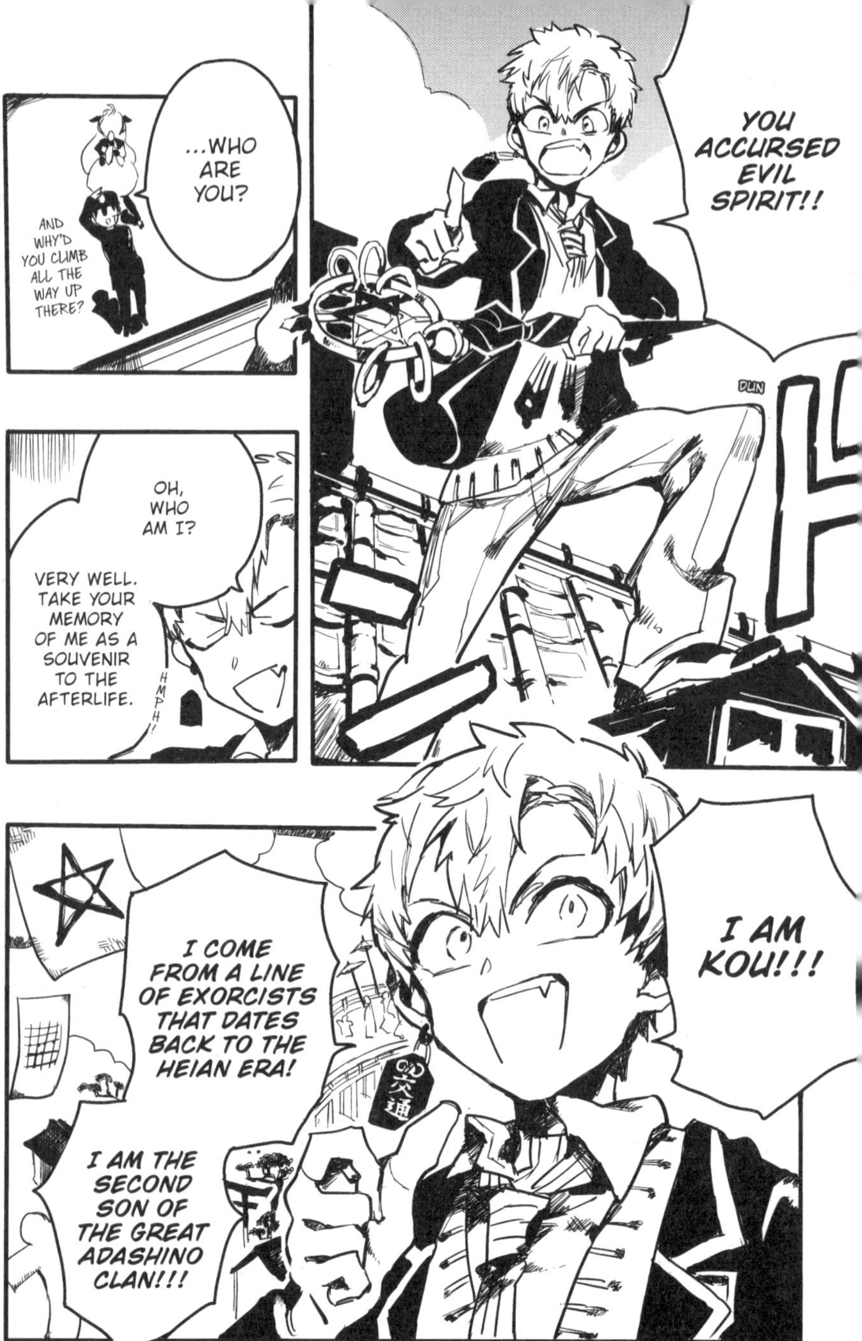
YOU ACCURSED EVIL SPIRIT!!
DUN
...WHO ARE YOU?
AND WHY'D YOU CLIMB ALL THE WAY UP THERE?
OH, WHO AM I?
VERY WELL. TAKE YOUR MEMORY OF ME AS A SOUVENIR TO THE AFTERLIFE.
HMPH!
I AM KOU!!!
I COME FROM A LINE OF EXORCISTS THAT DATES BACK TO THE HEIAN ERA!
I AM THE SECOND SON OF THE GREAT ADASHINO CLAN!!!

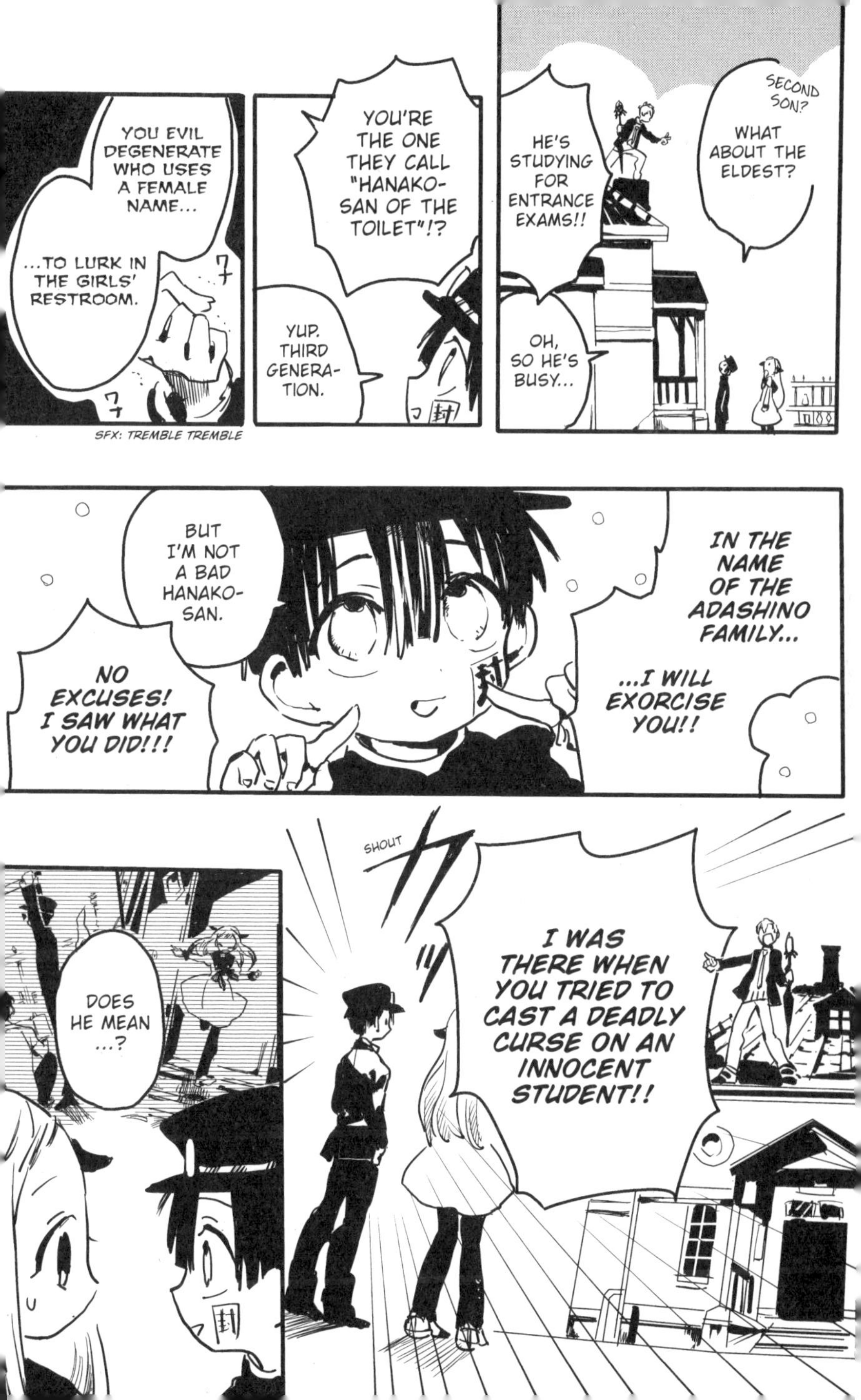
SECOND SON?
WHAT ABOUT THE ELDEST?
HE'S STUDYING FOR ENTRANCE EXAMS!!
OH, SO HE'S BUSY...
YOU'RE THE ONE THEY CALL "HANAKO-SAN OF THE TOILET"!?
YUP. THIRD GENERATION.
YOU EVIL DEGENERATE WHO USES A FEMALE NAME...
...TO LURK IN THE GIRLS' RESTROOM.
SFX: TREMBLE TREMBLE
IN THE NAME OF THE ADASHINO FAMILY...
...I WILL EXORCISE YOU!!
BUT I'M NOT A BAD HANAKO-SAN.
NO EXCUSES! I SAW WHAT YOU DID!!!
SHOUT
I WAS THERE WHEN YOU TRIED TO CAST A DEADLY CURSE ON AN INNOCENT STUDENT!!
DOES HE MEAN ...?

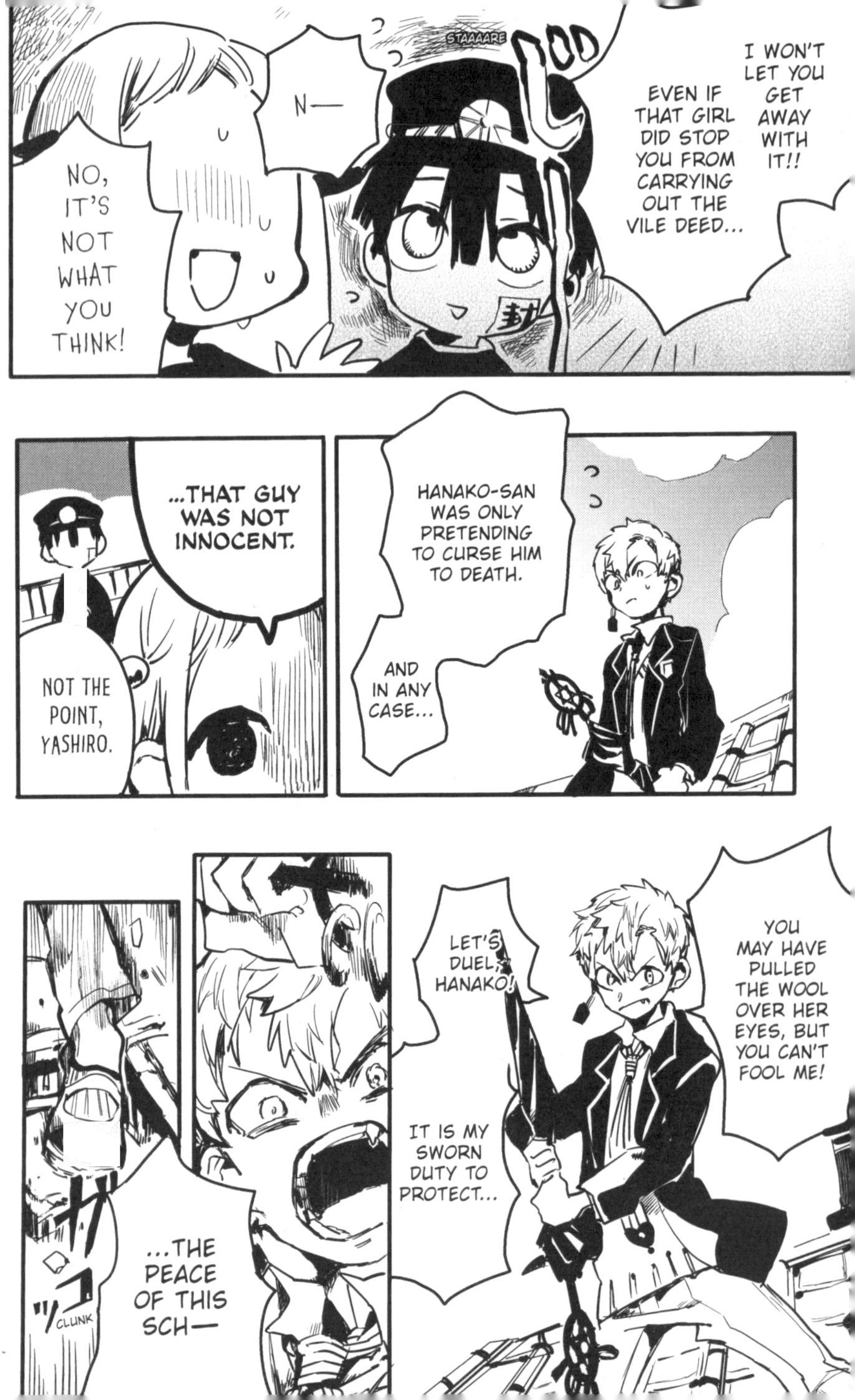

I WON'T LET YOU GET AWAY WITH IT!!
EVEN IF THAT GIRL DID STOP YOU FROM CARRYING OUT THE VILE DEED...
STAAAARE
N—
NO, IT'S NOT WHAT YOU THINK!
HANAKO-SAN WAS ONLY PRETENDING TO CURSE HIM TO DEATH.
AND IN ANY CASE...
...THAT GUY WAS NOT INNOCENT.
NOT THE POINT, YASHIRO.
YOU MAY HAVE PULLED THE WOOL OVER HER EYES, BUT YOU CAN'T FOOL ME!
LET'S DUEL, HANAKO!
IT IS MY SWORN DUTY TO PROTECT...
...THE PEACE OF THIS SCH—
CLUNK

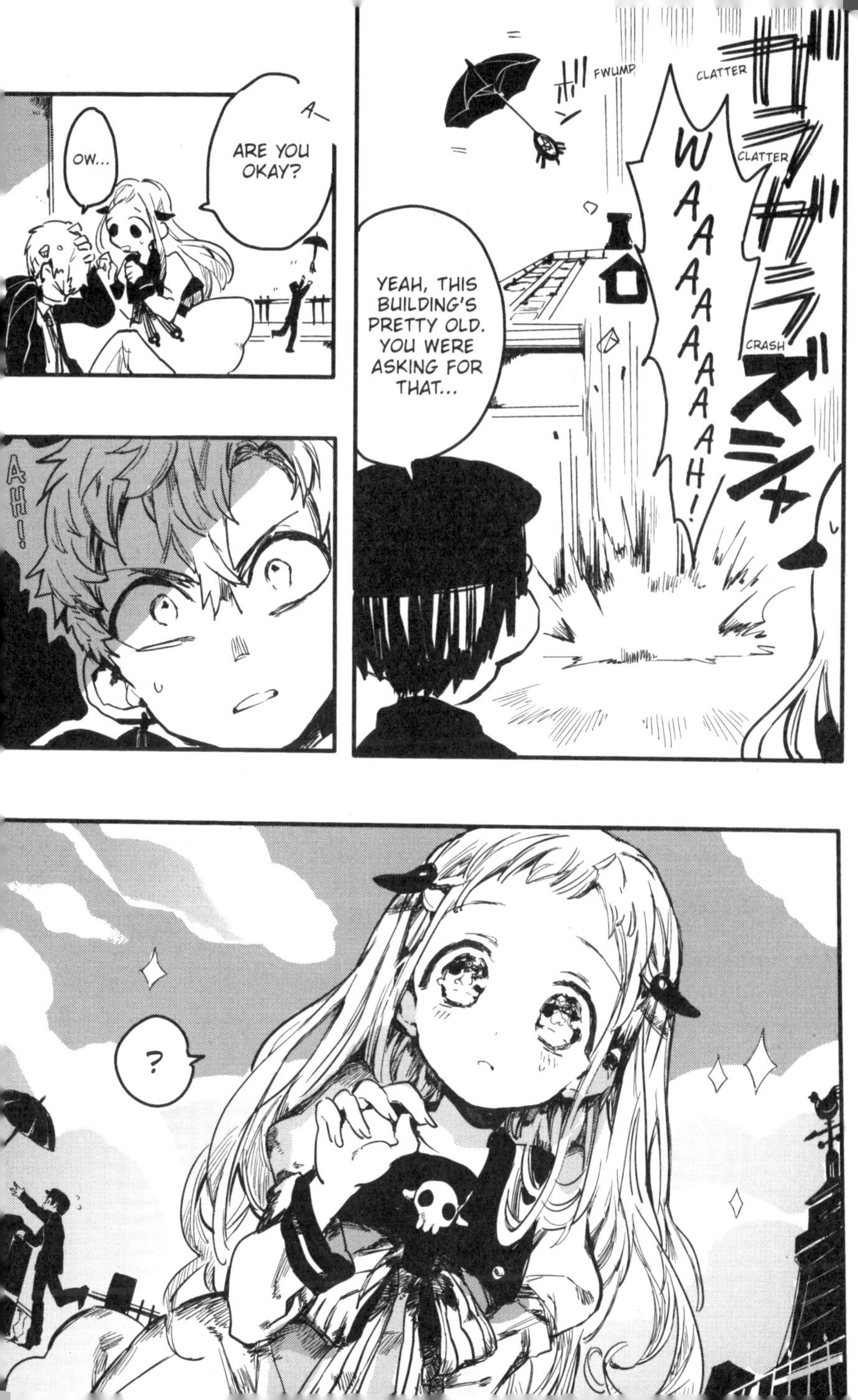
FWUMP
CLATTER
CLATTER
CRASH
WAAAAAAAAH!
YEAH, THIS BUILDING'S PRETTY OLD. YOU WERE ASKING FOR THAT...
A—
ARE YOU OKAY?
OW...
AH!
?

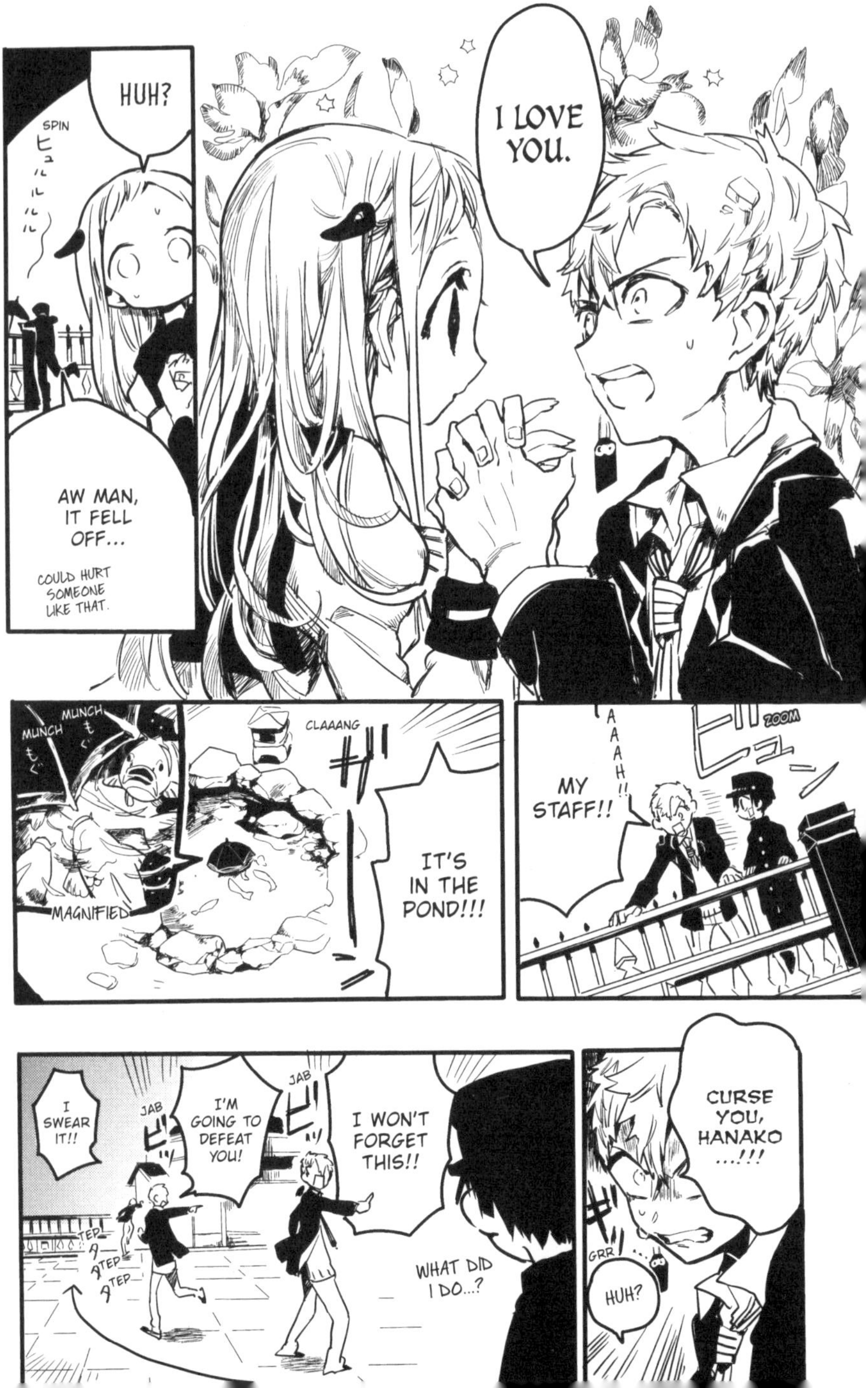

I LOVE YOU.
HUH?
SPIN
ヒュルルルル
AW MAN, IT FELL OFF...
COULD HURT SOMEONE LIKE THAT.
ZOOM
AAAH!!
MY STAFF!!
CLAAANG
IT'S IN THE POND!!!
MUNCH MUNCH
もぐもぐ
MAGNIFIED
CURSE YOU, HANAKO ...!!!
GRR
HUH?
I WON'T FORGET THIS!!
WHAT DID I DO...?
JAB
I'M GOING TO DEFEAT YOU!
JAB
I SWEAR IT!!
TEP TEP TEP

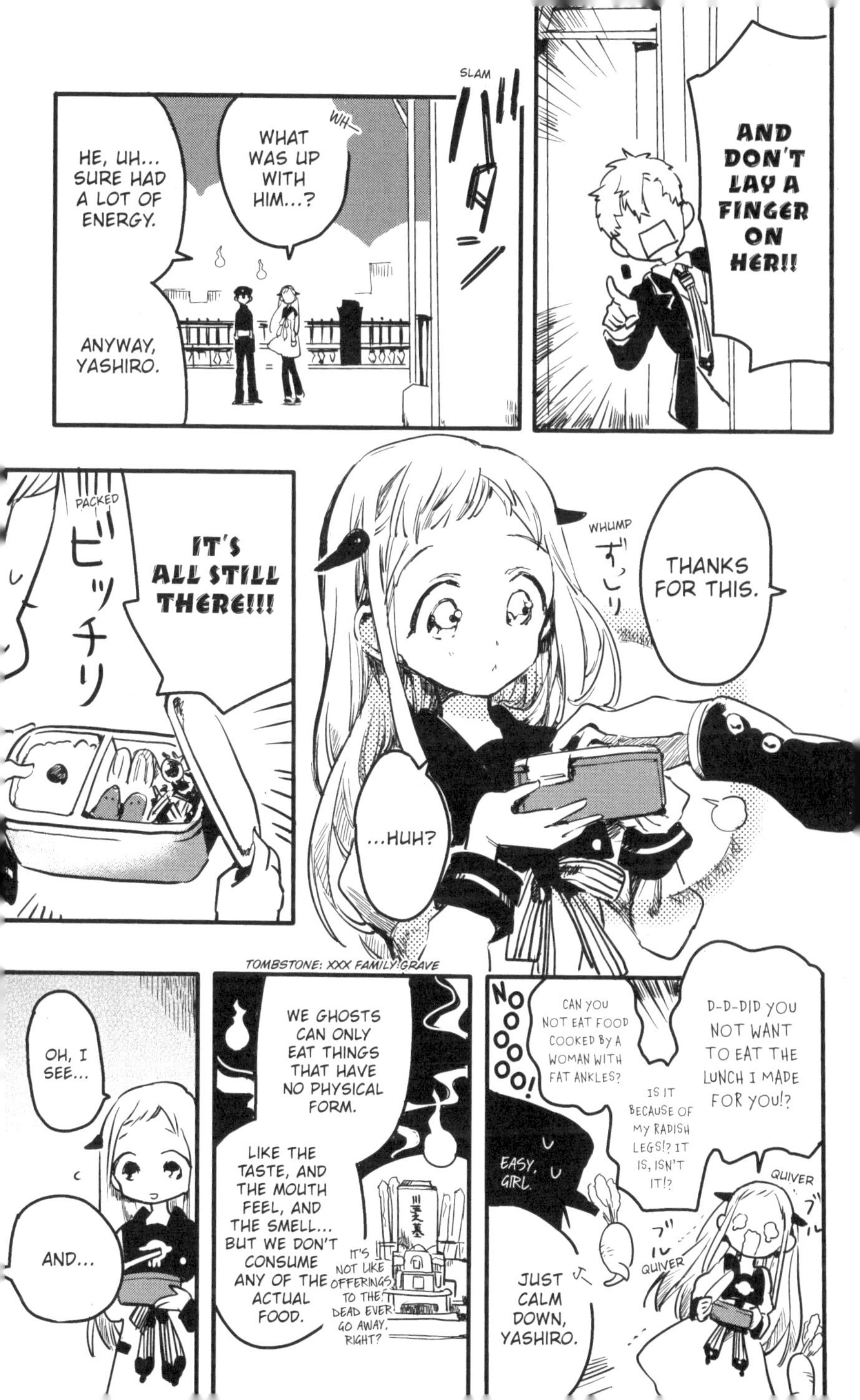
SLAM
AND DON'T LAY A FINGER ON HER!!
WH—
WHAT WAS UP WITH HIM...?
HE, UH... SURE HAD A LOT OF ENERGY.
ANYWAY, YASHIRO.
WHUMP ずっしり
THANKS FOR THIS.
...HUH?
PACKED ビッチリ
IT'S ALL STILL THERE!!!
TOMBSTONE: XXX FAMILY GRAVE
D-D-DID YOU NOT WANT TO EAT THE LUNCH I MADE FOR YOU!?
CAN YOU NOT EAT FOOD COOKED BY A WOMAN WITH FAT ANKLES?
NOOOOOO!
IS IT BECAUSE OF MY RADISH LEGS!? IT IS, ISN'T IT!?
QUIVER ブル
QUIVER ブル
EASY, GIRL.
JUST CALM DOWN, YASHIRO.
WE GHOSTS CAN ONLY EAT THINGS THAT HAVE NO PHYSICAL FORM.
LIKE THE TASTE, AND THE MOUTH FEEL, AND THE SMELL... BUT WE DON'T CONSUME ANY OF THE ACTUAL FOOD.
IT'S NOT LIKE OFFERINGS TO THE DEAD EVER GO AWAY, RIGHT?
OH, I SEE...
AND...

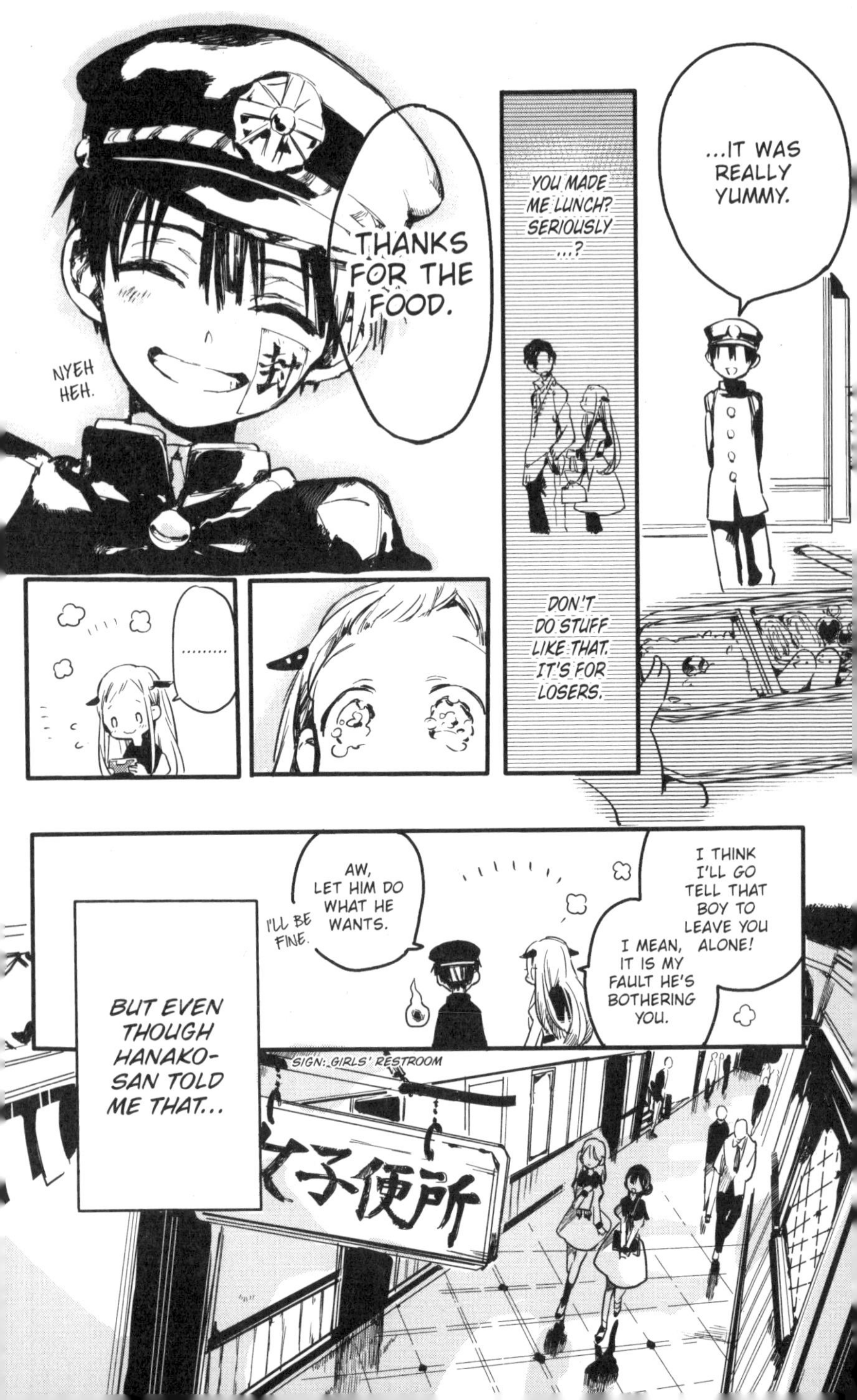
...IT WAS REALLY YUMMY.
YOU MADE ME LUNCH? SERIOUSLY ...?
DON'T DO STUFF LIKE THAT. IT'S FOR LOSERS.
THANKS FOR THE FOOD.
NYEH HEH.
....
I THINK I'LL GO TELL THAT BOY TO LEAVE YOU ALONE!
I MEAN, IT IS MY FAULT HE'S BOTHERING YOU.
AW, LET HIM DO WHAT HE WANTS.
I'LL BE FINE.
SIGN: GIRLS' RESTROOM
BUT EVEN THOUGH HANAKO-SAN TOLD ME THAT...

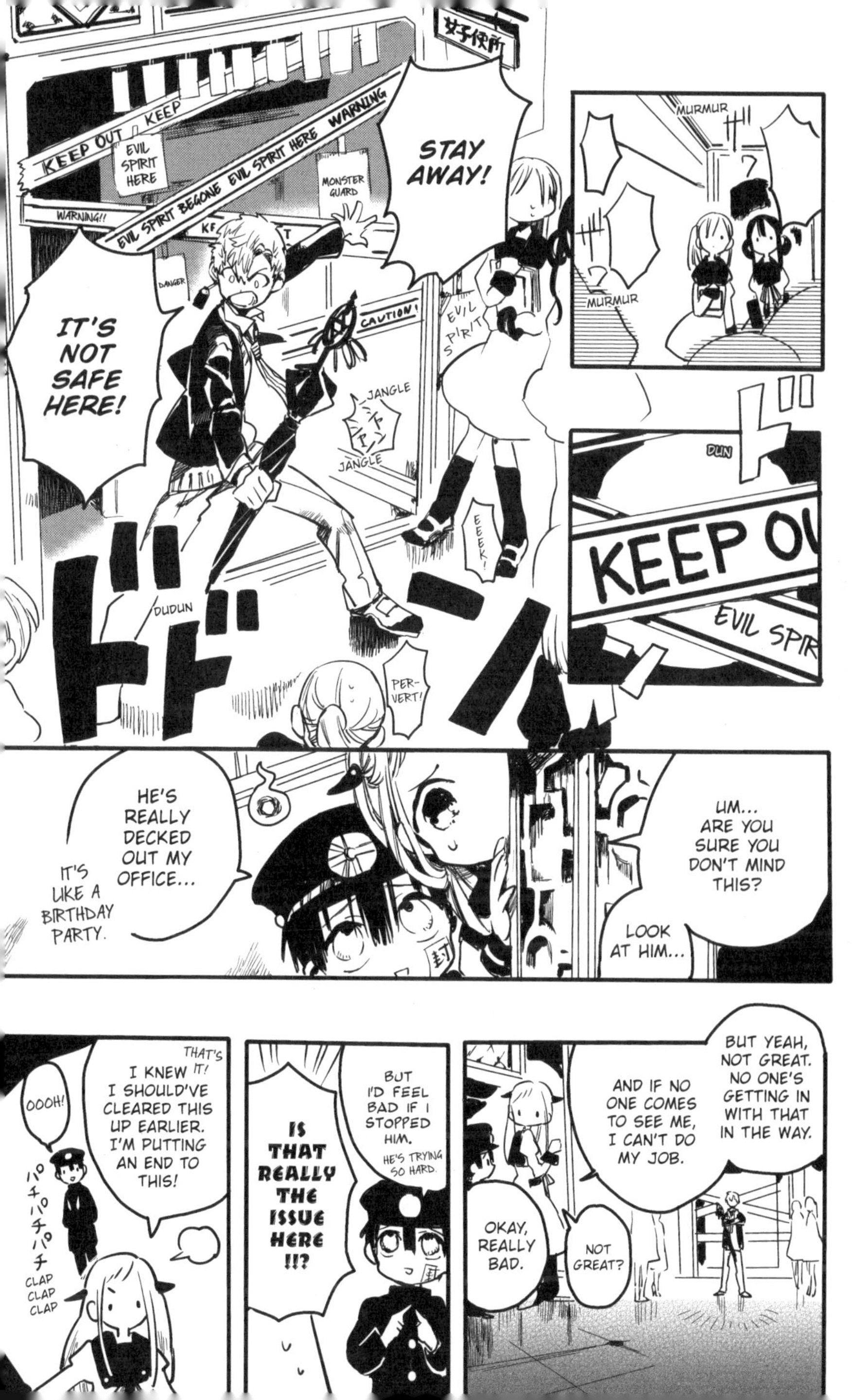

MURMUR
MURMUR
DUN
KEEP OU
EVIL SPIR
女子便所
KEEP OUT
KEEP
EVIL SPIRIT HERE
EVIL SPIRIT BEGONE
EVIL SPIRIT HERE
WARNING
MONSTER GUARD
WARNING!!
DANGER
CAUTION!
STAY AWAY!
IT'S NOT SAFE HERE!
JANGLE
JANGLE
EVIL SPIRIT
EEEEK!
DUDUN
PER-VERT!
UM... ARE YOU SURE YOU DON'T MIND THIS?
LOOK AT HIM...
HE'S REALLY DECKED OUT MY OFFICE...
IT'S LIKE A BIRTHDAY PARTY.
BUT YEAH, NOT GREAT. NO ONE'S GETTING IN WITH THAT IN THE WAY.
AND IF NO ONE COMES TO SEE ME, I CAN'T DO MY JOB.
NOT GREAT?
OKAY, REALLY BAD.
BUT I'D FEEL BAD IF I STOPPED HIM.
HE'S TRYING SO HARD.
IS THAT REALLY THE ISSUE HERE!!?
THAT'S IT!
I KNEW IT! I SHOULD'VE CLEARED THIS UP EARLIER. I'M PUTTING AN END TO THIS!
OOOH!
パチパチパチ
CLAP CLAP CLAP

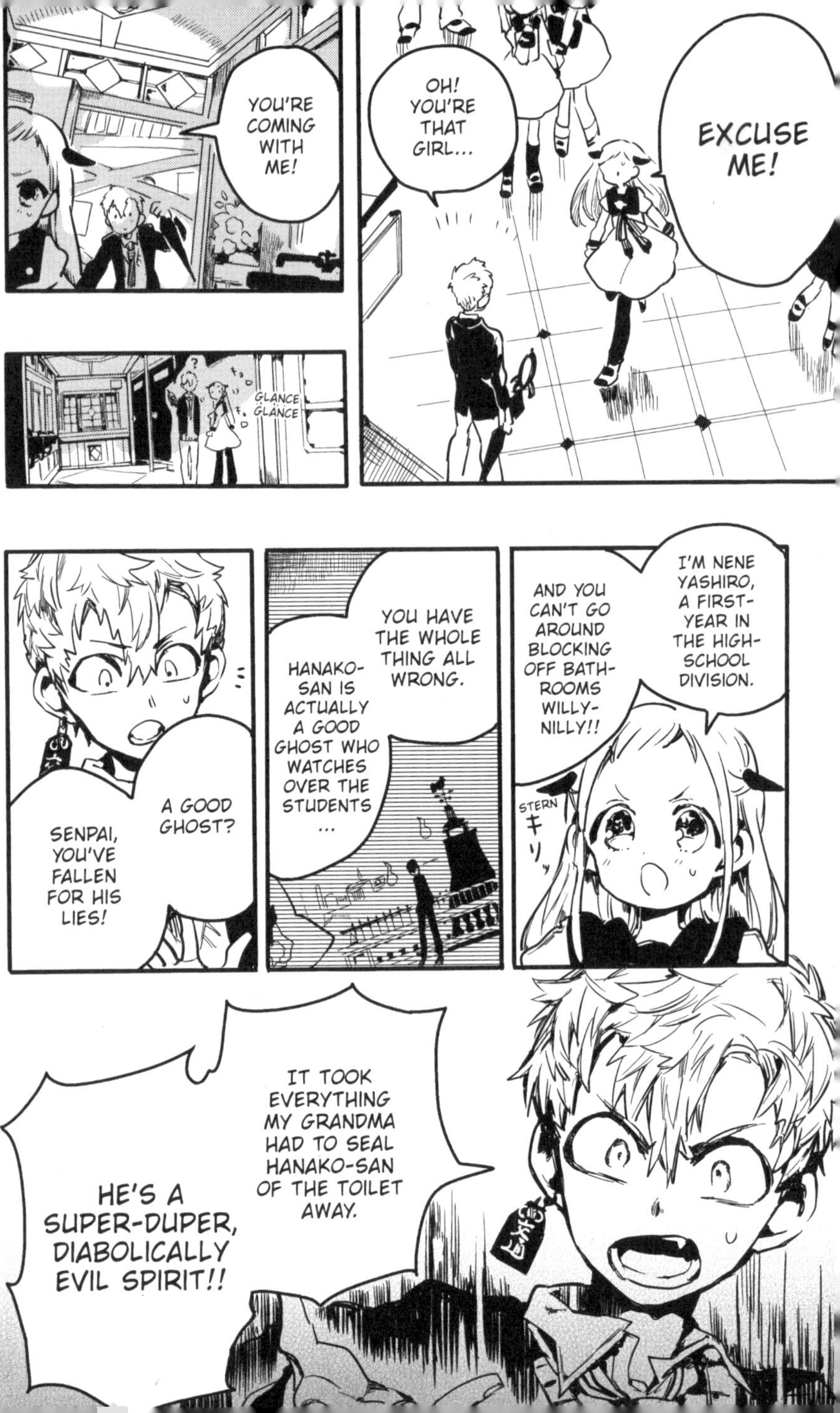
EXCUSE ME!
OH! YOU'RE THAT GIRL...
YOU'RE COMING WITH ME!
GLANCE GLANCE
I'M NENE YASHIRO, A FIRST-YEAR IN THE HIGH-SCHOOL DIVISION.
AND YOU CAN'T GO AROUND BLOCKING OFF BATHROOMS WILLY-NILLY!!
STERN
YOU HAVE THE WHOLE THING ALL WRONG.
HANAKO-SAN IS ACTUALLY A GOOD GHOST WHO WATCHES OVER THE STUDENTS...
A GOOD GHOST?
SENPAI, YOU'VE FALLEN FOR HIS LIES!
IT TOOK EVERYTHING MY GRANDMA HAD TO SEAL HANAKO-SAN OF THE TOILET AWAY.
HE'S A SUPER-DUPER, DIABOLICALLY EVIL SPIRIT!!

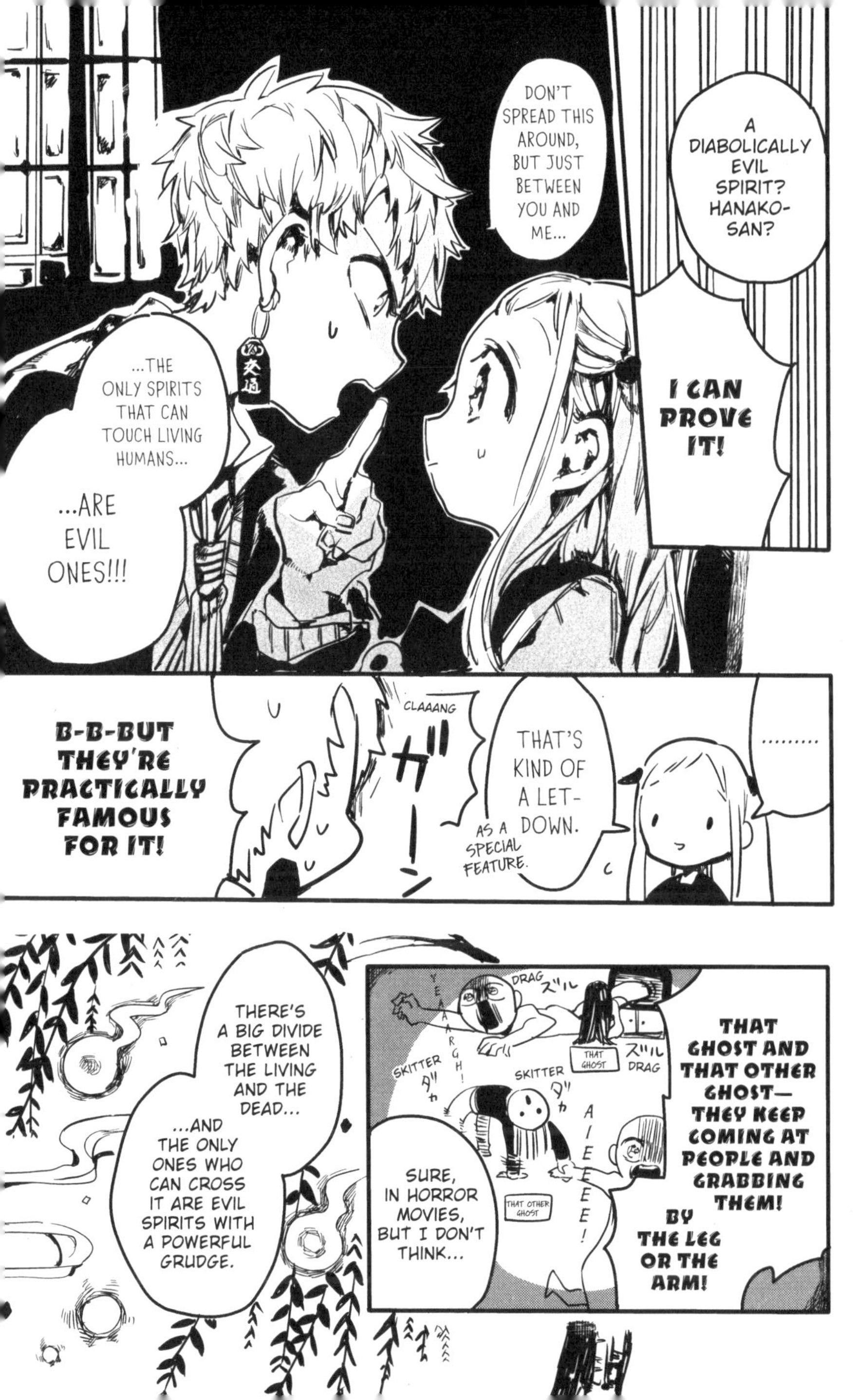
A DIABOLICALLY EVIL SPIRIT? HANAKO-SAN?
I CAN PROVE IT!
DON'T SPREAD THIS AROUND, BUT JUST BETWEEN YOU AND ME...
...THE ONLY SPIRITS THAT CAN TOUCH LIVING HUMANS...
...ARE EVIL ONES!!!
....
THAT'S KIND OF A LET-DOWN.
AS A SPECIAL FEATURE.
CLAAANG
ガーン
B-B-BUT THEY'RE PRACTICALLY FAMOUS FOR IT!
THAT GHOST AND THAT OTHER GHOST—THEY KEEP COMING AT PEOPLE AND GRABBING THEM!
BY THE LEG OR THE ARM!
DRAG ズル
YEAAARGH!
ズル DRAG
THAT GHOST
SKITTER ダッ
SKITTER ダッ
AIEEEEE!
THAT OTHER GHOST
SURE, IN HORROR MOVIES, BUT I DON'T THINK...
THERE'S A BIG DIVIDE BETWEEN THE LIVING AND THE DEAD...
...AND THE ONLY ONES WHO CAN CROSS IT ARE EVIL SPIRITS WITH A POWERFUL GRUDGE.

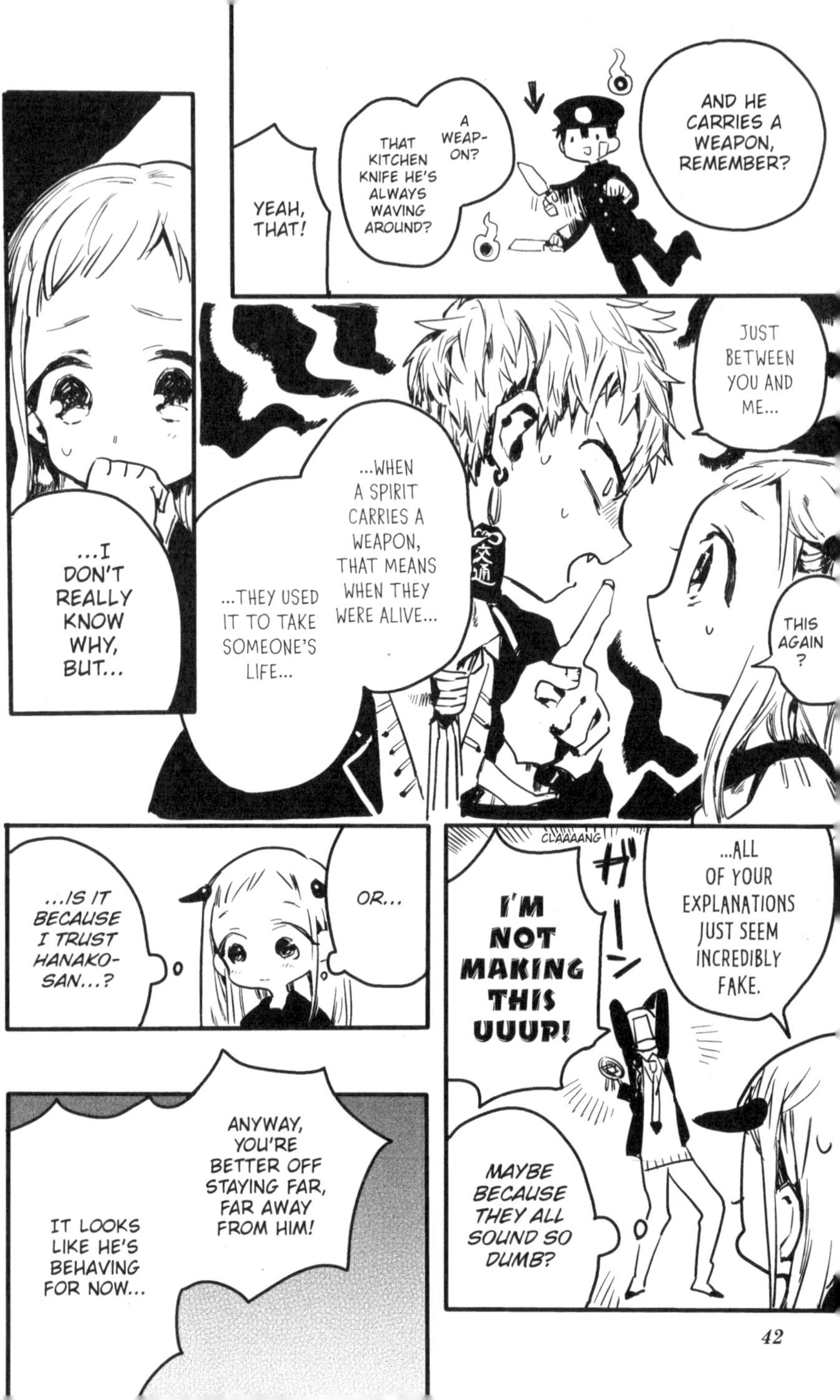
AND HE CARRIES A WEAPON, REMEMBER?
A WEAPON?
THAT KITCHEN KNIFE HE'S ALWAYS WAVING AROUND?
YEAH, THAT!
JUST BETWEEN YOU AND ME...
THIS AGAIN?
...WHEN A SPIRIT CARRIES A WEAPON, THAT MEANS WHEN THEY WERE ALIVE...
...THEY USED IT TO TAKE SOMEONE'S LIFE...
...I DON'T REALLY KNOW WHY, BUT...
...ALL OF YOUR EXPLANATIONS JUST SEEM INCREDIBLY FAKE.
CLAAAANG
I'M NOT MAKING THIS UUUP!
MAYBE BECAUSE THEY ALL SOUND SO DUMB?
OR...
...IS IT BECAUSE I TRUST HANAKO-SAN...?
ANYWAY, YOU'RE BETTER OFF STAYING FAR, FAR AWAY FROM HIM!
IT LOOKS LIKE HE'S BEHAVING FOR NOW...

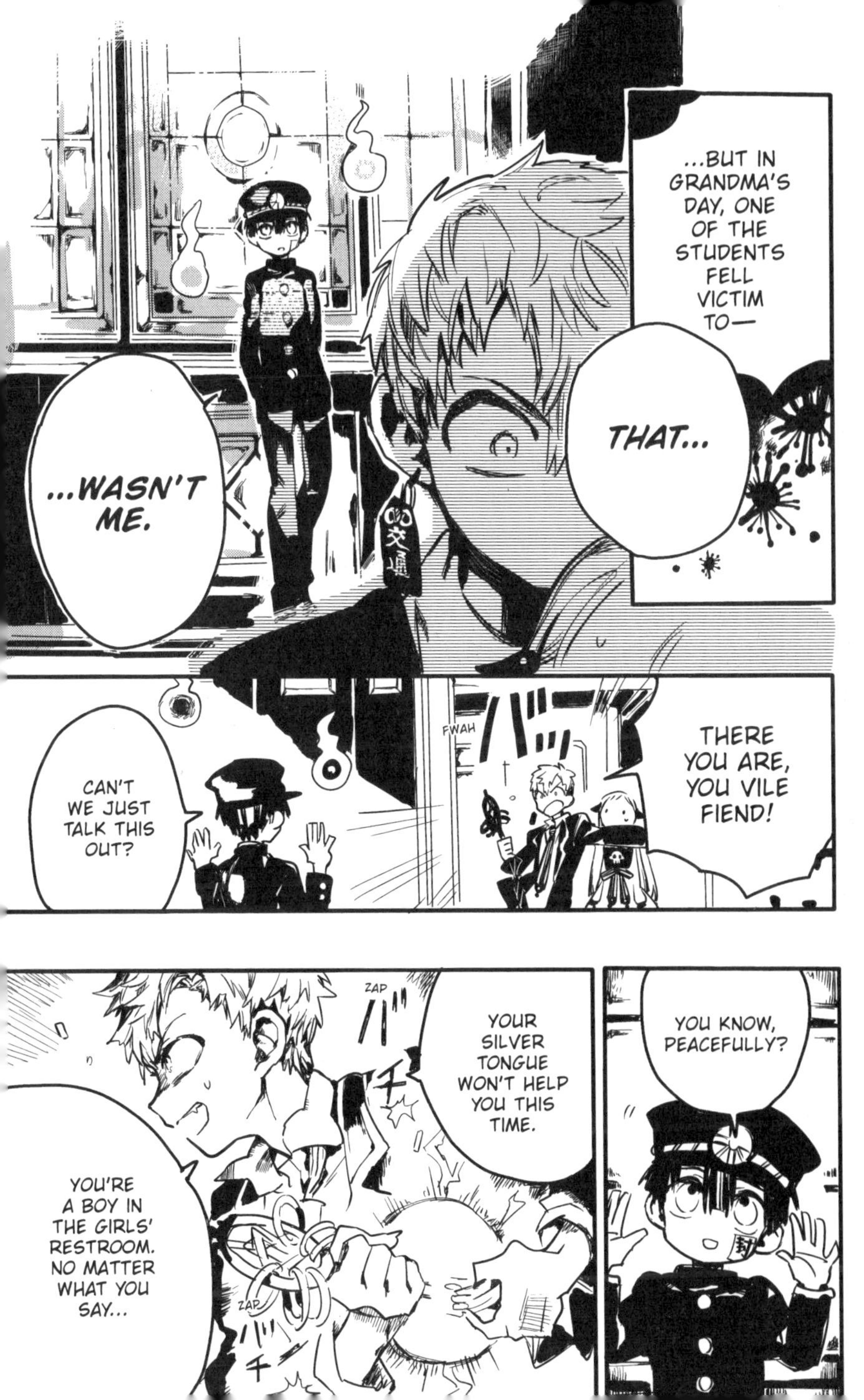
...BUT IN GRANDMA'S DAY, ONE OF THE STUDENTS FELL VICTIM TO—
THAT...
...WASN'T ME.
THERE YOU ARE, YOU VILE FIEND!
FWAH
CAN'T WE JUST TALK THIS OUT?
YOU KNOW, PEACEFULLY?
ZAP
YOUR SILVER TONGUE WON'T HELP YOU THIS TIME.
YOU'RE A BOY IN THE GIRLS' RESTROOM. NO MATTER WHAT YOU SAY...
ZAP

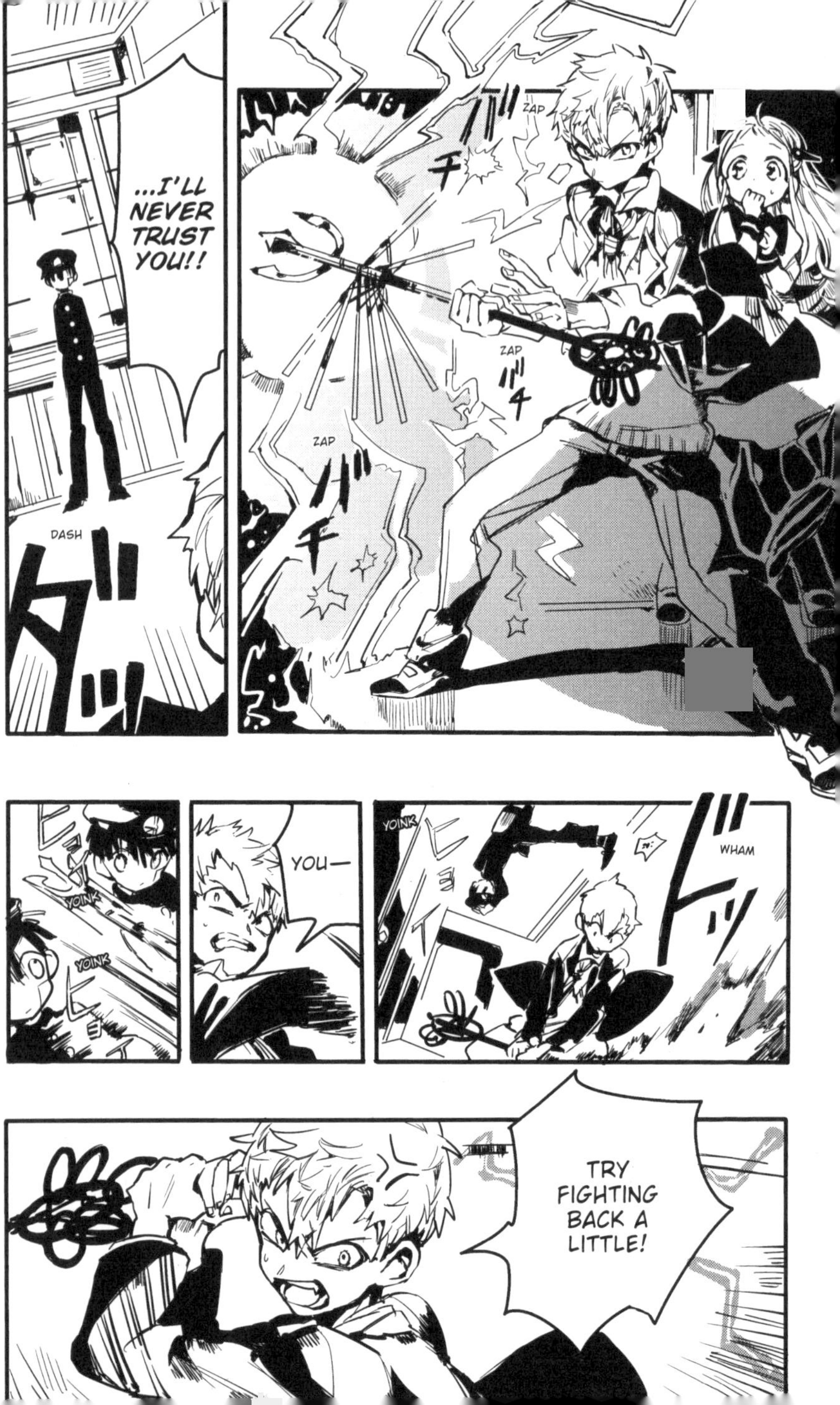
ZAP
ZAP
ZAP
...I'LL NEVER TRUST YOU!!
DASH
WHAM
YOINK
YOU—
YOINK
YOINK
TRY FIGHTING BACK A LITTLE!

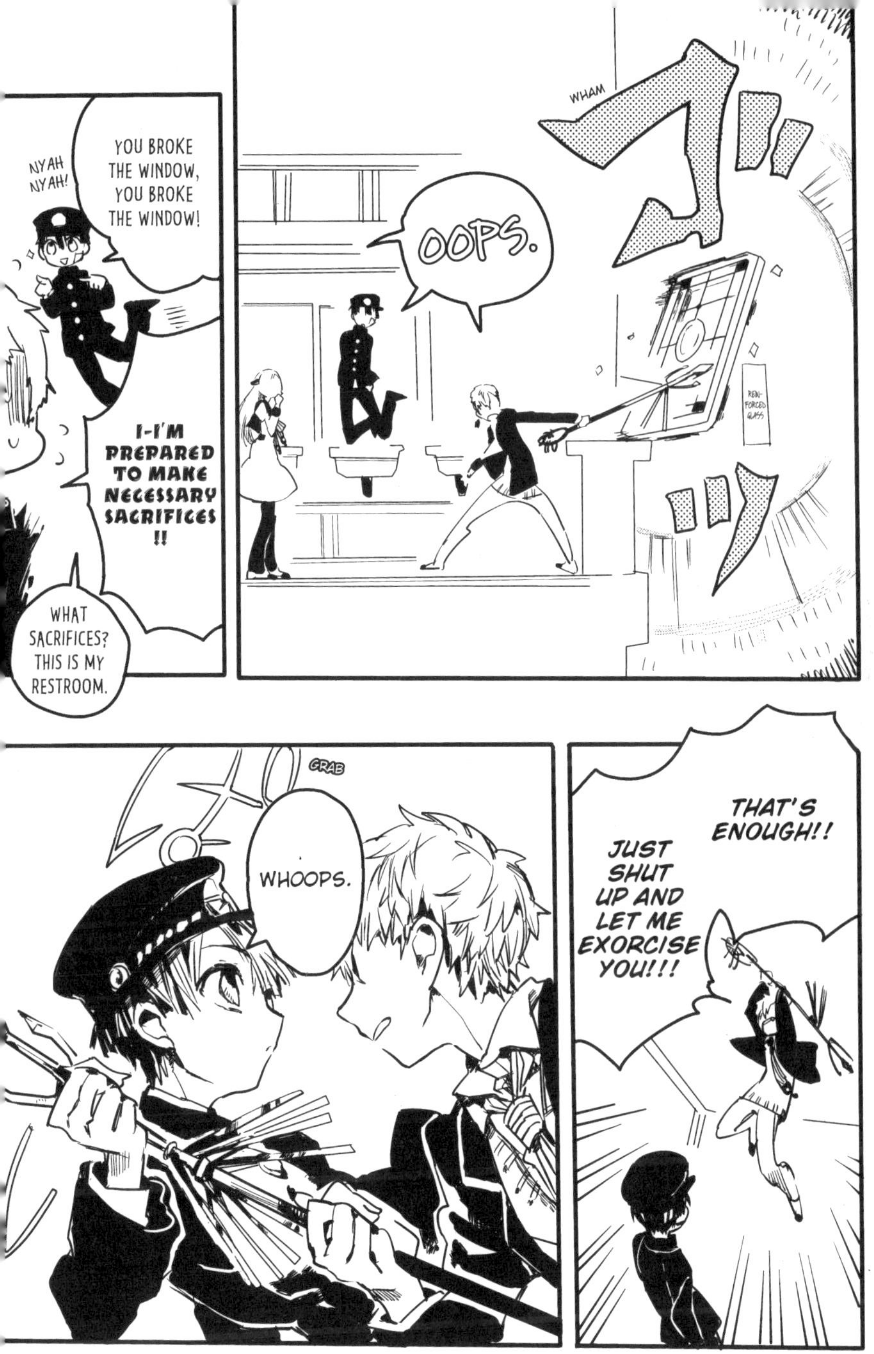
WHAM
OOPS.
REIN-FORCED GLASS
YOU BROKE THE WINDOW, YOU BROKE THE WINDOW!
NYAH NYAH!
I-I'M PREPARED TO MAKE NECESSARY SACRIFICES !!
WHAT SACRIFICES? THIS IS MY RESTROOM.
THAT'S ENOUGH!!
JUST SHUT UP AND LET ME EXORCISE YOU!!!
GRAB
WHOOPS.

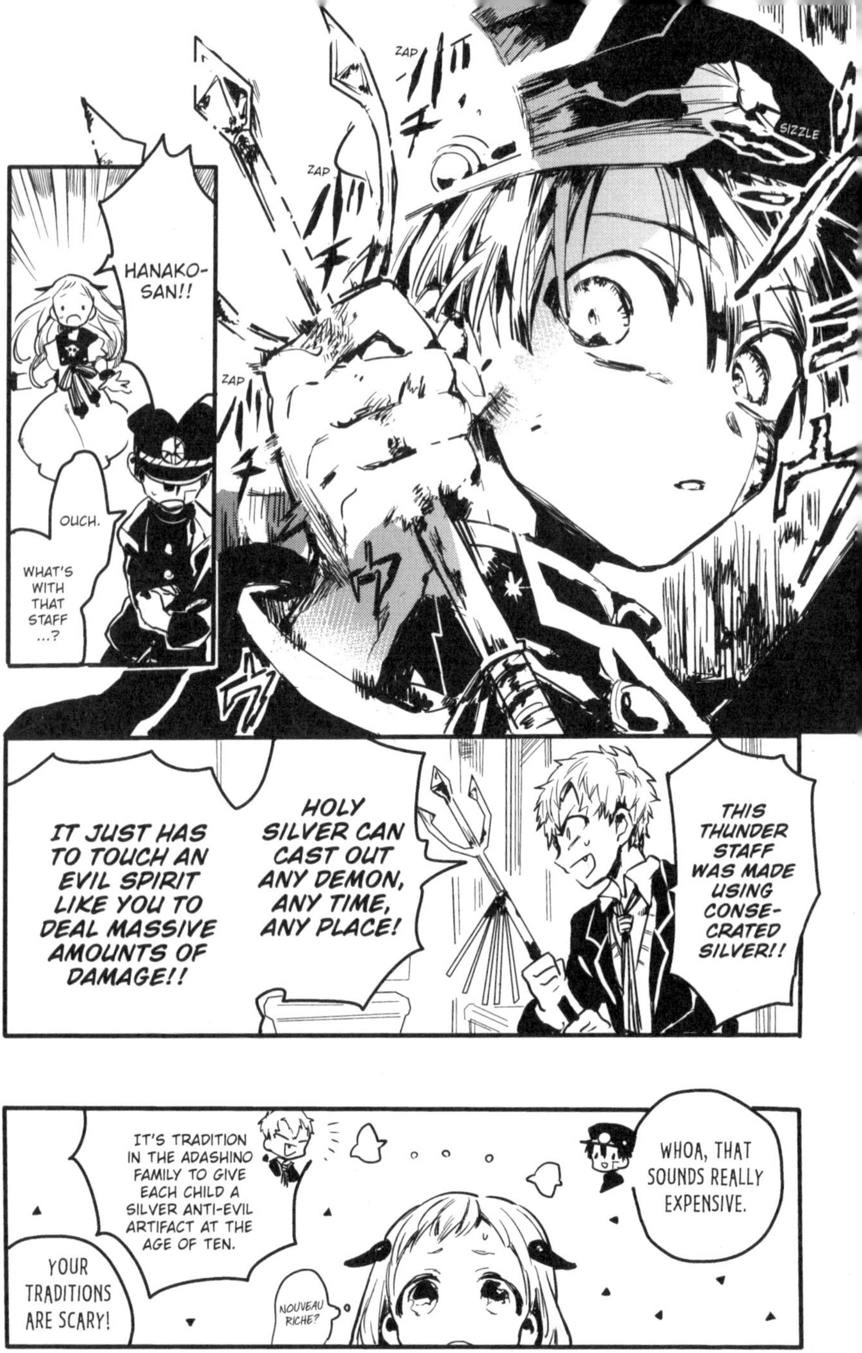
ZAP
SIZZLE
ZAP
ZAP
HANAKO-SAN!!
OUCH.
WHAT'S WITH THAT STAFF ...?
THIS THUNDER STAFF WAS MADE USING CONSE-CRATED SILVER!!
HOLY SILVER CAN CAST OUT ANY DEMON, ANY TIME, ANY PLACE!
IT JUST HAS TO TOUCH AN EVIL SPIRIT LIKE YOU TO DEAL MASSIVE AMOUNTS OF DAMAGE!!
WHOA, THAT SOUNDS REALLY EXPENSIVE.
IT'S TRADITION IN THE ADASHINO FAMILY TO GIVE EACH CHILD A SILVER ANTI-EVIL ARTIFACT AT THE AGE OF TEN.
NOUVEAU RICHE?
YOUR TRADITIONS ARE SCARY!

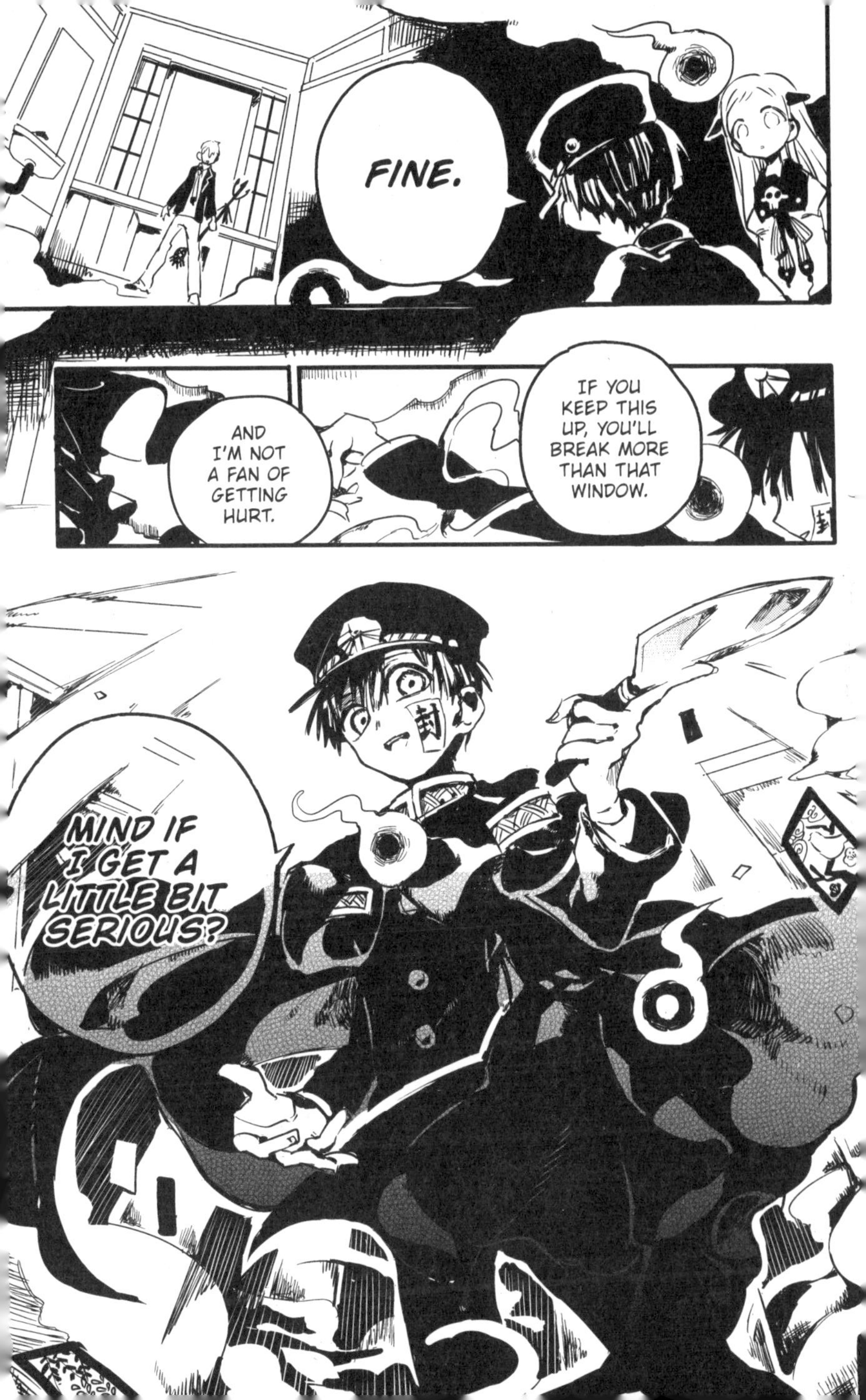
FINE.
IF YOU KEEP THIS UP, YOU'LL BREAK MORE THAN THAT WINDOW.
AND I'M NOT A FAN OF GETTING HURT.
MIND IF I GET A LITTLE BIT SERIOUS?

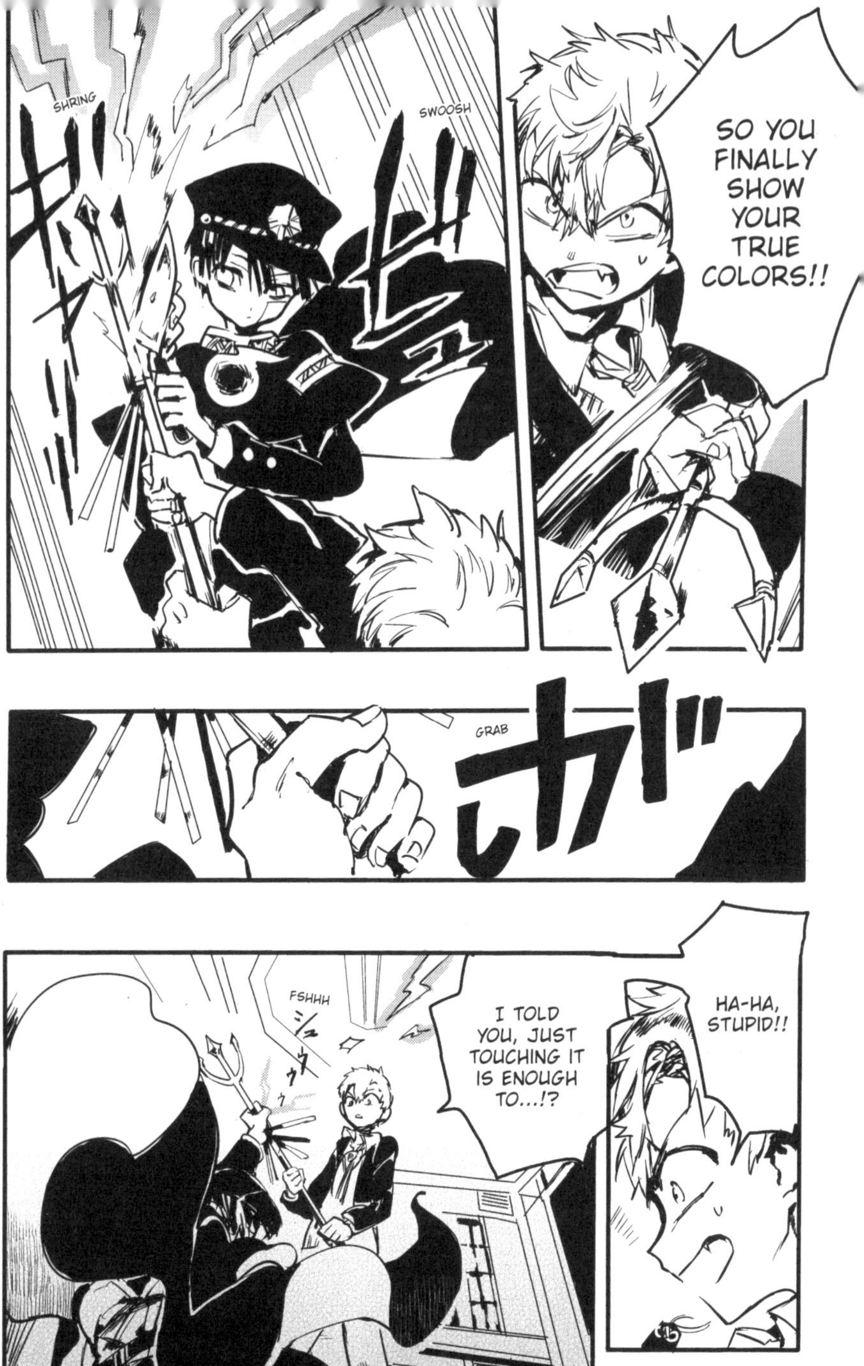
SO YOU FINALLY SHOW YOUR TRUE COLORS!!
SWOOSH
SHRING
GRAB
HA-HA, STUPID!!
I TOLD YOU, JUST TOUCHING IT IS ENOUGH TO...!?
FSHHH

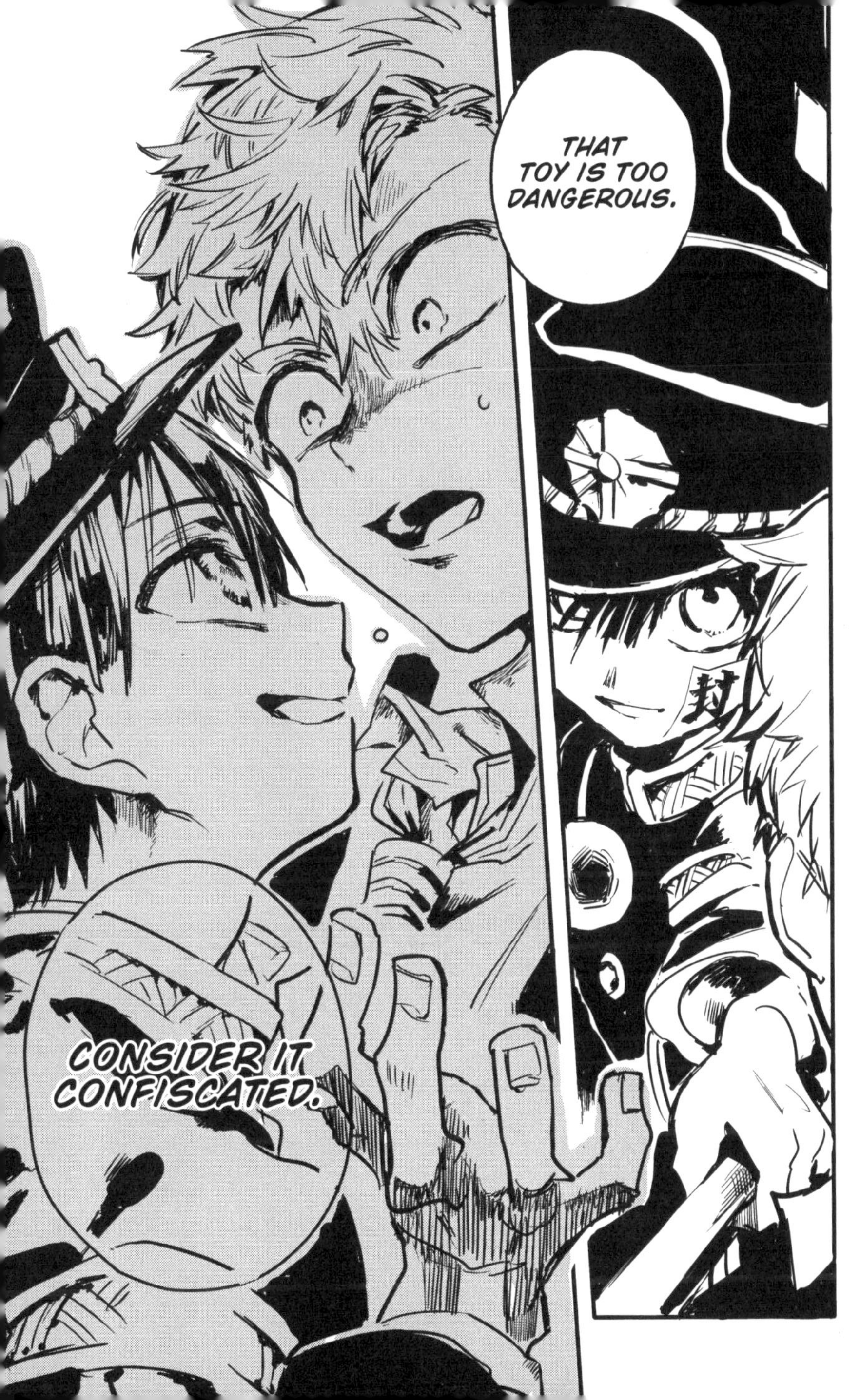
THAT TOY IS TOO DANGEROUS.
CONSIDER IT CONFISCATED.

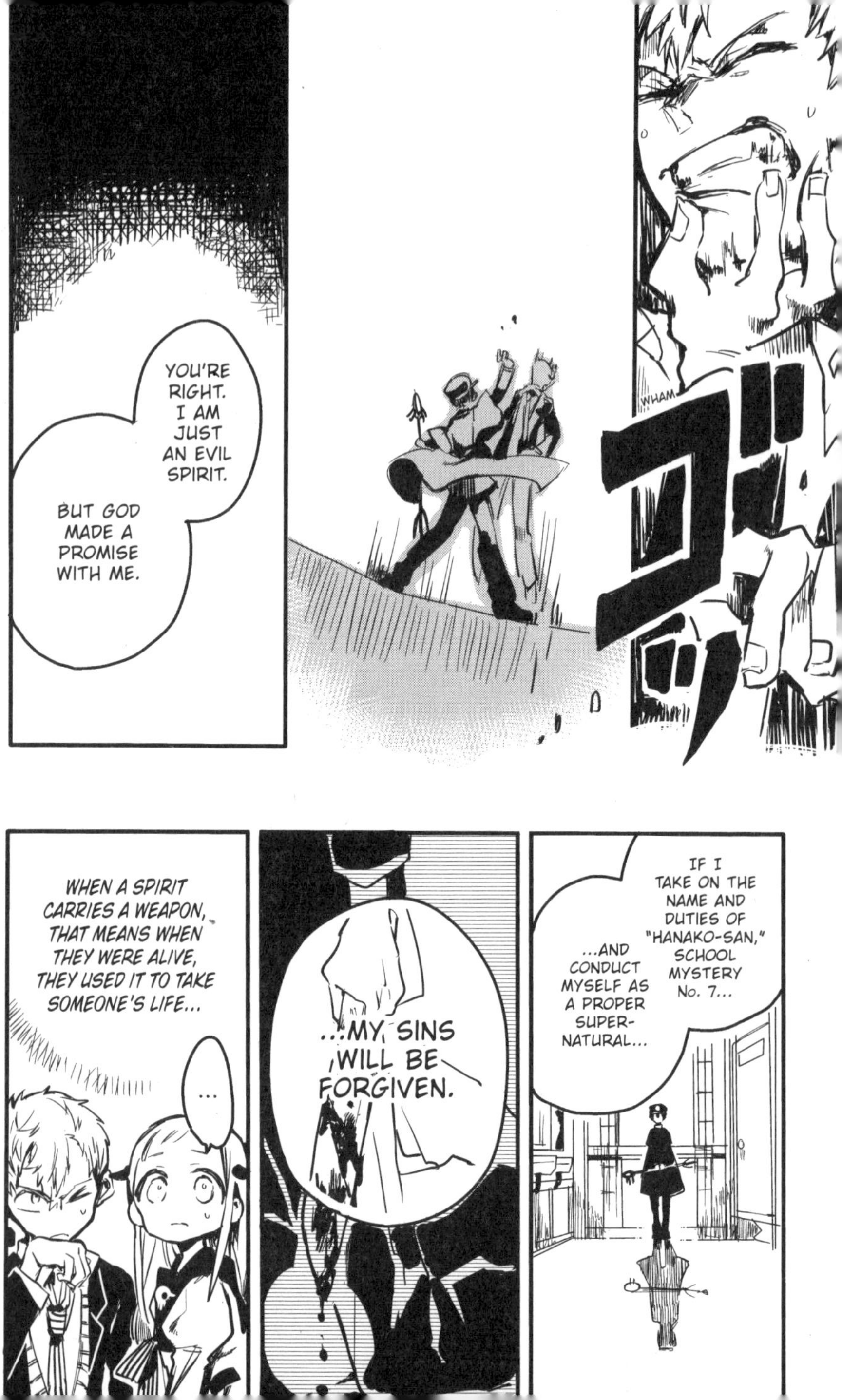
WHAM
YOU'RE RIGHT. I AM JUST AN EVIL SPIRIT.
BUT GOD MADE A PROMISE WITH ME.
IF I TAKE ON THE NAME AND DUTIES OF "HANAKO-SAN," SCHOOL MYSTERY No. 7...
...AND CONDUCT MYSELF AS A PROPER SUPER-NATURAL...
...MY SINS WILL BE FORGIVEN.
WHEN A SPIRIT CARRIES A WEAPON, THAT MEANS WHEN THEY WERE ALIVE, THEY USED IT TO TAKE SOMEONE'S LIFE...
...

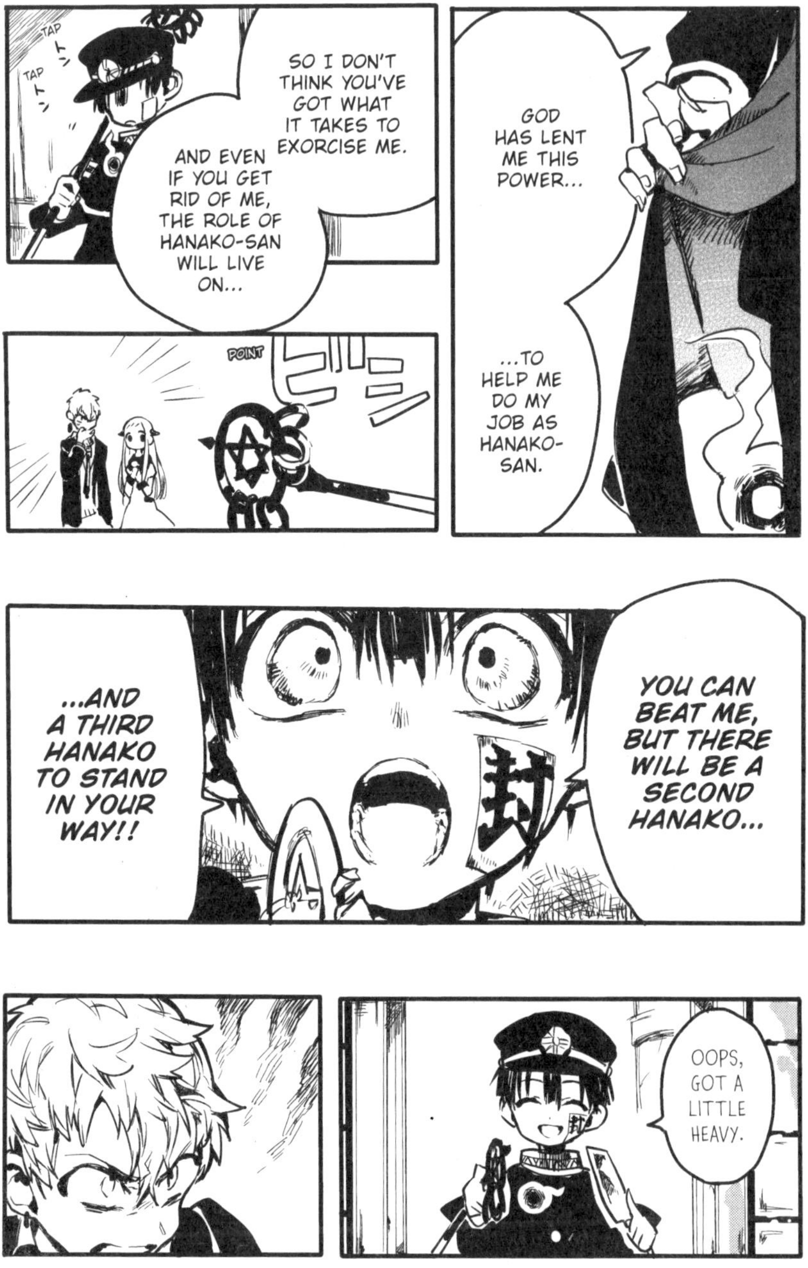
GOD HAS LENT ME THIS POWER...
...TO HELP ME DO MY JOB AS HANAKO-SAN.
SO I DON'T THINK YOU'VE GOT WHAT IT TAKES TO EXORCISE ME.
AND EVEN IF YOU GET RID OF ME, THE ROLE OF HANAKO-SAN WILL LIVE ON...
TAP
TAP
POINT
YOU CAN BEAT ME, BUT THERE WILL BE A SECOND HANAKO...
...AND A THIRD HANAKO TO STAND IN YOUR WAY!!
OOPS, GOT A LITTLE HEAVY.

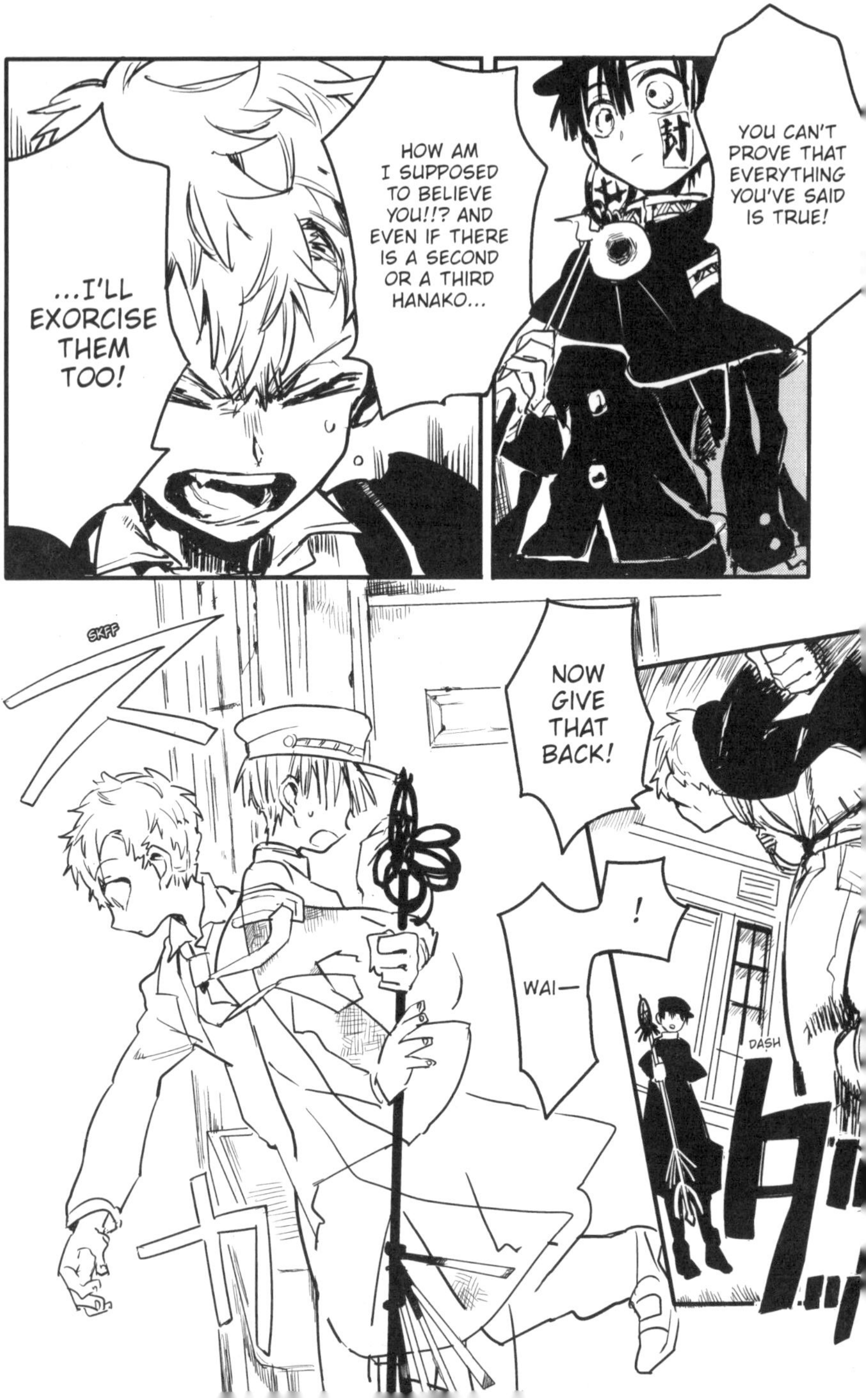
YOU CAN'T PROVE THAT EVERYTHING YOU'VE SAID IS TRUE!
HOW AM I SUPPOSED TO BELIEVE YOU!!? AND EVEN IF THERE IS A SECOND OR A THIRD HANAKO...
...I'LL EXORCISE THEM TOO!
NOW GIVE THAT BACK!
SKFF
!
WAI—
DASH

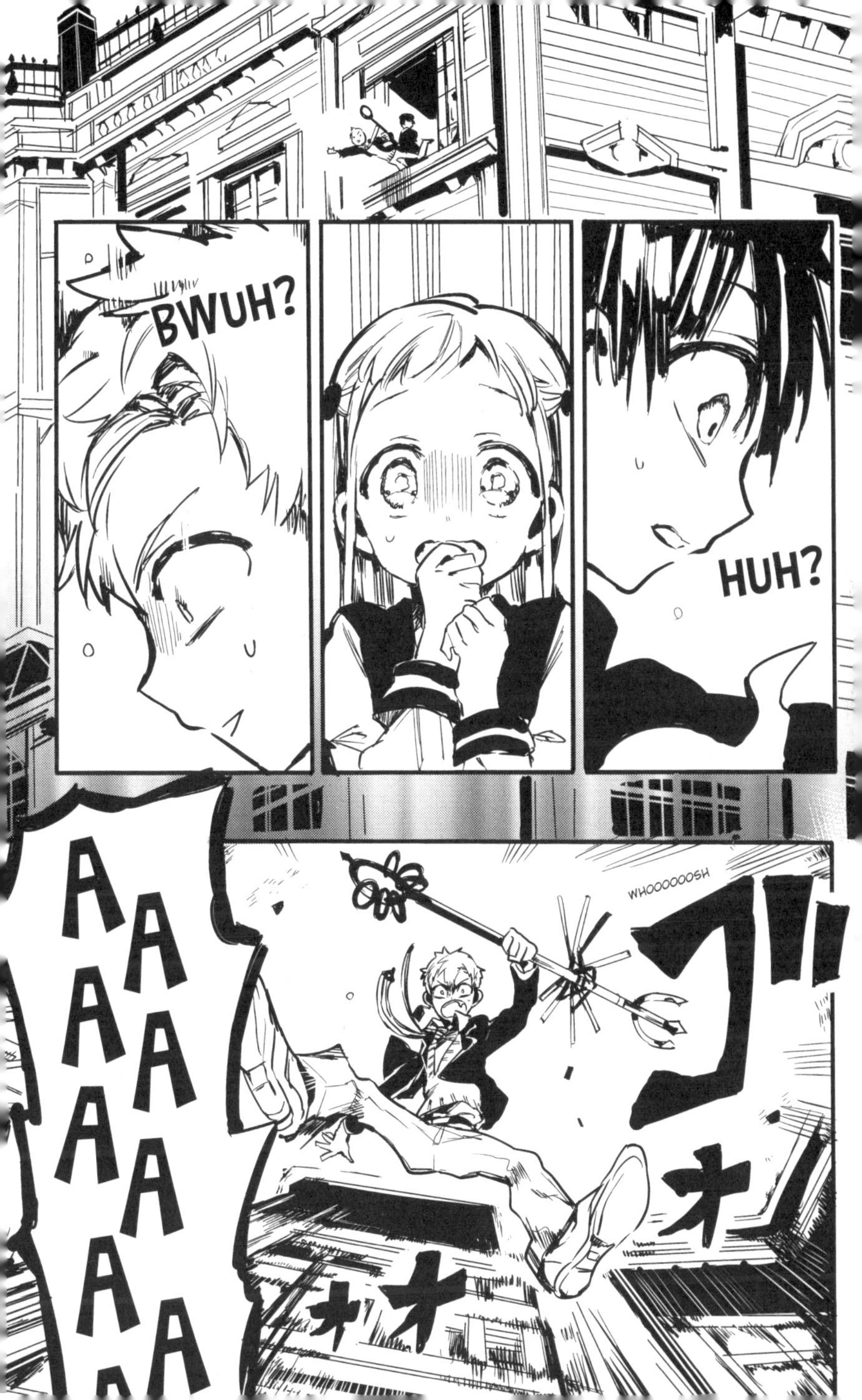
HUH?
BWUH?
WHOOOOOOSH
ゴオオオ
AAAAAAAAAAAA

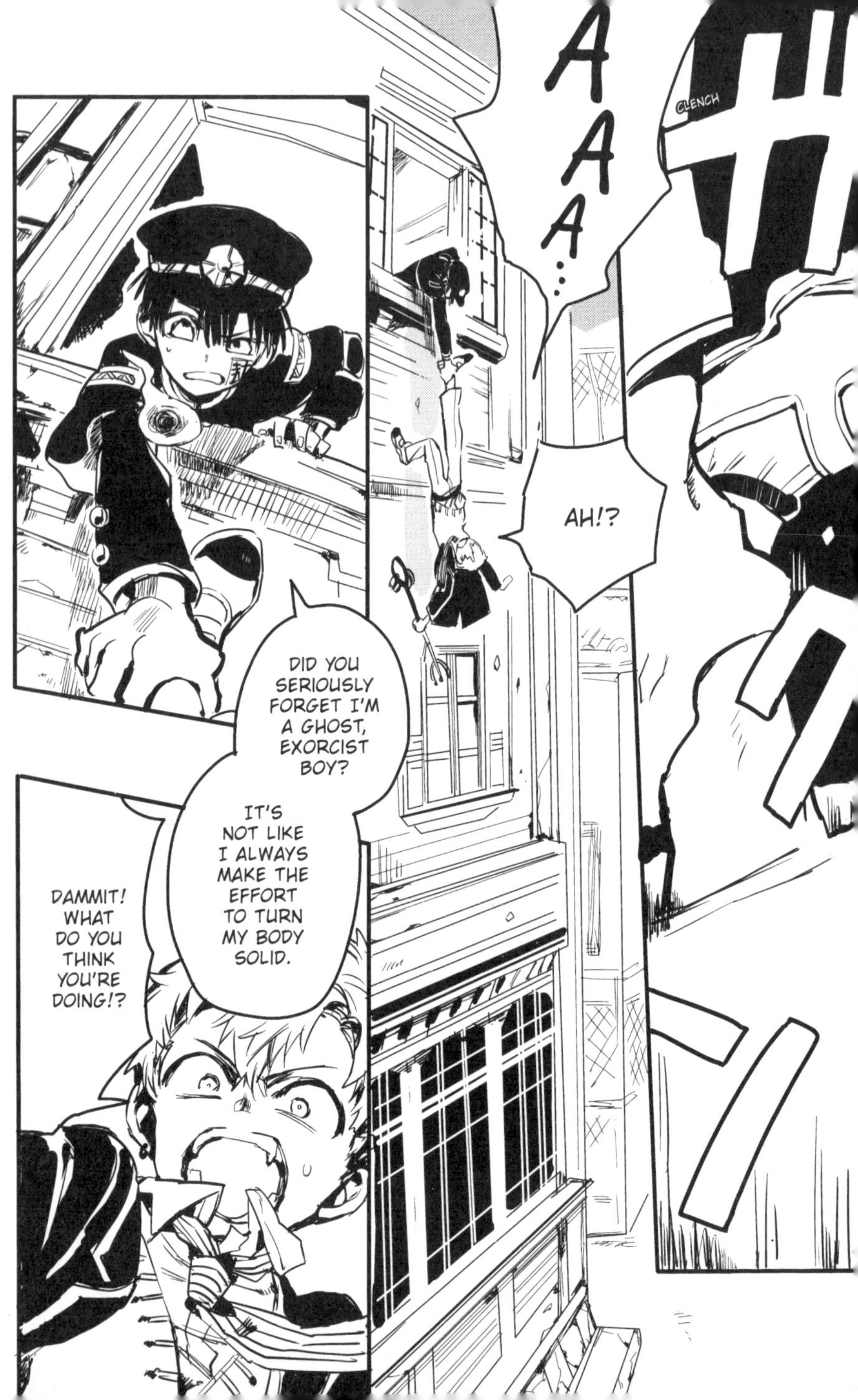
CLENCH
AAAA...
AH!?
DID YOU SERIOUSLY FORGET I'M A GHOST, EXORCIST BOY?
IT'S NOT LIKE I ALWAYS MAKE THE EFFORT TO TURN MY BODY SOLID.
DAMMIT! WHAT DO YOU THINK YOU'RE DOING!?

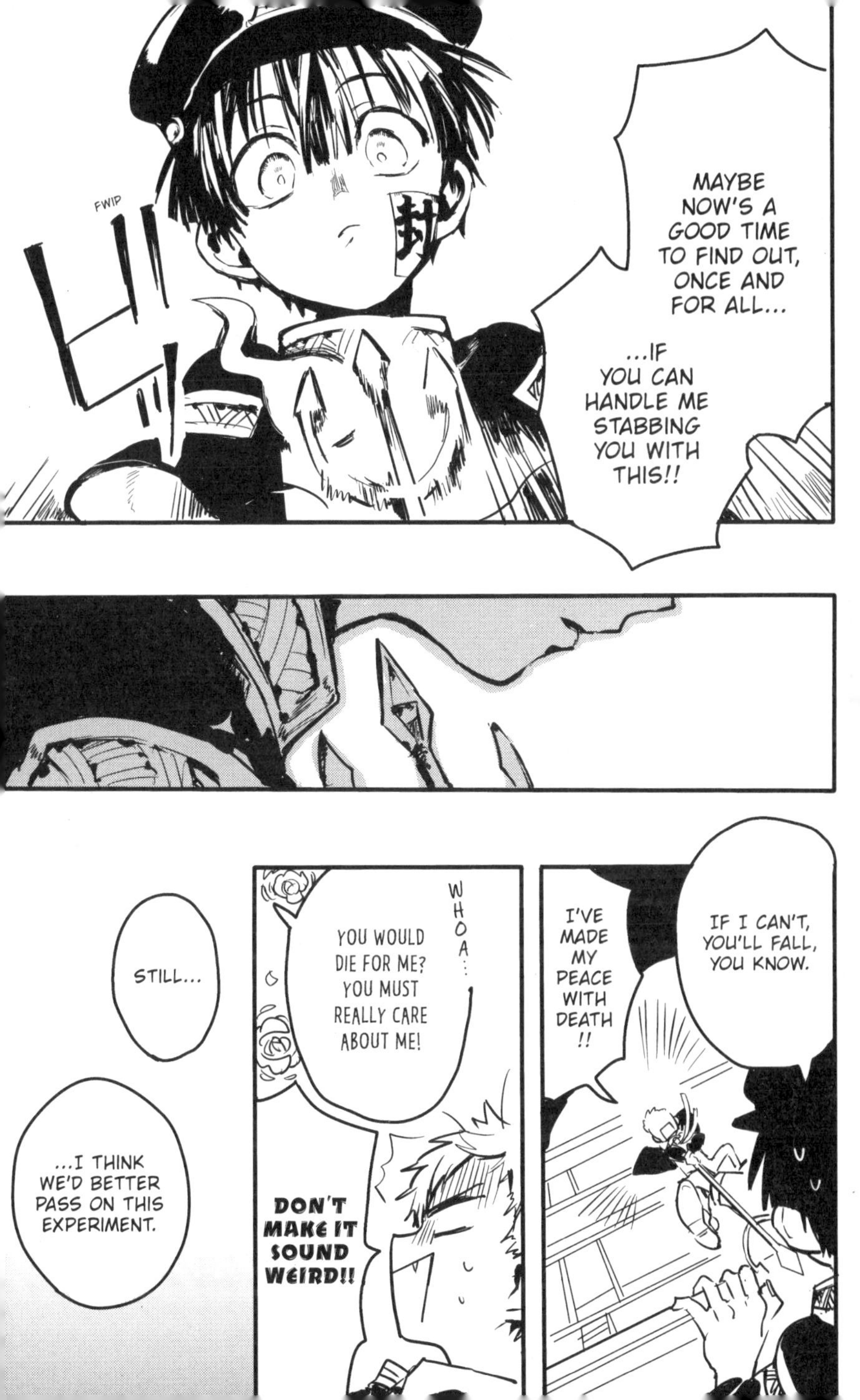
MAYBE NOW'S A GOOD TIME TO FIND OUT, ONCE AND FOR ALL... ...IF YOU CAN HANDLE ME STABBING YOU WITH THIS!!
FWIP
IF I CAN'T, YOU'LL FALL, YOU KNOW.
I'VE MADE MY PEACE WITH DEATH!!
WHOA...
YOU WOULD DIE FOR ME? YOU MUST REALLY CARE ABOUT ME!
DON'T MAKE IT SOUND WEIRD!!
STILL...
...I THINK WE'D BETTER PASS ON THIS EXPERIMENT.

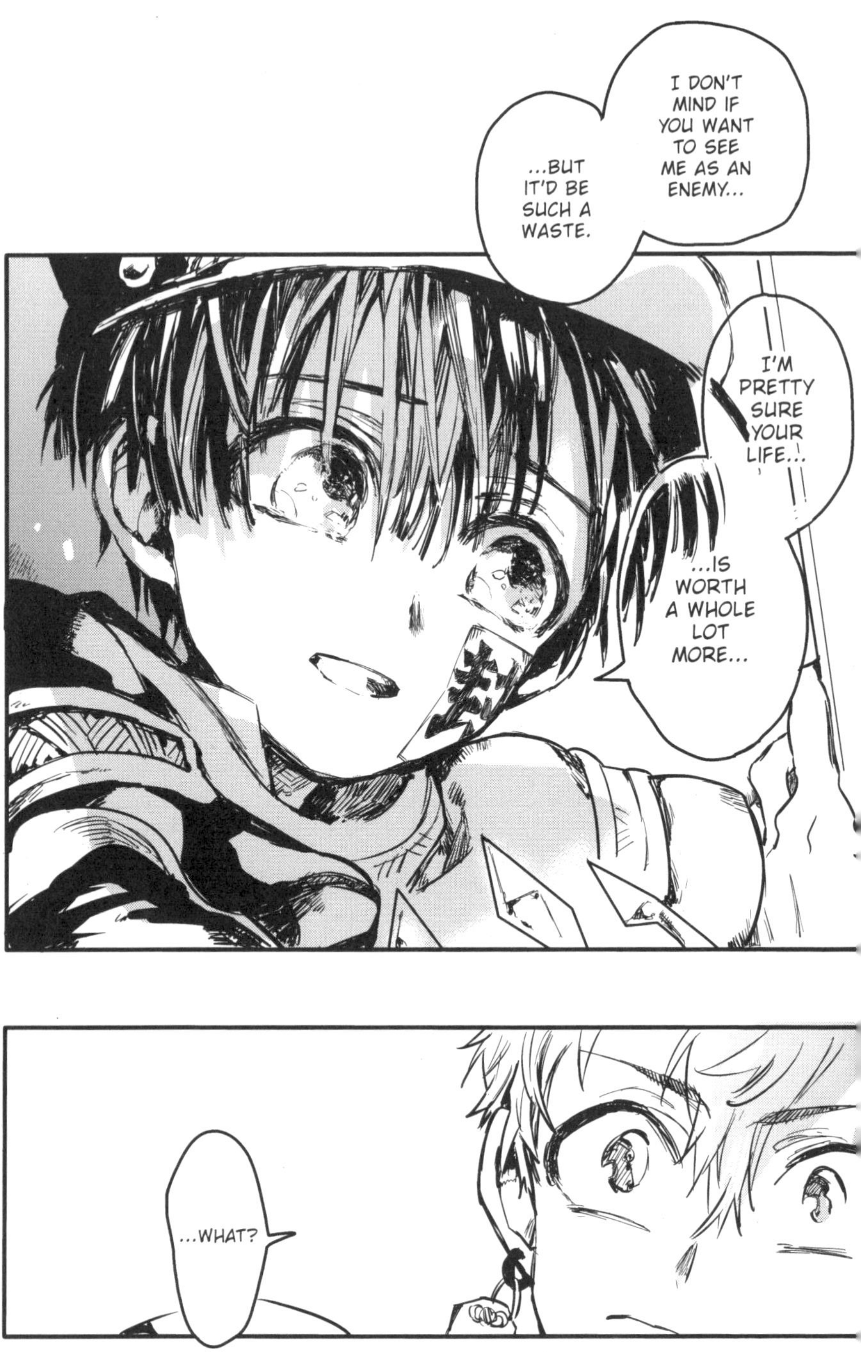
I DON'T MIND IF YOU WANT TO SEE ME AS AN ENEMY...
...BUT IT'D BE SUCH A WASTE.
I'M PRETTY SURE YOUR LIFE...
...IS WORTH A WHOLE LOT MORE...
...WHAT?

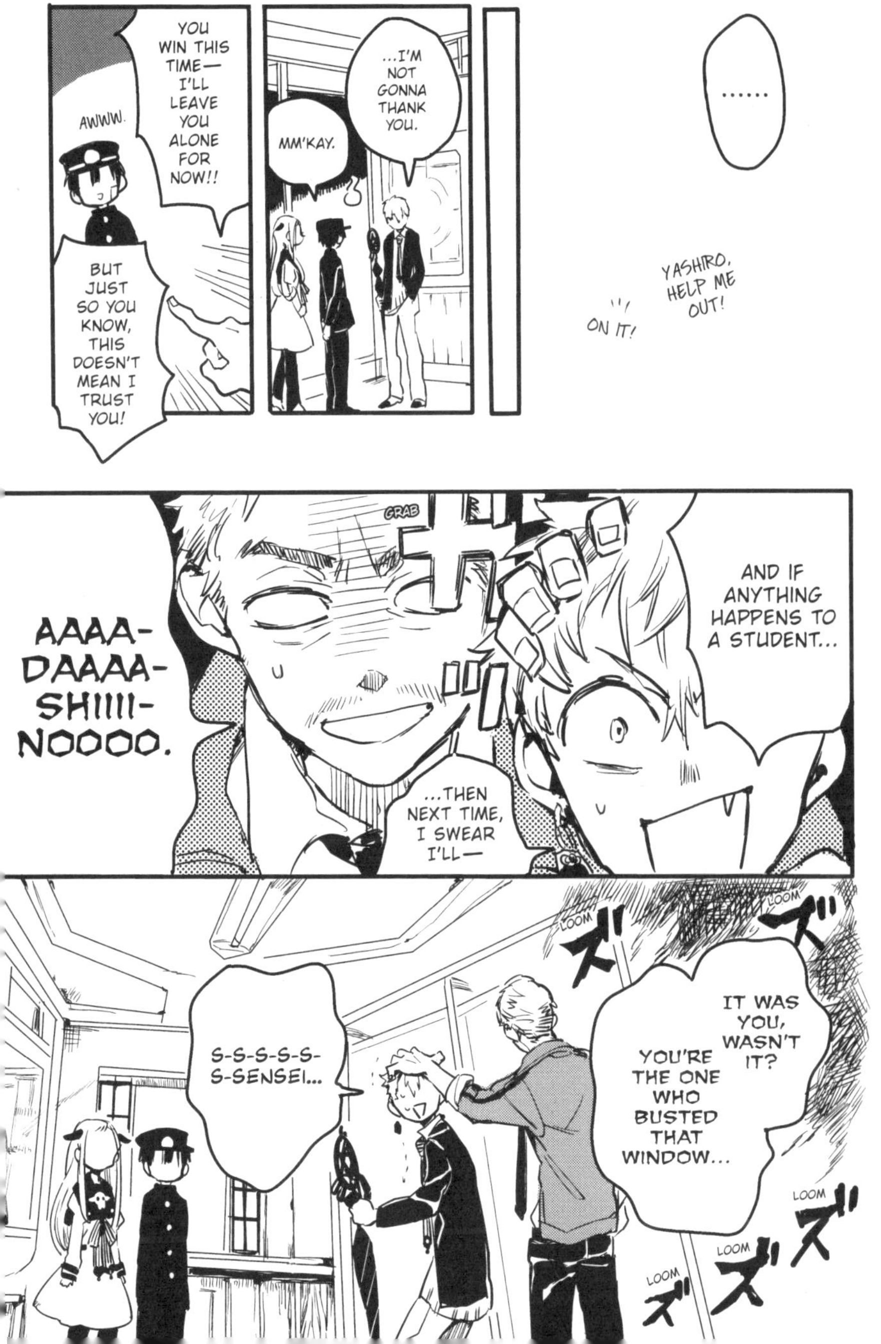
......
YASHIRO, HELP ME OUT!
ON IT!
...I'M NOT GONNA THANK YOU.
MM'KAY.
YOU WIN THIS TIME— I'LL LEAVE YOU ALONE FOR NOW!!
AWWW.
BUT JUST SO YOU KNOW, THIS DOESN'T MEAN I TRUST YOU!
GRAB
AND IF ANYTHING HAPPENS TO A STUDENT...
...THEN NEXT TIME, I SWEAR I'LL—
AAAA-DAAAA-SHIIII-NOOOO.
LOOM
LOOM
IT WAS YOU, WASN'T IT?
YOU'RE THE ONE WHO BUSTED THAT WINDOW...
S-S-S-S-S-S-SENSEI...
LOOM
LOOM
LOOM

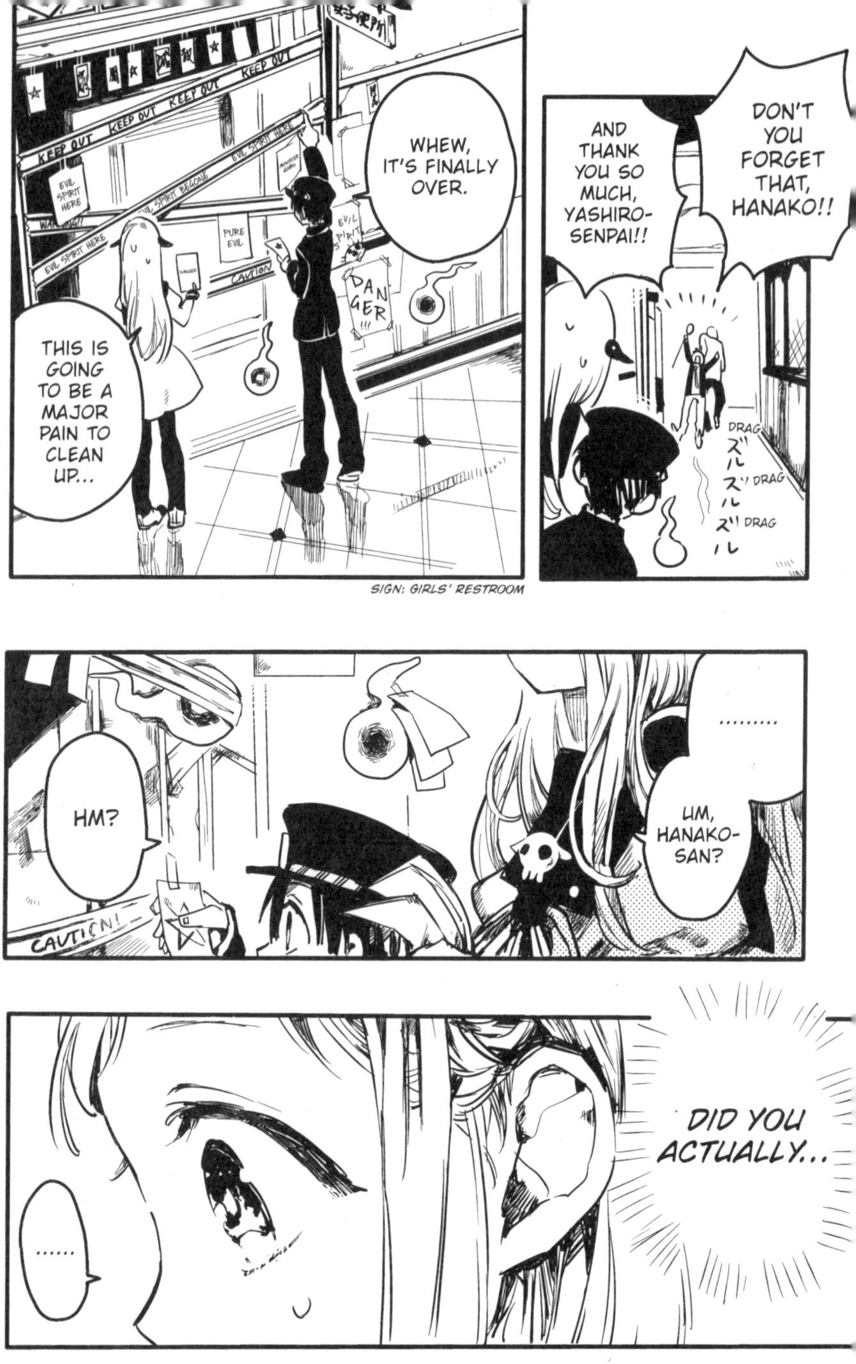
DON'T YOU FORGET THAT, HANAKO!!
AND THANK YOU SO MUCH, YASHIRO-SENPAI!!
DRAG ズルズルズル DRAG DRAG
WHEW, IT'S FINALLY OVER.
THIS IS GOING TO BE A MAJOR PAIN TO CLEAN UP...
SIGN: GIRLS' RESTROOM
....
UM, HANAKO-SAN?
HM?
DID YOU ACTUALLY...
......

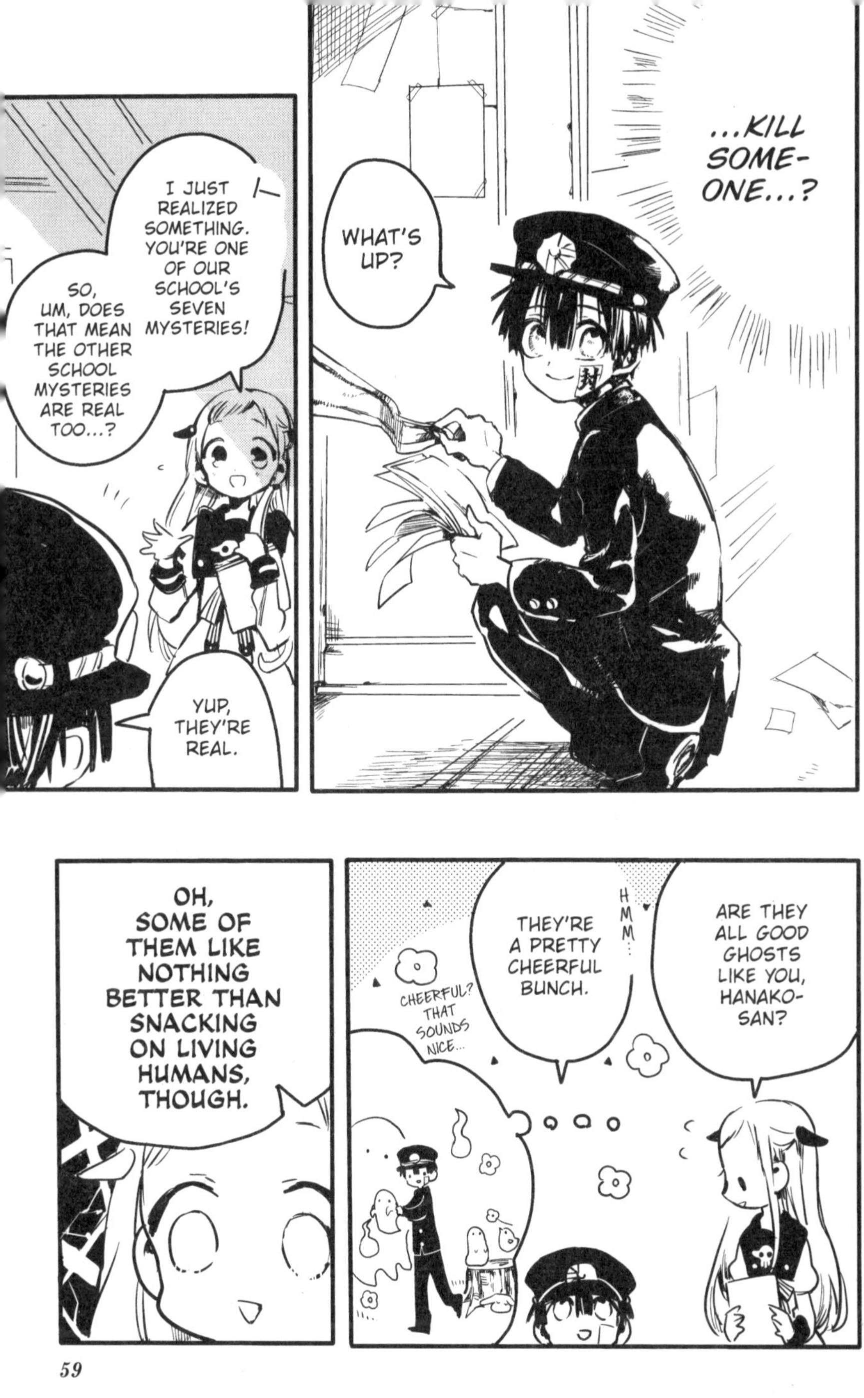
...KILL SOME-ONE...?
WHAT'S UP?
I JUST REALIZED SOMETHING. YOU'RE ONE OF OUR SCHOOL'S SEVEN MYSTERIES!
SO, UM, DOES THAT MEAN THE OTHER SCHOOL MYSTERIES ARE REAL TOO...?
YUP, THEY'RE REAL.
ARE THEY ALL GOOD GHOSTS LIKE YOU, HANAKO-SAN?
HMM...
THEY'RE A PRETTY CHEERFUL BUNCH.
CHEERFUL? THAT SOUNDS NICE...
OH, SOME OF THEM LIKE NOTHING BETTER THAN SNACKING ON LIVING HUMANS, THOUGH.

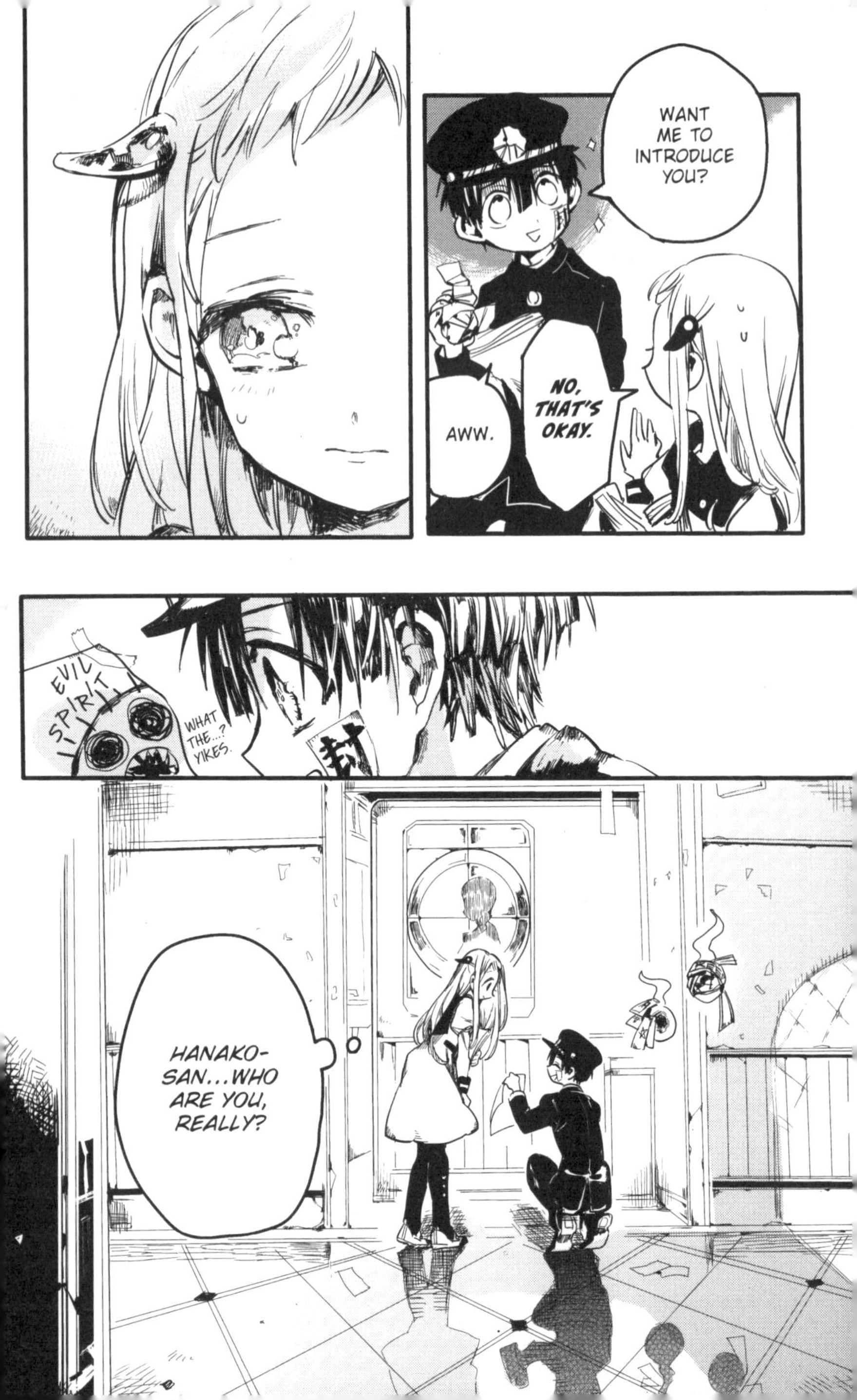
WANT ME TO INTRODUCE YOU?
NO, THAT'S OKAY.
AWW.
EVIL SPIRIT
WHAT THE...? YIKES.
HANAKO-SAN...WHO ARE YOU, REALLY?

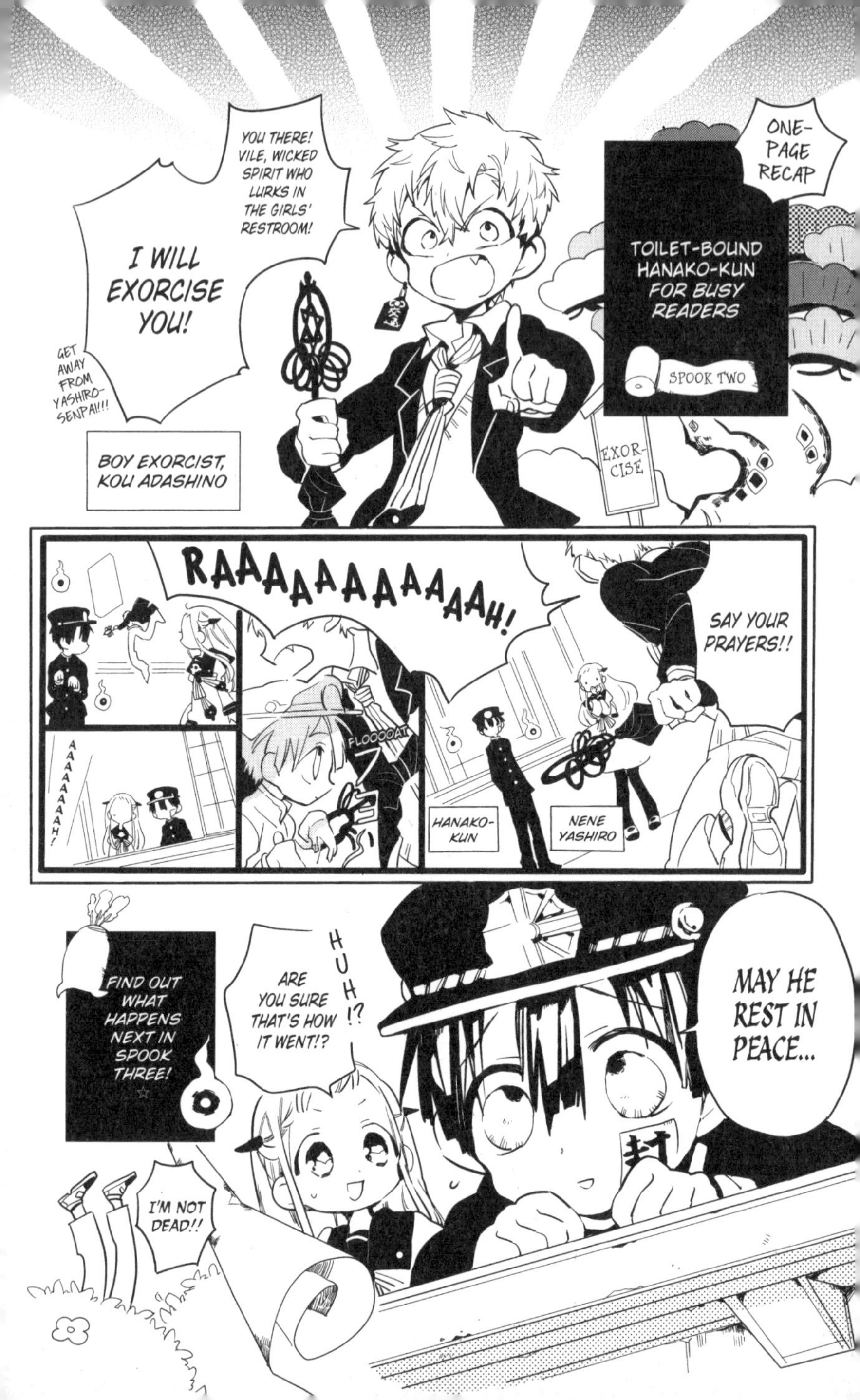
ONE-PAGE RECAP
TOILET-BOUND HANAKO-KUN FOR BUSY READERS
SPOOK TWO
EXOR-CISE
YOU THERE! VILE, WICKED SPIRIT WHO LURKS IN THE GIRLS' RESTROOM!
I WILL EXORCISE YOU!
GET AWAY FROM YASHIRO-SENPAI!!!
BOY EXORCIST, KOU ADASHINO
SAY YOUR PRAYERS!!
NENE YASHIRO
HANAKO-KUN
RAAAAAAAAAAAH!
FLOOOOAT
AAAAAAAAAH!
MAY HE REST IN PEACE...
HUH!?
ARE YOU SURE THAT'S HOW IT WENT!?
FIND OUT WHAT HAPPENS NEXT IN SPOOK THREE! ☆
I'M NOT DEAD!!

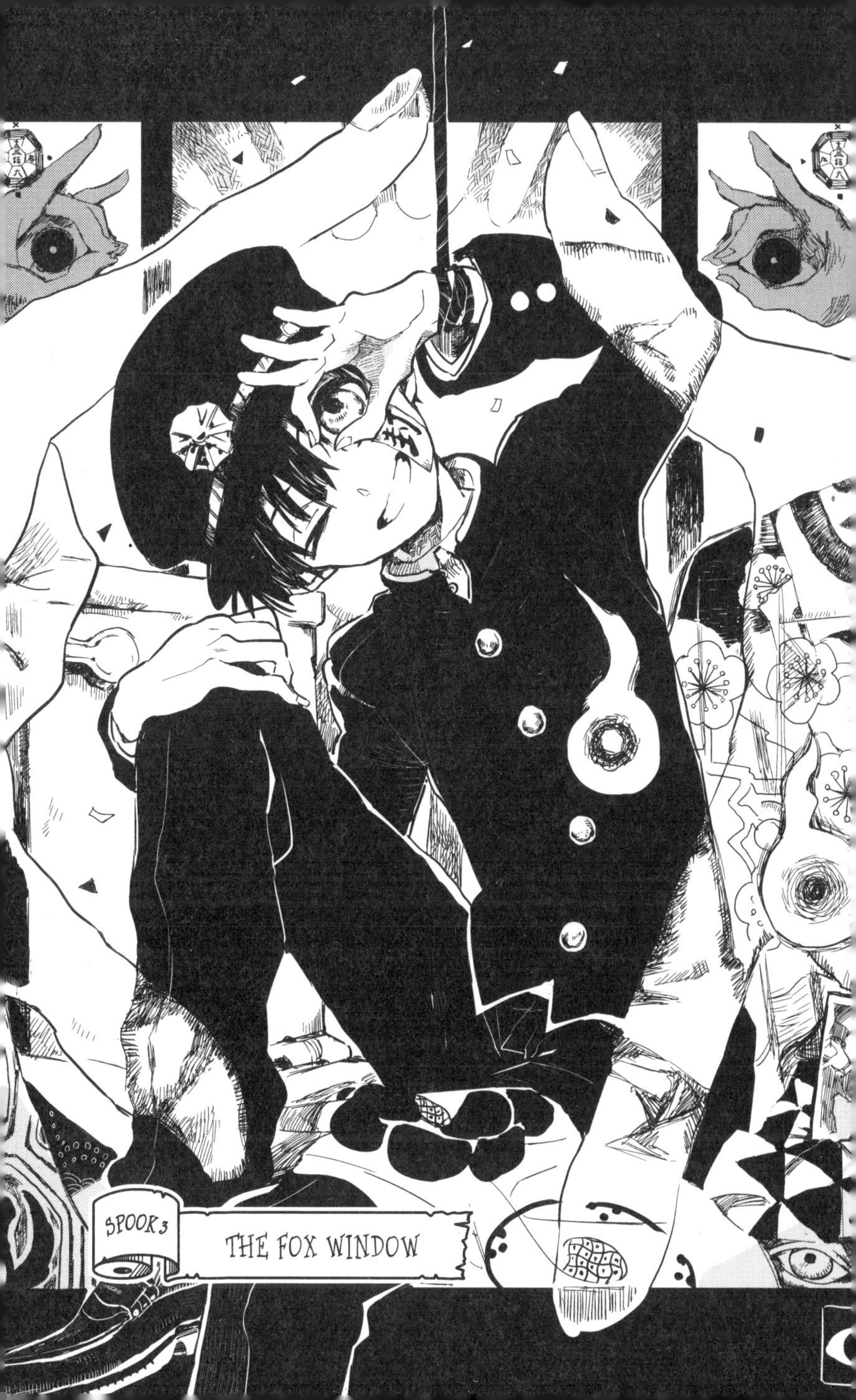
SPOOK 3
THE FOX WINDOW

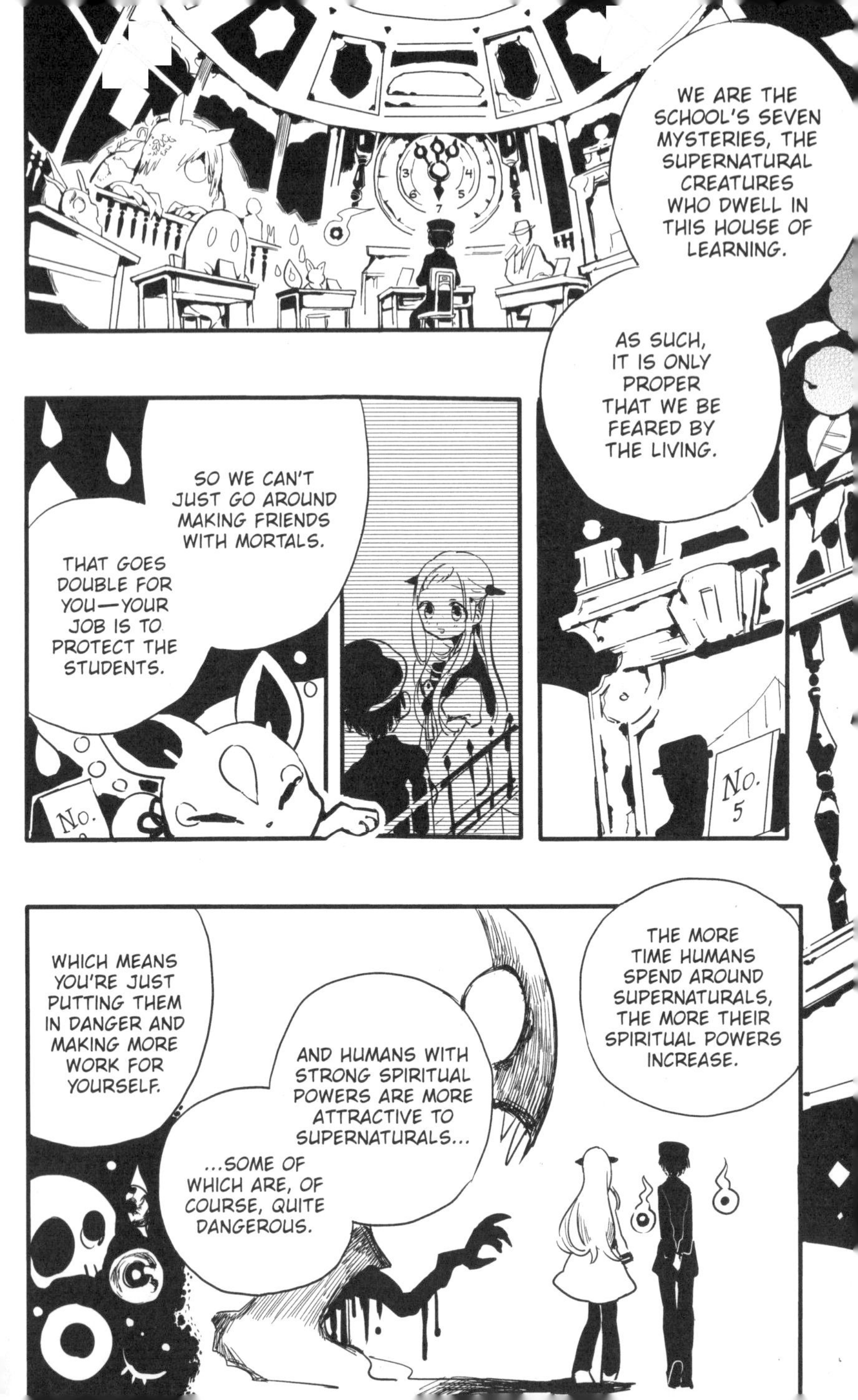
WE ARE THE SCHOOL'S SEVEN MYSTERIES, THE SUPERNATURAL CREATURES WHO DWELL IN THIS HOUSE OF LEARNING.
AS SUCH, IT IS ONLY PROPER THAT WE BE FEARED BY THE LIVING.
No. 5
SO WE CAN'T JUST GO AROUND MAKING FRIENDS WITH MORTALS.
THAT GOES DOUBLE FOR YOU—YOUR JOB IS TO PROTECT THE STUDENTS.
No.
THE MORE TIME HUMANS SPEND AROUND SUPERNATURALS, THE MORE THEIR SPIRITUAL POWERS INCREASE.
AND HUMANS WITH STRONG SPIRITUAL POWERS ARE MORE ATTRACTIVE TO SUPERNATURALS...
...SOME OF WHICH ARE, OF COURSE, QUITE DANGEROUS.
WHICH MEANS YOU'RE JUST PUTTING THEM IN DANGER AND MAKING MORE WORK FOR YOURSELF.

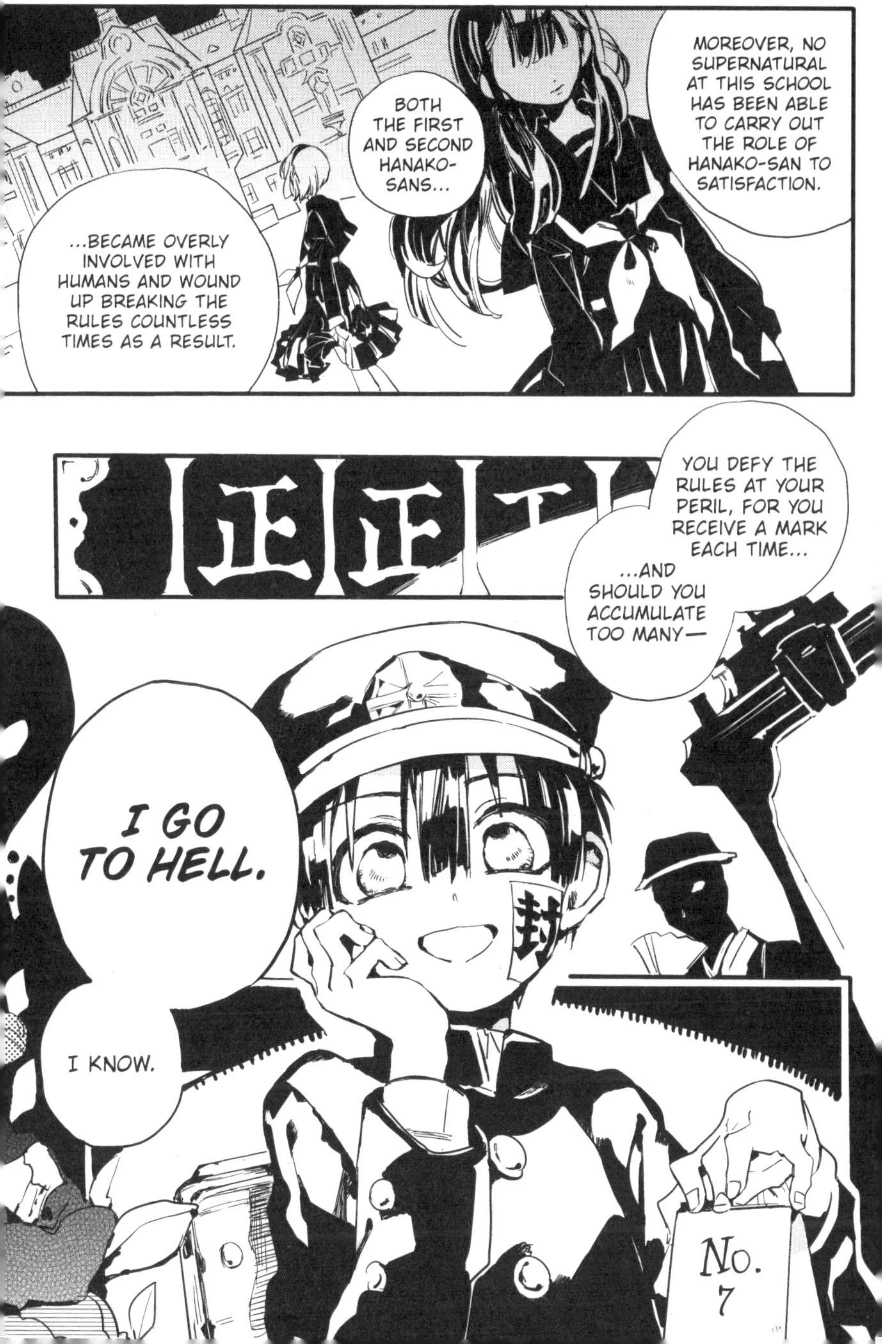
MOREOVER, NO SUPERNATURAL AT THIS SCHOOL HAS BEEN ABLE TO CARRY OUT THE ROLE OF HANAKO-SAN TO SATISFACTION.
BOTH THE FIRST AND SECOND HANAKO-SANS...
...BECAME OVERLY INVOLVED WITH HUMANS AND WOUND UP BREAKING THE RULES COUNTLESS TIMES AS A RESULT.
YOU DEFY THE RULES AT YOUR PERIL, FOR YOU RECEIVE A MARK EACH TIME...
...AND SHOULD YOU ACCUMULATE TOO MANY—
I GO TO HELL.
I KNOW.
No. 7

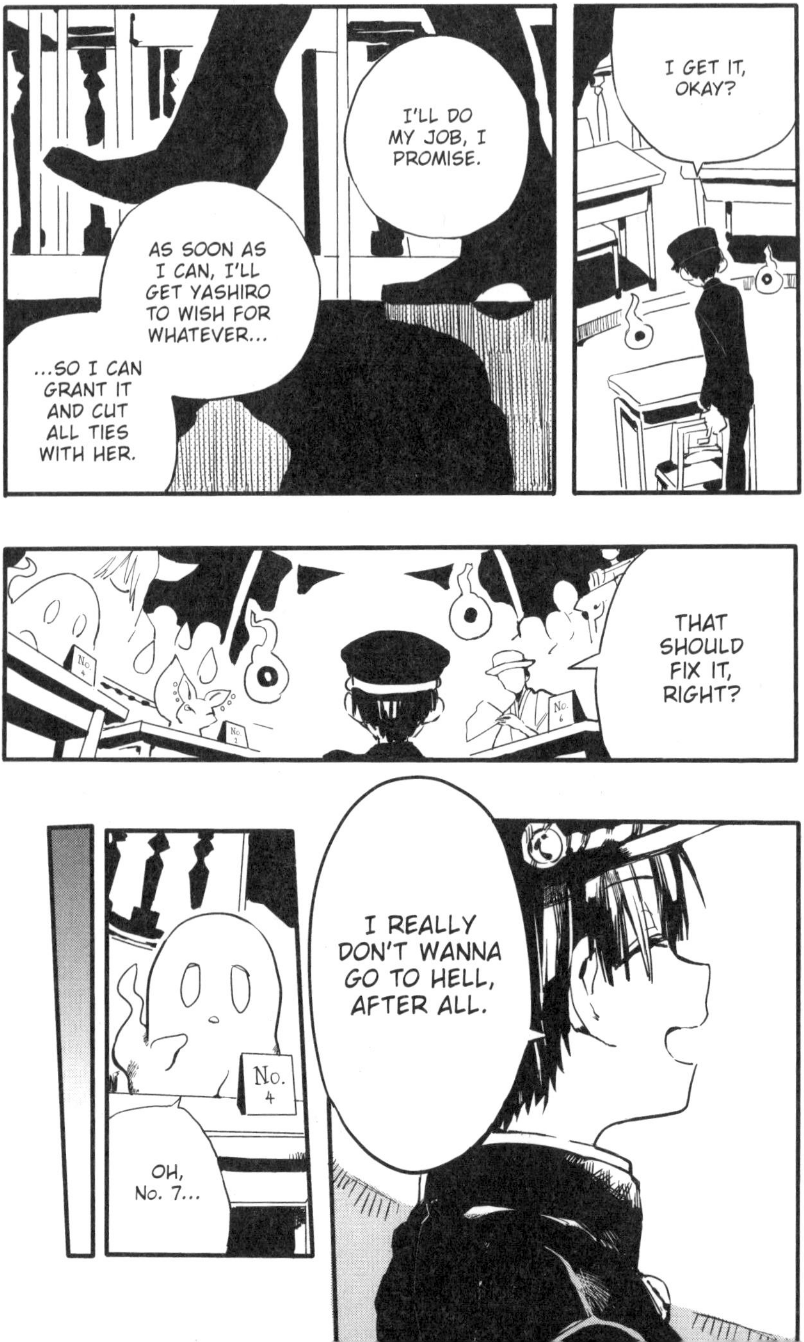
I GET IT, OKAY?
I'LL DO MY JOB, I PROMISE.
AS SOON AS I CAN, I'LL GET YASHIRO TO WISH FOR WHATEVER...
...SO I CAN GRANT IT AND CUT ALL TIES WITH HER.
THAT SHOULD FIX IT, RIGHT?
I REALLY DON'T WANNA GO TO HELL, AFTER ALL.
No. 4
OH, No. 7...

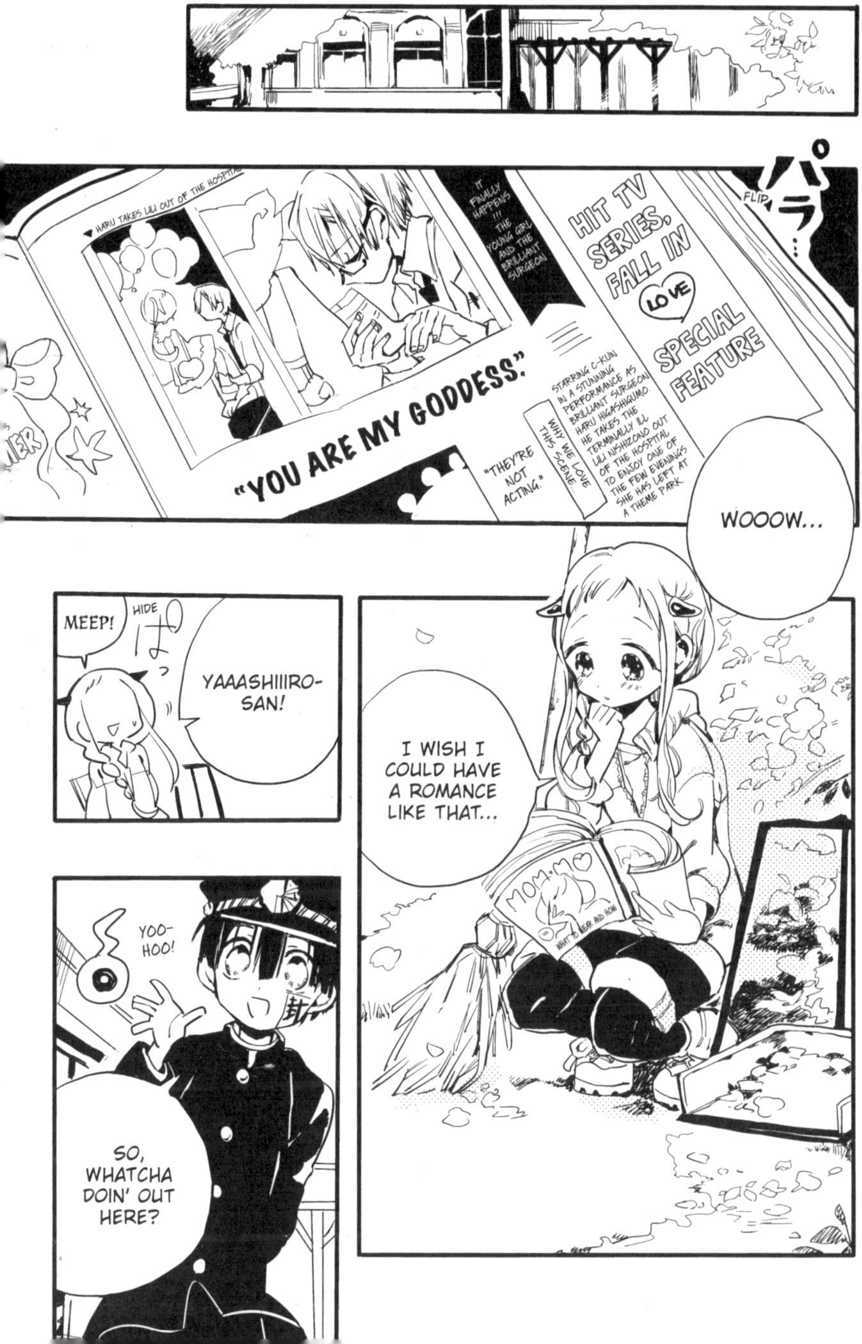
パラ
FLIP
HIT TV SERIES, FALL IN LOVE SPECIAL FEATURE
IT FINALLY HAPPENS!!! THE YOUNG GIRL AND THE BRILLIANT SURGEON
HARU TAKES LILI OUT OF THE HOSPITAL
"YOU ARE MY GODDESS."
STARRING C-KUN IN A STUNNING PERFORMANCE AS BRILLIANT SURGEON HARU HIGASHIGUMO. HE TAKES THE TERMINALLY ILL LILI NISHIZONO OUT OF THE HOSPITAL TO ENJOY ONE OF THE FEW EVENINGS SHE HAS LEFT AT A THEME PARK
WHY WE LOVE THIS SCENE
"THEY'RE NOT ACTING."
WOOOW...
I WISH I COULD HAVE A ROMANCE LIKE THAT...
MOM·MO
WHAT TO WEAR AND HOW
YAAASHIIIRO-SAN!
HIDE
MEEP!
YOO-HOO!
SO, WHATCHA DOIN' OUT HERE?

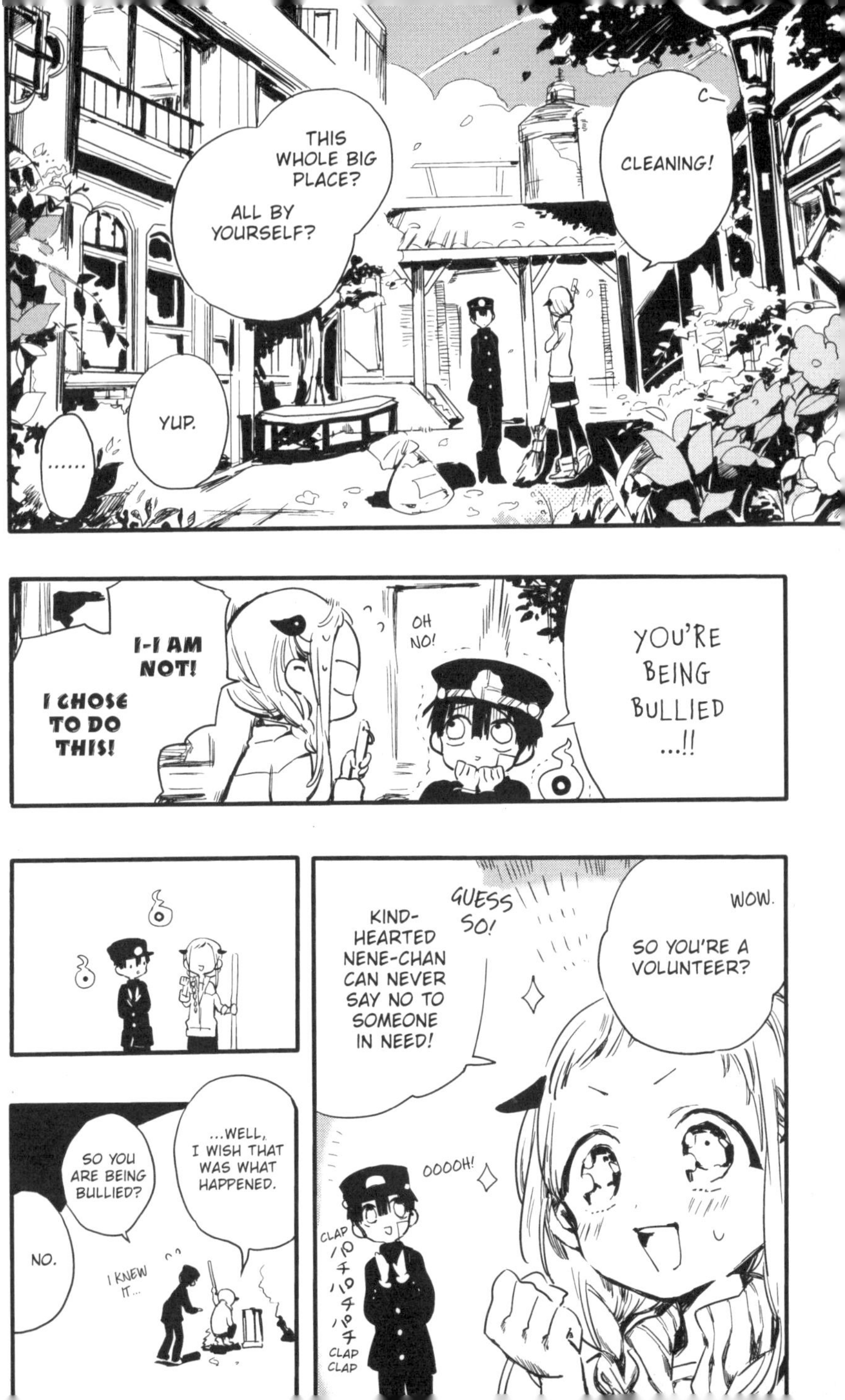
C—
CLEANING!
THIS WHOLE BIG PLACE?
ALL BY YOURSELF?
YUP.
......
YOU'RE BEING BULLIED ...!!
OH NO!
I-I AM NOT!
I CHOSE TO DO THIS!
WOW.
SO YOU'RE A VOLUNTEER?
GUESS SO!
KIND-HEARTED NENE-CHAN CAN NEVER SAY NO TO SOMEONE IN NEED!
OOOOH!
CLAP パチ パチ パチ CLAP CLAP
...WELL, I WISH THAT WAS WHAT HAPPENED.
SO YOU ARE BEING BULLIED?
NO.
I KNEW IT...

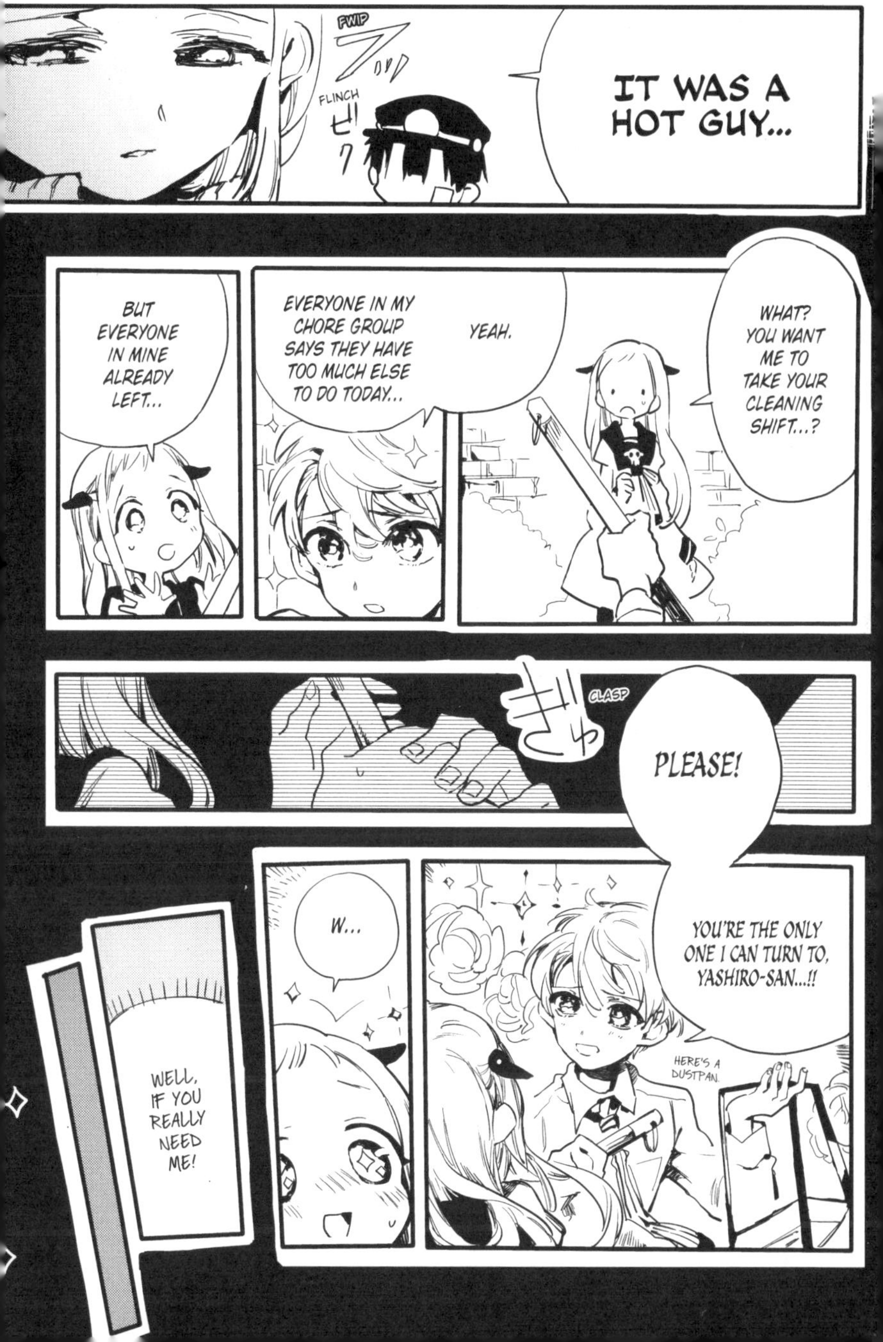
IT WAS A HOT GUY...
FWIP
FLINCH
WHAT? YOU WANT ME TO TAKE YOUR CLEANING SHIFT...?
YEAH.
EVERYONE IN MY CHORE GROUP SAYS THEY HAVE TOO MUCH ELSE TO DO TODAY...
BUT EVERYONE IN MINE ALREADY LEFT...
PLEASE!
CLASP
YOU'RE THE ONLY ONE I CAN TURN TO, YASHIRO-SAN...!!
HERE'S A DUSTPAN.
W...
WELL, IF YOU REALLY NEED ME!

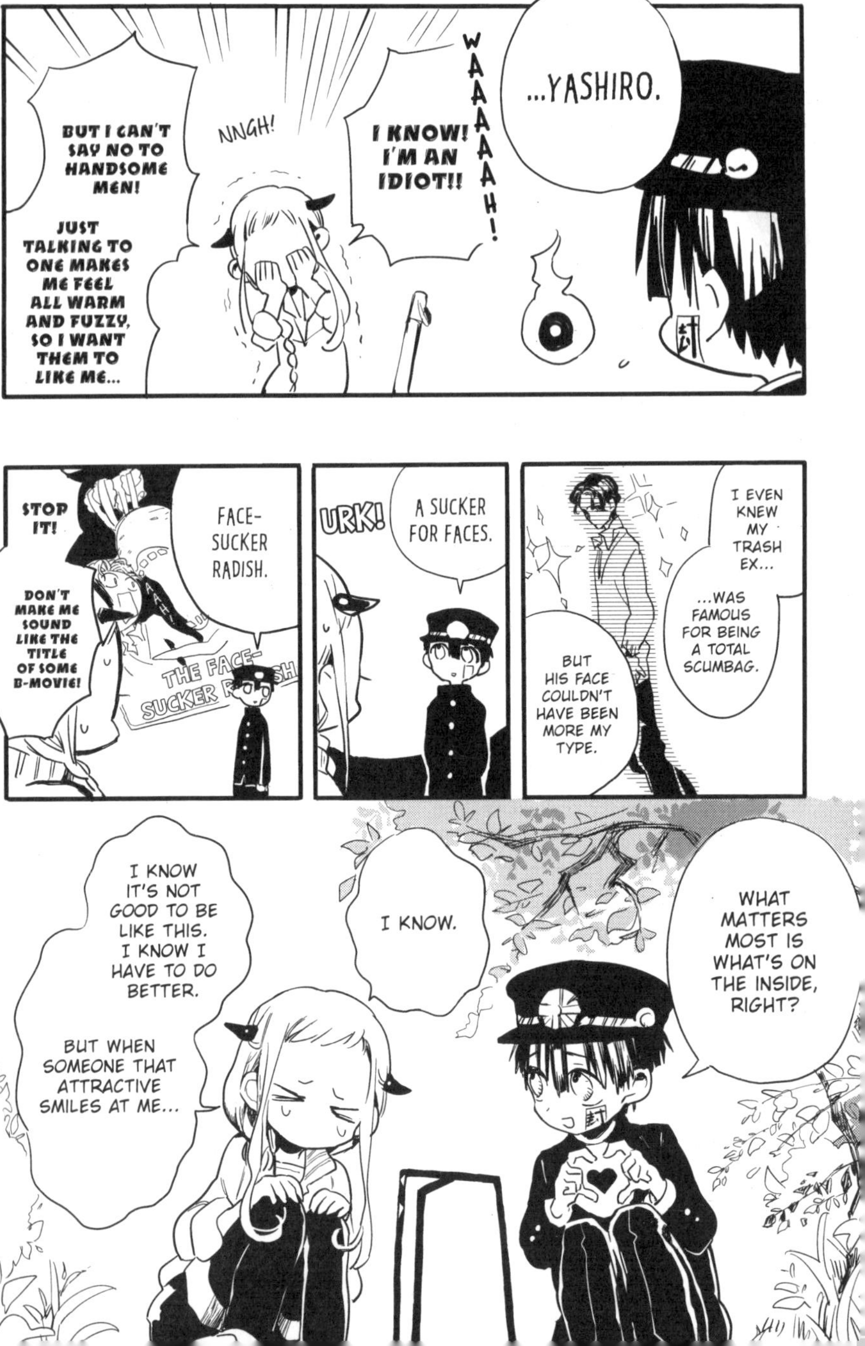
...YASHIRO.
WAAAAAAH!
I KNOW! I'M AN IDIOT!!
NNGH!
BUT I CAN'T SAY NO TO HANDSOME MEN!
JUST TALKING TO ONE MAKES ME FEEL ALL WARM AND FUZZY, SO I WANT THEM TO LIKE ME...
I EVEN KNEW MY TRASH EX...
...WAS FAMOUS FOR BEING A TOTAL SCUMBAG.
BUT HIS FACE COULDN'T HAVE BEEN MORE MY TYPE.
A SUCKER FOR FACES.
URK!
FACE-SUCKER RADISH.
STOP IT!
DON'T MAKE ME SOUND LIKE THE TITLE OF SOME B-MOVIE!
WHAT MATTERS MOST IS WHAT'S ON THE INSIDE, RIGHT?
I KNOW.
I KNOW IT'S NOT GOOD TO BE LIKE THIS. I KNOW I HAVE TO DO BETTER.
BUT WHEN SOMEONE THAT ATTRACTIVE SMILES AT ME...

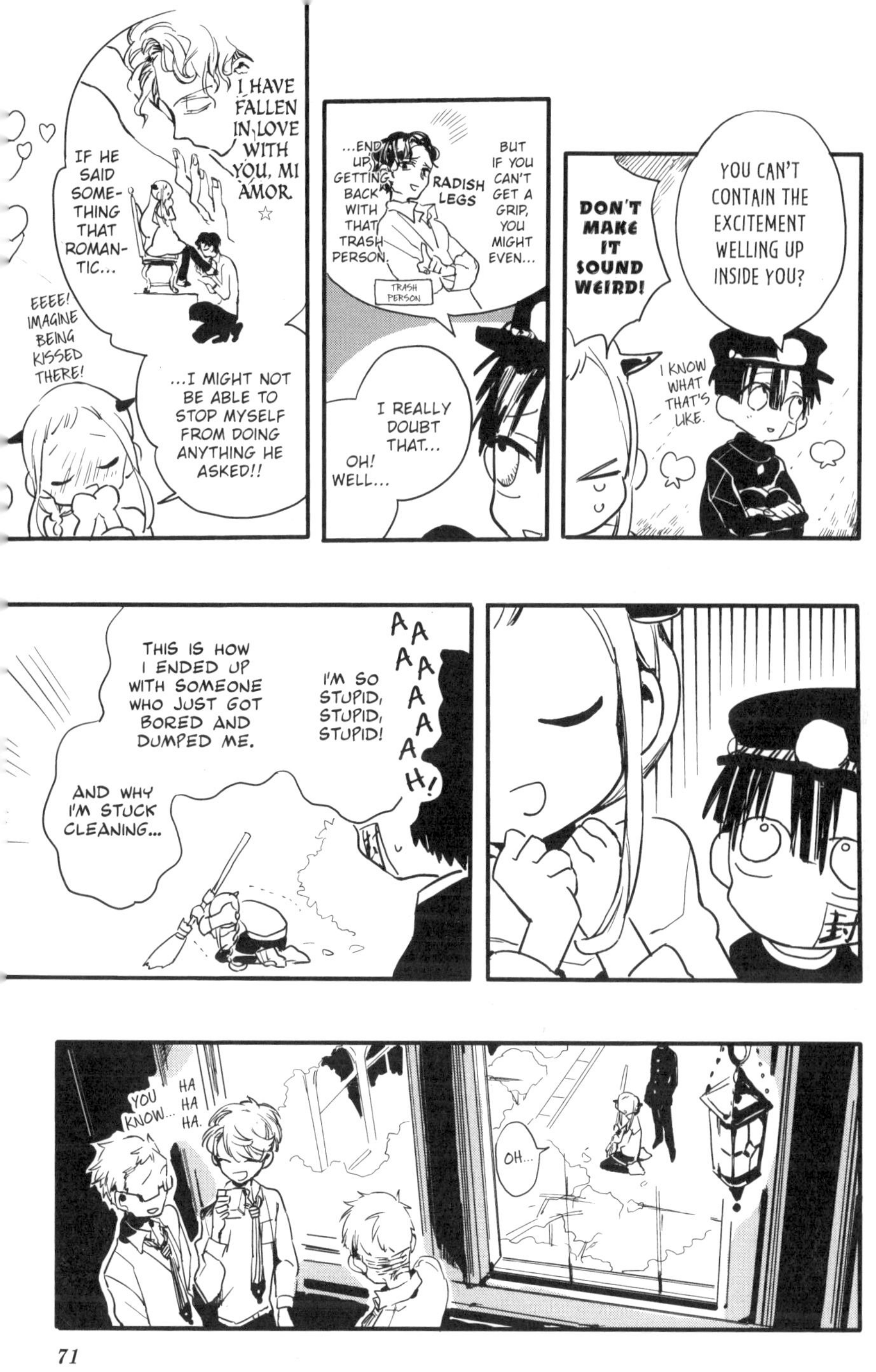
YOU CAN'T CONTAIN THE EXCITEMENT WELLING UP INSIDE YOU?
I KNOW WHAT THAT'S LIKE.
DON'T MAKE IT SOUND WEIRD!
BUT IF YOU CAN'T GET A GRIP, YOU MIGHT EVEN...
RADISH LEGS
...END UP GETTING BACK WITH THAT TRASH PERSON.
TRASH PERSON
I REALLY DOUBT THAT...
OH! WELL...
I HAVE FALLEN IN LOVE WITH YOU, MI AMOR. ☆
IF HE SAID SOMETHING THAT ROMANTIC...
...I MIGHT NOT BE ABLE TO STOP MYSELF FROM DOING ANYTHING HE ASKED!!
EEEE! IMAGINE BEING KISSED THERE!
AAAAAAAH!
I'M SO STUPID, STUPID, STUPID!
THIS IS HOW I ENDED UP WITH SOMEONE WHO JUST GOT BORED AND DUMPED ME.
AND WHY I'M STUCK CLEANING...
OH...
HA HA HA.
YOU KNOW...

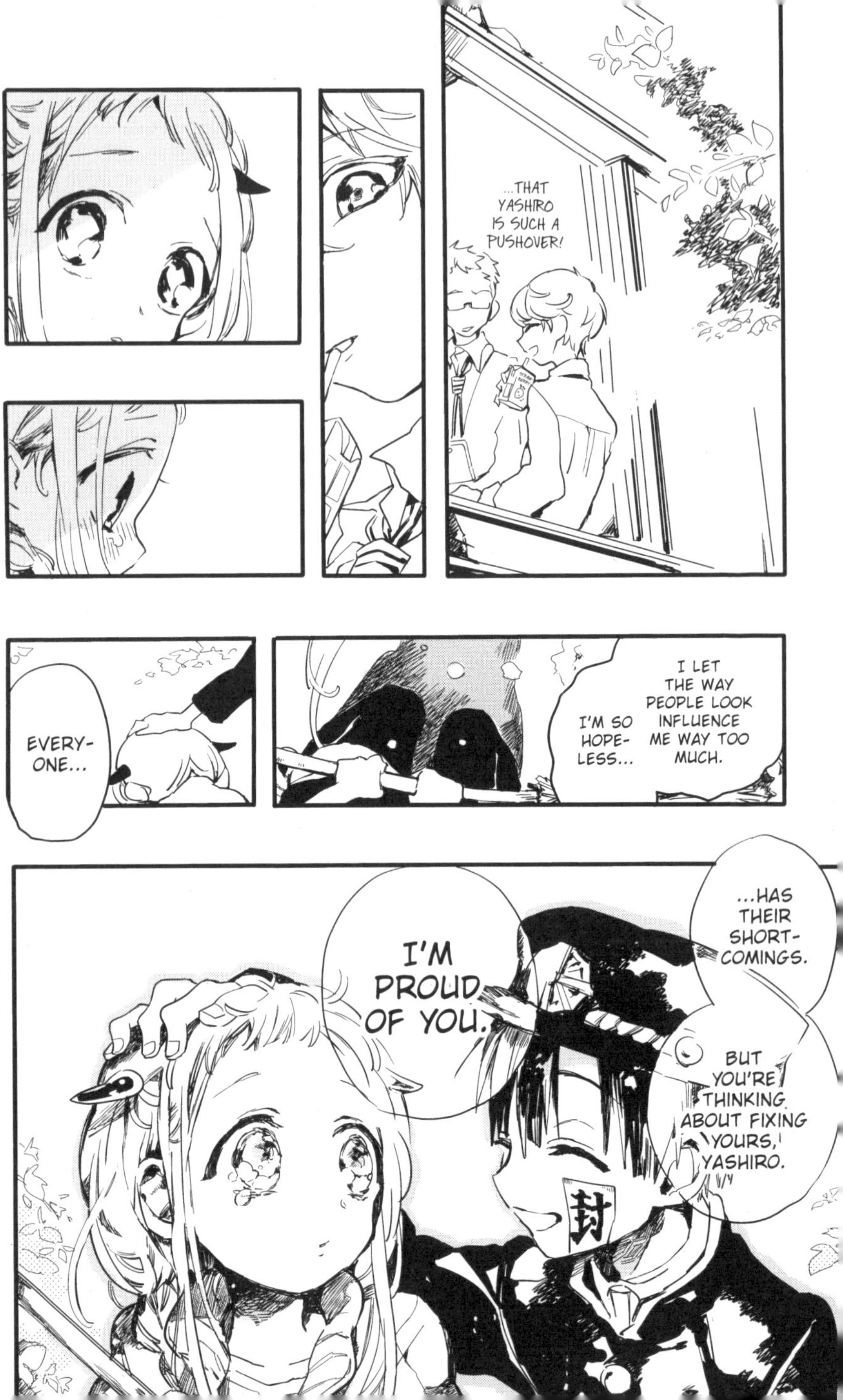
...THAT YASHIRO IS SUCH A PUSHOVER!
I LET THE WAY PEOPLE LOOK INFLUENCE ME WAY TOO MUCH.
I'M SO HOPE-LESS...
EVERY-ONE...
...HAS THEIR SHORT-COMINGS.
BUT YOU'RE THINKING ABOUT FIXING YOURS, YASHIRO.
I'M PROUD OF YOU.

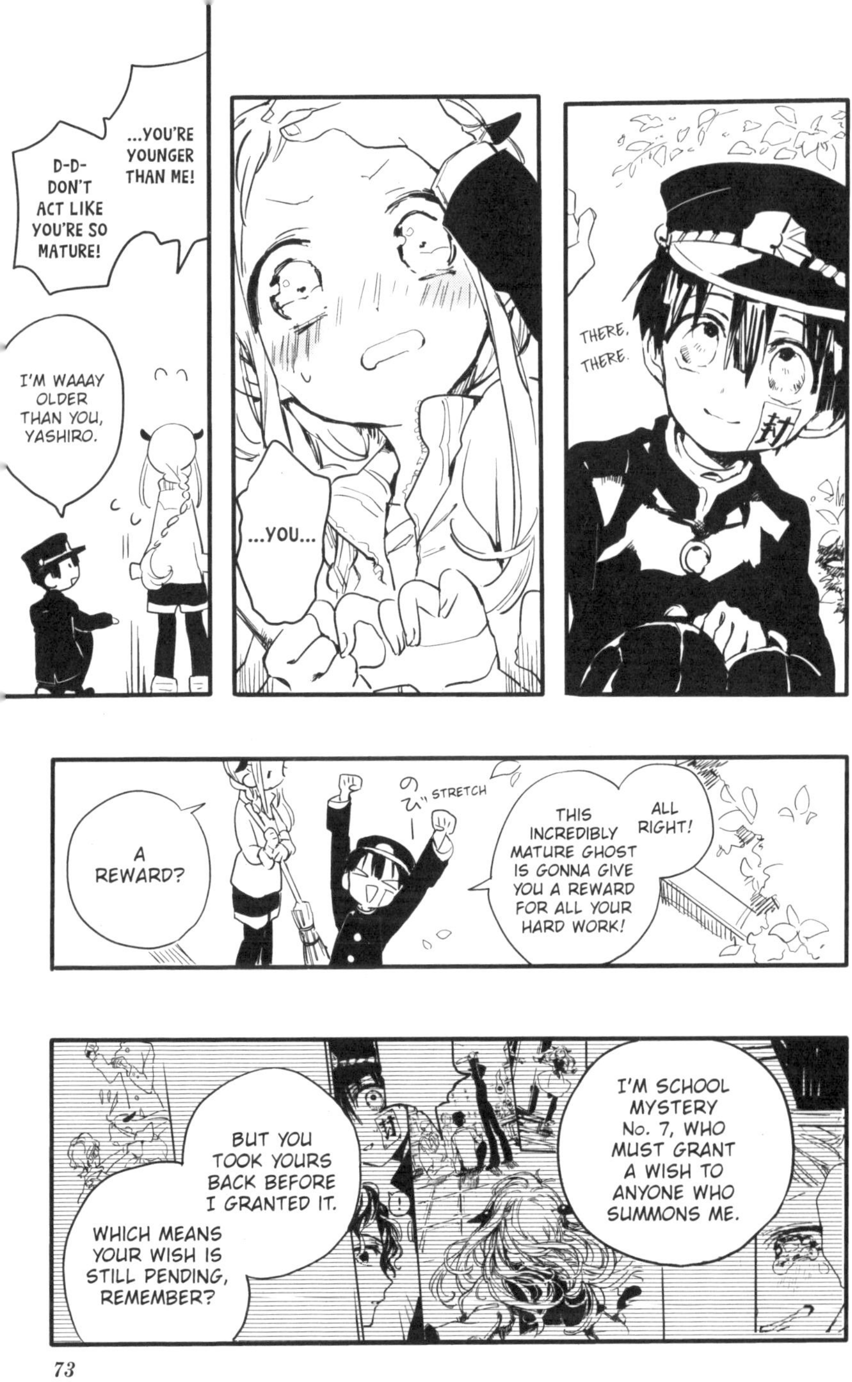
THERE, THERE.
...YOU...
...YOU'RE YOUNGER THAN ME!
D-D-DON'T ACT LIKE YOU'RE SO MATURE!
I'M WAAAY OLDER THAN YOU, YASHIRO.
ALL RIGHT!
THIS INCREDIBLY MATURE GHOST IS GONNA GIVE YOU A REWARD FOR ALL YOUR HARD WORK!
のび STRETCH
A REWARD?
I'M SCHOOL MYSTERY No. 7, WHO MUST GRANT A WISH TO ANYONE WHO SUMMONS ME.
BUT YOU TOOK YOURS BACK BEFORE I GRANTED IT.
WHICH MEANS YOUR WISH IS STILL PENDING, REMEMBER?

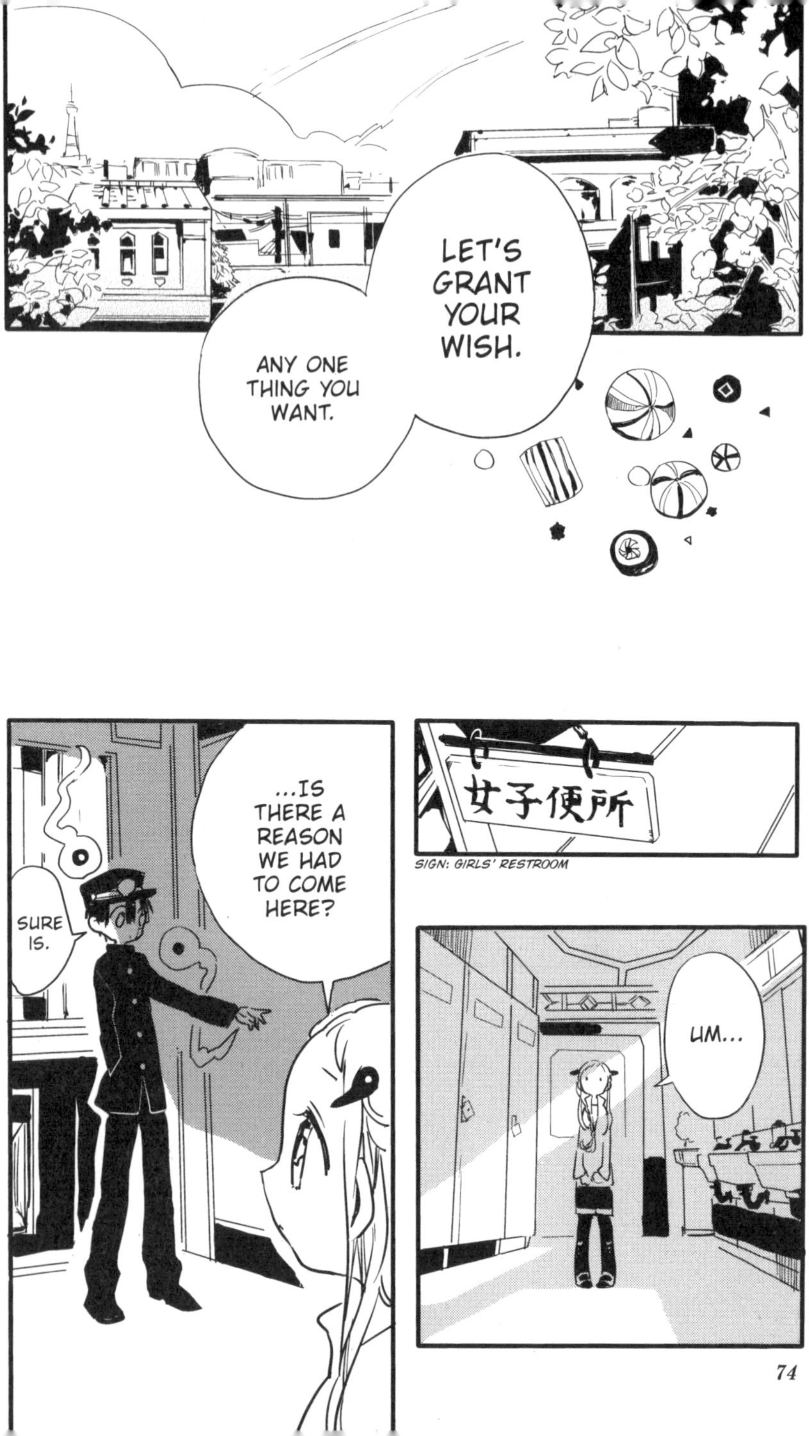
LET'S GRANT YOUR WISH.
ANY ONE THING YOU WANT.
女子便所
SIGN: GIRLS' RESTROOM
UM...
...IS THERE A REASON WE HAD TO COME HERE?
SURE IS.

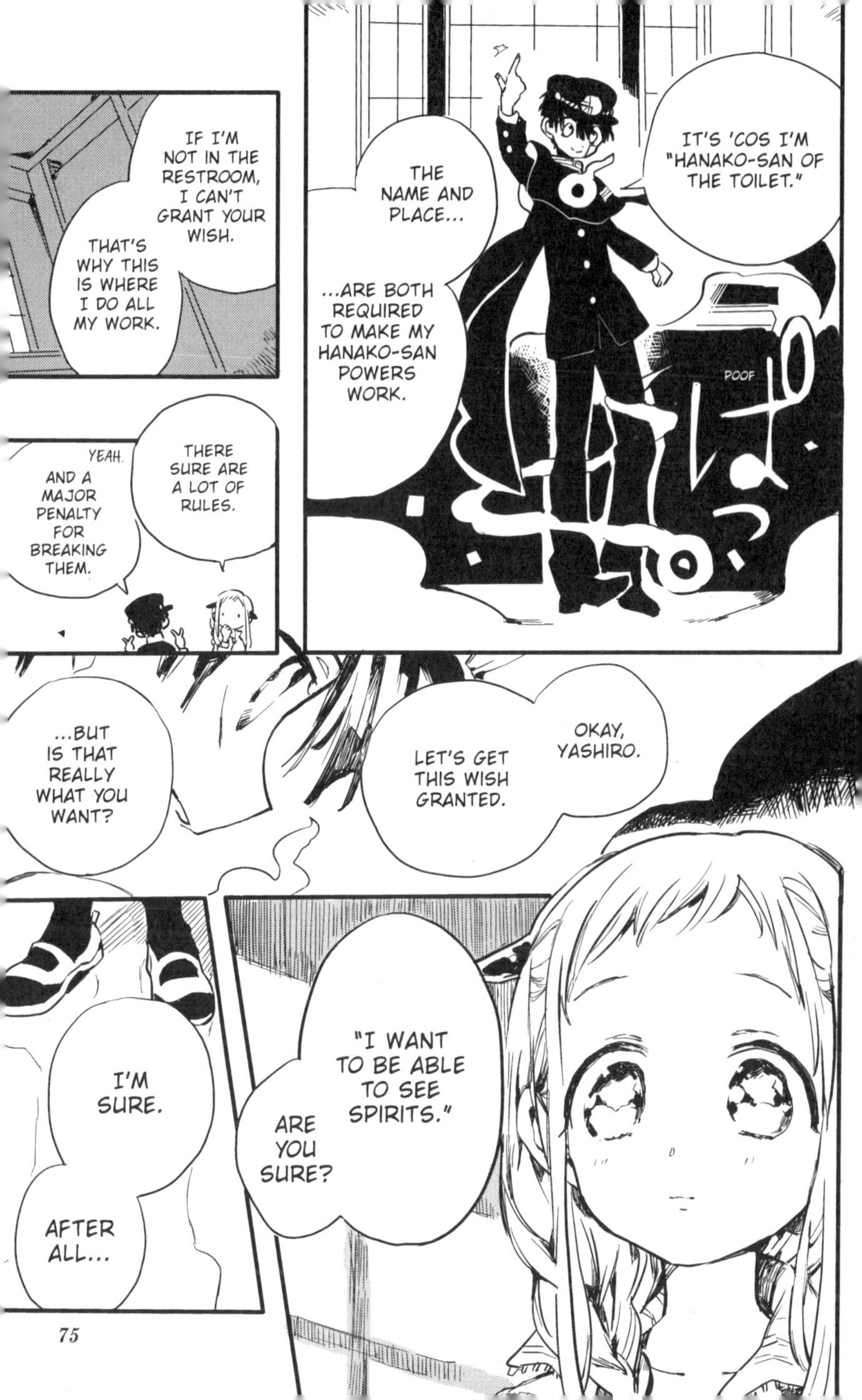
IT'S 'COS I'M "HANAKO-SAN OF THE TOILET."
THE NAME AND PLACE...
...ARE BOTH REQUIRED TO MAKE MY HANAKO-SAN POWERS WORK.
POOF
IF I'M NOT IN THE RESTROOM, I CAN'T GRANT YOUR WISH.
THAT'S WHY THIS IS WHERE I DO ALL MY WORK.
THERE SURE ARE A LOT OF RULES.
YEAH.
AND A MAJOR PENALTY FOR BREAKING THEM.
OKAY, YASHIRO.
LET'S GET THIS WISH GRANTED.
...BUT IS THAT REALLY WHAT YOU WANT?
"I WANT TO BE ABLE TO SEE SPIRITS."
ARE YOU SURE?
I'M SURE.
AFTER ALL...

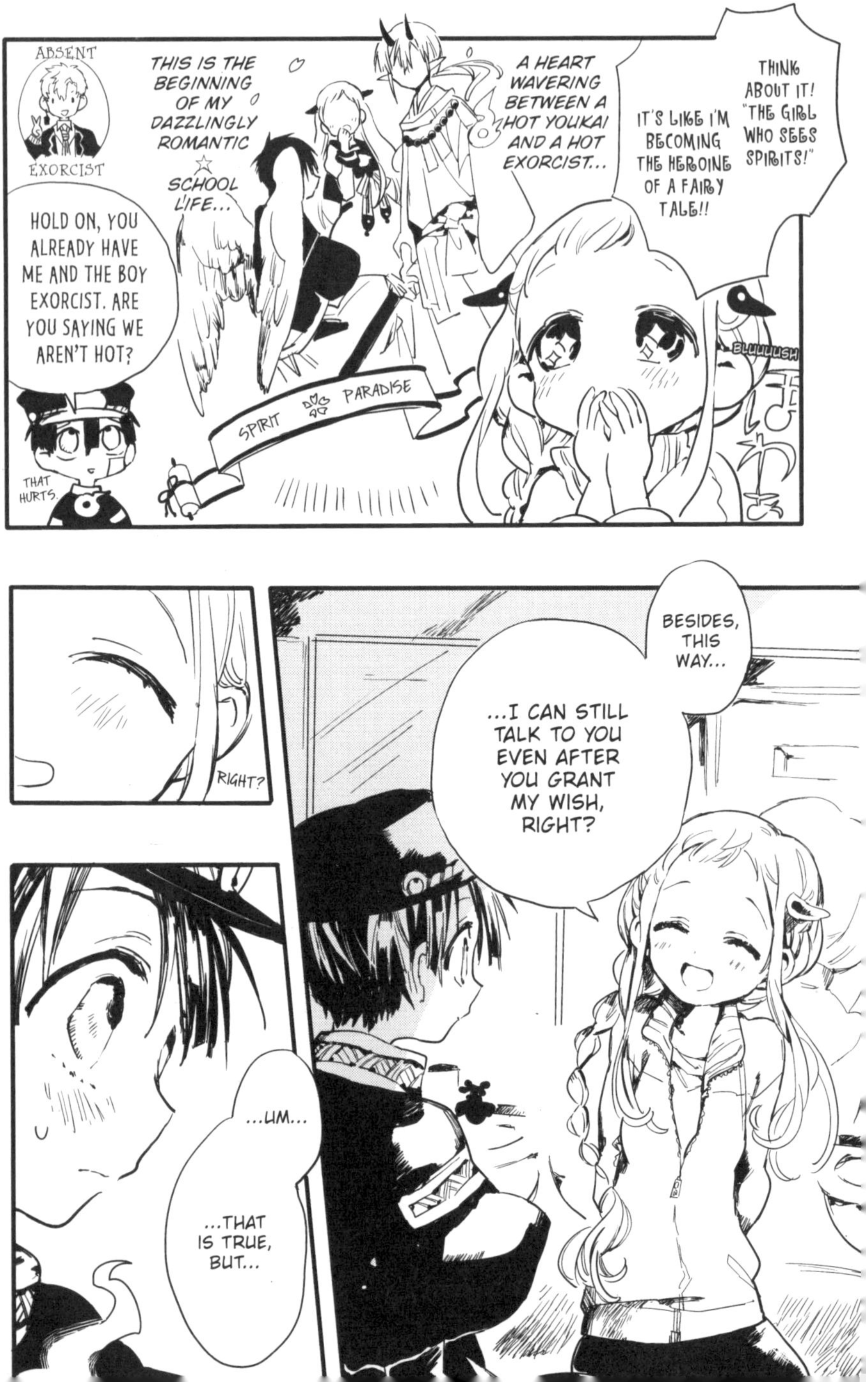

THINK ABOUT IT! "THE GIRL WHO SEES SPIRITS!"
IT'S LIKE I'M BECOMING THE HEROINE OF A FAIRY TALE!!
A HEART WAVERING BETWEEN A HOT YOUKAI AND A HOT EXORCIST...
THIS IS THE BEGINNING OF MY DAZZLINGLY ROMANTIC ☆ SCHOOL LIFE...
ABSENT EXORCIST
BLUUUUSH
SPIRIT PARADISE
HOLD ON, YOU ALREADY HAVE ME AND THE BOY EXORCIST. ARE YOU SAYING WE AREN'T HOT?
THAT HURTS.
BESIDES, THIS WAY...
...I CAN STILL TALK TO YOU EVEN AFTER YOU GRANT MY WISH, RIGHT?
RIGHT?
...UM...
...THAT IS TRUE, BUT...

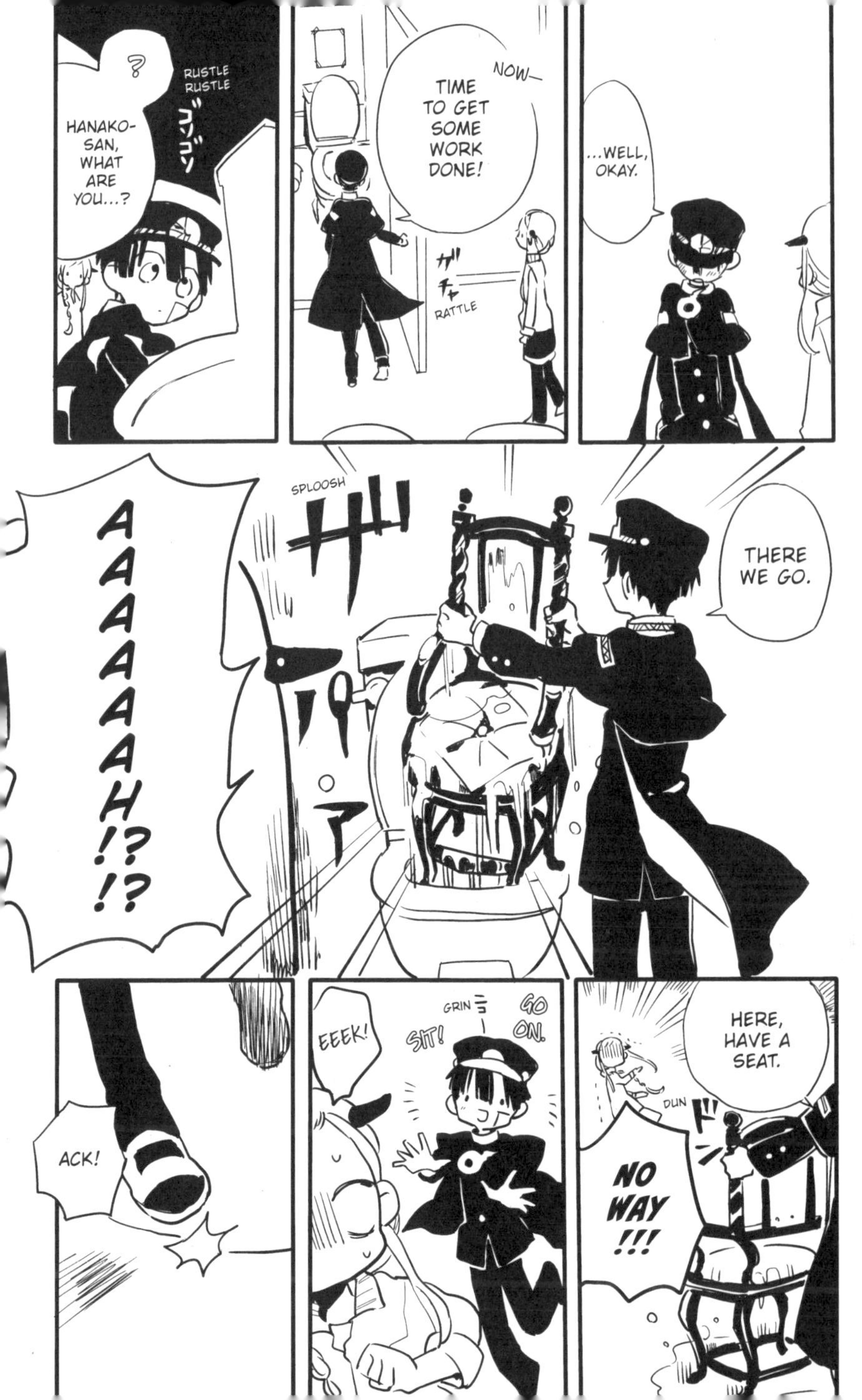
...WELL, OKAY.
NOW—
TIME TO GET SOME WORK DONE!
ガチャ
RATTLE
?
RUSTLE RUSTLE
ゴソゴソ
HANAKO-SAN, WHAT ARE YOU...?
THERE WE GO.
SPLOOSH
ザバァ
AAAAAAAAH!?!?
HERE, HAVE A SEAT.
DUN
ド
NO WAY!!!
GRIN
ニコ
GO ON.
SIT!
EEEK!
ACK!

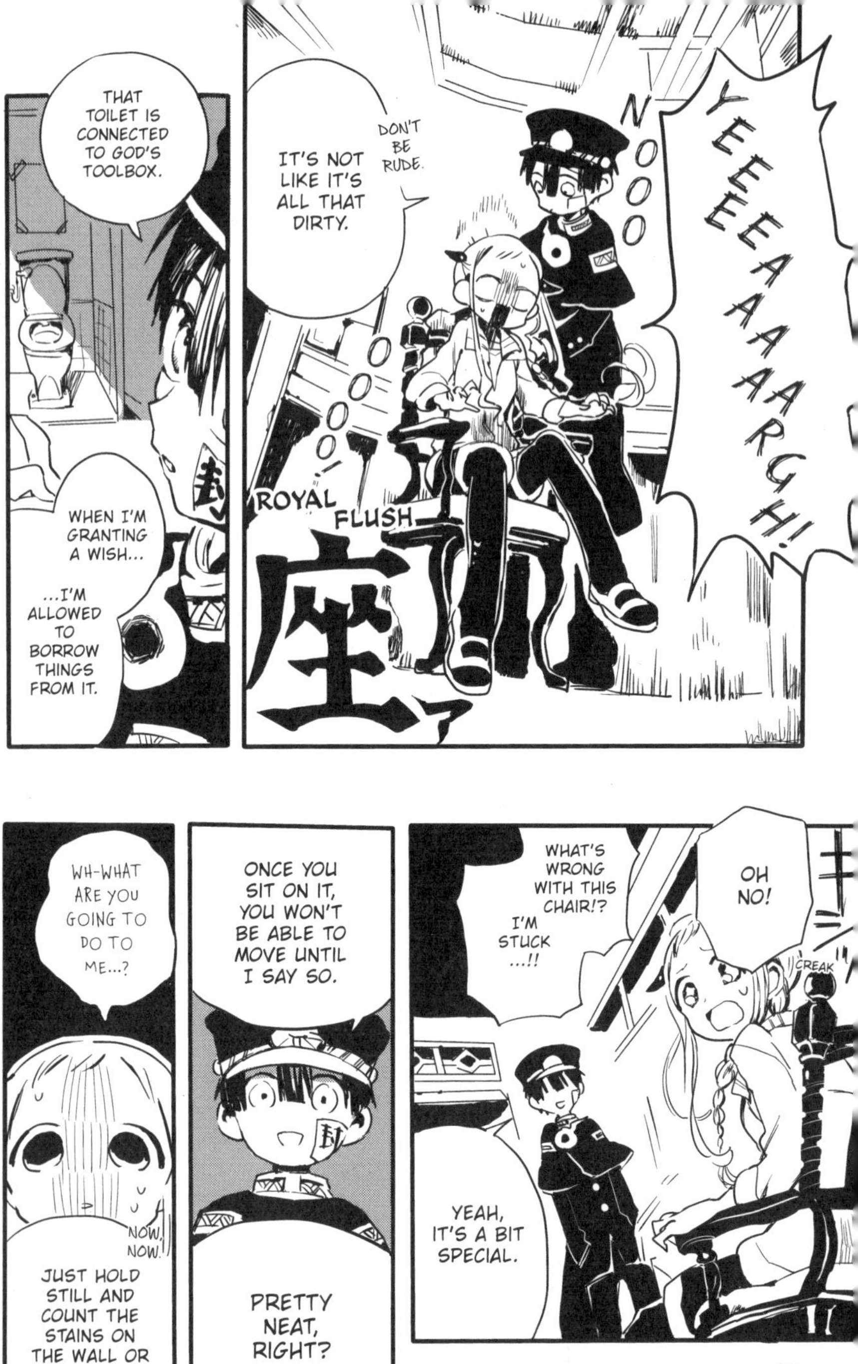
YEEEEAAAAAARGH!
NOOOO
IT'S NOT LIKE IT'S ALL THAT DIRTY.
DON'T BE RUDE.
OOOOO...
ROYAL FLUSH
座
THAT TOILET IS CONNECTED TO GOD'S TOOLBOX.
WHEN I'M GRANTING A WISH...
...I'M ALLOWED TO BORROW THINGS FROM IT.
OH NO!
WHAT'S WRONG WITH THIS CHAIR!?
I'M STUCK ...!!
CREAK
YEAH, IT'S A BIT SPECIAL.
ONCE YOU SIT ON IT, YOU WON'T BE ABLE TO MOVE UNTIL I SAY SO.
PRETTY NEAT, RIGHT?
WH-WHAT ARE YOU GOING TO DO TO ME...?
NOW, NOW.
JUST HOLD STILL AND COUNT THE STAINS ON THE WALL OR SOMETHING.

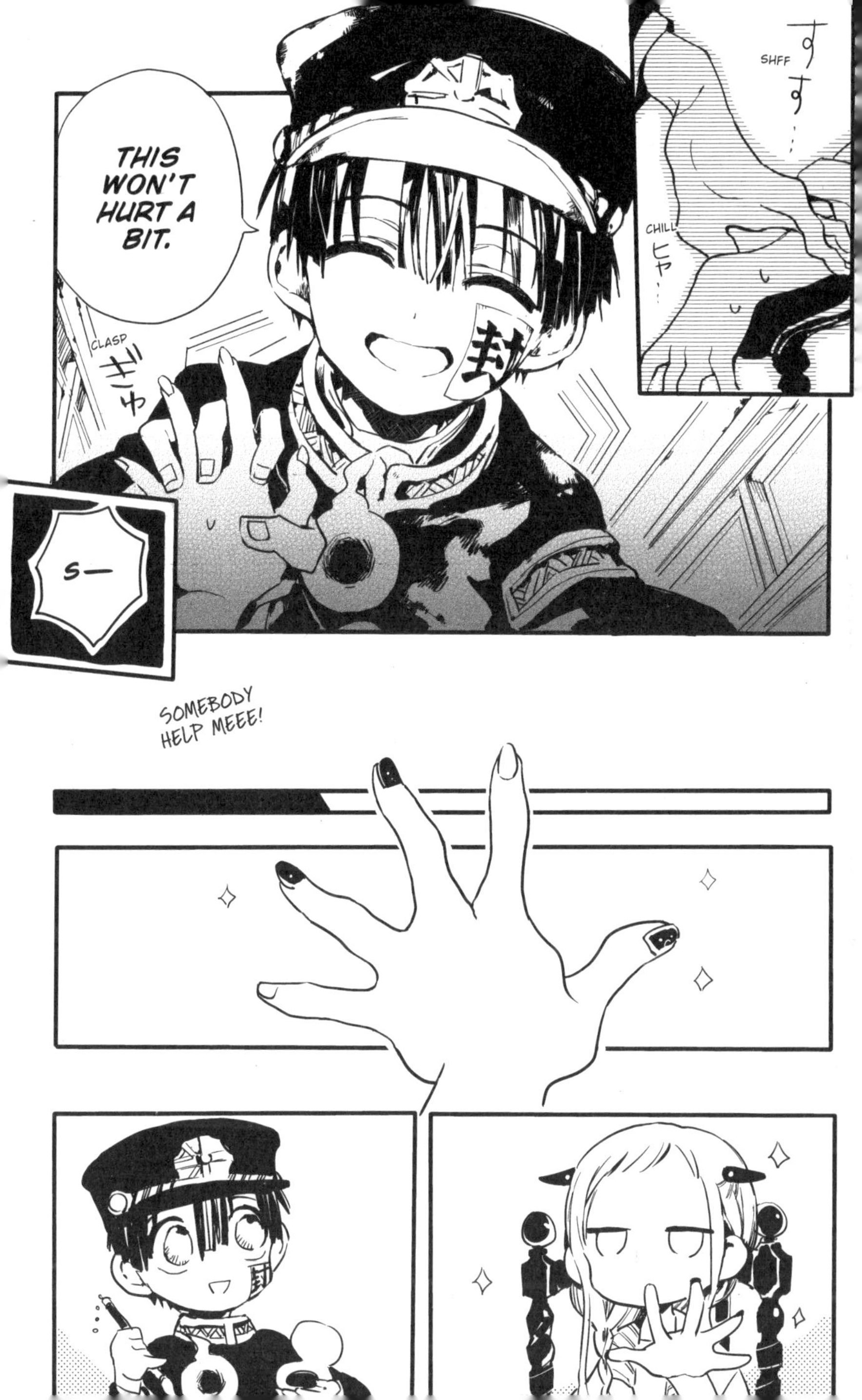

SHFF
すす
CHILL
ヒヤ
THIS WON'T HURT A BIT.
CLASP
ぎゅ
S—
SOMEBODY HELP MEEE!

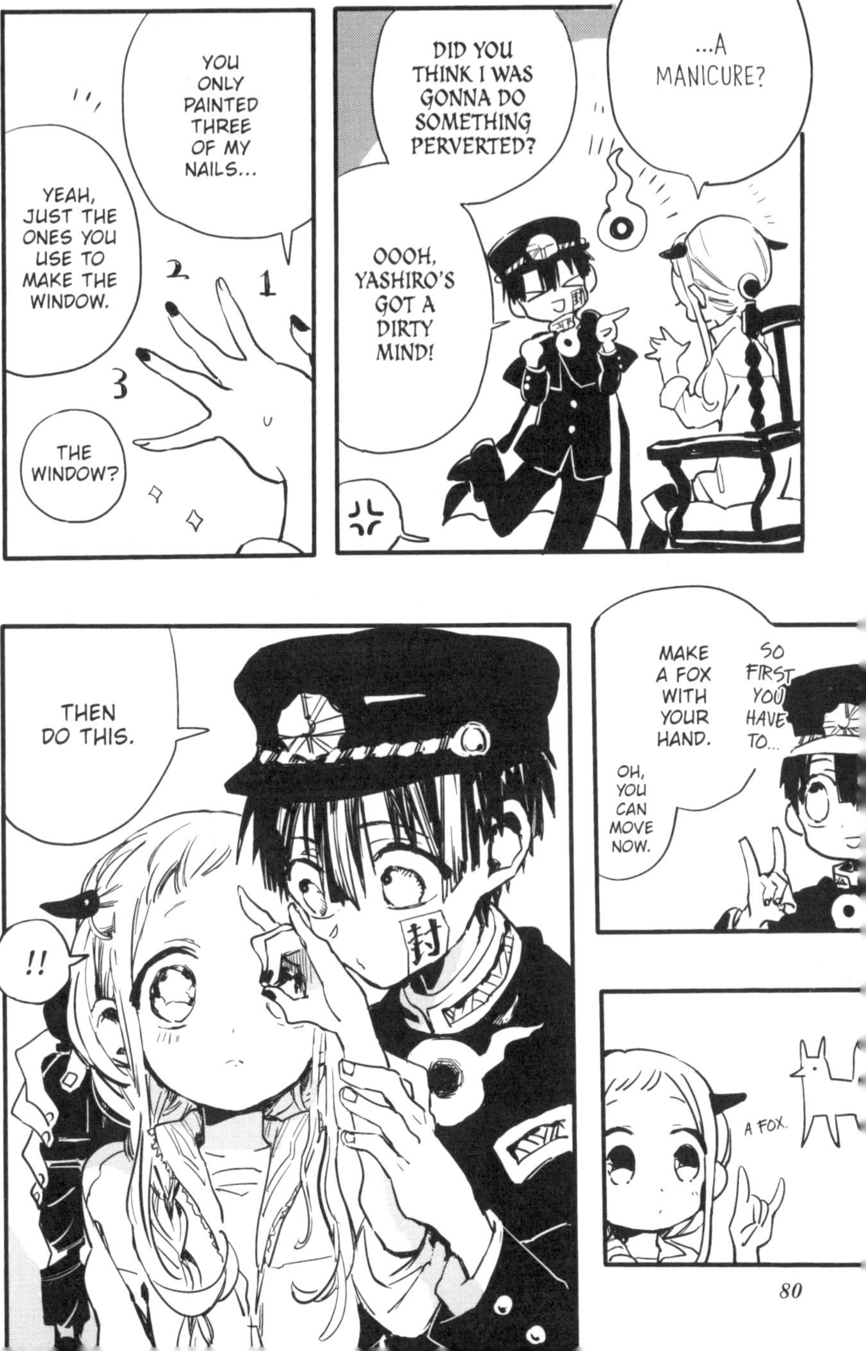
...A MANICURE?
DID YOU THINK I WAS GONNA DO SOMETHING PERVERTED?
OOOH, YASHIRO'S GOT A DIRTY MIND!
YOU ONLY PAINTED THREE OF MY NAILS...
YEAH, JUST THE ONES YOU USE TO MAKE THE WINDOW.
1
2
3
THE WINDOW?
SO FIRST YOU HAVE TO...
MAKE A FOX WITH YOUR HAND.
OH, YOU CAN MOVE NOW.
A FOX.
THEN DO THIS.
!!

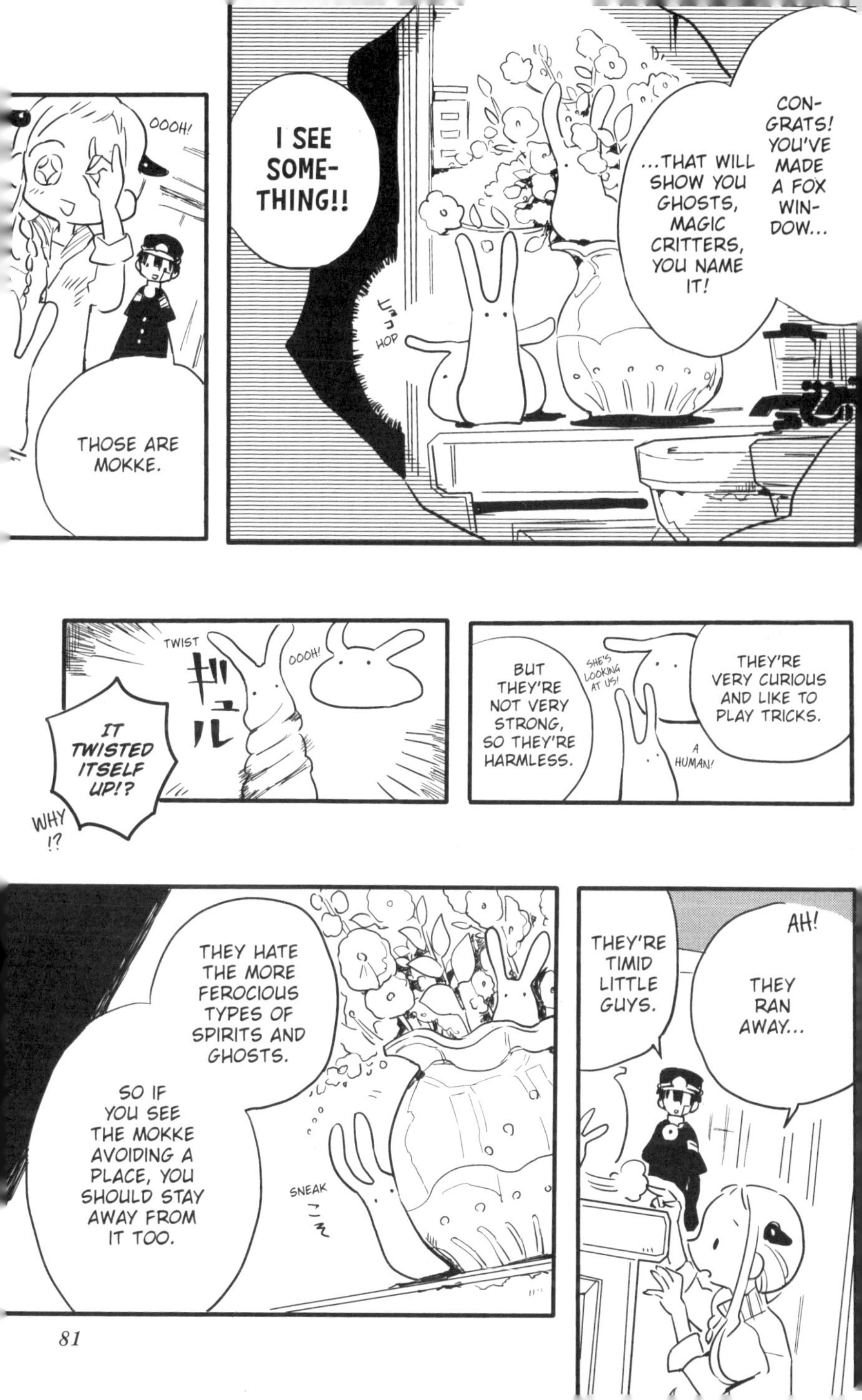
CON-GRATS! YOU'VE MADE A FOX WIN-DOW...
...THAT WILL SHOW YOU GHOSTS, MAGIC CRITTERS, YOU NAME IT!
I SEE SOME-THING!!
HOP
OOOH!
THOSE ARE MOKKE.
THEY'RE VERY CURIOUS AND LIKE TO PLAY TRICKS.
SHE'S LOOKING AT US!
A HUMAN!
BUT THEY'RE NOT VERY STRONG, SO THEY'RE HARMLESS.
TWIST
OOOH!
IT TWISTED ITSELF UP!?
WHY !?
AH!
THEY RAN AWAY...
THEY'RE TIMID LITTLE GUYS.
THEY HATE THE MORE FEROCIOUS TYPES OF SPIRITS AND GHOSTS.
SO IF YOU SEE THE MOKKE AVOIDING A PLACE, YOU SHOULD STAY AWAY FROM IT TOO.
SNEAK

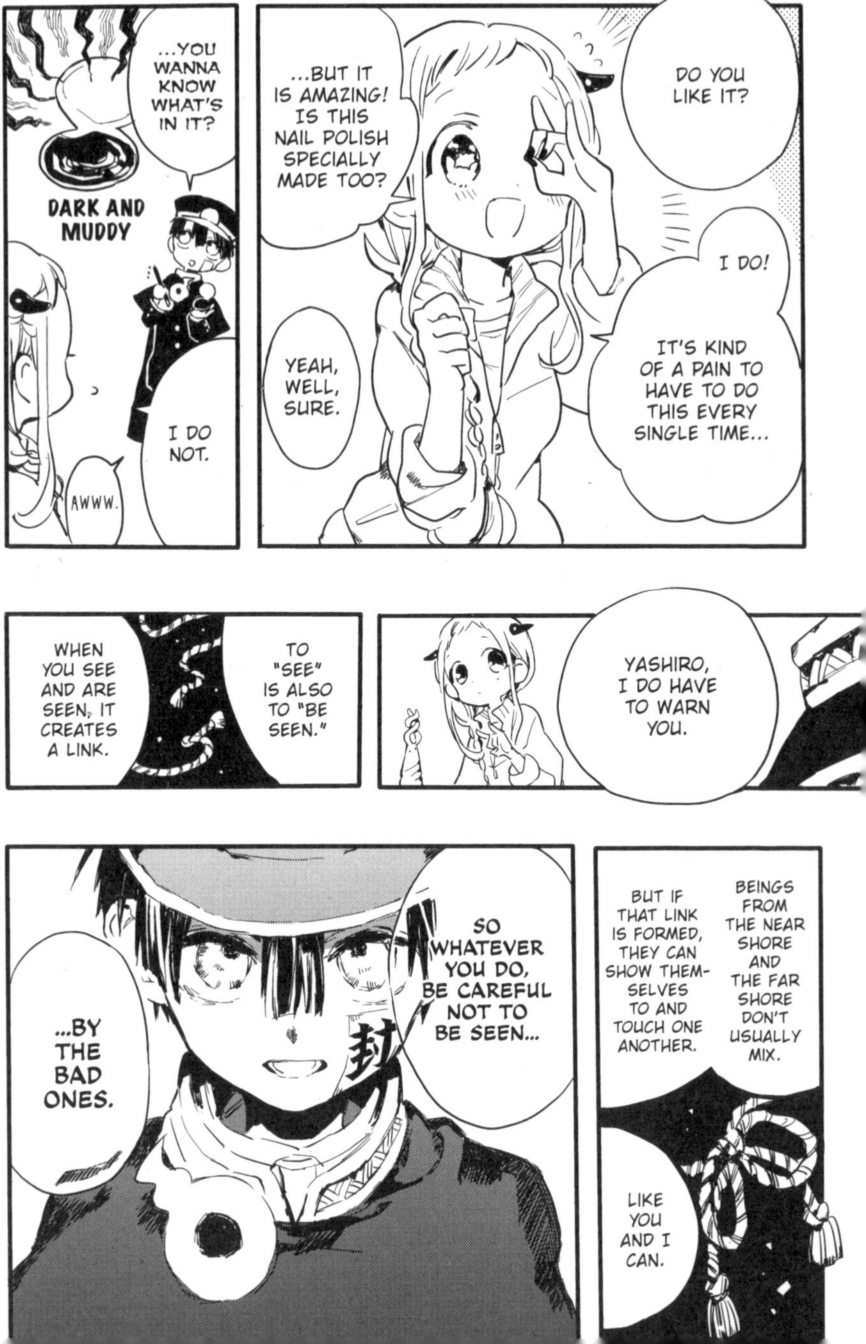
DO YOU LIKE IT?
...BUT IT IS AMAZING! IS THIS NAIL POLISH SPECIALLY MADE TOO?
I DO!
IT'S KIND OF A PAIN TO HAVE TO DO THIS EVERY SINGLE TIME...
YEAH, WELL, SURE.
...YOU WANNA KNOW WHAT'S IN IT?
DARK AND MUDDY
I DO NOT.
AWWW.
YASHIRO, I DO HAVE TO WARN YOU.
TO "SEE" IS ALSO TO "BE SEEN."
WHEN YOU SEE AND ARE SEEN, IT CREATES A LINK.
BEINGS FROM THE NEAR SHORE AND THE FAR SHORE DON'T USUALLY MIX.
BUT IF THAT LINK IS FORMED, THEY CAN SHOW THEM-SELVES TO AND TOUCH ONE ANOTHER.
LIKE YOU AND I CAN.
SO WHATEVER YOU DO, BE CAREFUL NOT TO BE SEEN...
...BY THE BAD ONES.

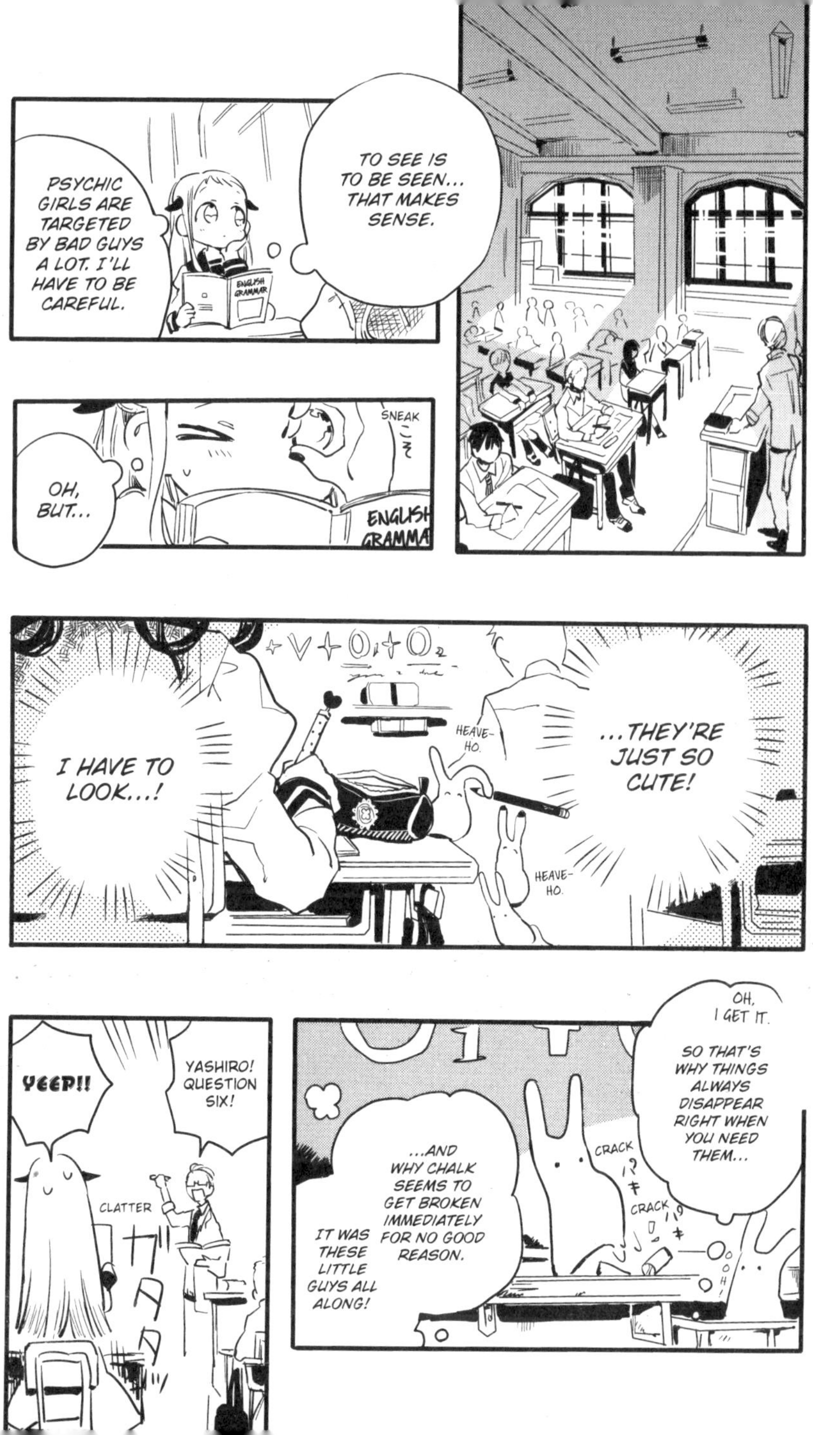
TO SEE IS TO BE SEEN... THAT MAKES SENSE.
PSYCHIC GIRLS ARE TARGETED BY BAD GUYS A LOT. I'LL HAVE TO BE CAREFUL.
ENGLISH GRAMMAR
SNEAK
OH, BUT...
ENGLISH GRAMMA
...THEY'RE JUST SO CUTE!
HEAVE-HO.
HEAVE-HO.
I HAVE TO LOOK...!
OH, I GET IT.
SO THAT'S WHY THINGS ALWAYS DISAPPEAR RIGHT WHEN YOU NEED THEM...
CRACK
CRACK
OOH!
...AND WHY CHALK SEEMS TO GET BROKEN IMMEDIATELY FOR NO GOOD REASON.
IT WAS THESE LITTLE GUYS ALL ALONG!
YASHIRO! QUESTION SIX!
YEEP!!
CLATTER

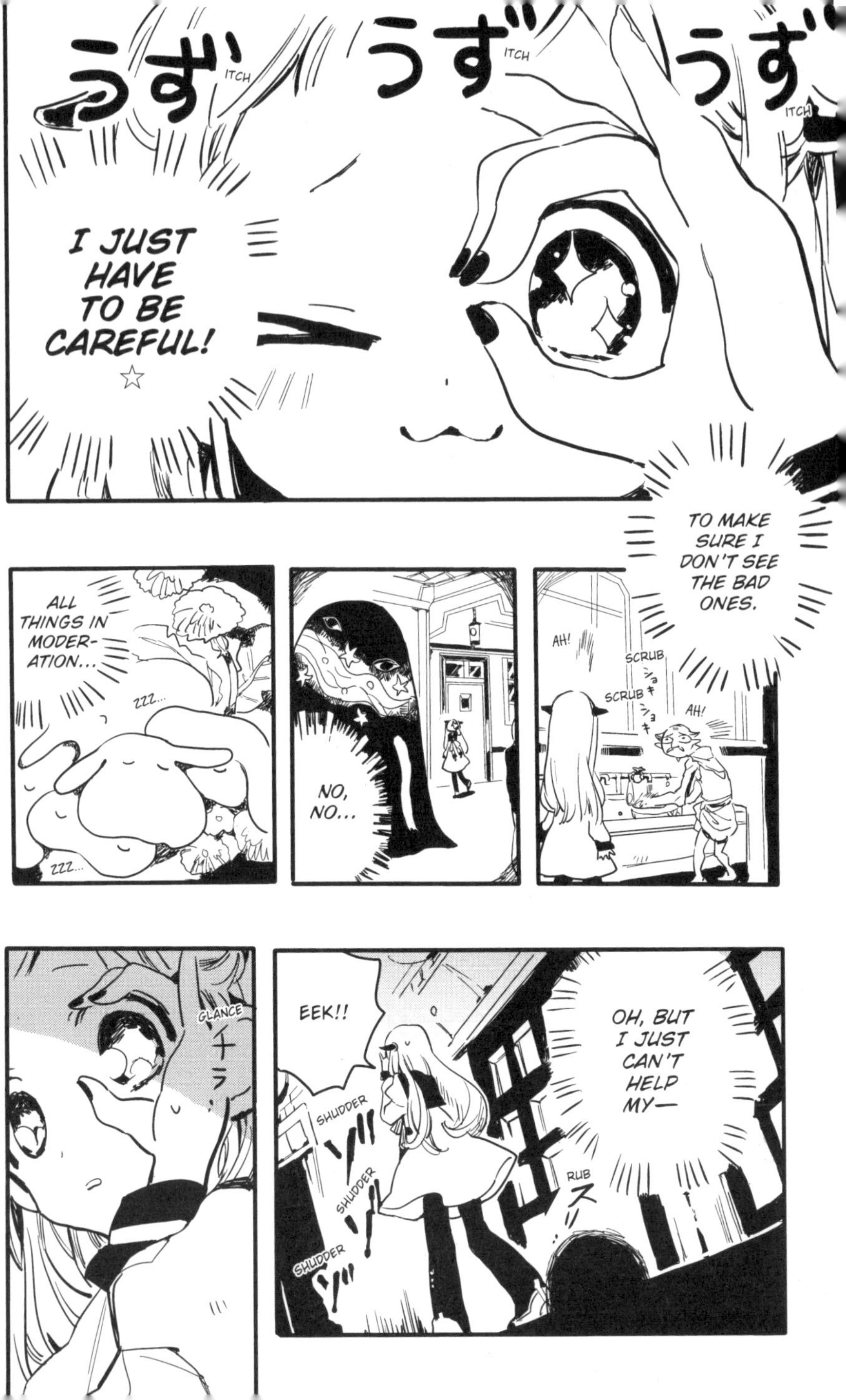
うず
ITCH
うず
ITCH
うず
ITCH
I JUST HAVE TO BE CAREFUL! ☆
TO MAKE SURE I DON'T SEE THE BAD ONES.
AH!
SCRUB ショキ
SCRUB ショキ
AH!
NO, NO...
ALL THINGS IN MODER-ATION...
ZZZ...
ZZZ...
OH, BUT I JUST CAN'T HELP MY—
EEK!!
SHUDDER
SHUDDER
SHUDDER
RUB スッ
GLANCE チラ

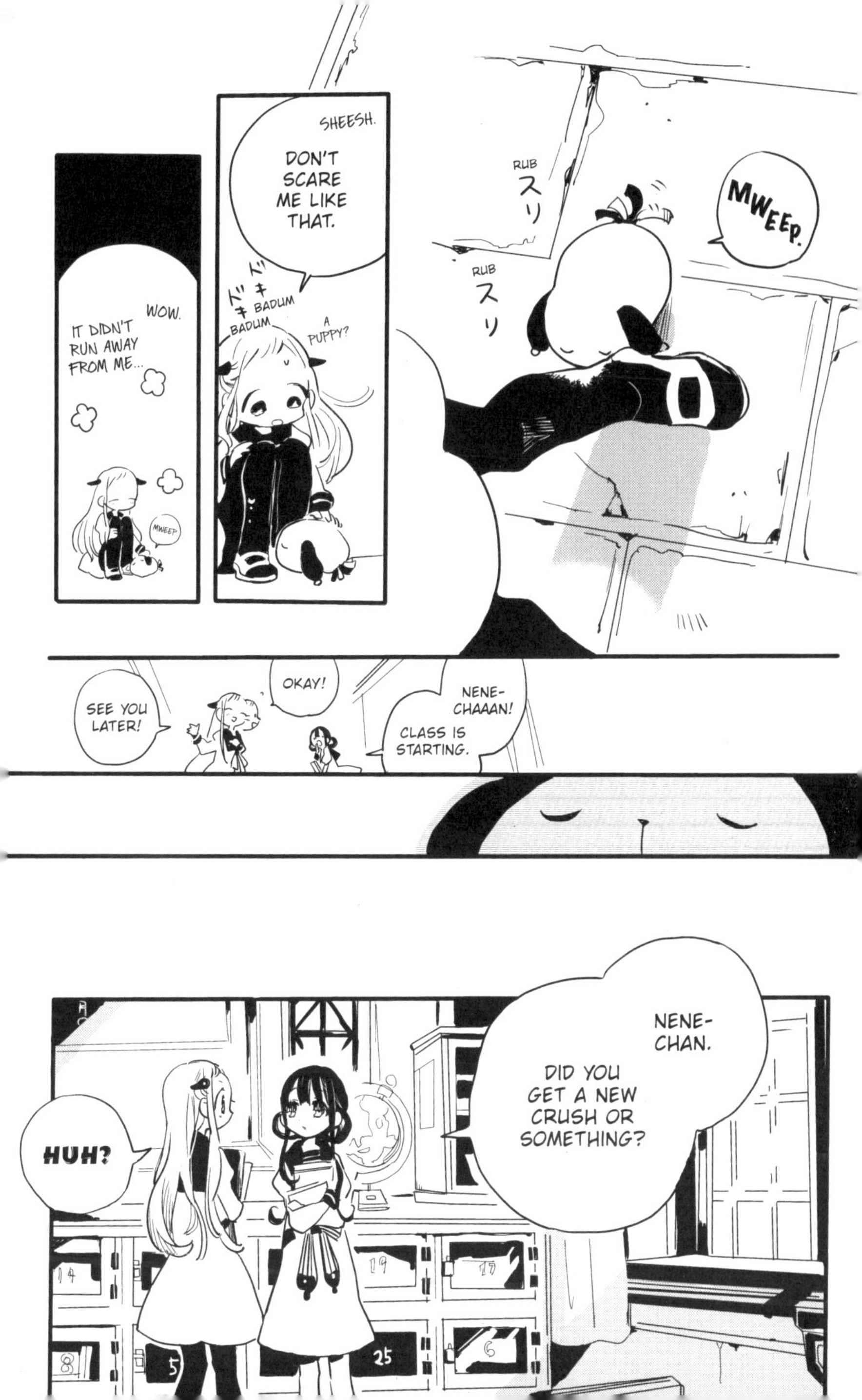
MWEEP.
RUB スリ
RUB スリ
SHEESH.
DON'T SCARE ME LIKE THAT.
ドキドキ BADUM BADUM
A PUPPY?
WOW.
IT DIDN'T RUN AWAY FROM ME...
MWEEP
NENE-CHAAAN!
CLASS IS STARTING.
OKAY!
SEE YOU LATER!
NENE-CHAN.
DID YOU GET A NEW CRUSH OR SOMETHING?
HUH?

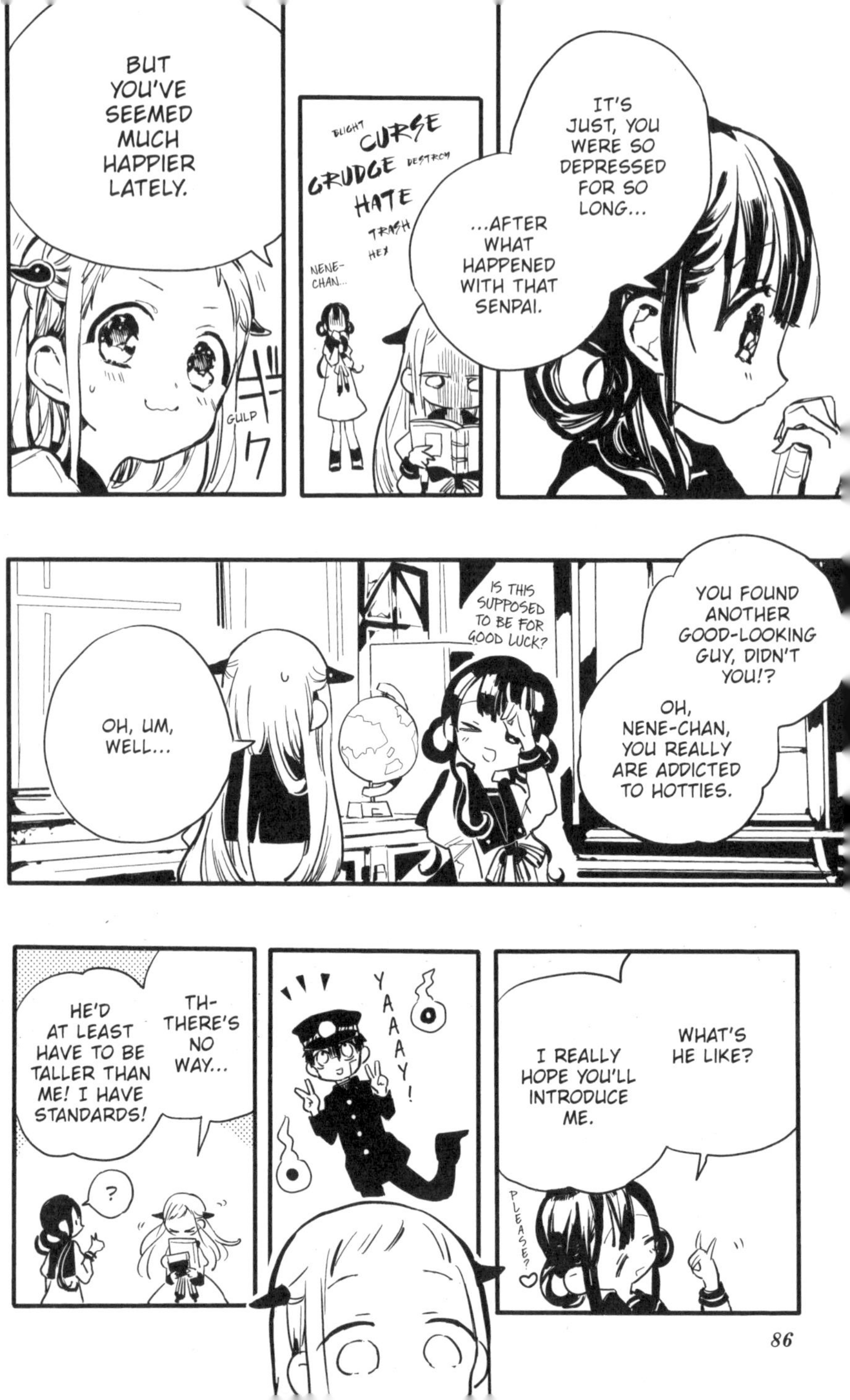
IT'S JUST, YOU WERE SO DEPRESSED FOR SO LONG...
...AFTER WHAT HAPPENED WITH THAT SENPAI.
BLIGHT
CURSE
GRUDGE
DESTROY
HATE
TRASH
HEX
NENE-CHAN...
BUT YOU'VE SEEMED MUCH HAPPIER LATELY.
GULP
YOU FOUND ANOTHER GOOD-LOOKING GUY, DIDN'T YOU!?
OH, NENE-CHAN, YOU REALLY ARE ADDICTED TO HOTTIES.
IS THIS SUPPOSED TO BE FOR GOOD LUCK?
OH, UM, WELL...
WHAT'S HE LIKE?
I REALLY HOPE YOU'LL INTRODUCE ME.
PLEASE?♡
YAAAAY!
TH-THERE'S NO WAY...
HE'D AT LEAST HAVE TO BE TALLER THAN ME! I HAVE STANDARDS!
?

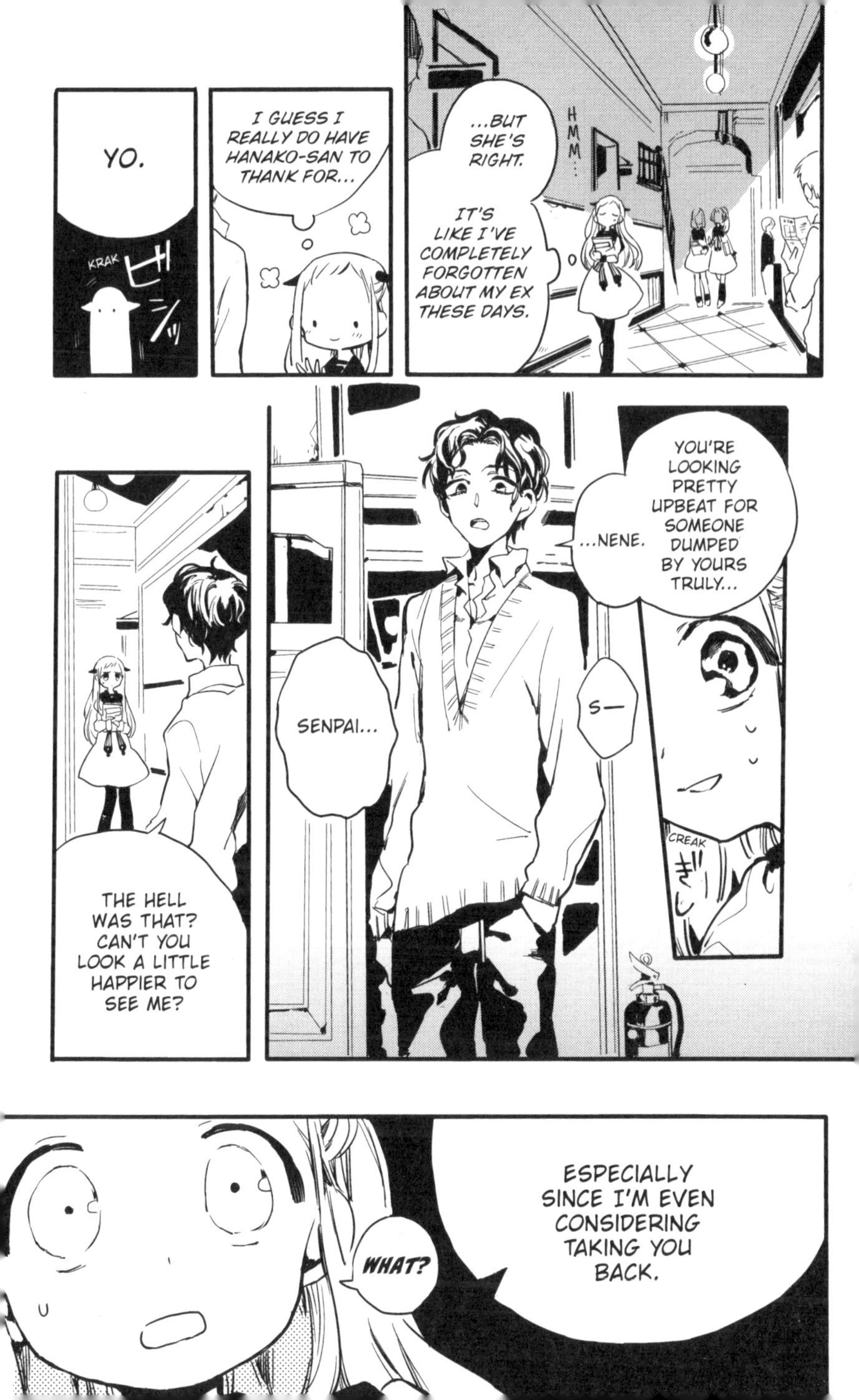

HMM...
...BUT SHE'S RIGHT.
IT'S LIKE I'VE COMPLETELY FORGOTTEN ABOUT MY EX THESE DAYS.
I GUESS I REALLY DO HAVE HANAKO-SAN TO THANK FOR...
YO.
KRAK
YOU'RE LOOKING PRETTY UPBEAT FOR SOMEONE DUMPED BY YOURS TRULY...
S—
CREAK
...NENE.
SENPAI...
THE HELL WAS THAT? CAN'T YOU LOOK A LITTLE HAPPIER TO SEE ME?
ESPECIALLY SINCE I'M EVEN CONSIDERING TAKING YOU BACK.
WHAT?

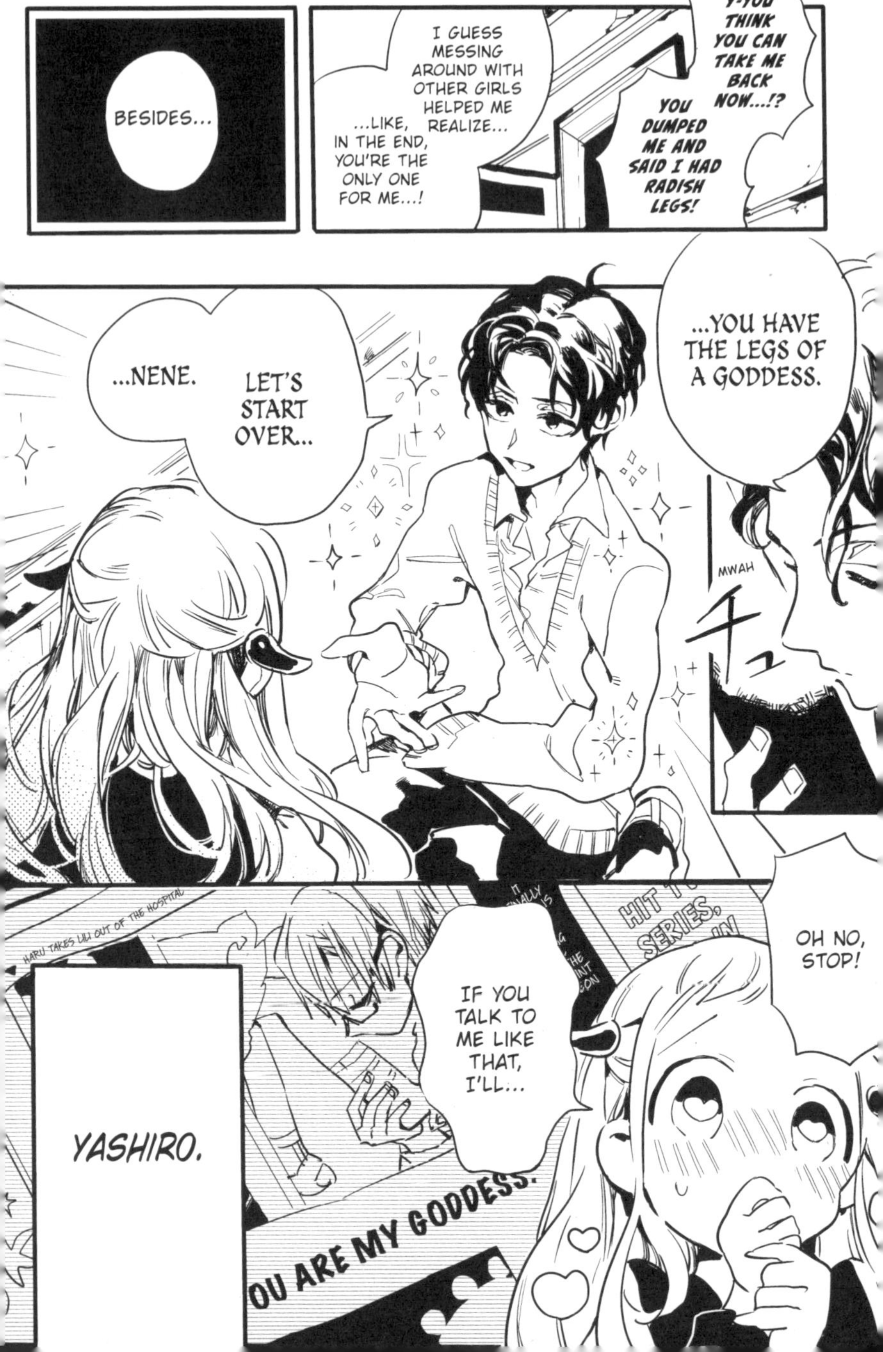
Y-YOU THINK YOU CAN TAKE ME BACK NOW...!?
YOU DUMPED ME AND SAID I HAD RADISH LEGS!
I GUESS MESSING AROUND WITH OTHER GIRLS HELPED ME REALIZE...
...LIKE, IN THE END, YOU'RE THE ONLY ONE FOR ME...!
BESIDES...
...YOU HAVE THE LEGS OF A GODDESS.
MWAH
チュ
...NENE.
LET'S START OVER...
OH NO, STOP!
IF YOU TALK TO ME LIKE THAT, I'LL...
OU ARE MY GODDESS.
HARU TAKES LILI OUT OF THE HOSPITAL
YASHIRO.

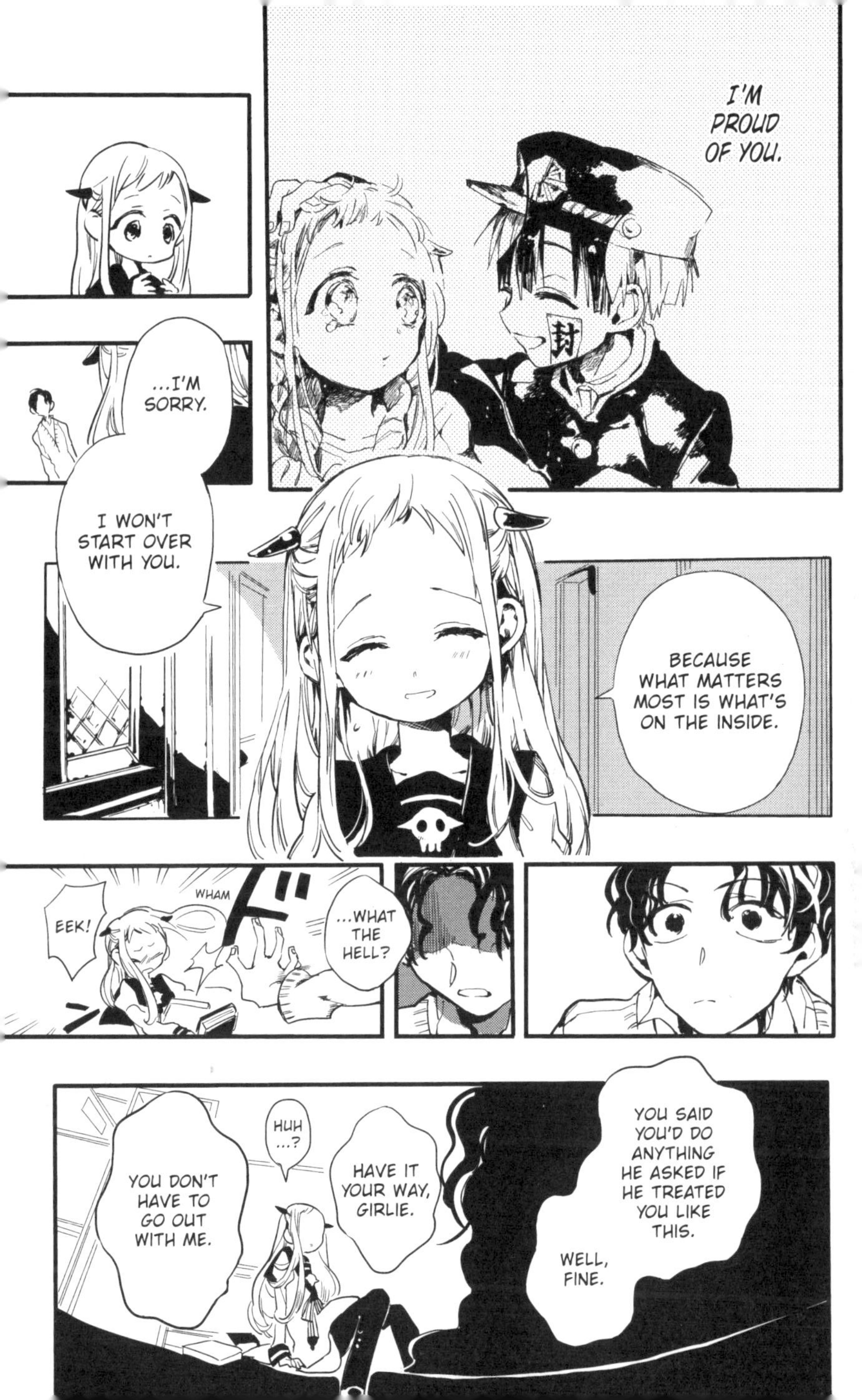
I'M PROUD OF YOU.
...I'M SORRY.
BECAUSE WHAT MATTERS MOST IS WHAT'S ON THE INSIDE.
I WON'T START OVER WITH YOU.
...WHAT THE HELL?
WHAM
EEK!
YOU SAID YOU'D DO ANYTHING HE ASKED IF HE TREATED YOU LIKE THIS.
WELL, FINE.
HAVE IT YOUR WAY, GIRLIE.
HUH ...?
YOU DON'T HAVE TO GO OUT WITH ME.

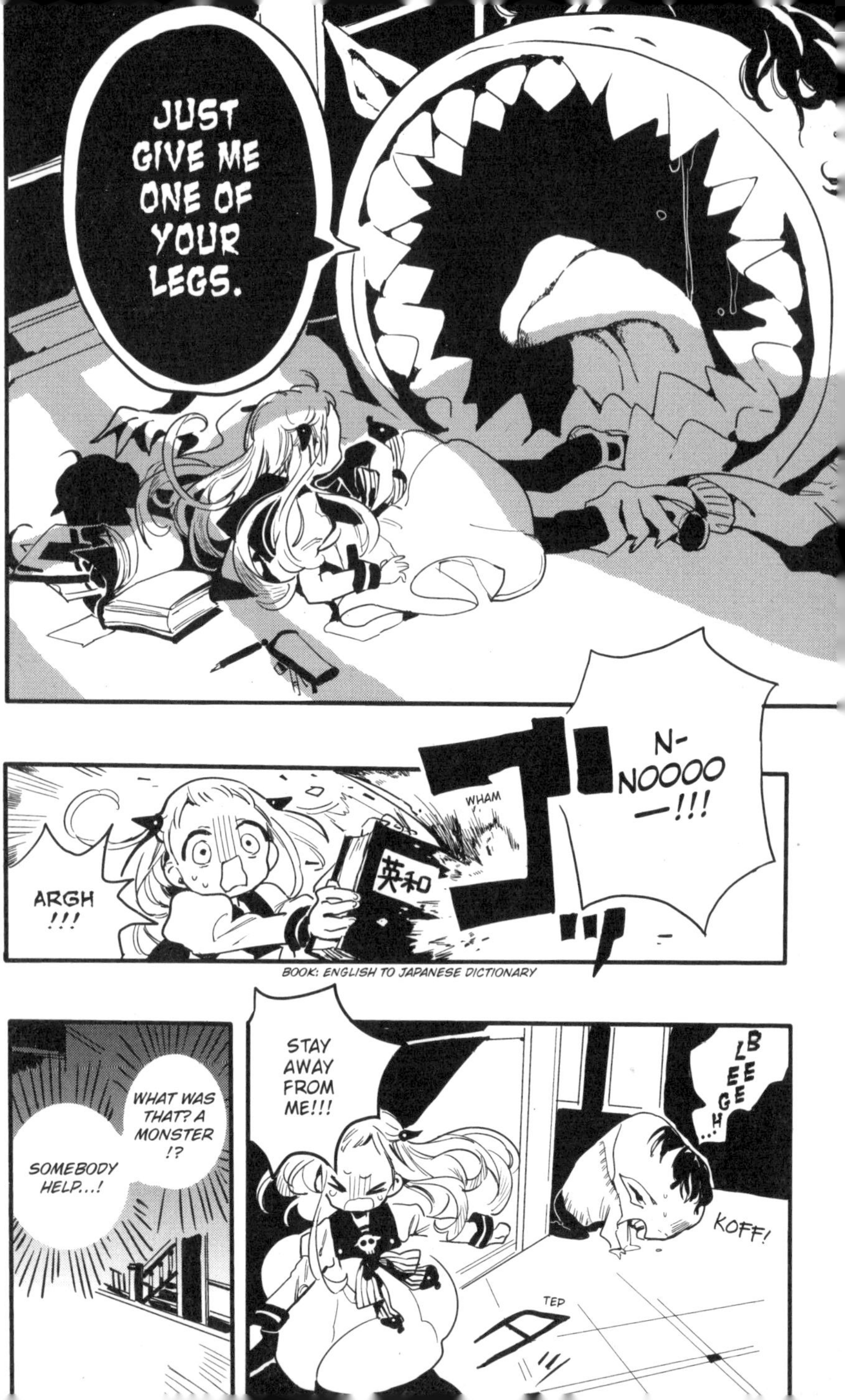
JUST GIVE ME ONE OF YOUR LEGS.
N-NOOOO—!!!
WHAM
英和
ARGH!!!
BOOK: ENGLISH TO JAPANESE DICTIONARY
BLEEEEGH...
KOFF!
STAY AWAY FROM ME!!!
TEP
WHAT WAS THAT? A MONSTER!?
SOMEBODY HELP...!

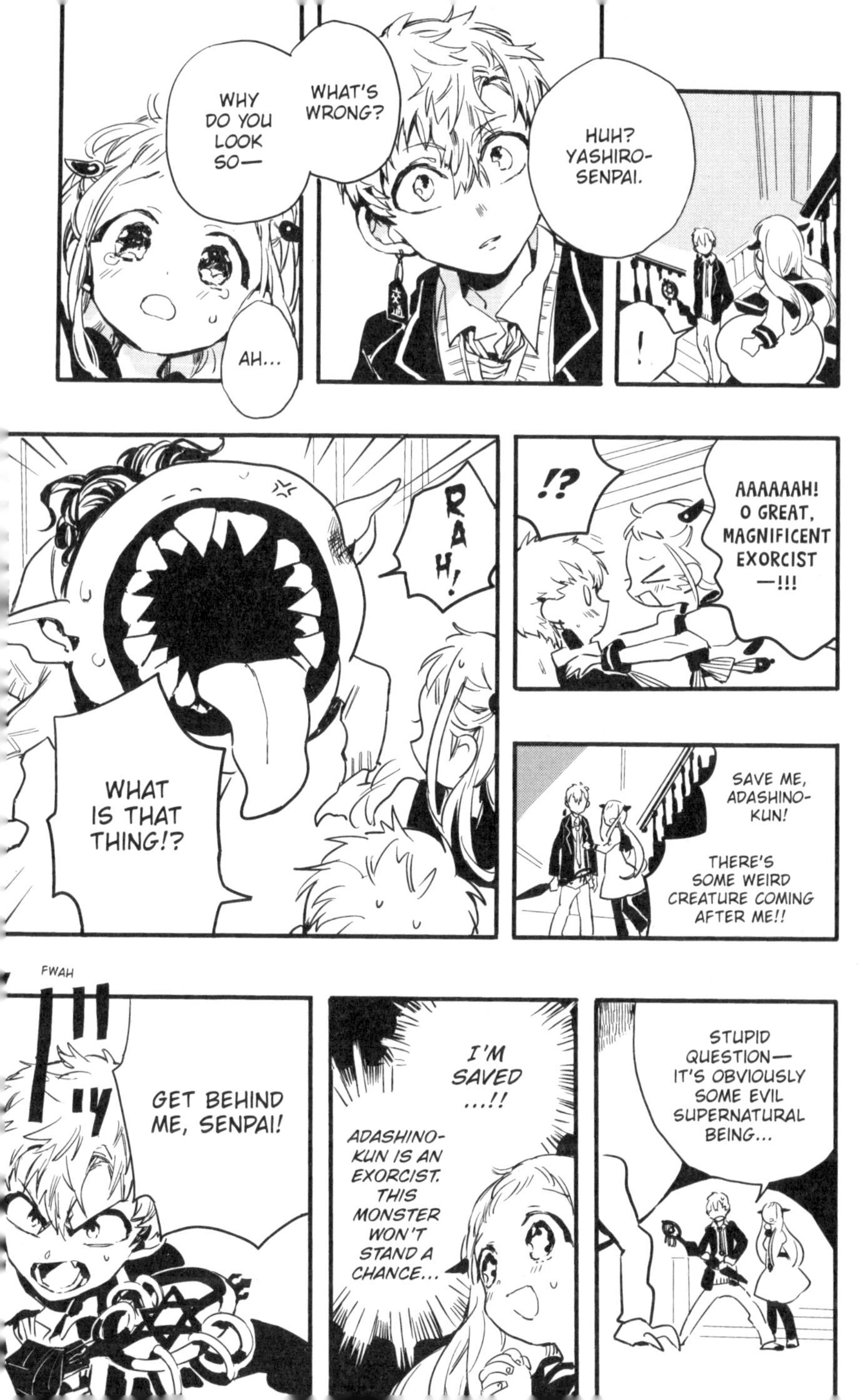
HUH? YASHIRO-SENPAI.
!
WHAT'S WRONG?
WHY DO YOU LOOK SO—
AH...
!?
AAAAAAH! O GREAT, MAGNIFICENT EXORCIST—!!!
SAVE ME, ADASHINO-KUN!
THERE'S SOME WEIRD CREATURE COMING AFTER ME!!
RAH!
WHAT IS THAT THING!?
STUPID QUESTION— IT'S OBVIOUSLY SOME EVIL SUPERNATURAL BEING...
I'M SAVED...!!
ADASHINO-KUN IS AN EXORCIST. THIS MONSTER WON'T STAND A CHANCE...
FWAH
GET BEHIND ME, SENPAI!

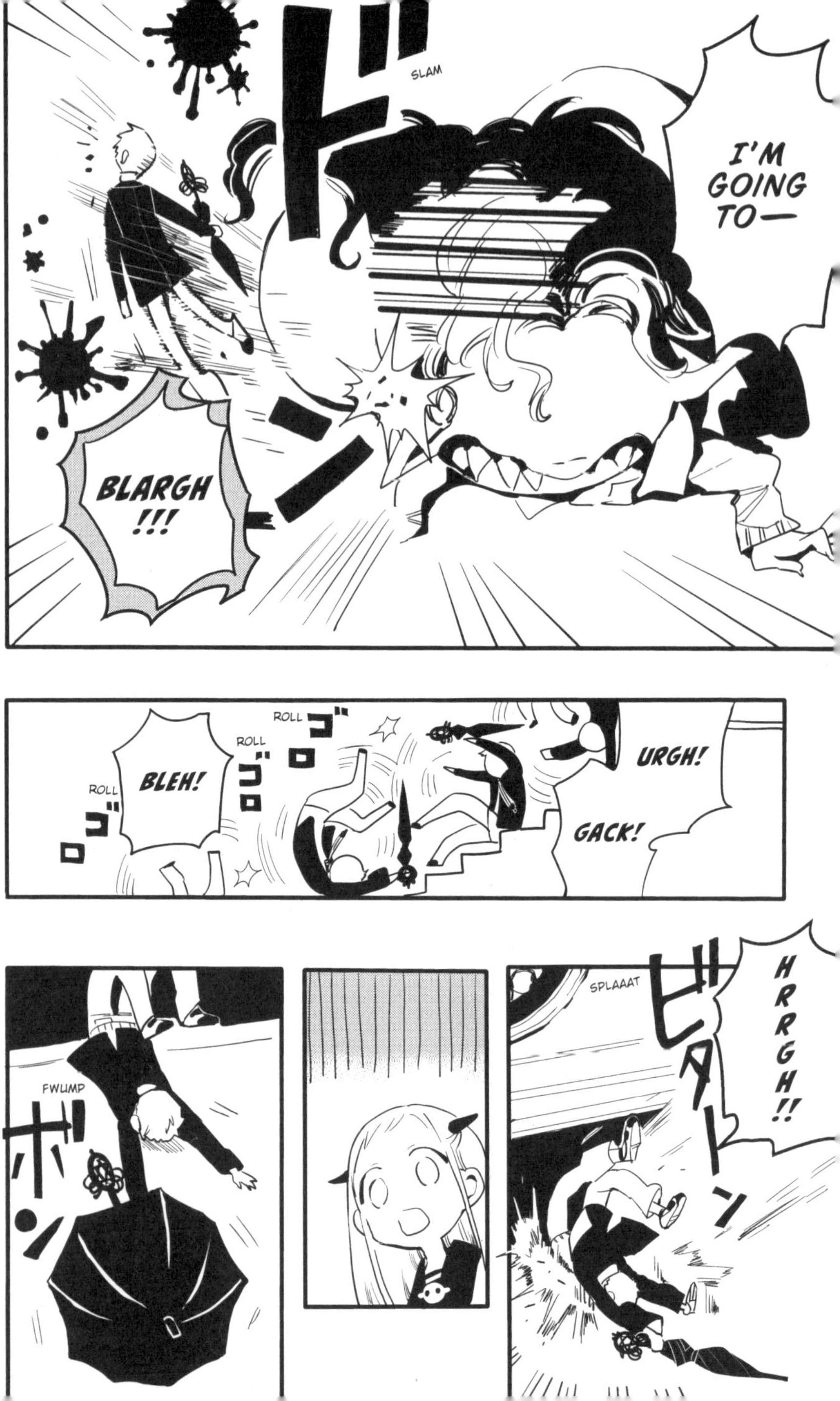
I'M GOING TO—
SLAM
BLARGH!!!
URGH!
GACK!
ROLL
ROLL
BLEH!
ROLL
HRRGH!!
SPLAAAT
FWUMP

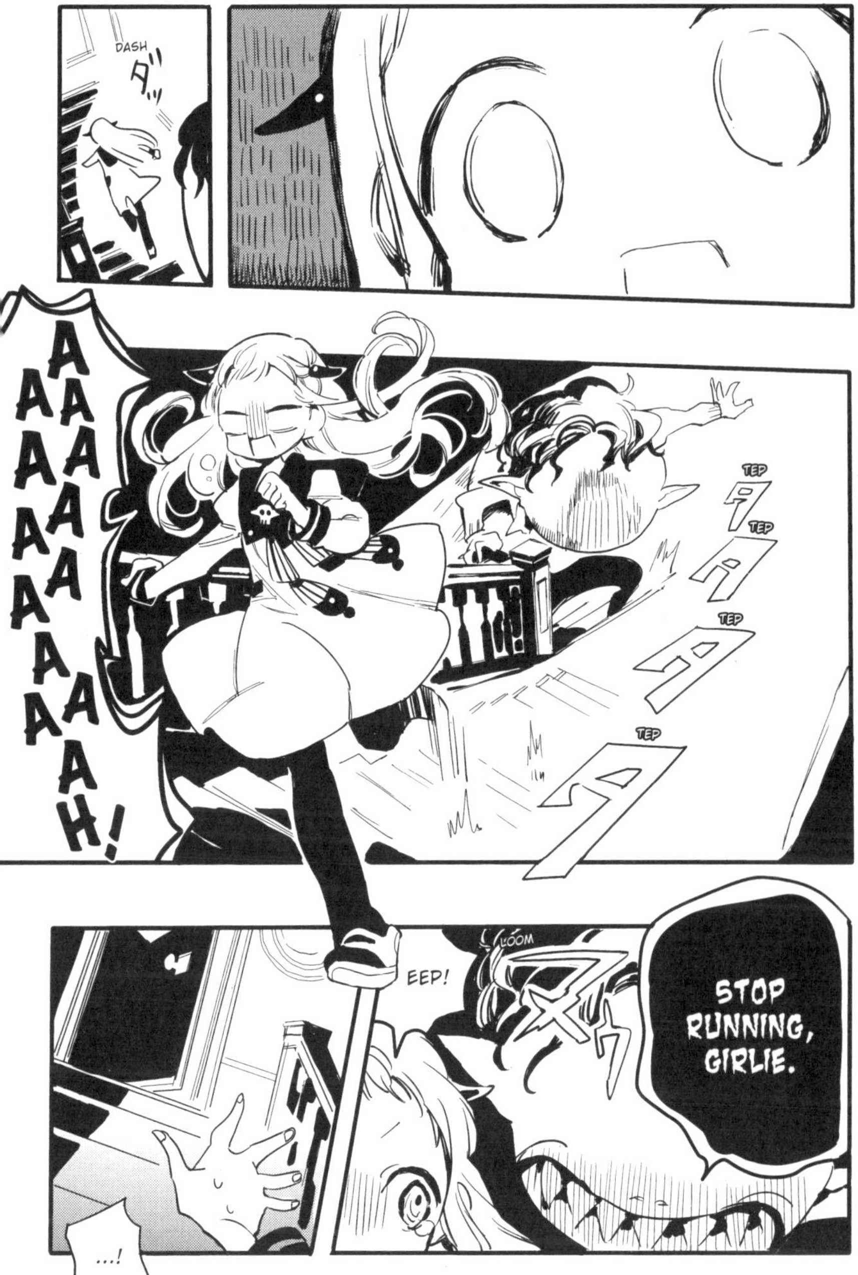
DASH
ダッ
TEP
タ
TEP
タ
TEP
タ
TEP
タ
AAAAAAAAAAAAAH!
LOOM
EEP!
STOP RUNNING, GIRLIE.
...!

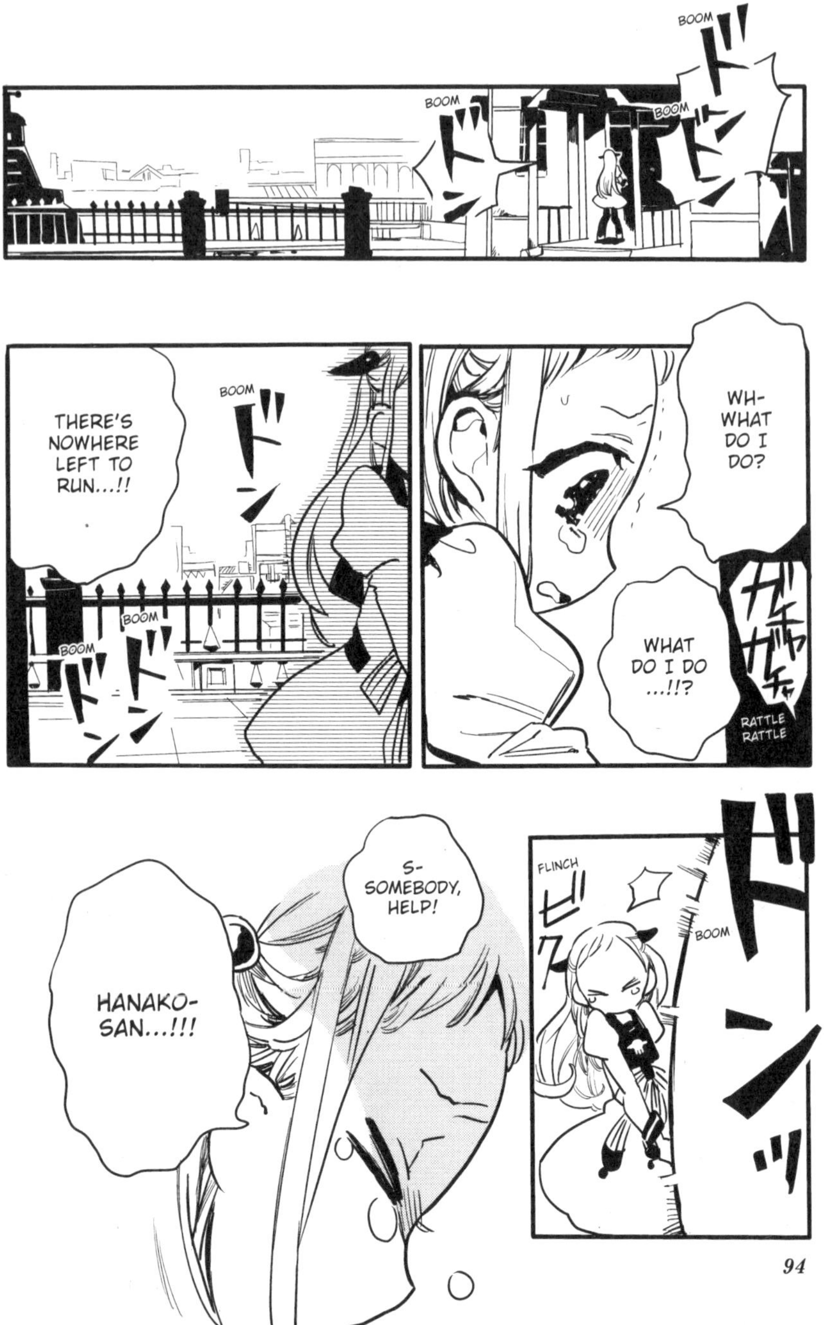
BOOM
BOOM
BOOM
WH-WHAT DO I DO?
WHAT DO I DO ...!!?
RATTLE RATTLE
BOOM
THERE'S NOWHERE LEFT TO RUN...!!
BOOM
BOOM
BOOM
FLINCH
S-SOMEBODY, HELP!
HANAKO-SAN...!!!

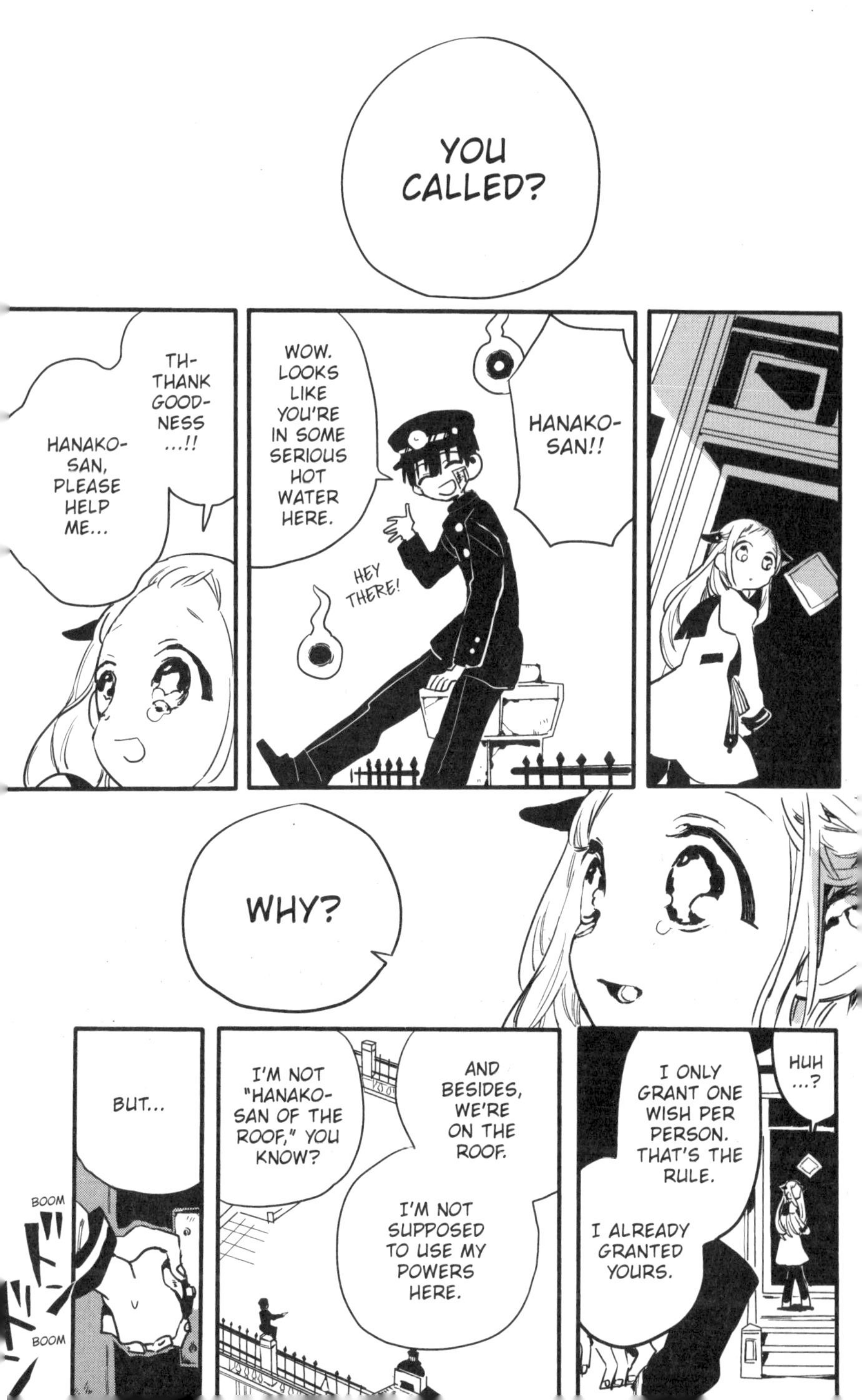
YOU CALLED?
HANAKO-SAN!!
WOW. LOOKS LIKE YOU'RE IN SOME SERIOUS HOT WATER HERE.
HEY THERE!
TH-THANK GOODNESS...!!
HANAKO-SAN, PLEASE HELP ME...
WHY?
HUH...?
I ONLY GRANT ONE WISH PER PERSON. THAT'S THE RULE.
I ALREADY GRANTED YOURS.
AND BESIDES, WE'RE ON THE ROOF.
I'M NOT "HANAKO-SAN OF THE ROOF," YOU KNOW?
I'M NOT SUPPOSED TO USE MY POWERS HERE.
BUT...
BOOM
BOOM

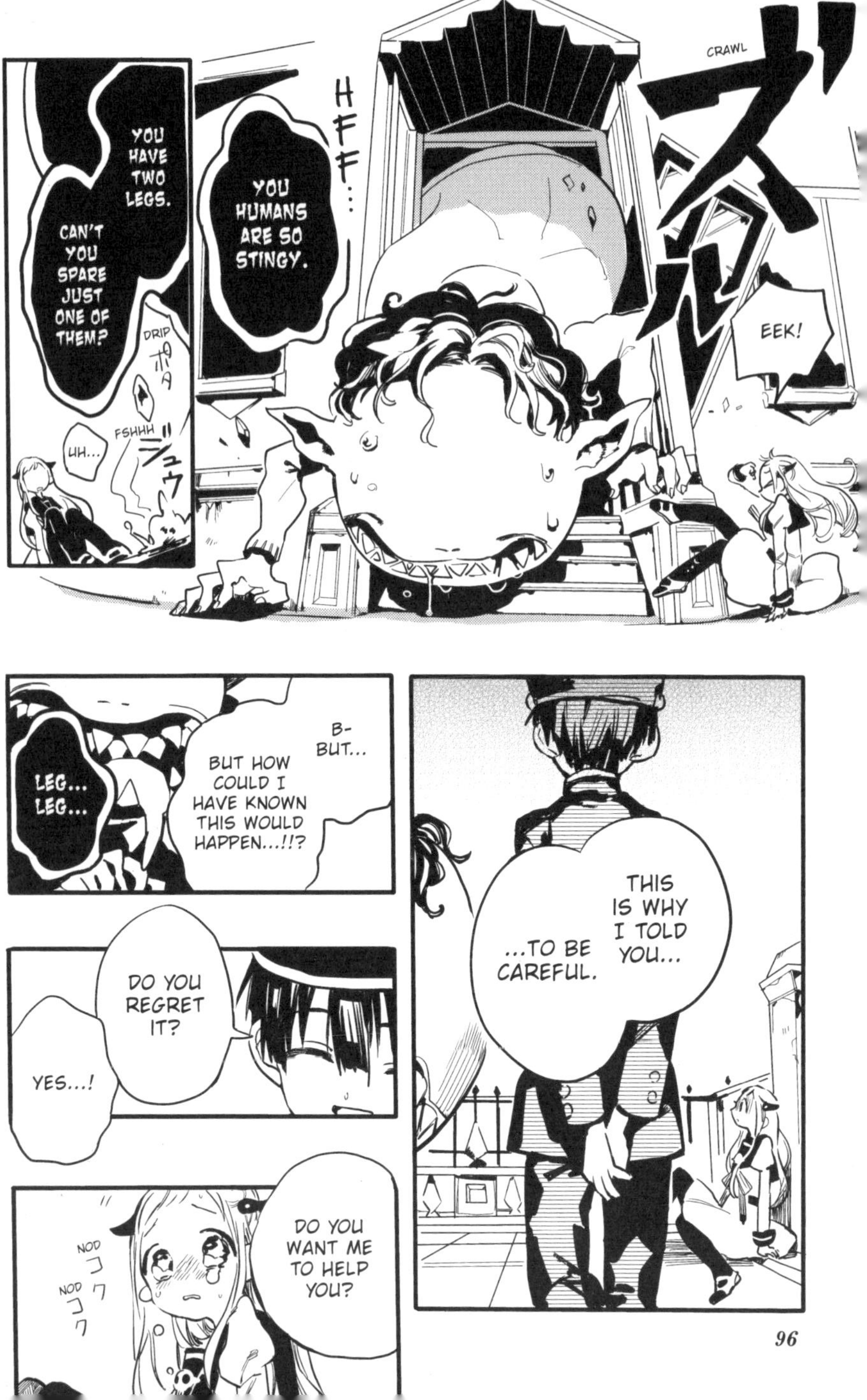
CRAWL
EEK!
HFF...
YOU HUMANS ARE SO STINGY.
YOU HAVE TWO LEGS.
CAN'T YOU SPARE JUST ONE OF THEM?
DRIP
FSHHH
UH...
THIS IS WHY I TOLD YOU...
...TO BE CAREFUL.
LEG... LEG...
B-BUT...
BUT HOW COULD I HAVE KNOWN THIS WOULD HAPPEN...!!?
DO YOU REGRET IT?
YES...!
DO YOU WANT ME TO HELP YOU?
NOD
NOD

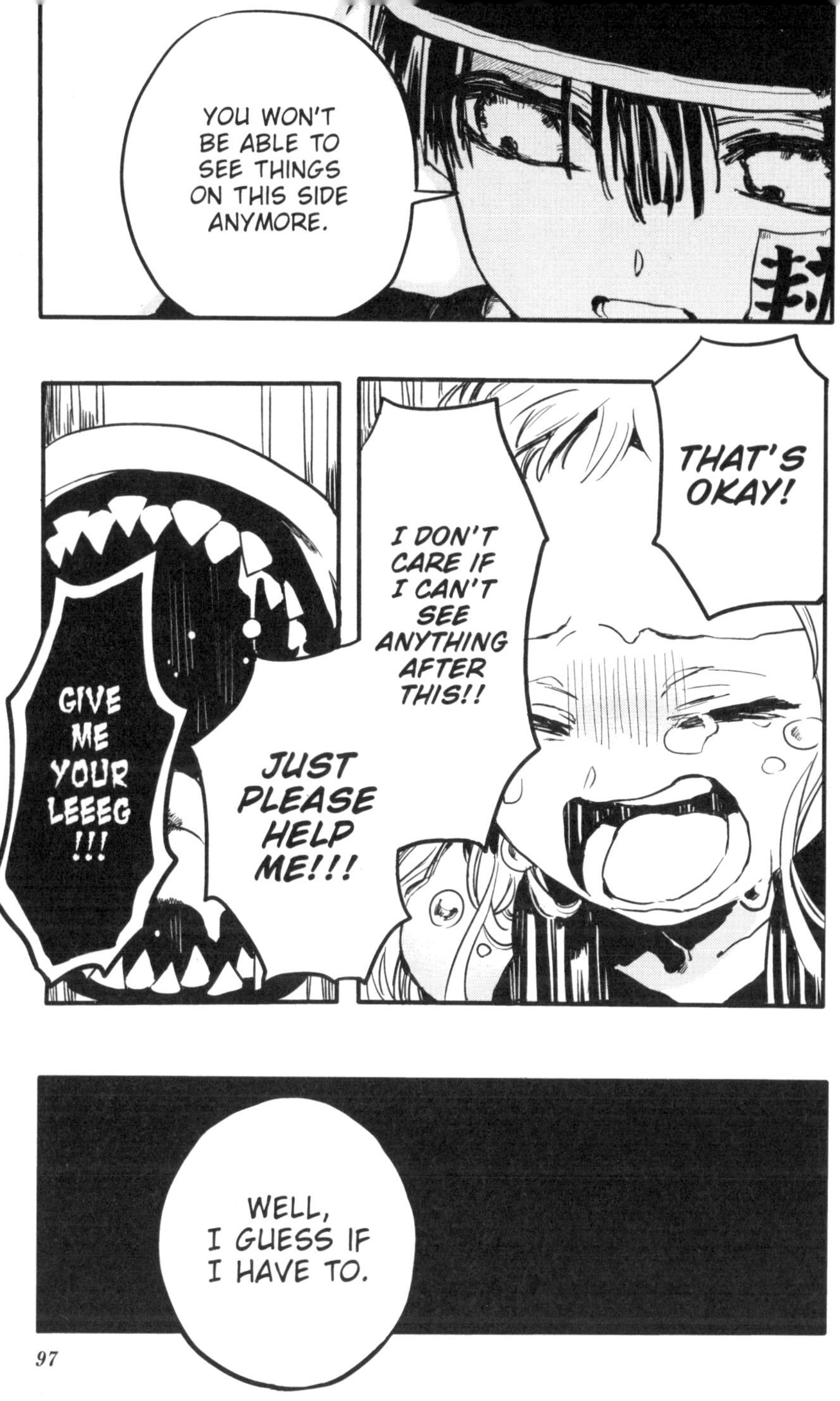
YOU WON'T BE ABLE TO SEE THINGS ON THIS SIDE ANYMORE.
THAT'S OKAY!
I DON'T CARE IF I CAN'T SEE ANYTHING AFTER THIS!!
JUST PLEASE HELP ME!!!
GIVE ME YOUR LEEEG!!!
WELL, I GUESS IF I HAVE TO.

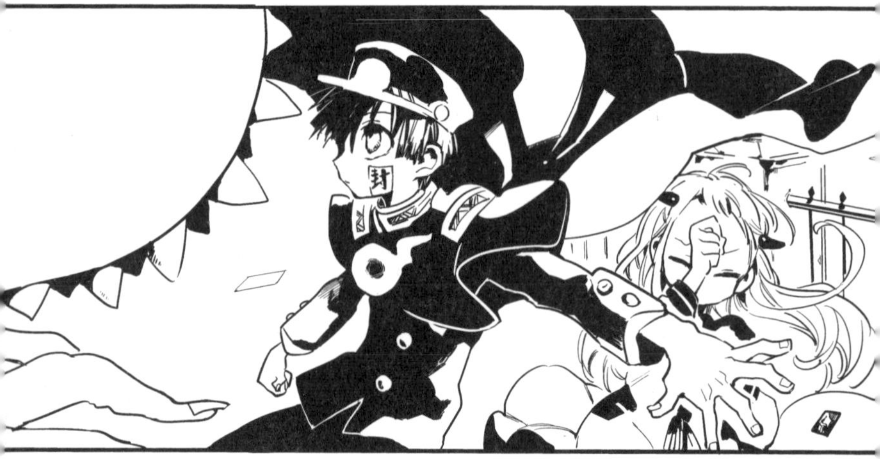
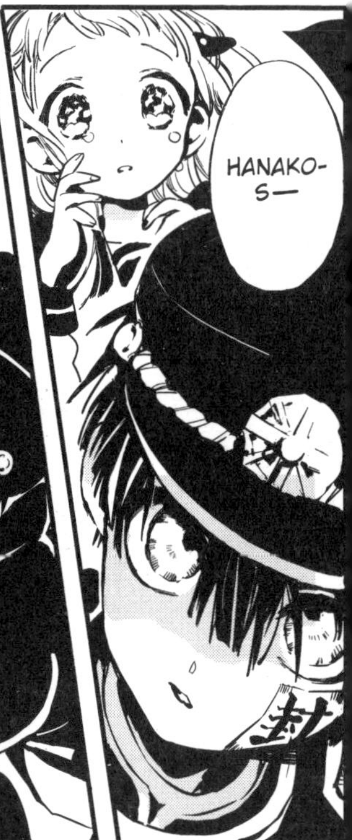
HANAKO-S—
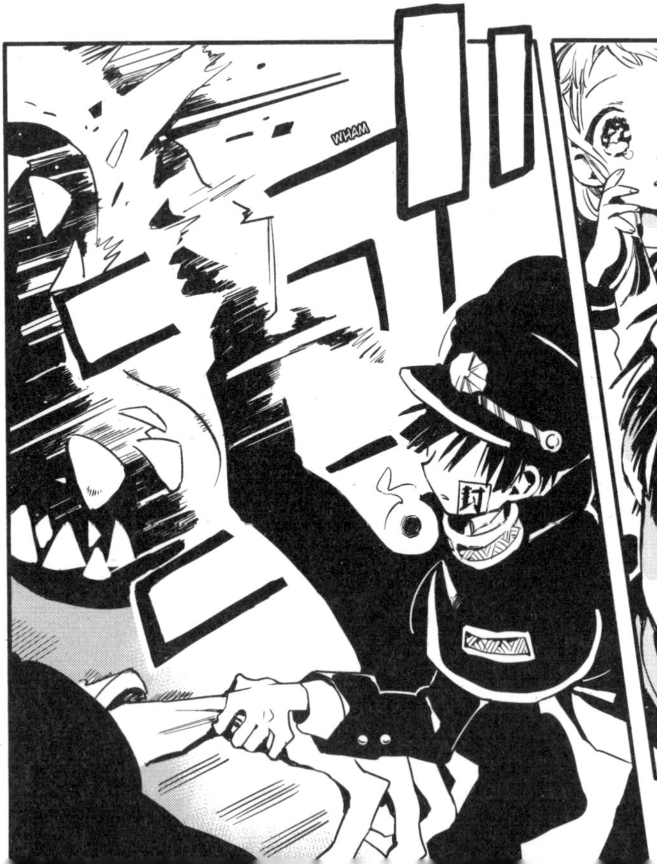
WHAM

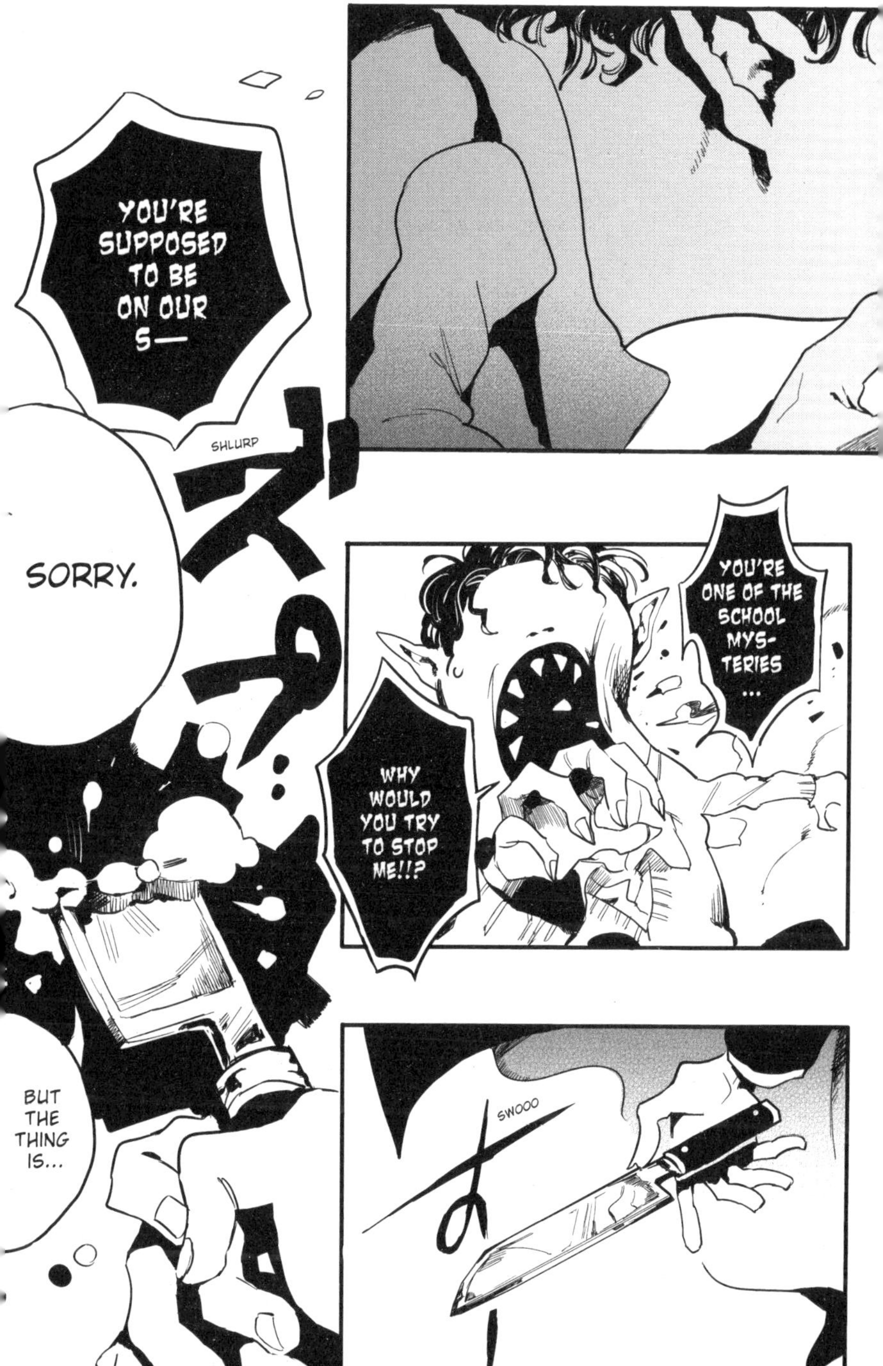
YOU'RE ONE OF THE SCHOOL MYSTERIES...
WHY WOULD YOU TRY TO STOP ME!!?
SWOOO
YOU'RE SUPPOSED TO BE ON OUR S—
SHLURP
SORRY.
BUT THE THING IS...

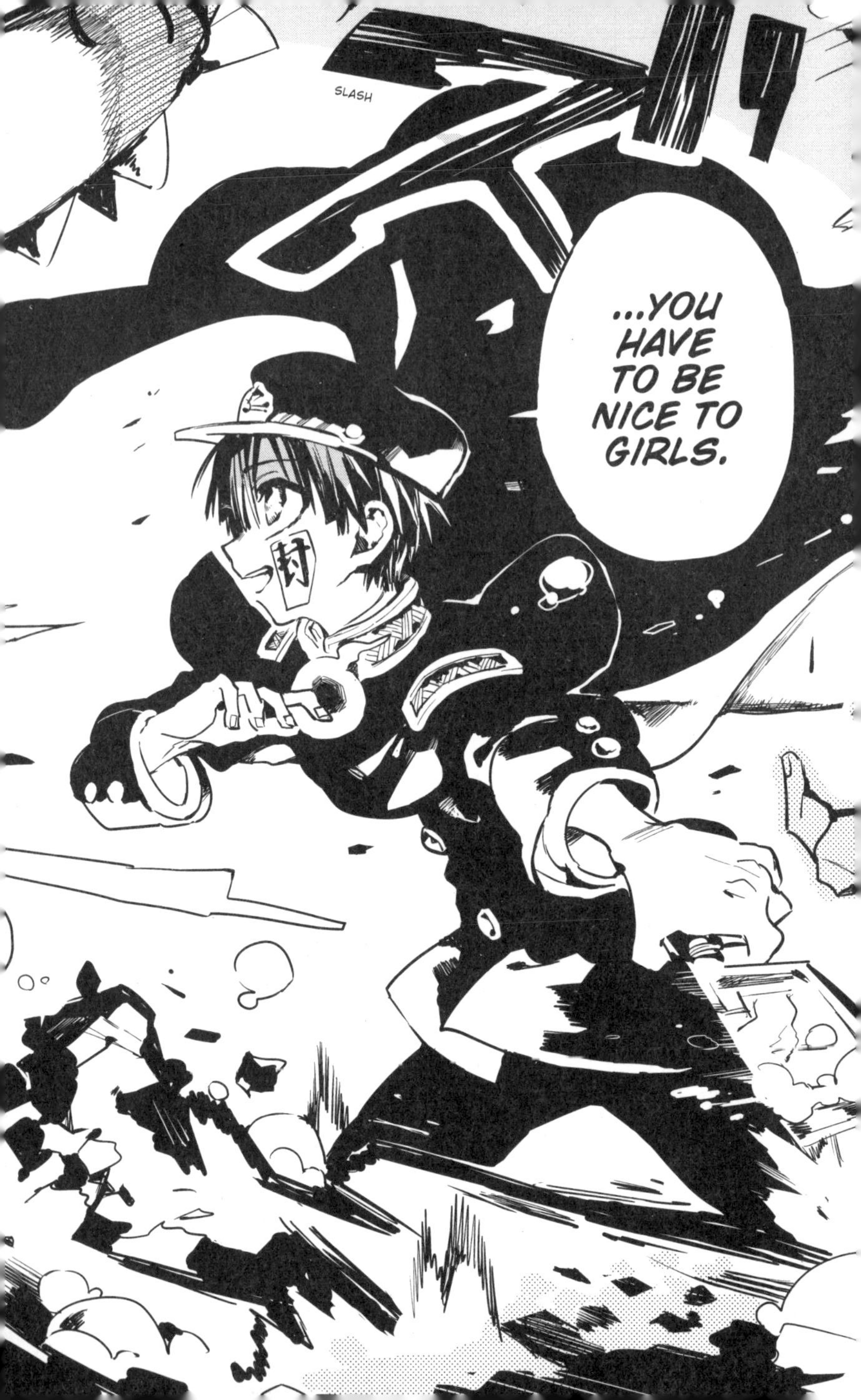
SLASH
...YOU HAVE TO BE NICE TO GIRLS.

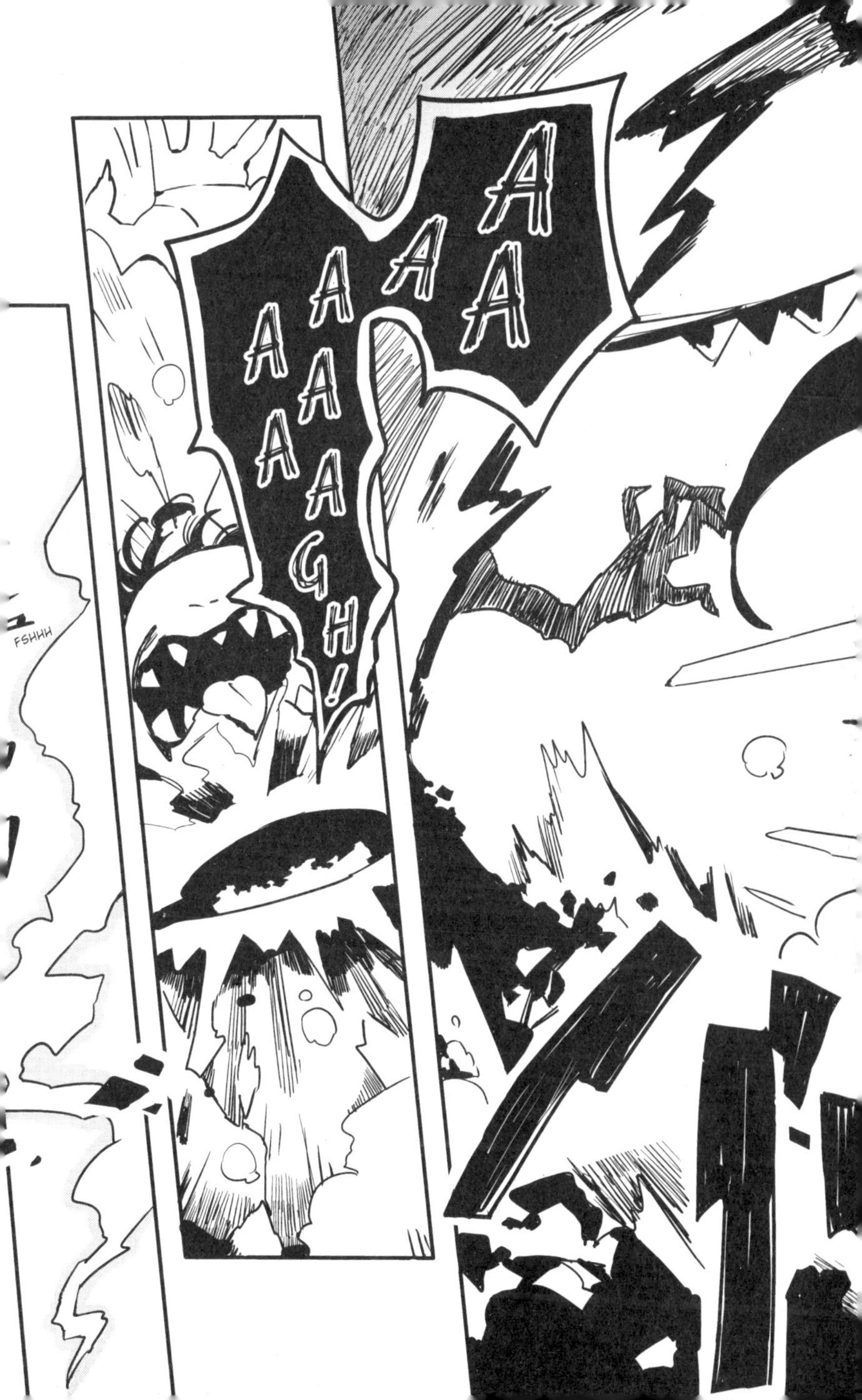
AAAAAAAAAAGH!
FSHHH

TUMBLE

THE RULE IS ONE WISH PER PERSON...

...AND I JUST GAVE YOU A FREEBIE.

STING

HNGH!!

ONE MORE MARK FOR EACH RULE I BREAK...

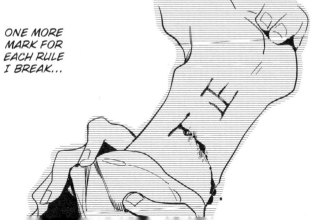

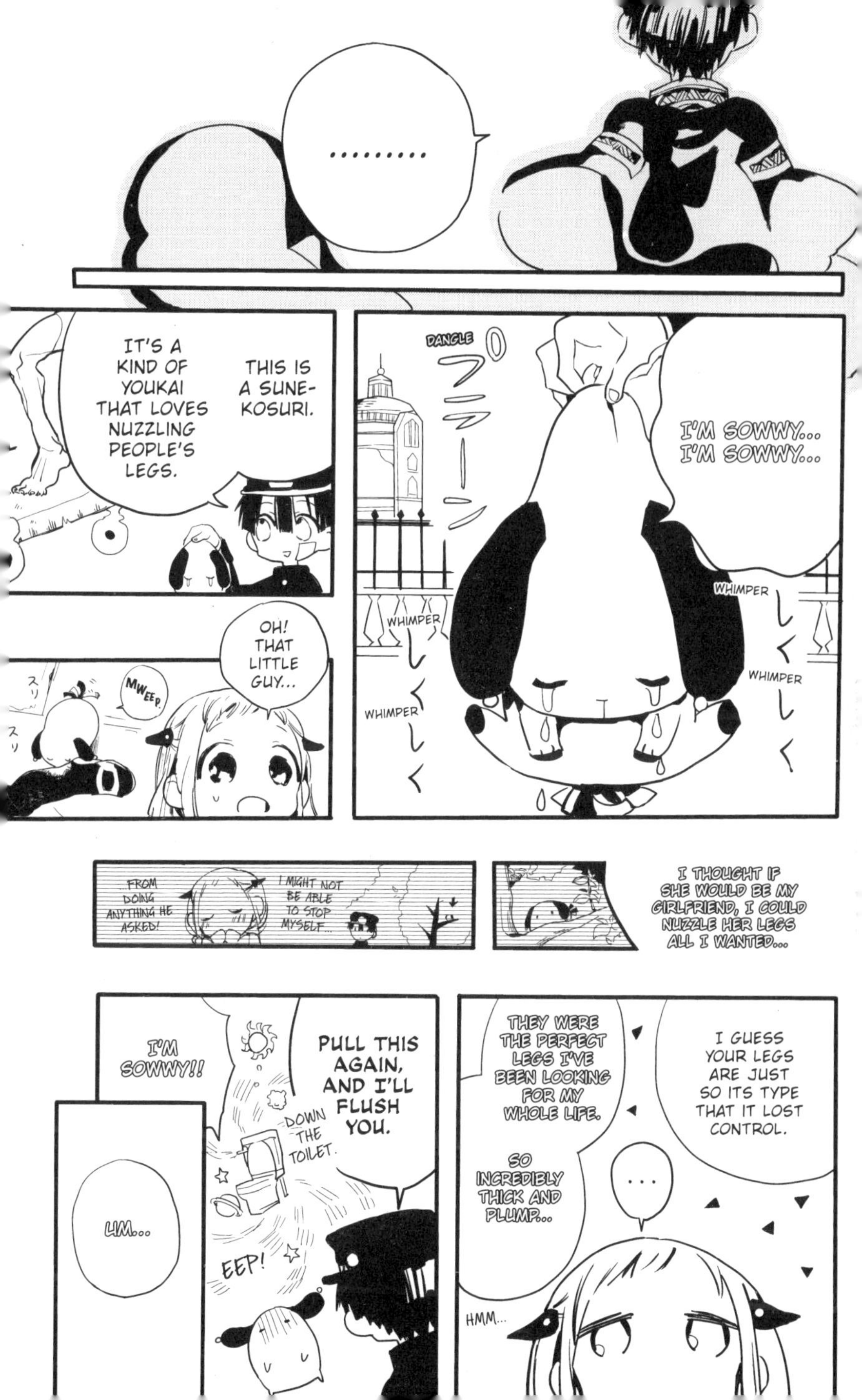
....
DANGLE
I'M SOWWY... I'M SOWWY...
WHIMPER
WHIMPER
WHIMPER
WHIMPER
THIS IS A SUNE-KOSURI.
IT'S A KIND OF YOUKAI THAT LOVES NUZZLING PEOPLE'S LEGS.
OH! THAT LITTLE GUY...
MWEEP
スリ
スリ
I THOUGHT IF SHE WOULD BE MY GIRLFRIEND, I COULD NUZZLE HER LEGS ALL I WANTED...
I MIGHT NOT BE ABLE TO STOP MYSELF...
...FROM DOING ANYTHING HE ASKED!
I GUESS YOUR LEGS ARE JUST SO ITS TYPE THAT IT LOST CONTROL.
THEY WERE THE PERFECT LEGS I'VE BEEN LOOKING FOR MY WHOLE LIFE.
SO INCREDIBLY THICK AND PLUMP...
...
HMM...
PULL THIS AGAIN, AND I'LL FLUSH YOU.
DOWN THE TOILET.
I'M SOWWY!!
EEP!
UM...

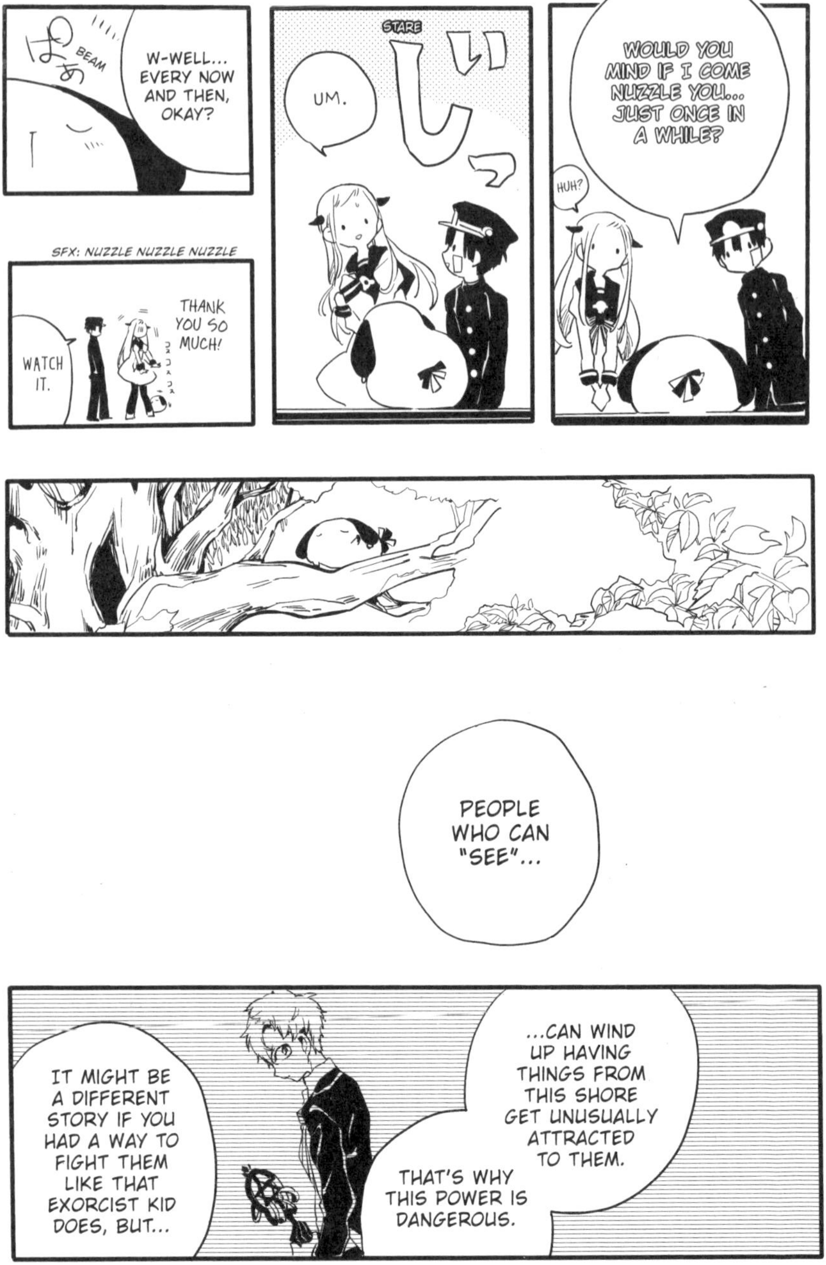
WOULD YOU MIND IF I COME NUZZLE YOU... JUST ONCE IN A WHILE?
HUH?
STARE
じいっ
UM.
はあ
BEAM
W-WELL... EVERY NOW AND THEN, OKAY?
SFX: NUZZLE NUZZLE NUZZLE
THANK YOU SO MUCH!
WATCH IT.
PEOPLE WHO CAN "SEE"...
...CAN WIND UP HAVING THINGS FROM THIS SHORE GET UNUSUALLY ATTRACTED TO THEM.
THAT'S WHY THIS POWER IS DANGEROUS.
IT MIGHT BE A DIFFERENT STORY IF YOU HAD A WAY TO FIGHT THEM LIKE THAT EXORCIST KID DOES, BUT...

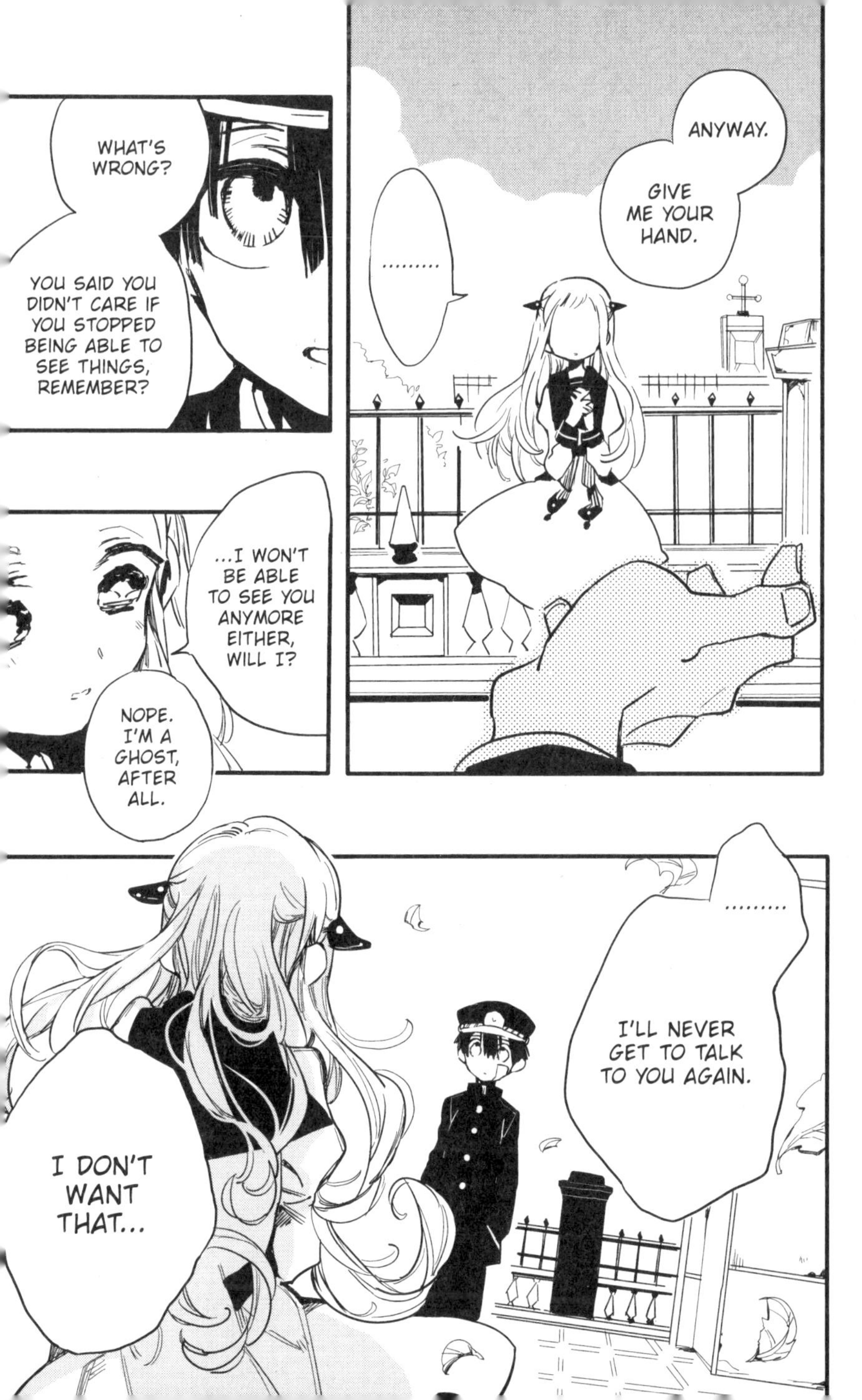
ANYWAY.
GIVE ME YOUR HAND.
....
WHAT'S WRONG?
YOU SAID YOU DIDN'T CARE IF YOU STOPPED BEING ABLE TO SEE THINGS, REMEMBER?
...I WON'T BE ABLE TO SEE YOU ANYMORE EITHER, WILL I?
NOPE. I'M A GHOST, AFTER ALL.
....
I'LL NEVER GET TO TALK TO YOU AGAIN.
I DON'T WANT THAT...

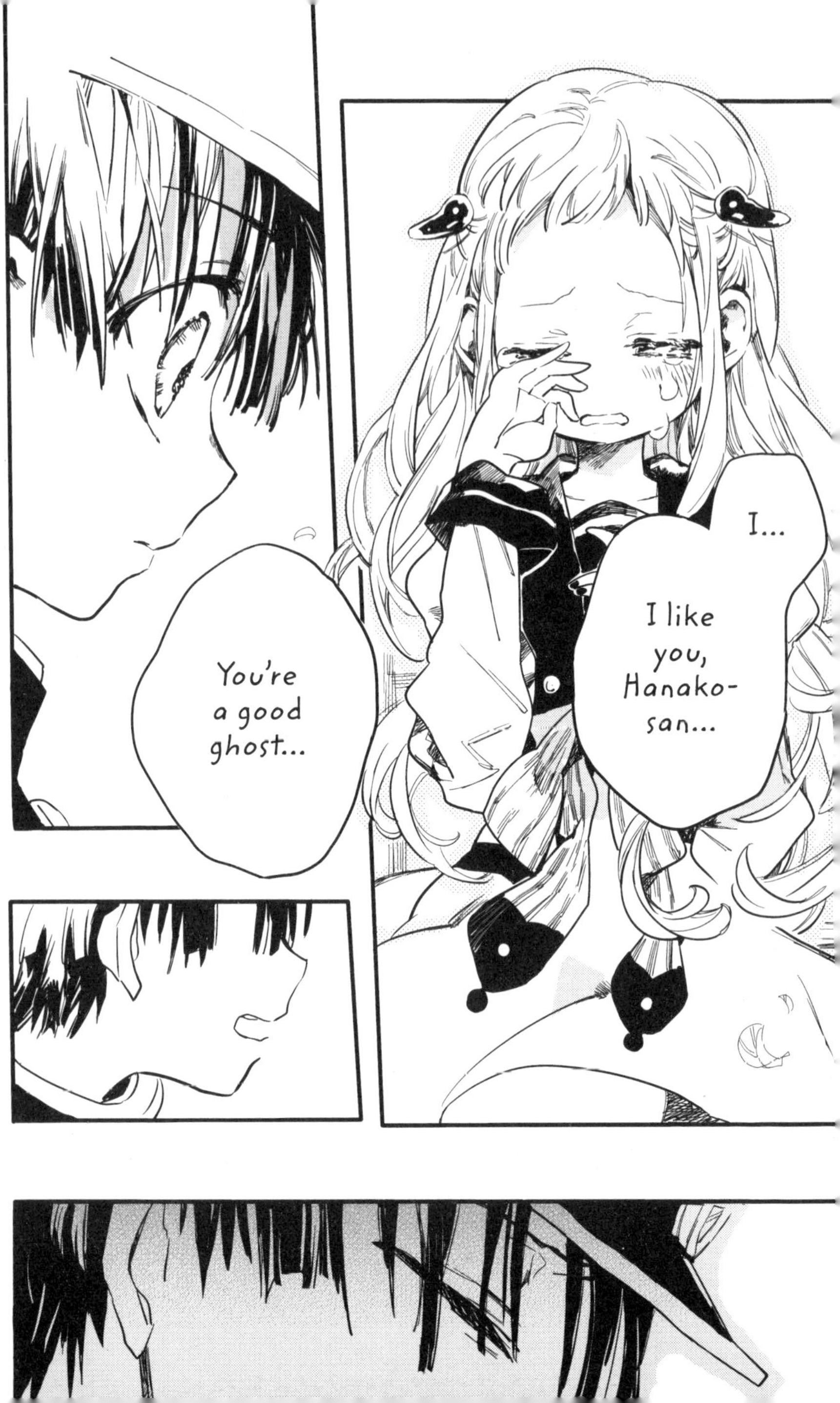
I...
I like you, Hanako-san...
You're a good ghost...

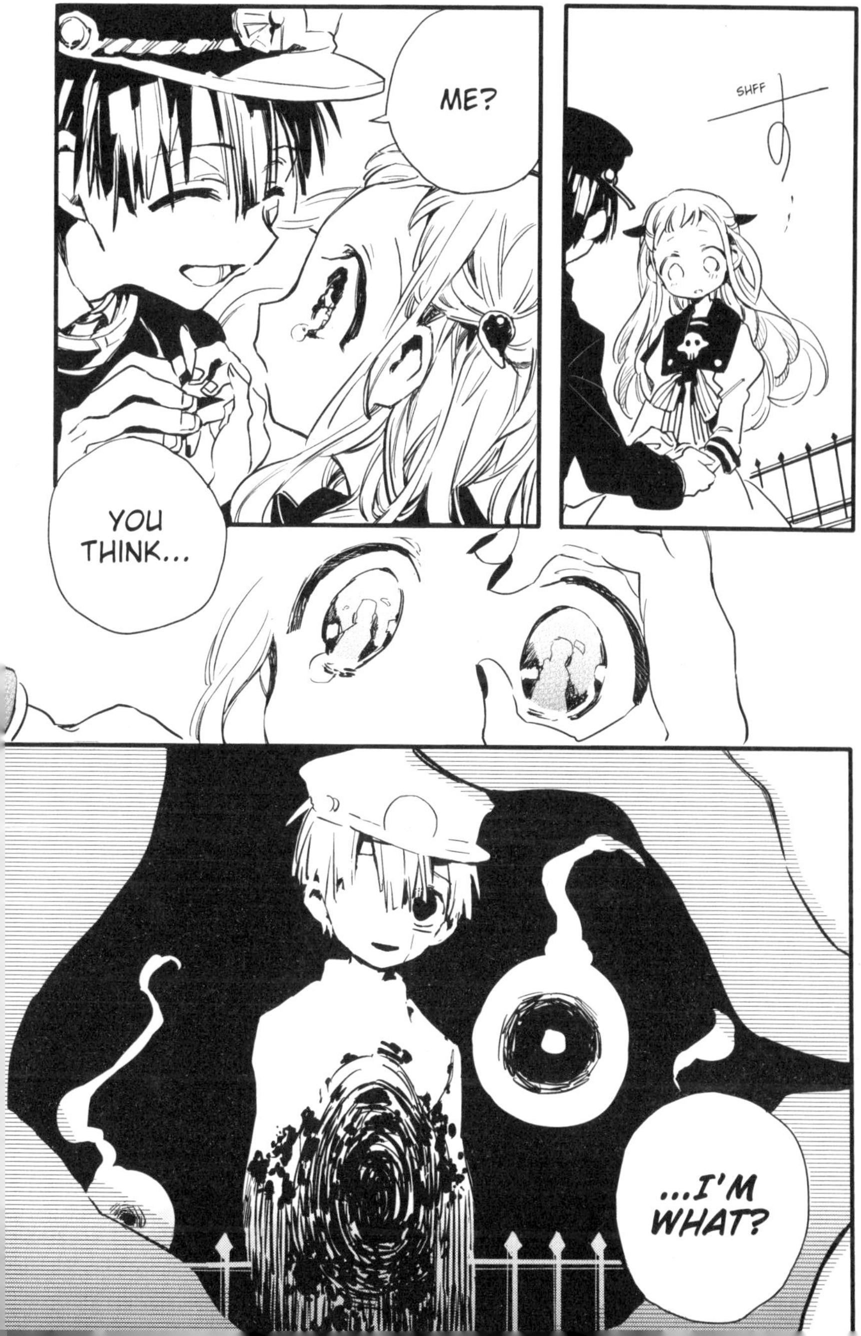
SHFF
ME?
YOU THINK...
...I'M WHAT?

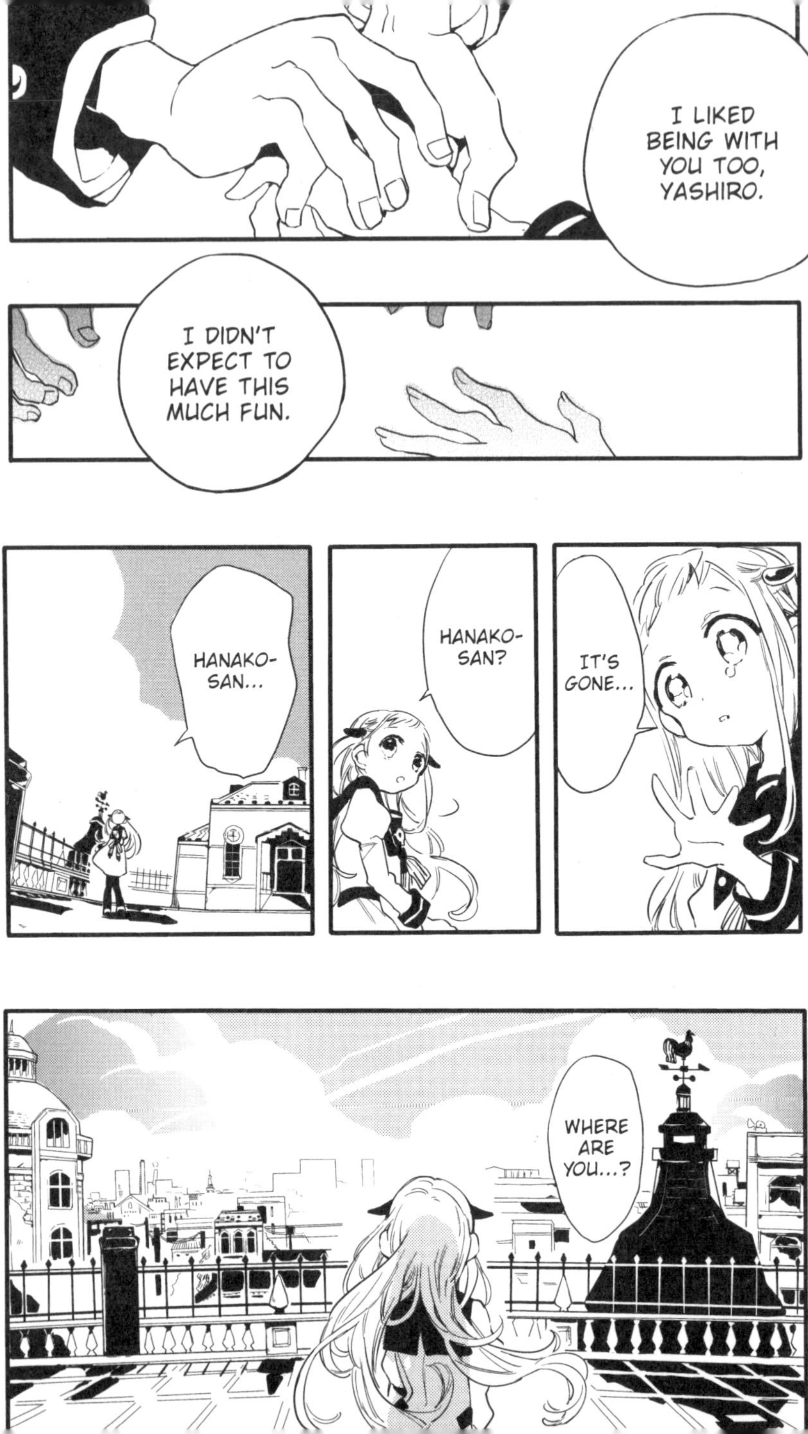
I LIKED BEING WITH YOU TOO, YASHIRO.
I DIDN'T EXPECT TO HAVE THIS MUCH FUN.
IT'S GONE...
HANAKO-SAN?
HANAKO-SAN...
WHERE ARE YOU...?

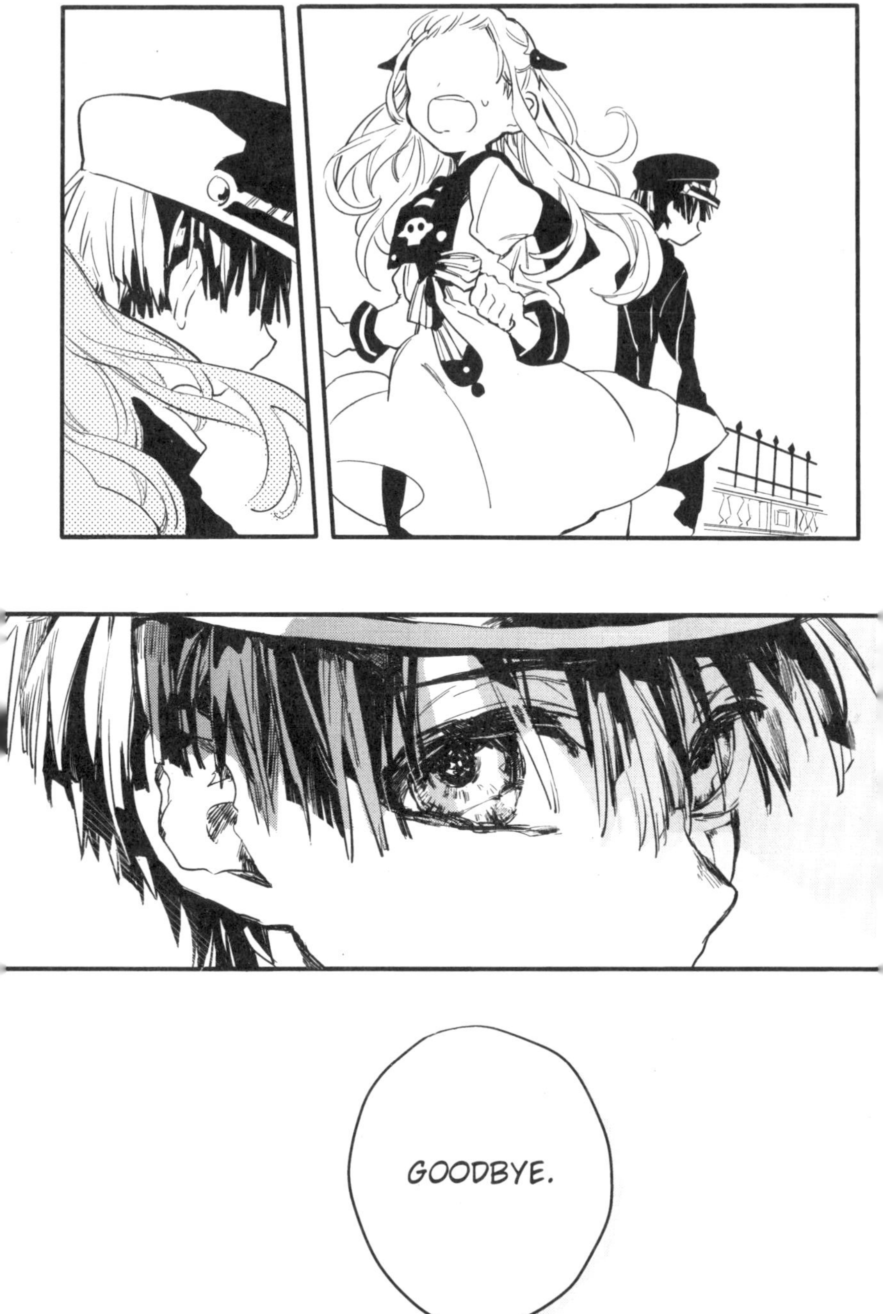
GOODBYE.

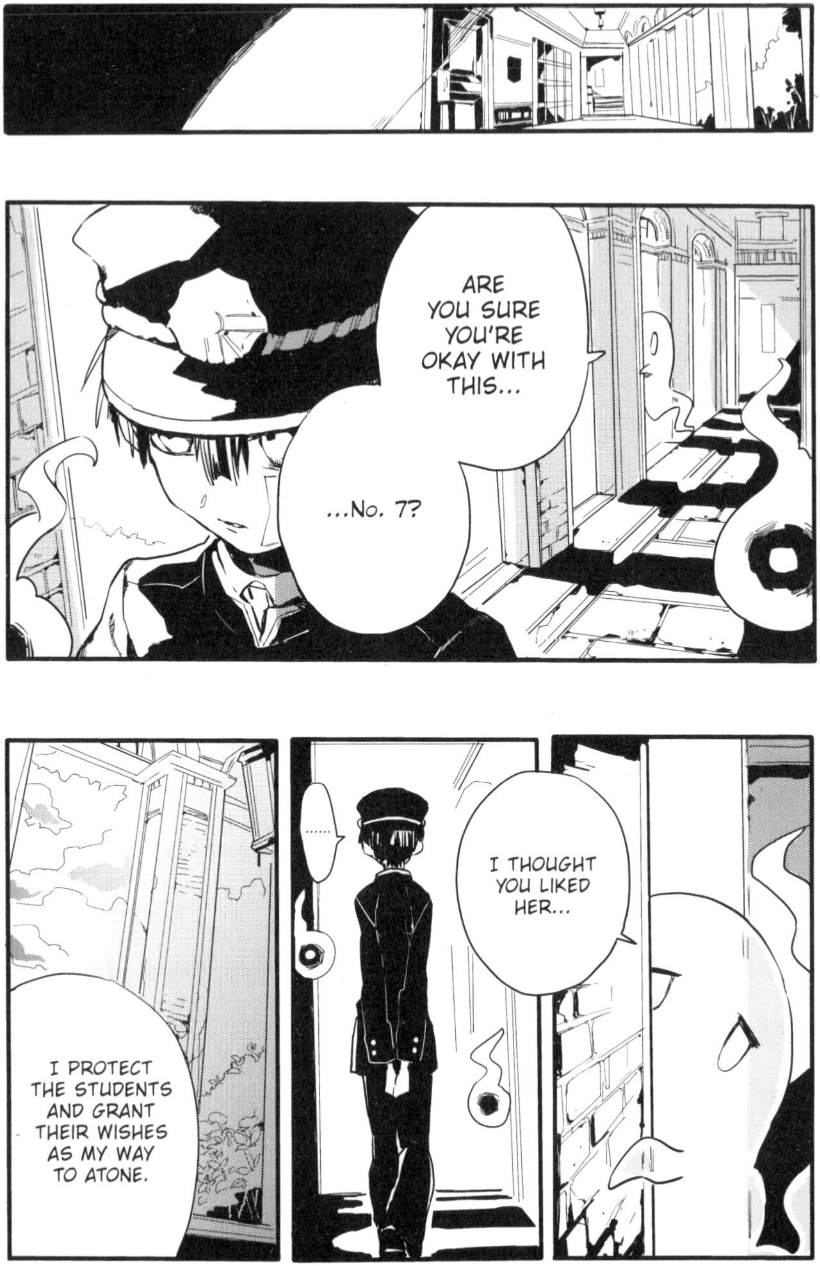
ARE YOU SURE YOU'RE OKAY WITH THIS...
...No. 7?
I THOUGHT YOU LIKED HER...
......
I PROTECT THE STUDENTS AND GRANT THEIR WISHES AS MY WAY TO ATONE.

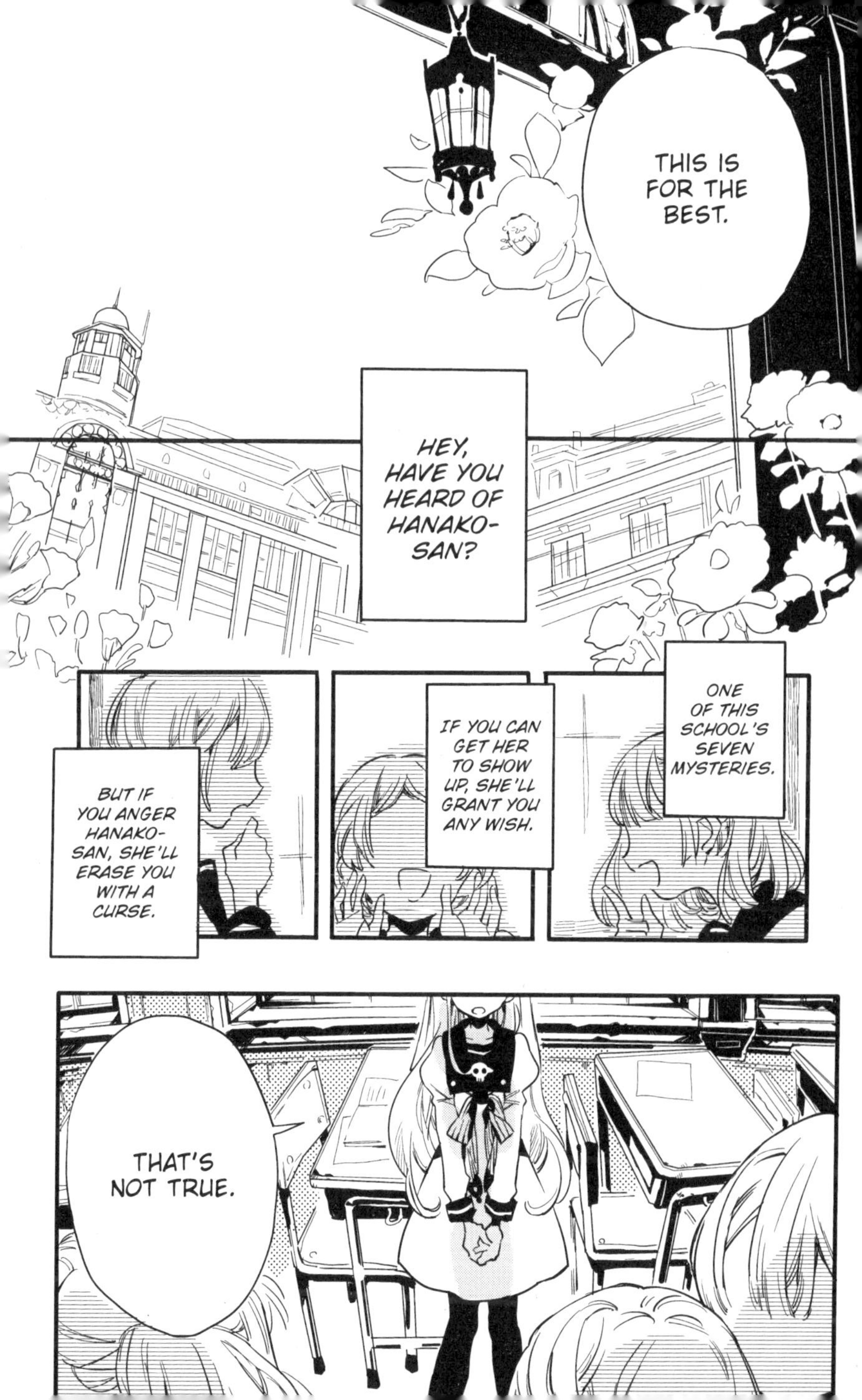
THIS IS FOR THE BEST.
HEY, HAVE YOU HEARD OF HANAKO-SAN?
ONE OF THIS SCHOOL'S SEVEN MYSTERIES.
IF YOU CAN GET HER TO SHOW UP, SHE'LL GRANT YOU ANY WISH.
BUT IF YOU ANGER HANAKO-SAN, SHE'LL ERASE YOU WITH A CURSE.
THAT'S NOT TRUE.

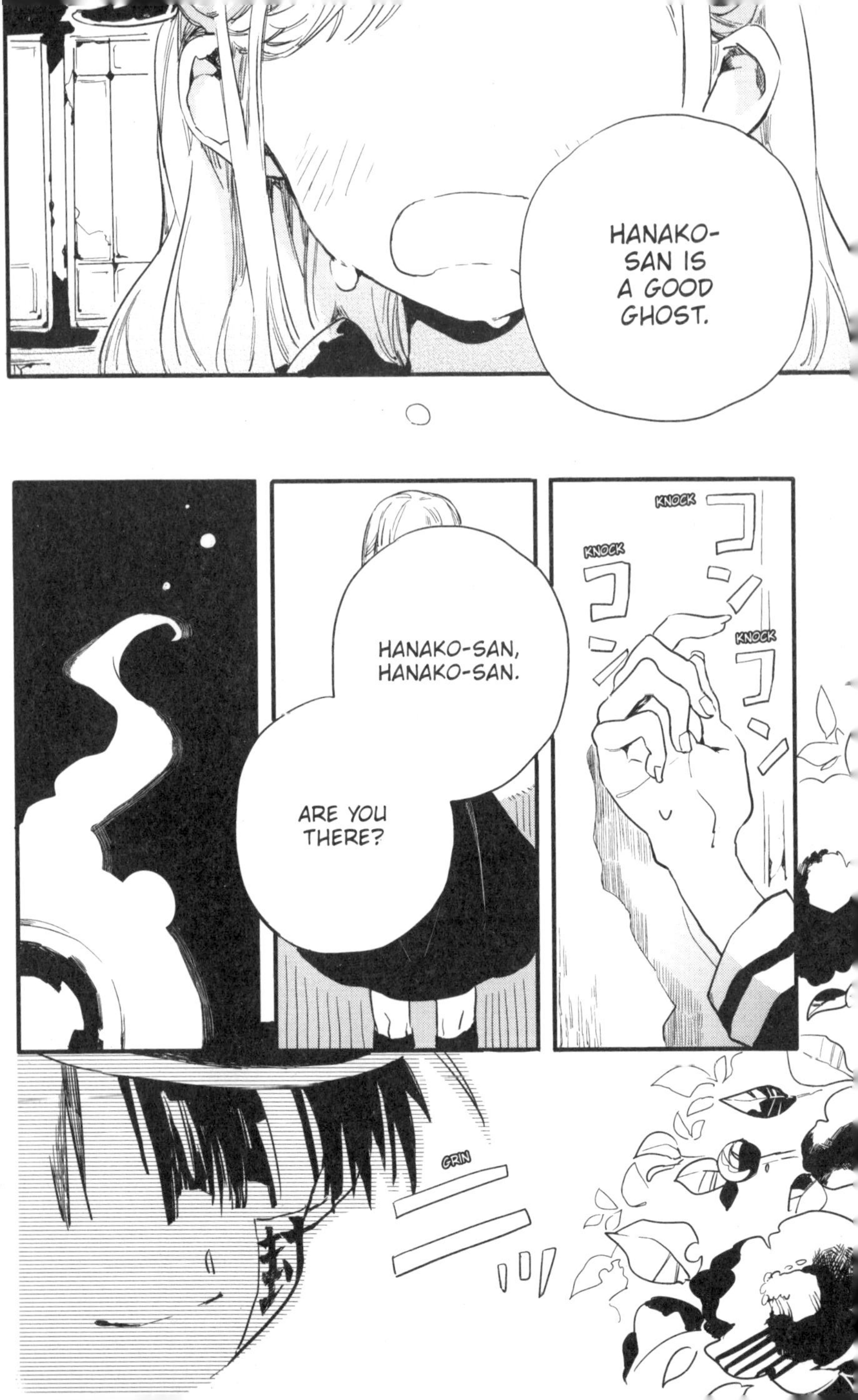
HANAKO-SAN IS A GOOD GHOST.
KNOCK
KNOCK
KNOCK
HANAKO-SAN, HANAKO-SAN.
ARE YOU THERE?
GRIN

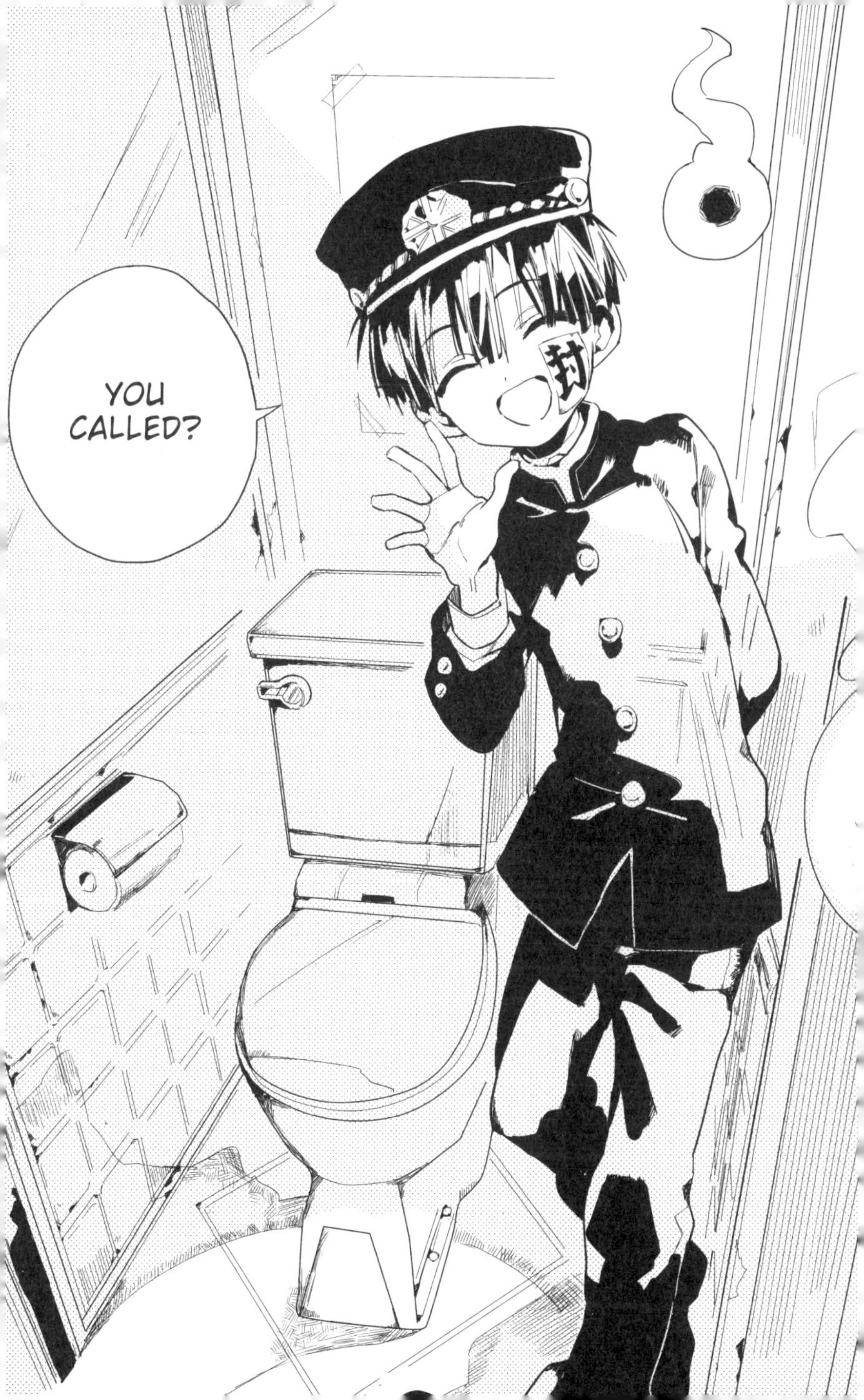
YOU CALLED?
封

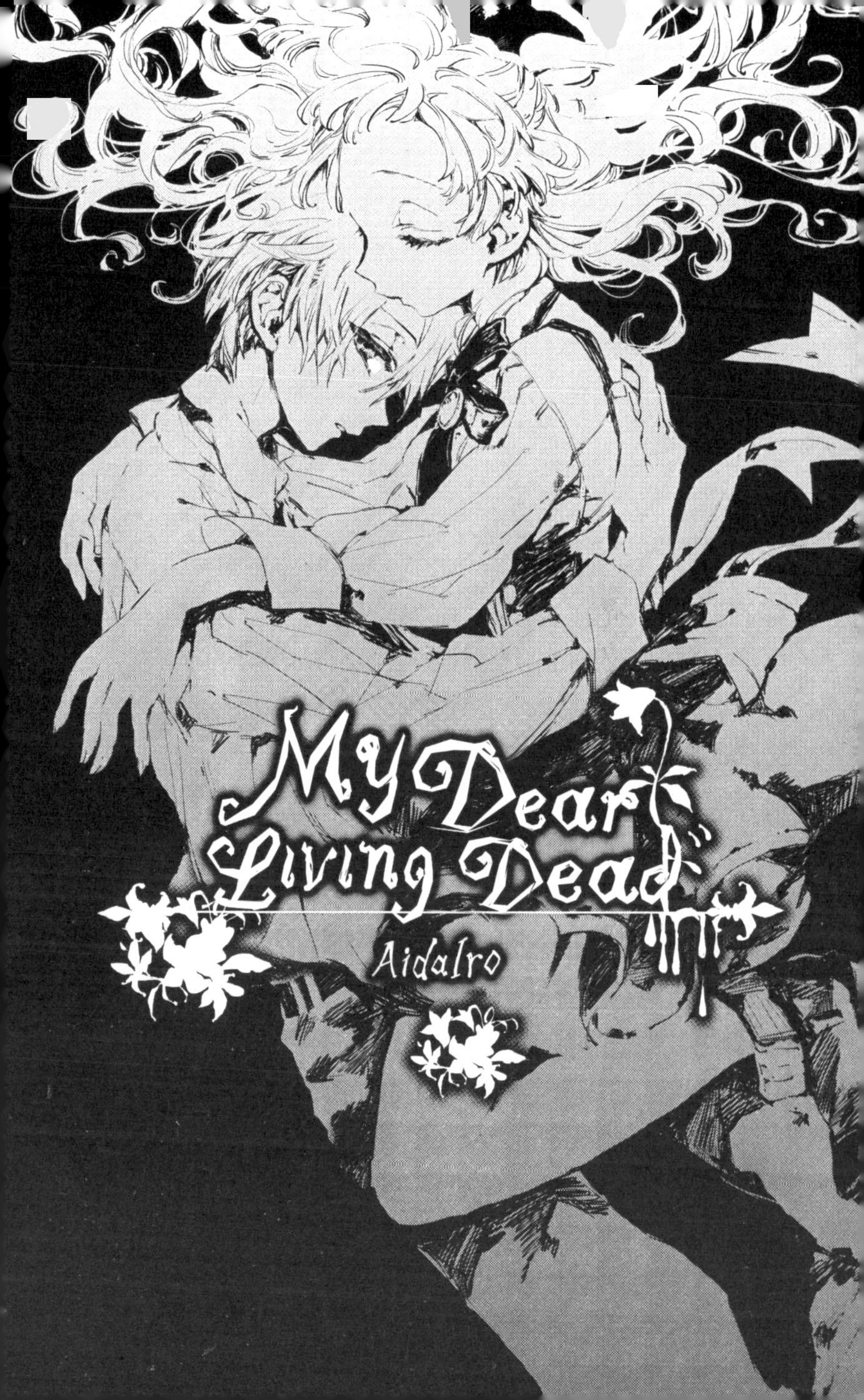
My Dear Living Dead
Aidalro

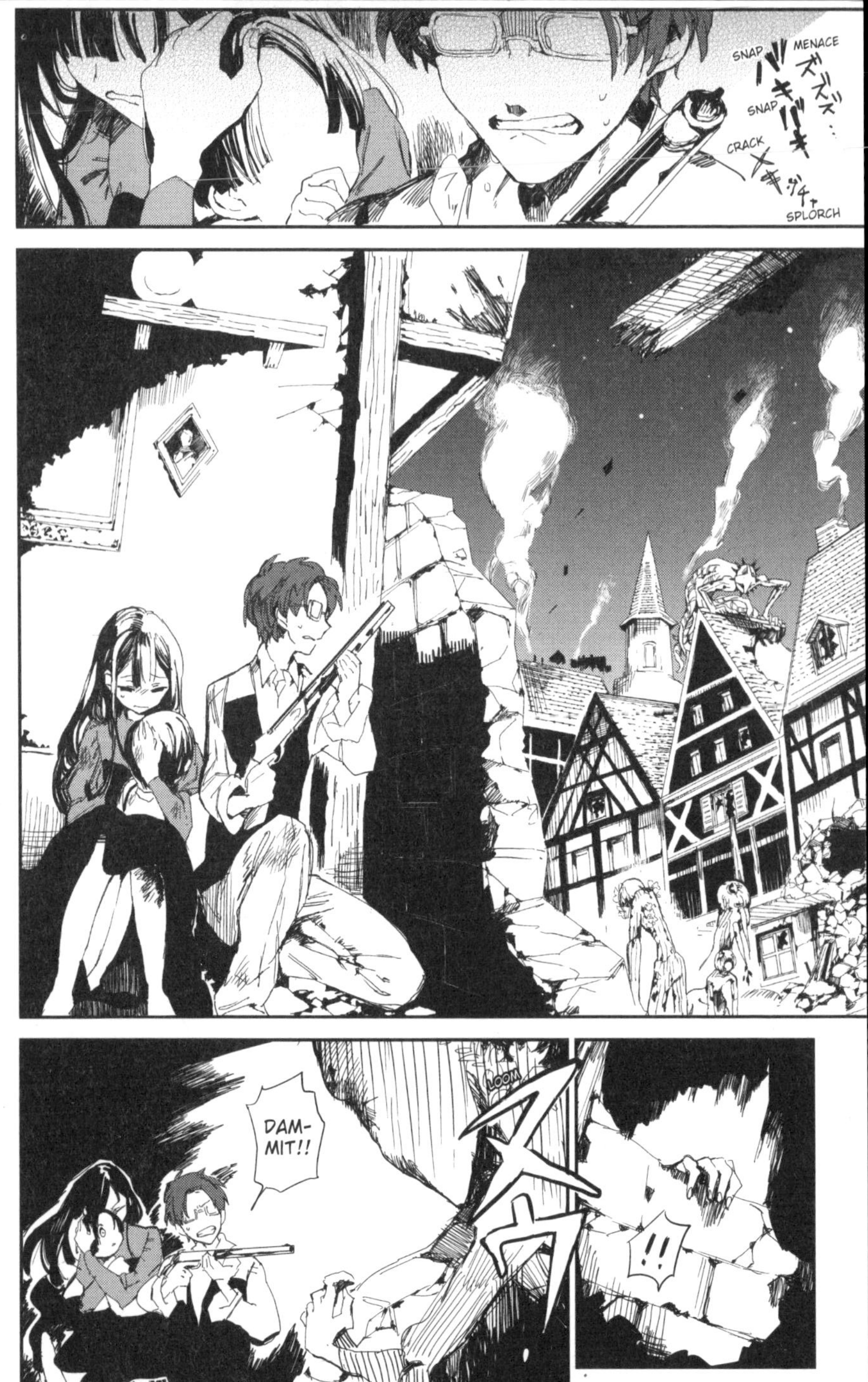
MENACE
ズズズ…
SNAP
バキ
SNAP
バキ
CRACK
メキ
グチャ
SPLORCH
!!
LOOM
DAM-
MIT!!

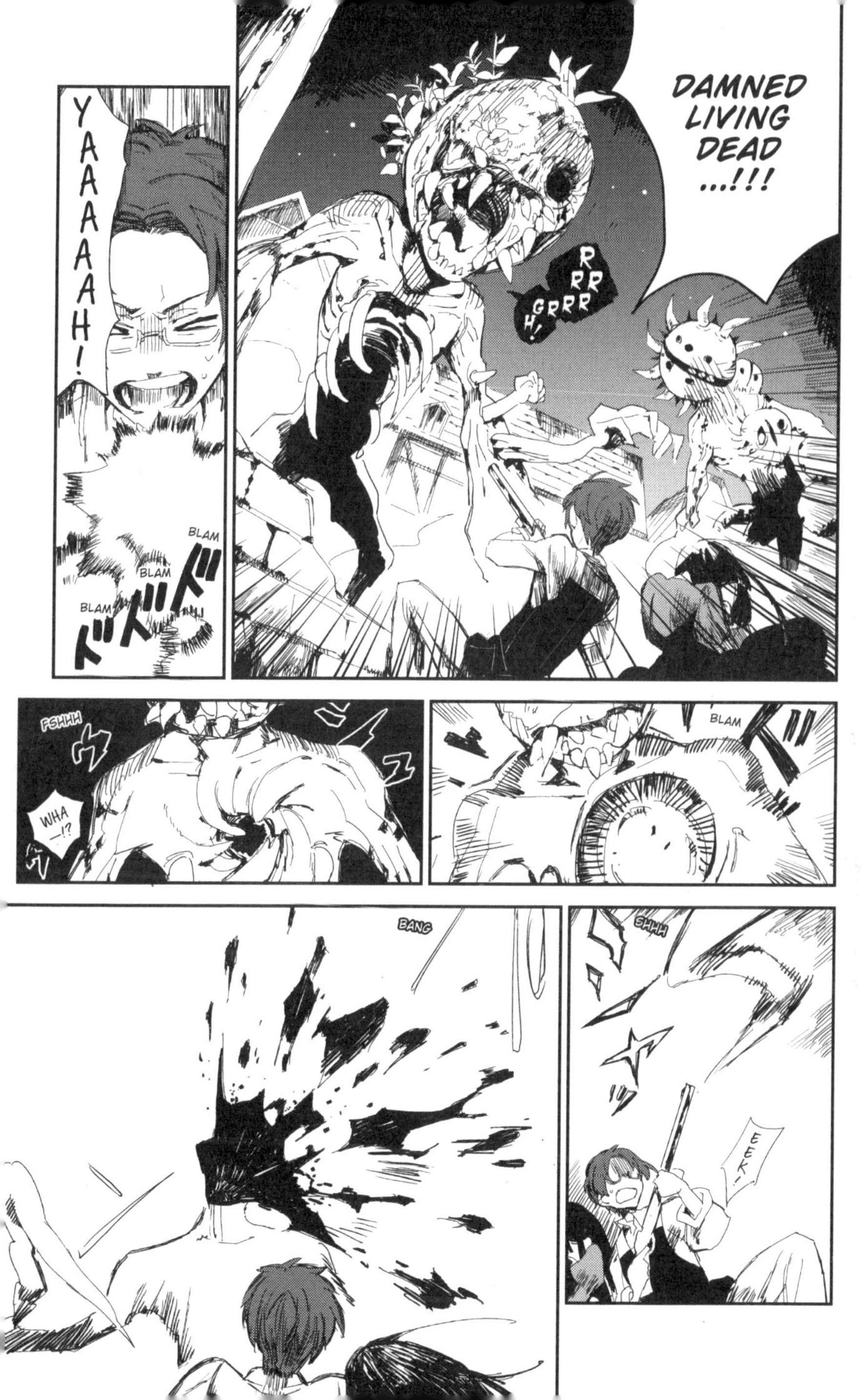
DAMNED LIVING DEAD ...!!!
GRRRRRRRH!
YAAAAAAH!
BLAM
BLAM
BLAM
BLAM
FSHHH
WHA—!?
SHHH
EEEK!
BANG

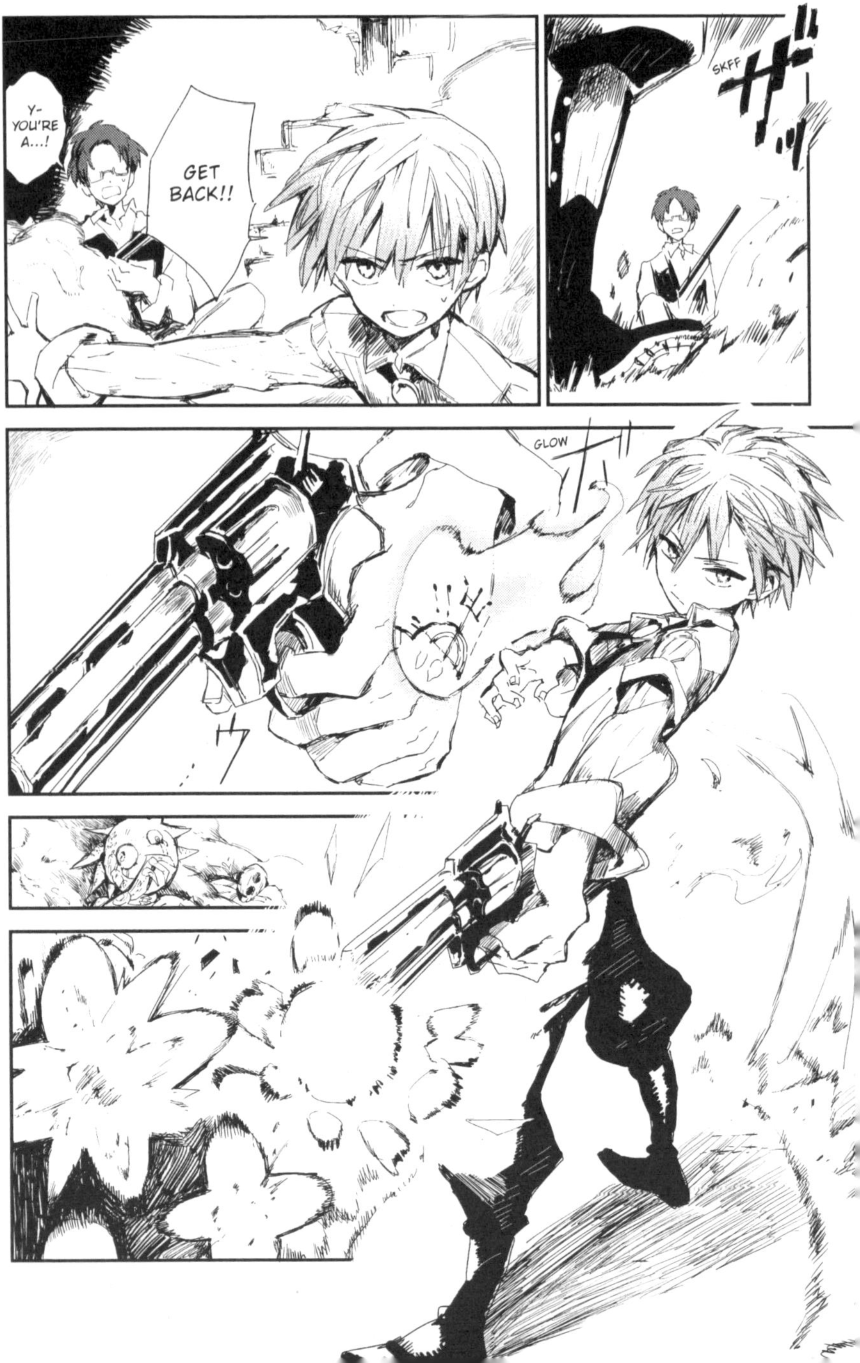
SKFF
GET BACK!!
Y-YOU'RE A...!
GLOW

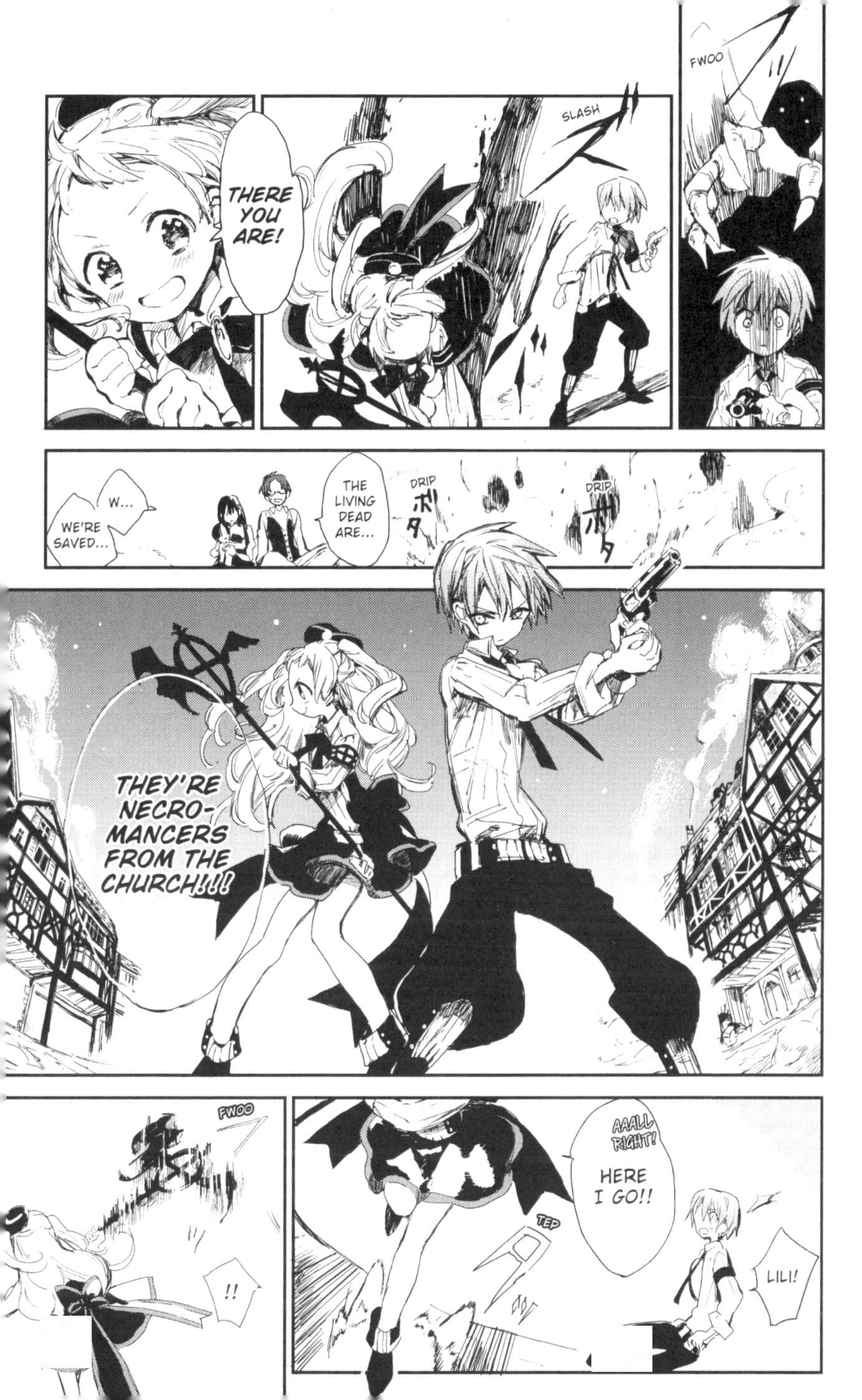

FWOO
!!
SLASH
THERE YOU ARE!
DRIP
ボタ
DRIP
ボタ
THE LIVING DEAD ARE...
W...
WE'RE SAVED...
THEY'RE NECRO-MANCERS FROM THE CHURCH!!!
LILI!
AAALL RIGHT!
HERE I GO!!
TEP
FWOO
!!
!!

GRAAAH!

EEEEEK!

EH HEH

UH.

GLORP

UH—

HUH?

HEY.

WHAM

DID YOU JUST TRY TO KILL LILI?

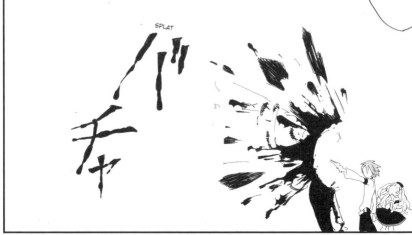

SPLAT

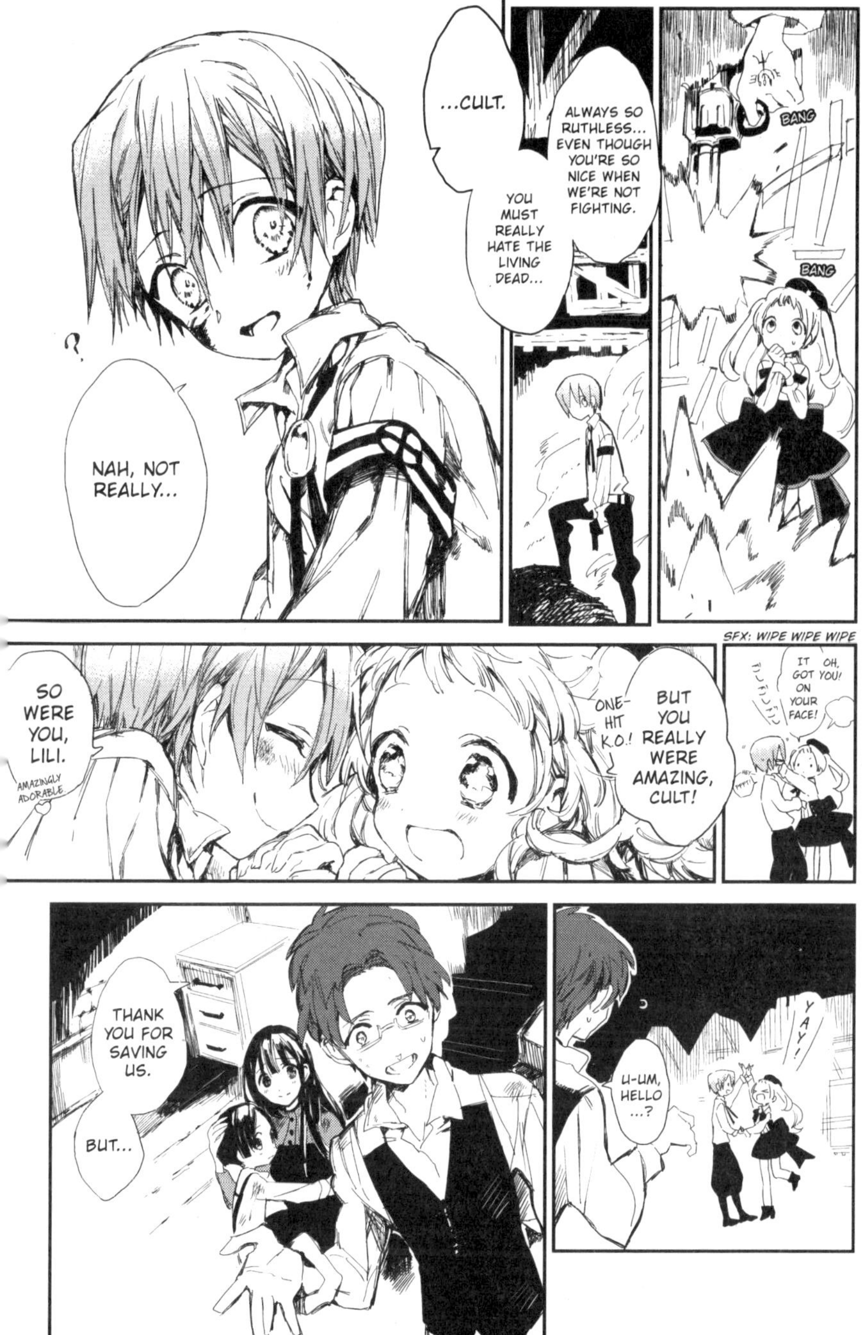
BANG
BANG
...CULT.
ALWAYS SO RUTHLESS... EVEN THOUGH YOU'RE SO NICE WHEN WE'RE NOT FIGHTING.
YOU MUST REALLY HATE THE LIVING DEAD...
?
NAH, NOT REALLY...
SFX: WIPE WIPE WIPE
OH, YOU!
IT GOT ON YOUR FACE!
HEY
PFFT!
BUT YOU REALLY WERE AMAZING, CULT!
ONE-HIT K.O.!
SO WERE YOU, LILI.
AMAZINGLY ADORABLE
YAY!
U-UM, HELLO ...?
THANK YOU FOR SAVING US.
BUT...

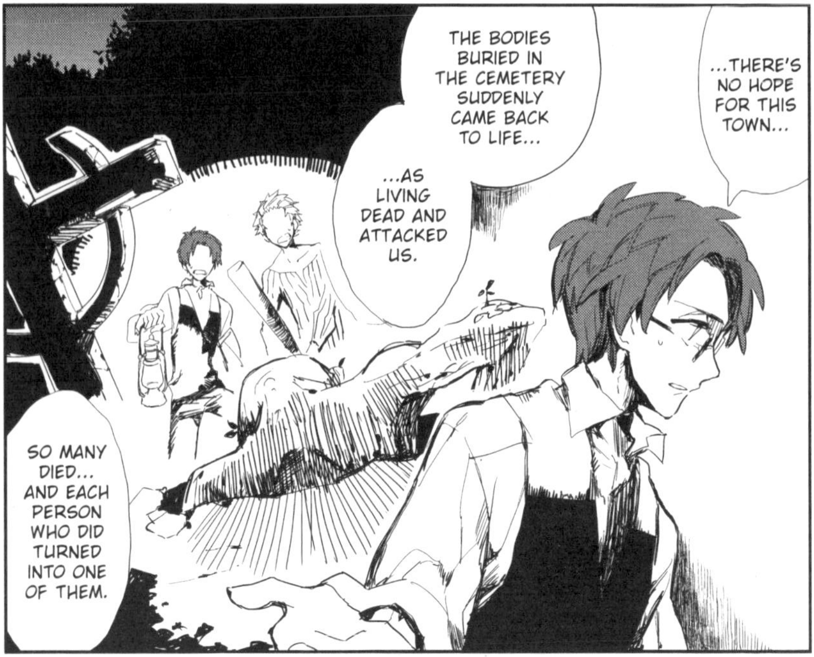
...THERE'S NO HOPE FOR THIS TOWN...
THE BODIES BURIED IN THE CEMETERY SUDDENLY CAME BACK TO LIFE...
...AS LIVING DEAD AND ATTACKED US.
SO MANY DIED... AND EACH PERSON WHO DID TURNED INTO ONE OF THEM.

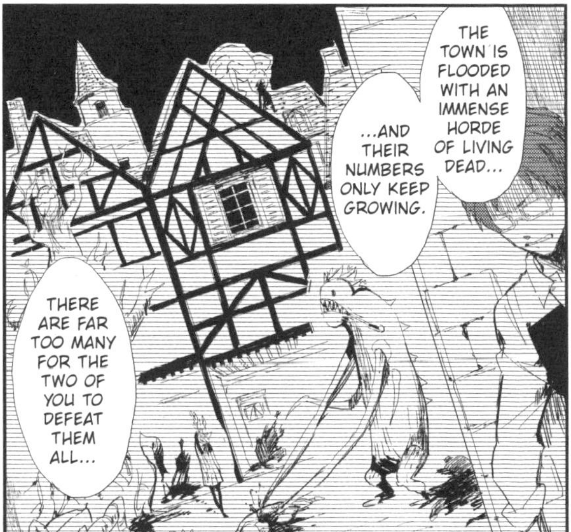
THE TOWN IS FLOODED WITH AN IMMENSE HORDE OF LIVING DEAD...
...AND THEIR NUMBERS ONLY KEEP GROWING.
THERE ARE FAR TOO MANY FOR THE TWO OF YOU TO DEFEAT THEM ALL...

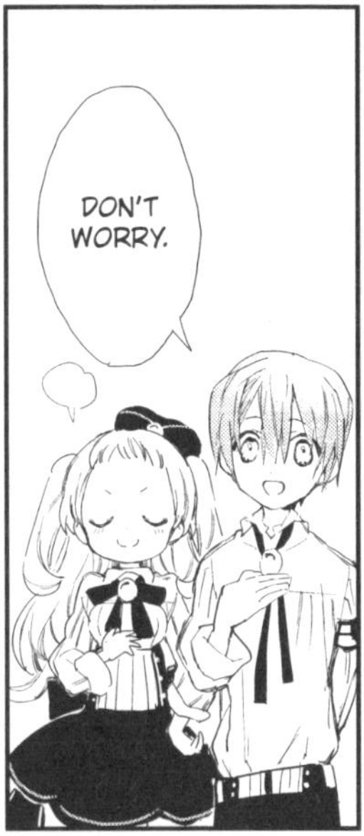
DON'T WORRY.

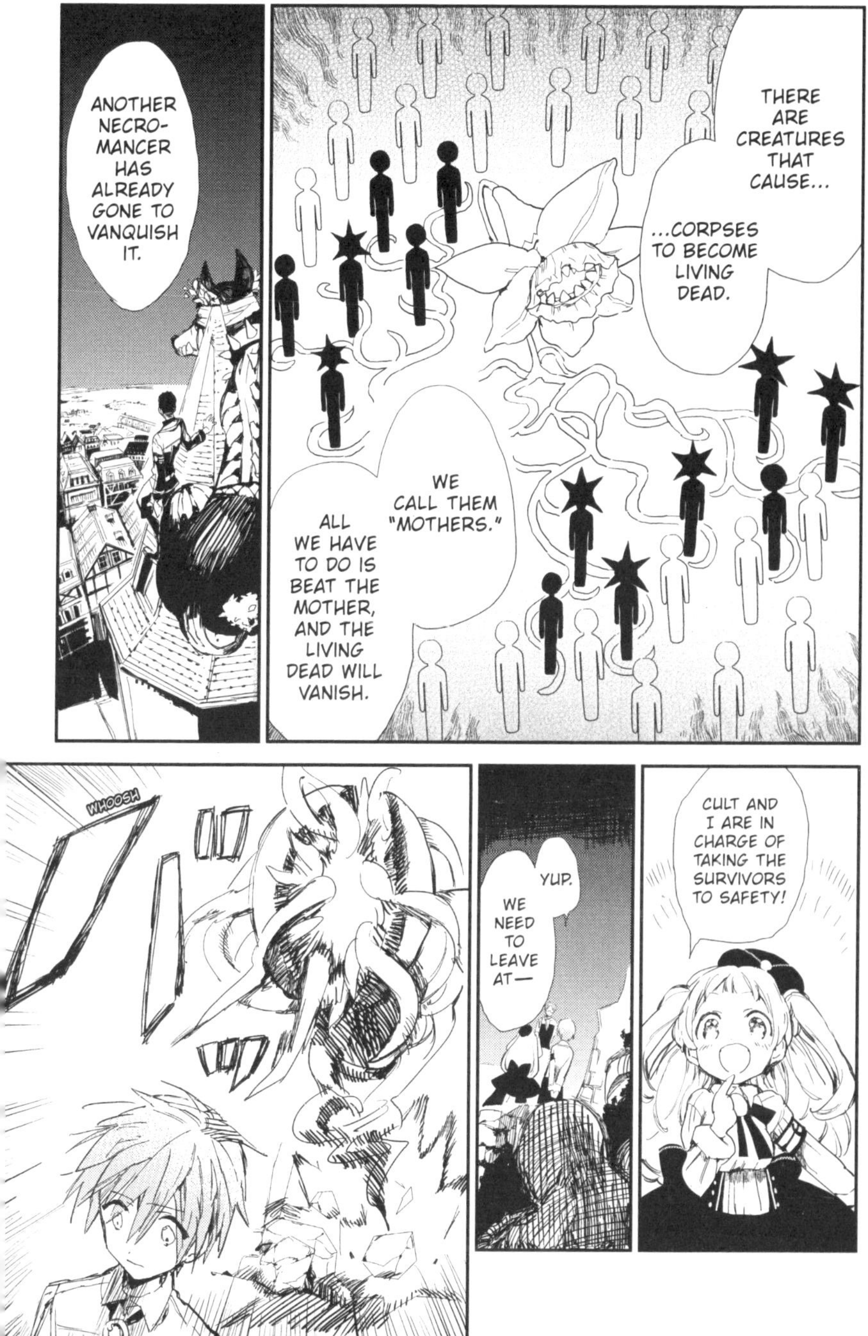
THERE ARE CREATURES THAT CAUSE...
...CORPSES TO BECOME LIVING DEAD.
WE CALL THEM "MOTHERS."
ALL WE HAVE TO DO IS BEAT THE MOTHER, AND THE LIVING DEAD WILL VANISH.
ANOTHER NECRO-MANCER HAS ALREADY GONE TO VANQUISH IT.
CULT AND I ARE IN CHARGE OF TAKING THE SURVIVORS TO SAFETY!
YUP.
WE NEED TO LEAVE AT—
WHOOSH

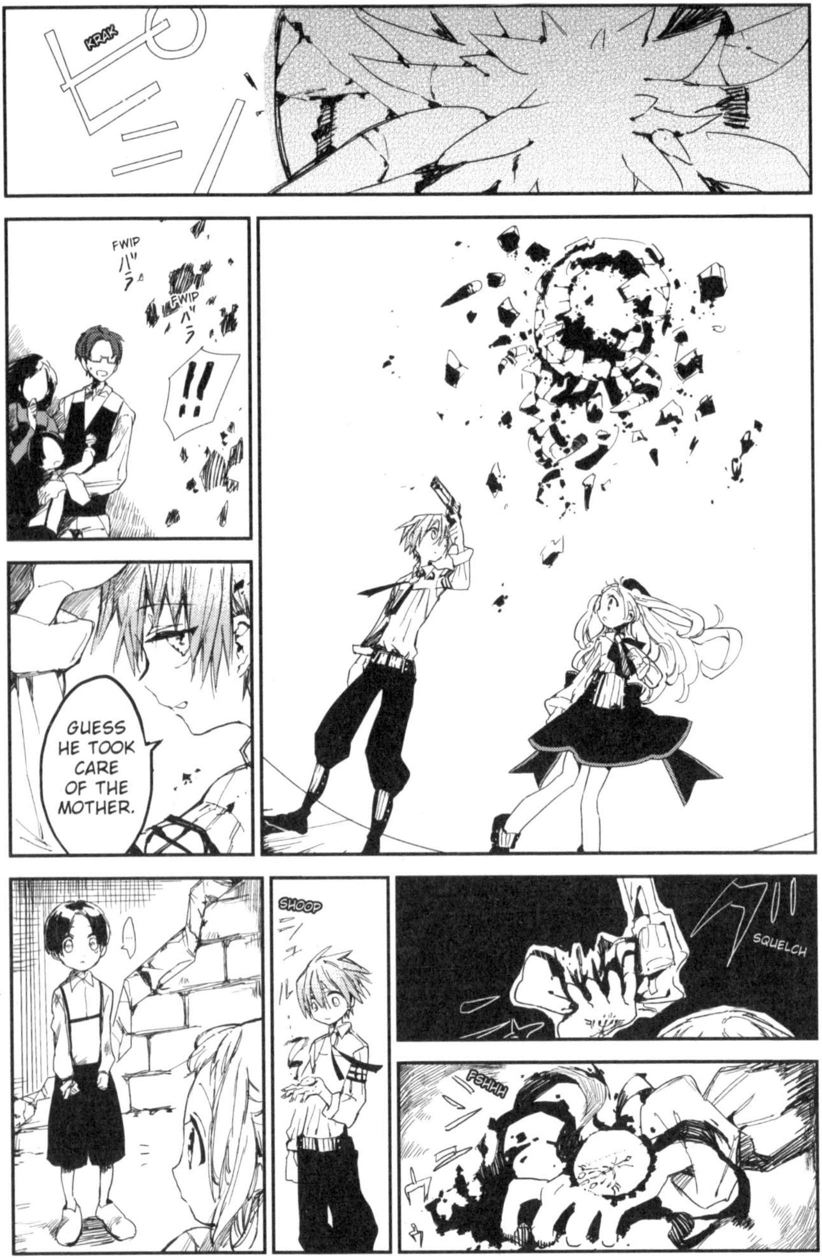
KRAK
FWIP
バラ
FWIP
バラ
!!
GUESS HE TOOK CARE OF THE MOTHER.
SQUELCH
PSHHH
SHOOP
...

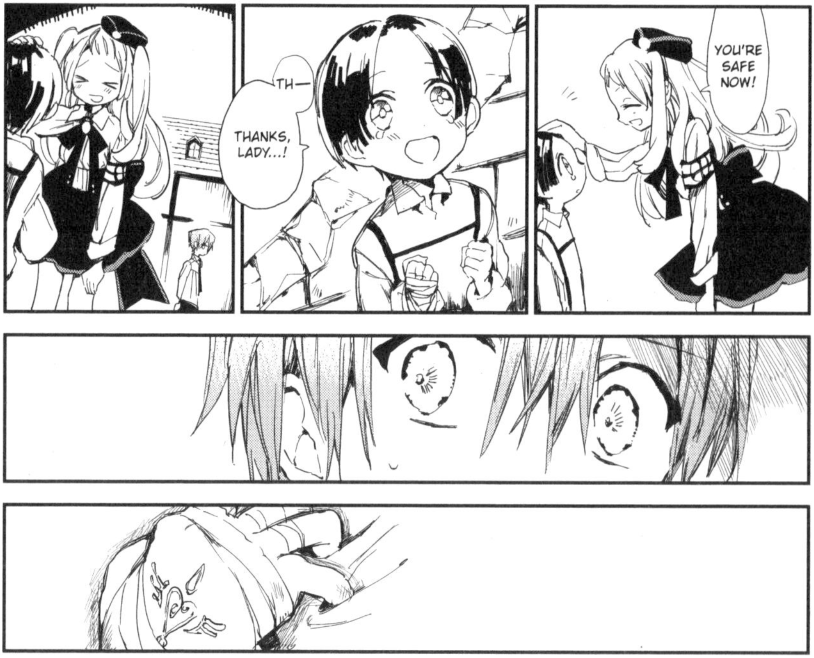
YOU'RE SAFE NOW!
TH—
THANKS, LADY...!
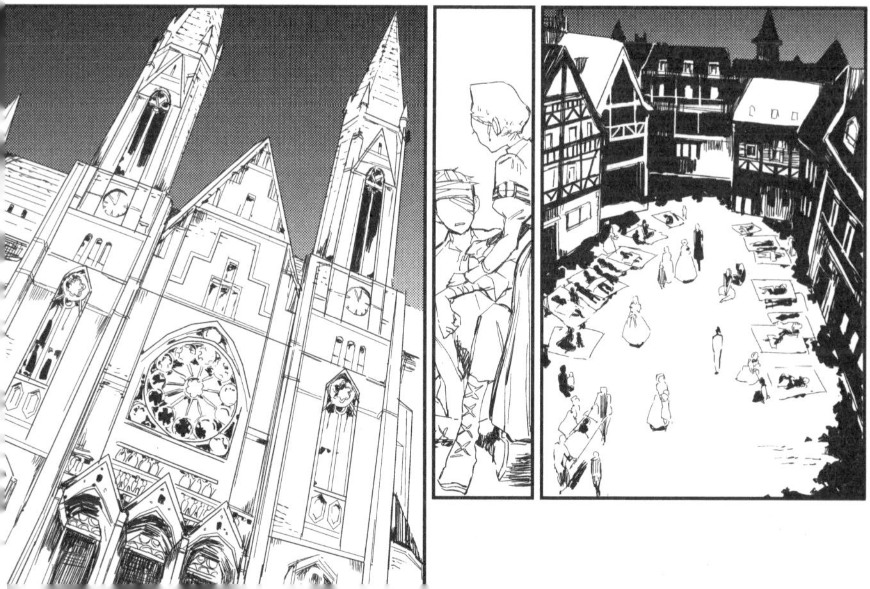

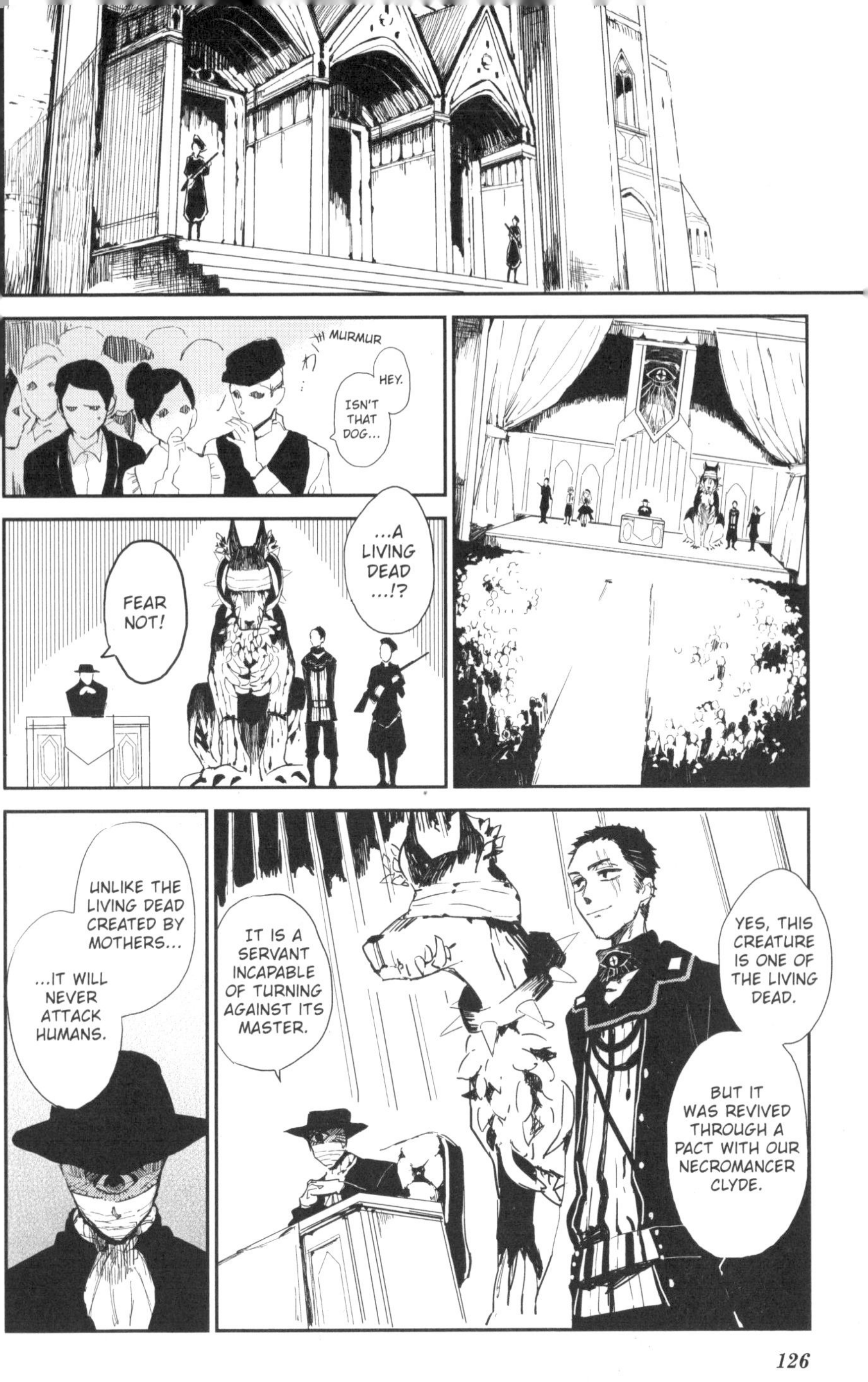
MURMUR
HEY. ISN'T THAT DOG...
...A LIVING DEAD...!?
FEAR NOT!
YES, THIS CREATURE IS ONE OF THE LIVING DEAD.
BUT IT WAS REVIVED THROUGH A PACT WITH OUR NECROMANCER CLYDE.
IT IS A SERVANT INCAPABLE OF TURNING AGAINST ITS MASTER.
UNLIKE THE LIVING DEAD CREATED BY MOTHERS...
...IT WILL NEVER ATTACK HUMANS.

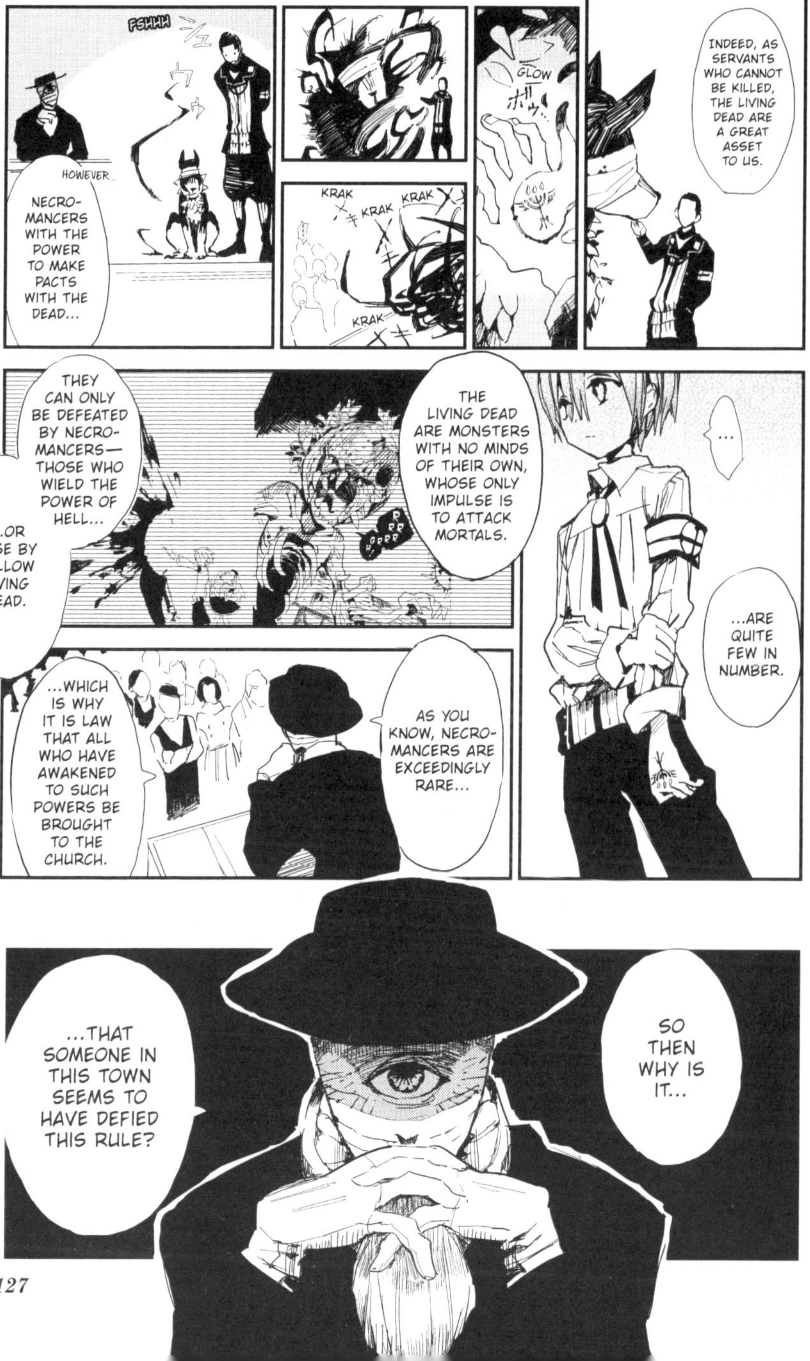
INDEED, AS SERVANTS WHO CANNOT BE KILLED, THE LIVING DEAD ARE A GREAT ASSET TO US.
GLOW
KRAK
KRAK
KRAK
KRAK
FSHHH
HOWEVER...
NECROMANCERS WITH THE POWER TO MAKE PACTS WITH THE DEAD...
...
...ARE QUITE FEW IN NUMBER.
THE LIVING DEAD ARE MONSTERS WITH NO MINDS OF THEIR OWN, WHOSE ONLY IMPULSE IS TO ATTACK MORTALS.
RRRR
THEY CAN ONLY BE DEFEATED BY NECROMANCERS—THOSE WHO WIELD THE POWER OF HELL...
...OR ELSE BY FELLOW LIVING DEAD.
AS YOU KNOW, NECROMANCERS ARE EXCEEDINGLY RARE...
...WHICH IS WHY IT IS LAW THAT ALL WHO HAVE AWAKENED TO SUCH POWERS BE BROUGHT TO THE CHURCH.
SO THEN WHY IS IT...
...THAT SOMEONE IN THIS TOWN SEEMS TO HAVE DEFIED THIS RULE?

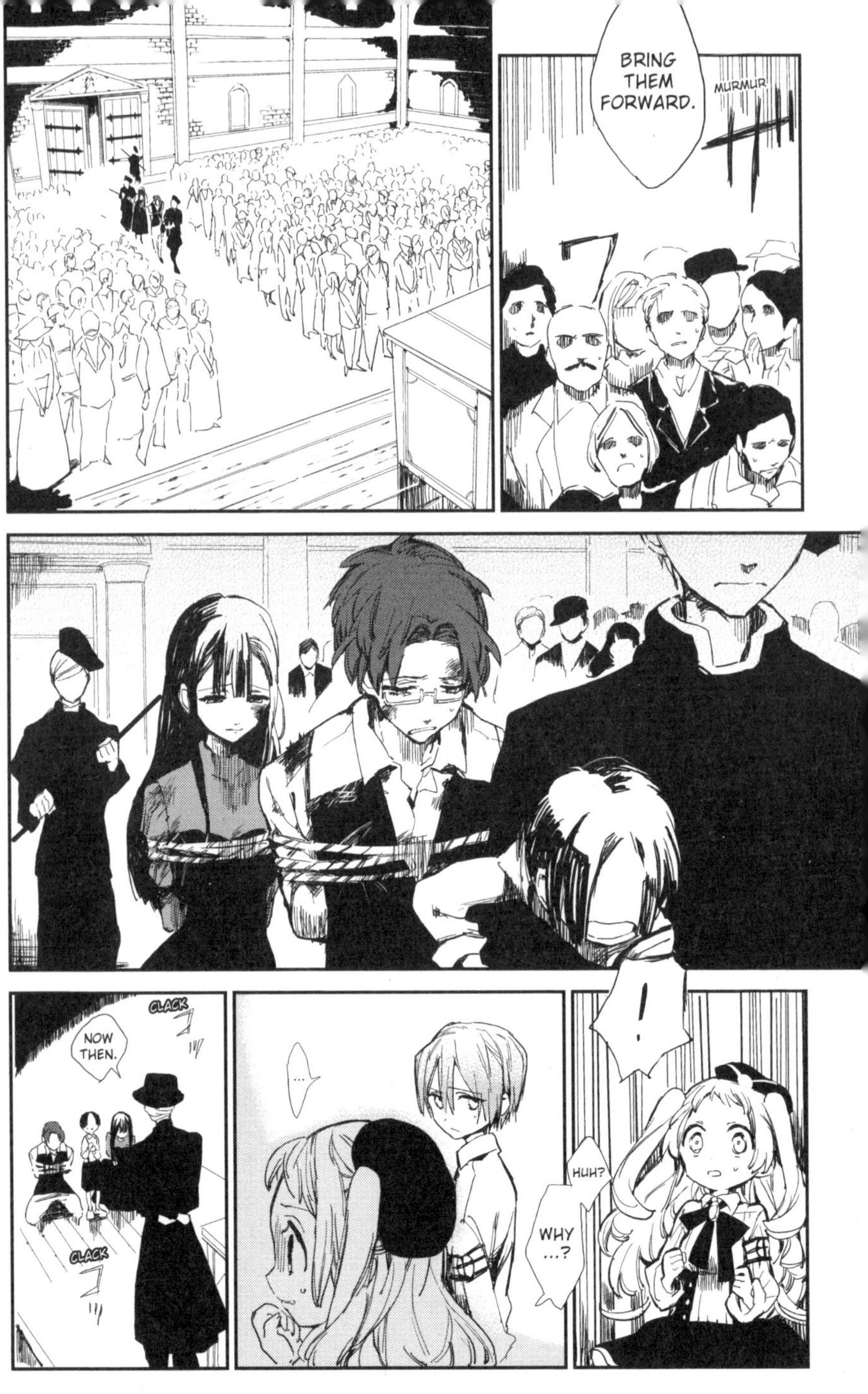
BRING THEM FORWARD.
MURMUR
!
HUH?
WHY ...?
...
CLACK
NOW THEN.
CLACK

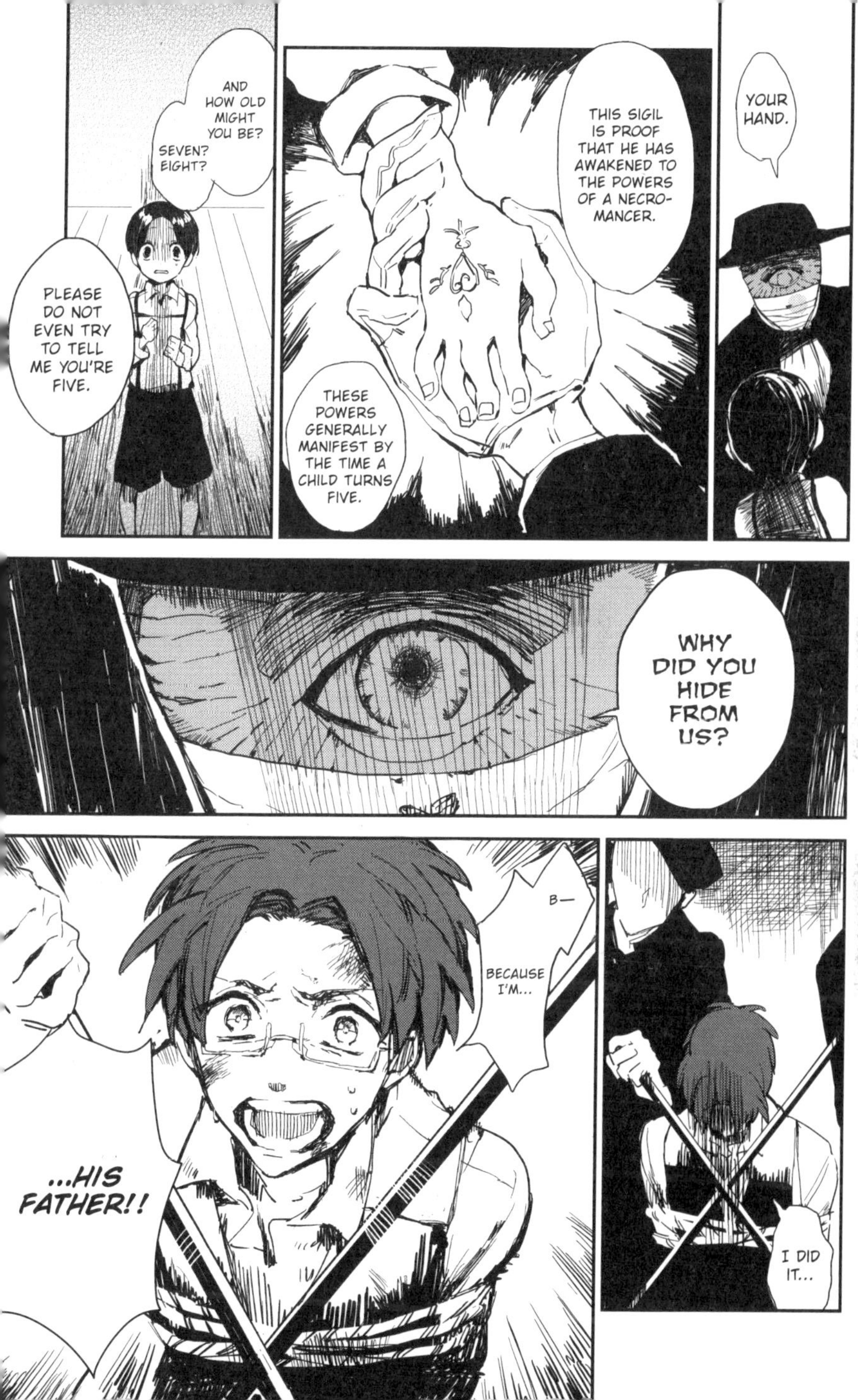
YOUR HAND.
THIS SIGIL IS PROOF THAT HE HAS AWAKENED TO THE POWERS OF A NECRO-MANCER.
THESE POWERS GENERALLY MANIFEST BY THE TIME A CHILD TURNS FIVE.
AND HOW OLD MIGHT YOU BE? SEVEN? EIGHT?
PLEASE DO NOT EVEN TRY TO TELL ME YOU'RE FIVE.
WHY DID YOU HIDE FROM US?
I DID IT...
B—
BECAUSE I'M...
...HIS FATHER!!

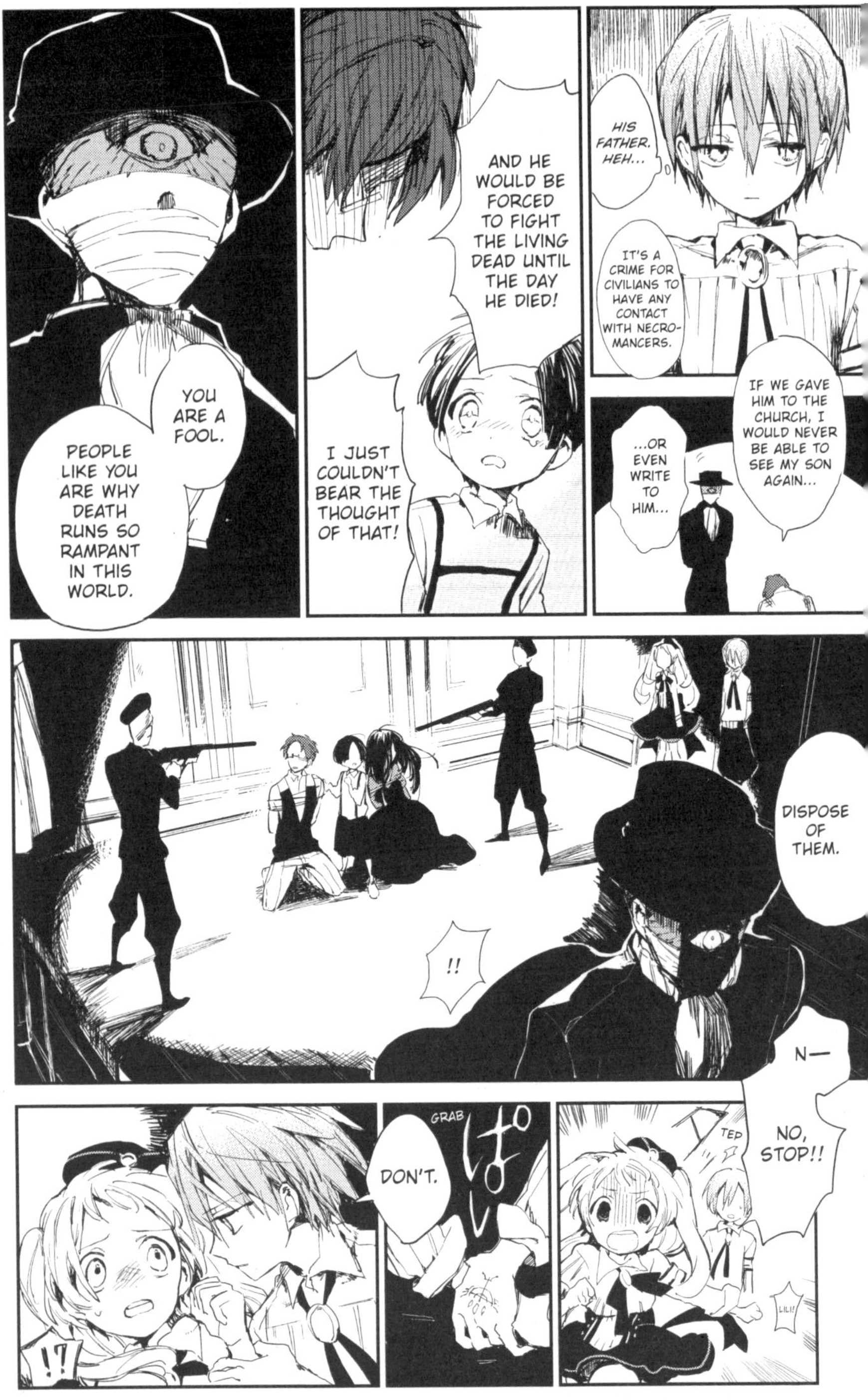
HIS FATHER. HEH...
IT'S A CRIME FOR CIVILIANS TO HAVE ANY CONTACT WITH NECRO-MANCERS.
IF WE GAVE HIM TO THE CHURCH, I WOULD NEVER BE ABLE TO SEE MY SON AGAIN...
...OR EVEN WRITE TO HIM...
AND HE WOULD BE FORCED TO FIGHT THE LIVING DEAD UNTIL THE DAY HE DIED!
I JUST COULDN'T BEAR THE THOUGHT OF THAT!
YOU ARE A FOOL.
PEOPLE LIKE YOU ARE WHY DEATH RUNS SO RAMPANT IN THIS WORLD.
DISPOSE OF THEM.
!!
N— NO, STOP!!
TEP
LILI!
GRAB
DON'T.
!?

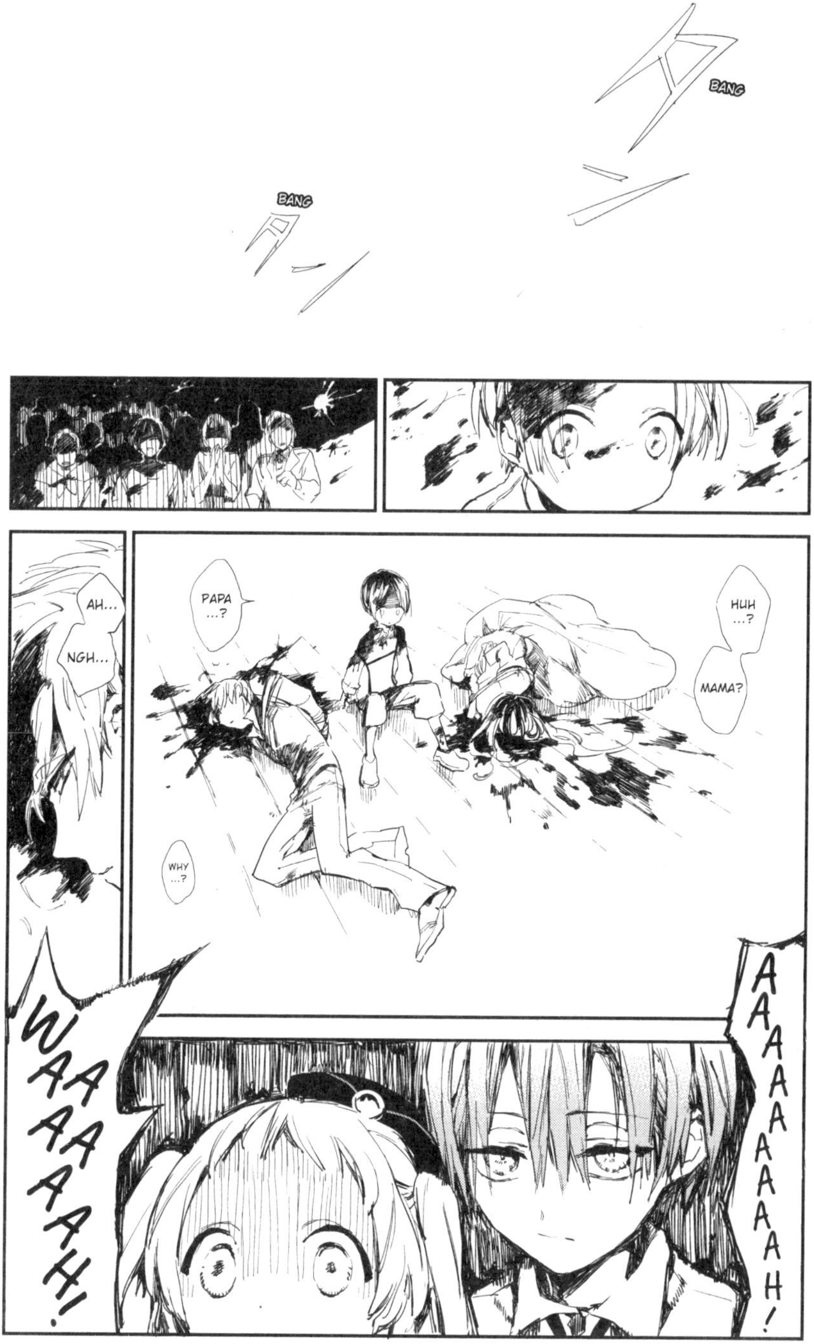
BANG
BANG
HUH ...?
MAMA?
PAPA ...?
WHY ...?
AH...
NGH...
AAAAAAAAAH!
WAAAAAAH!

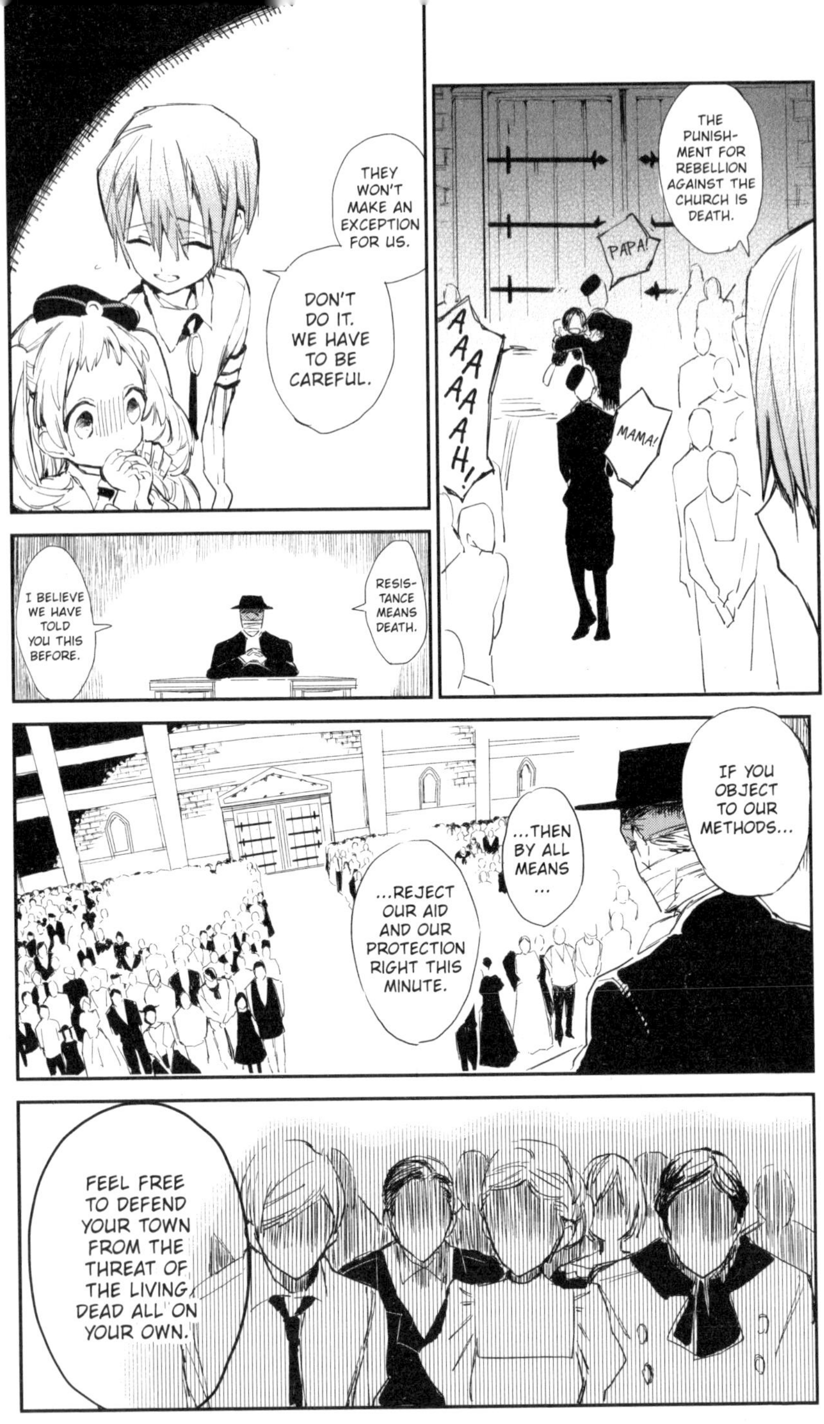

THE PUNISHMENT FOR REBELLION AGAINST THE CHURCH IS DEATH.
PAPA!
AAAAAAH!!
MAMA!
THEY WON'T MAKE AN EXCEPTION FOR US.
DON'T DO IT. WE HAVE TO BE CAREFUL.
RESISTANCE MEANS DEATH.
I BELIEVE WE HAVE TOLD YOU THIS BEFORE.
IF YOU OBJECT TO OUR METHODS...
...THEN BY ALL MEANS...
...REJECT OUR AID AND OUR PROTECTION RIGHT THIS MINUTE.
FEEL FREE TO DEFEND YOUR TOWN FROM THE THREAT OF THE LIVING DEAD ALL ON YOUR OWN.

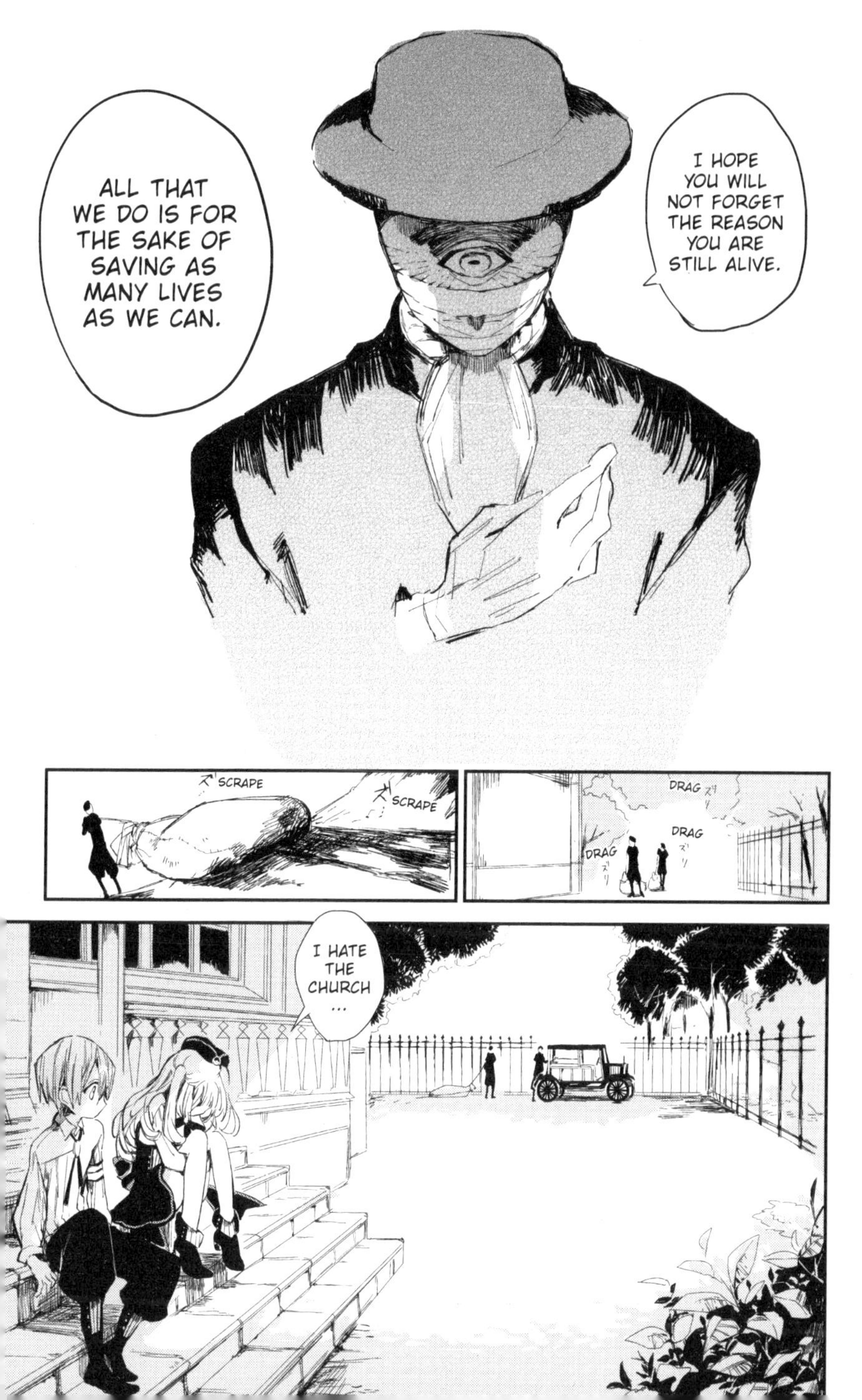

I HOPE YOU WILL NOT FORGET THE REASON YOU ARE STILL ALIVE.
ALL THAT WE DO IS FOR THE SAKE OF SAVING AS MANY LIVES AS WE CAN.
DRAG
DRAG
DRAG
SCRAPE
SCRAPE
I HATE THE CHURCH...

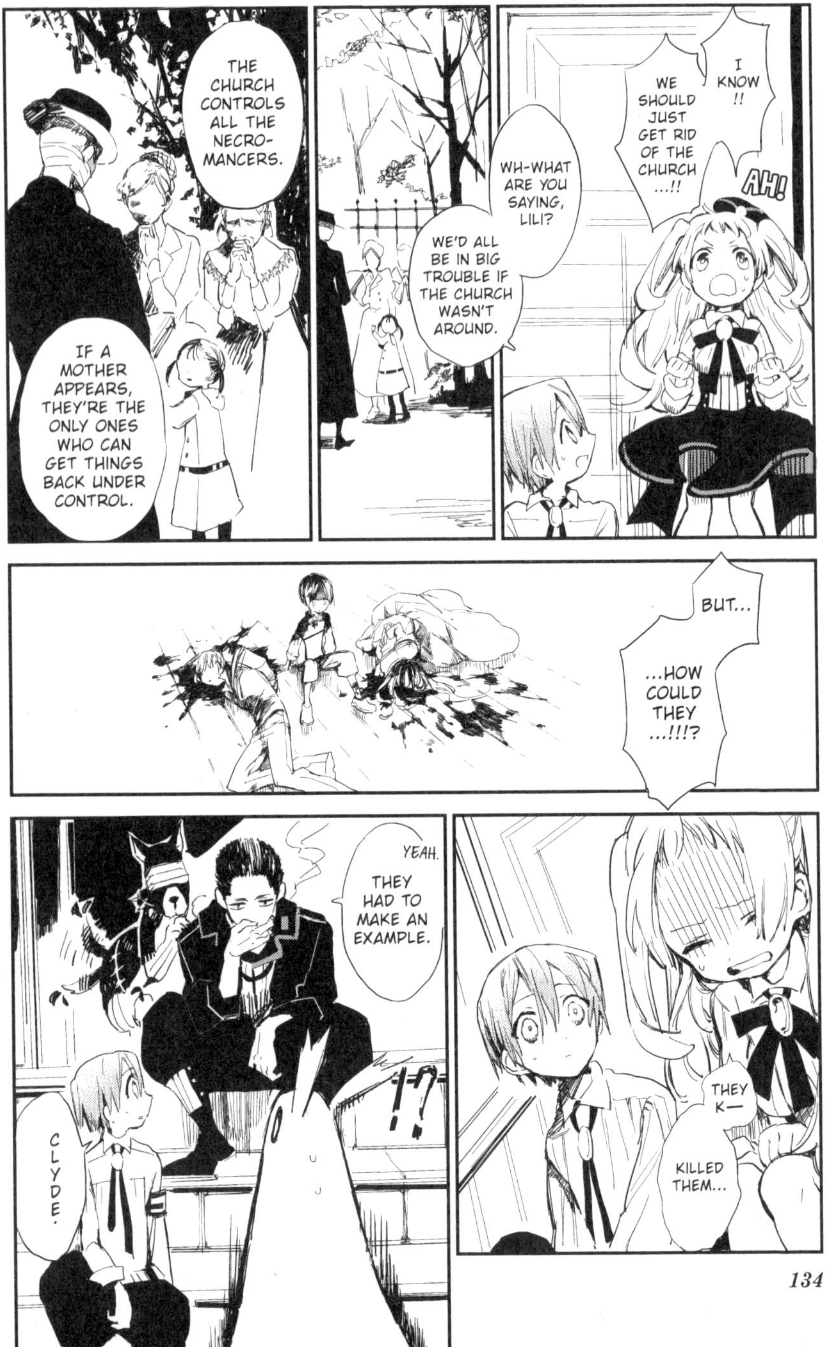
I KNOW !!
WE SHOULD JUST GET RID OF THE CHURCH ...!!
AH!
WH-WHAT ARE YOU SAYING, LILI?
WE'D ALL BE IN BIG TROUBLE IF THE CHURCH WASN'T AROUND.
THE CHURCH CONTROLS ALL THE NECRO-MANCERS.
IF A MOTHER APPEARS, THEY'RE THE ONLY ONES WHO CAN GET THINGS BACK UNDER CONTROL.
BUT...
...HOW COULD THEY ...!!!?
THEY K—
KILLED THEM...
YEAH.
THEY HAD TO MAKE AN EXAMPLE.
CLYDE.

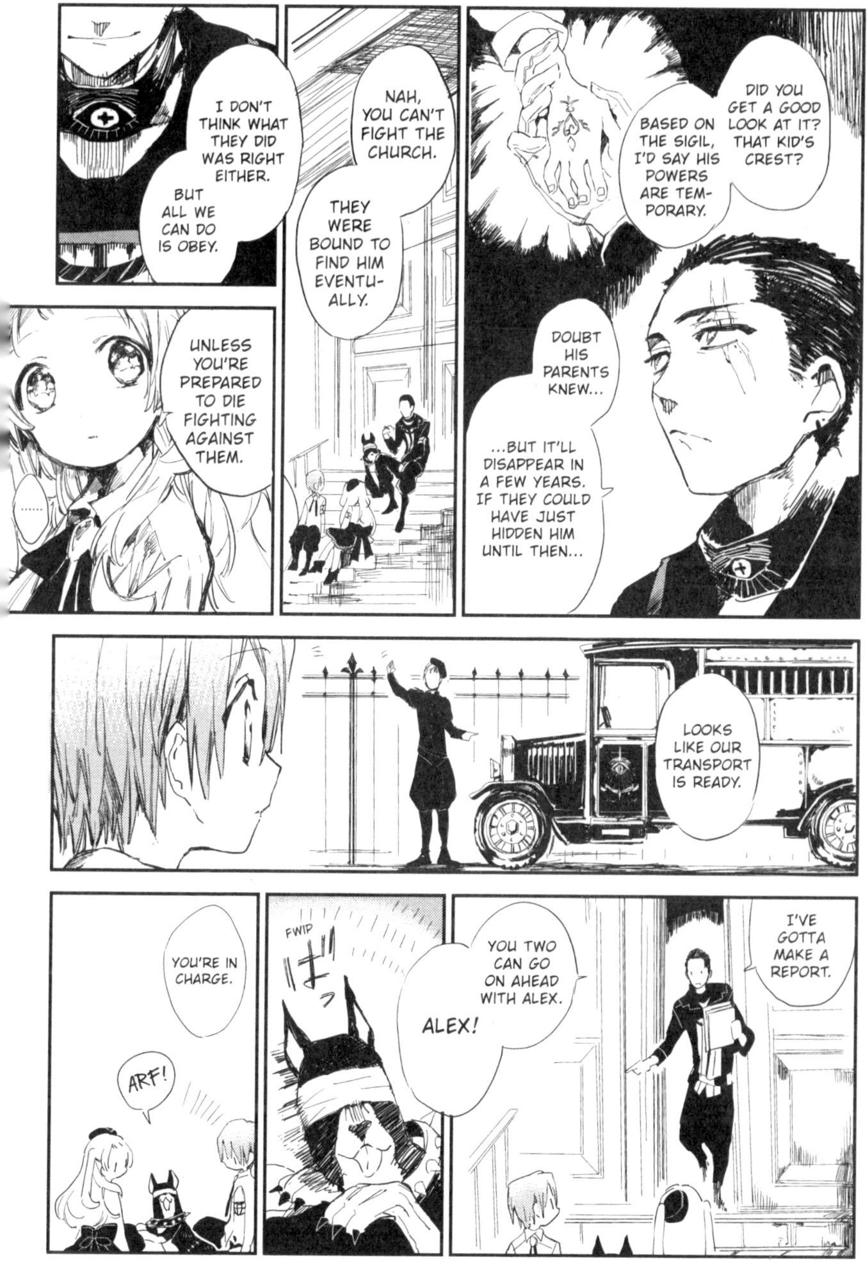
DID YOU GET A GOOD LOOK AT IT? THAT KID'S CREST?
BASED ON THE SIGIL, I'D SAY HIS POWERS ARE TEMPORARY.
DOUBT HIS PARENTS KNEW...
...BUT IT'LL DISAPPEAR IN A FEW YEARS. IF THEY COULD HAVE JUST HIDDEN HIM UNTIL THEN...
NAH, YOU CAN'T FIGHT THE CHURCH.
THEY WERE BOUND TO FIND HIM EVENTUALLY.
I DON'T THINK WHAT THEY DID WAS RIGHT EITHER.
BUT ALL WE CAN DO IS OBEY.
UNLESS YOU'RE PREPARED TO DIE FIGHTING AGAINST THEM.
......
LOOKS LIKE OUR TRANSPORT IS READY.
I'VE GOTTA MAKE A REPORT.
YOU TWO CAN GO ON AHEAD WITH ALEX.
FWIP
ALEX!
YOU'RE IN CHARGE.
ARF!

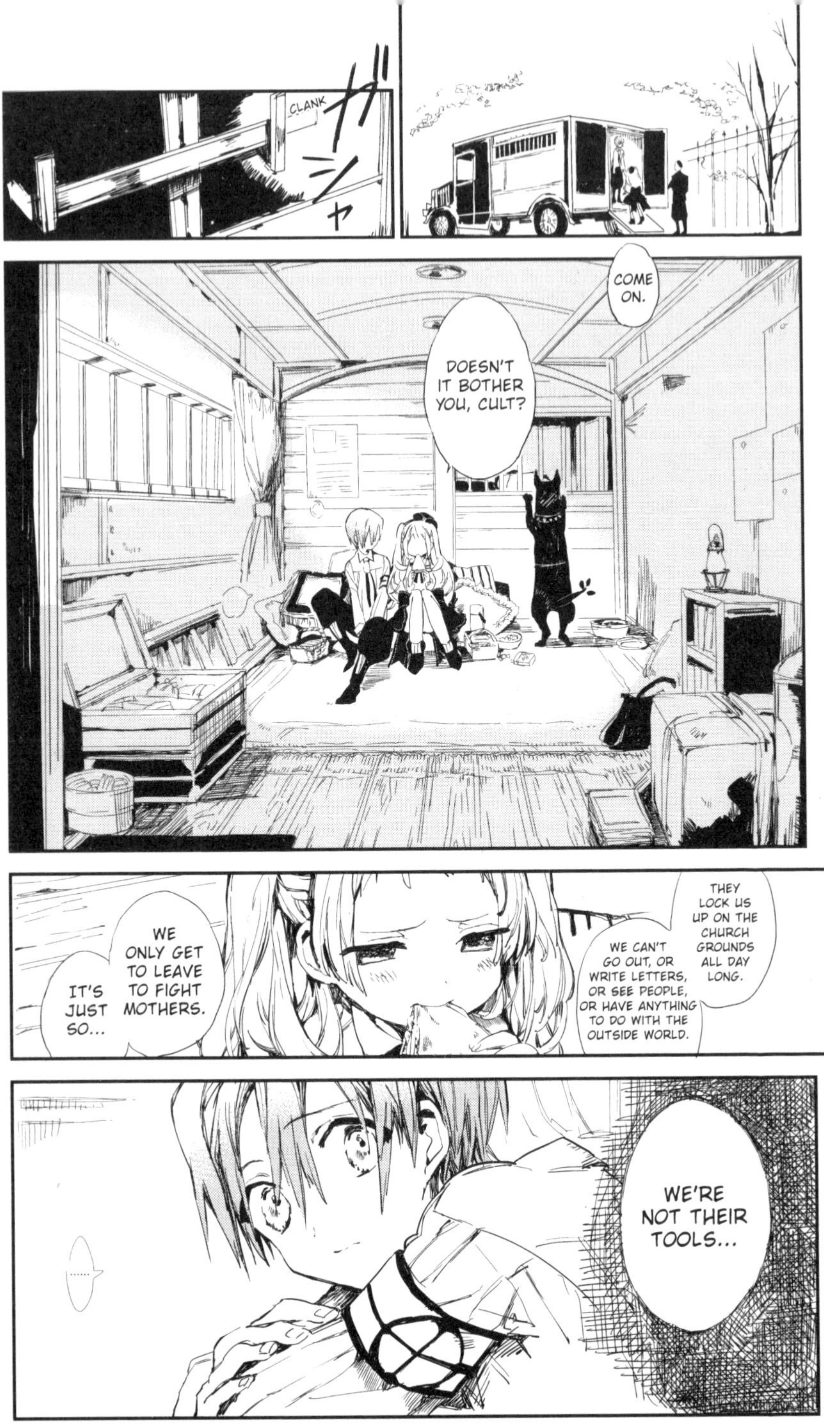
CLANK
ガシャ
COME ON.
DOESN'T IT BOTHER YOU, CULT?
THEY LOCK US UP ON THE CHURCH GROUNDS ALL DAY LONG.
WE CAN'T GO OUT, OR WRITE LETTERS, OR SEE PEOPLE, OR HAVE ANYTHING TO DO WITH THE OUTSIDE WORLD.
WE ONLY GET TO LEAVE TO FIGHT MOTHERS.
IT'S JUST SO...
WE'RE NOT THEIR TOOLS...
......

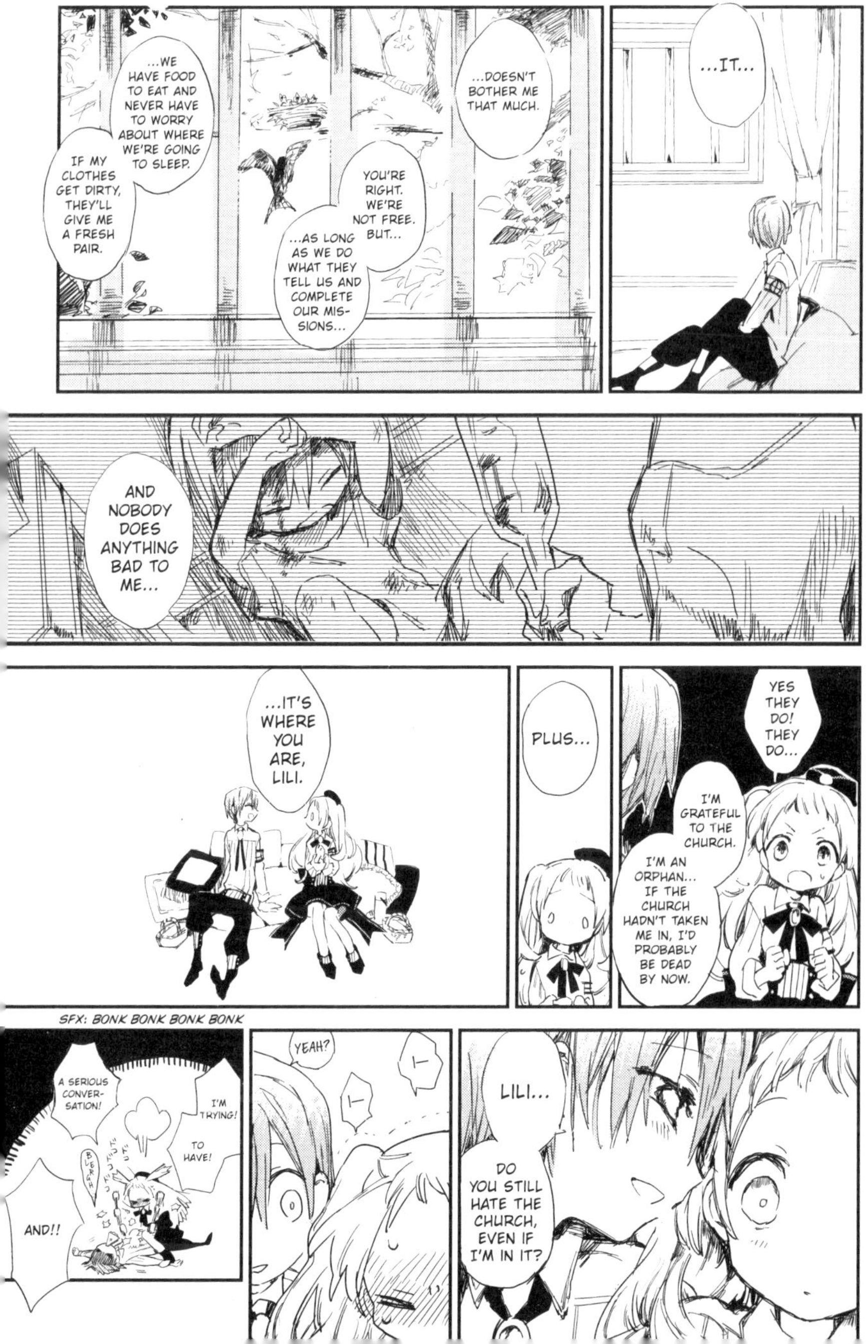
...IT...
...DOESN'T BOTHER ME THAT MUCH.
YOU'RE RIGHT. WE'RE NOT FREE. BUT...
...AS LONG AS WE DO WHAT THEY TELL US AND COMPLETE OUR MISSIONS...
...WE HAVE FOOD TO EAT AND NEVER HAVE TO WORRY ABOUT WHERE WE'RE GOING TO SLEEP.
IF MY CLOTHES GET DIRTY, THEY'LL GIVE ME A FRESH PAIR.
AND NOBODY DOES ANYTHING BAD TO ME...
YES THEY DO! THEY DO...
I'M GRATEFUL TO THE CHURCH.
I'M AN ORPHAN... IF THE CHURCH HADN'T TAKEN ME IN, I'D PROBABLY BE DEAD BY NOW.
PLUS...
...IT'S WHERE YOU ARE, LILI.
SFX: BONK BONK BONK BONK
LILI...
DO YOU STILL HATE THE CHURCH, EVEN IF I'M IN IT?
YEAH?
I-
I-
A SERIOUS CONVERSATION!
I'M TRYING!
TO HAVE!
AND!!

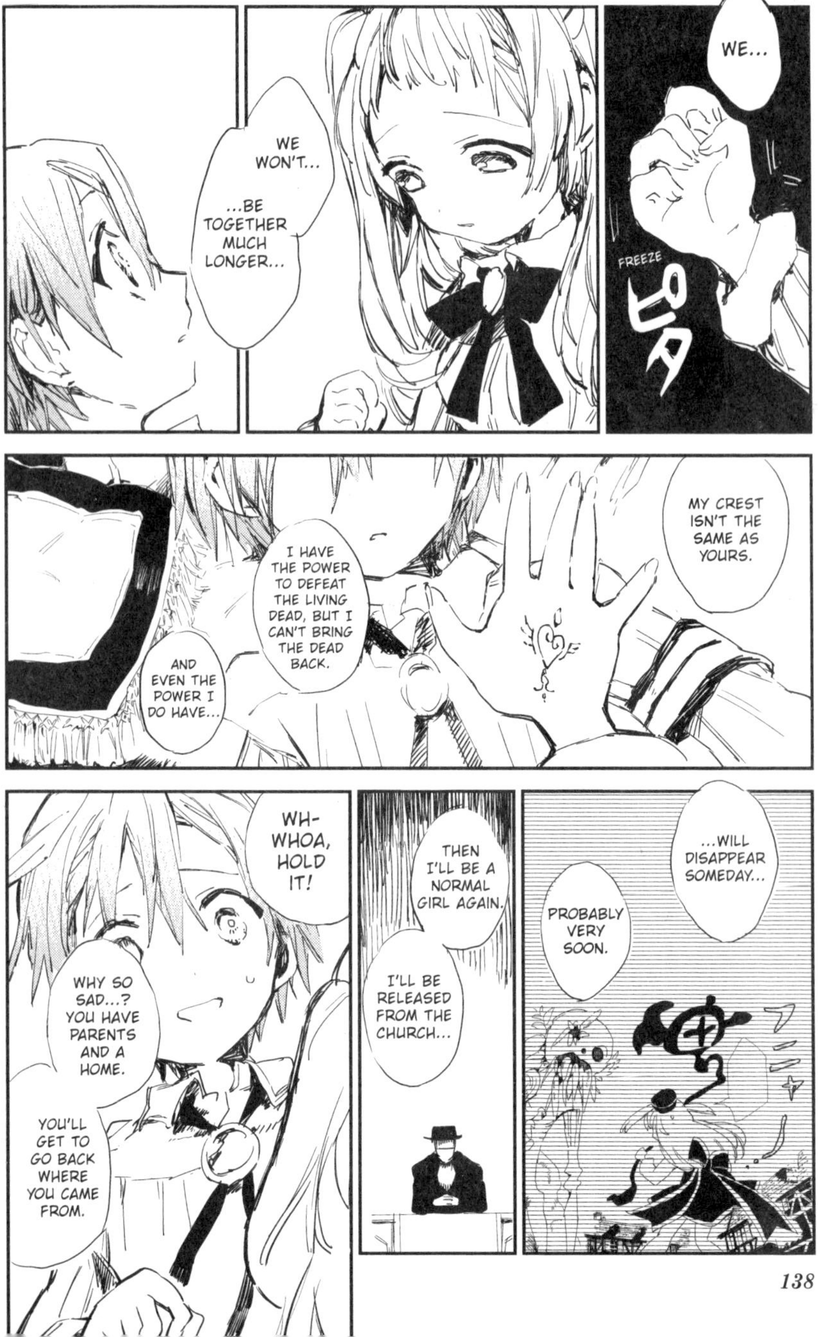
WE...
FREEZE
ピタ
WE WON'T...
...BE TOGETHER MUCH LONGER...
MY CREST ISN'T THE SAME AS YOURS.
I HAVE THE POWER TO DEFEAT THE LIVING DEAD, BUT I CAN'T BRING THE DEAD BACK.
AND EVEN THE POWER I DO HAVE...
...WILL DISAPPEAR SOMEDAY...
PROBABLY VERY SOON.
THEN I'LL BE A NORMAL GIRL AGAIN.
I'LL BE RELEASED FROM THE CHURCH...
WH-WHOA, HOLD IT!
WHY SO SAD...? YOU HAVE PARENTS AND A HOME.
YOU'LL GET TO GO BACK WHERE YOU CAME FROM.

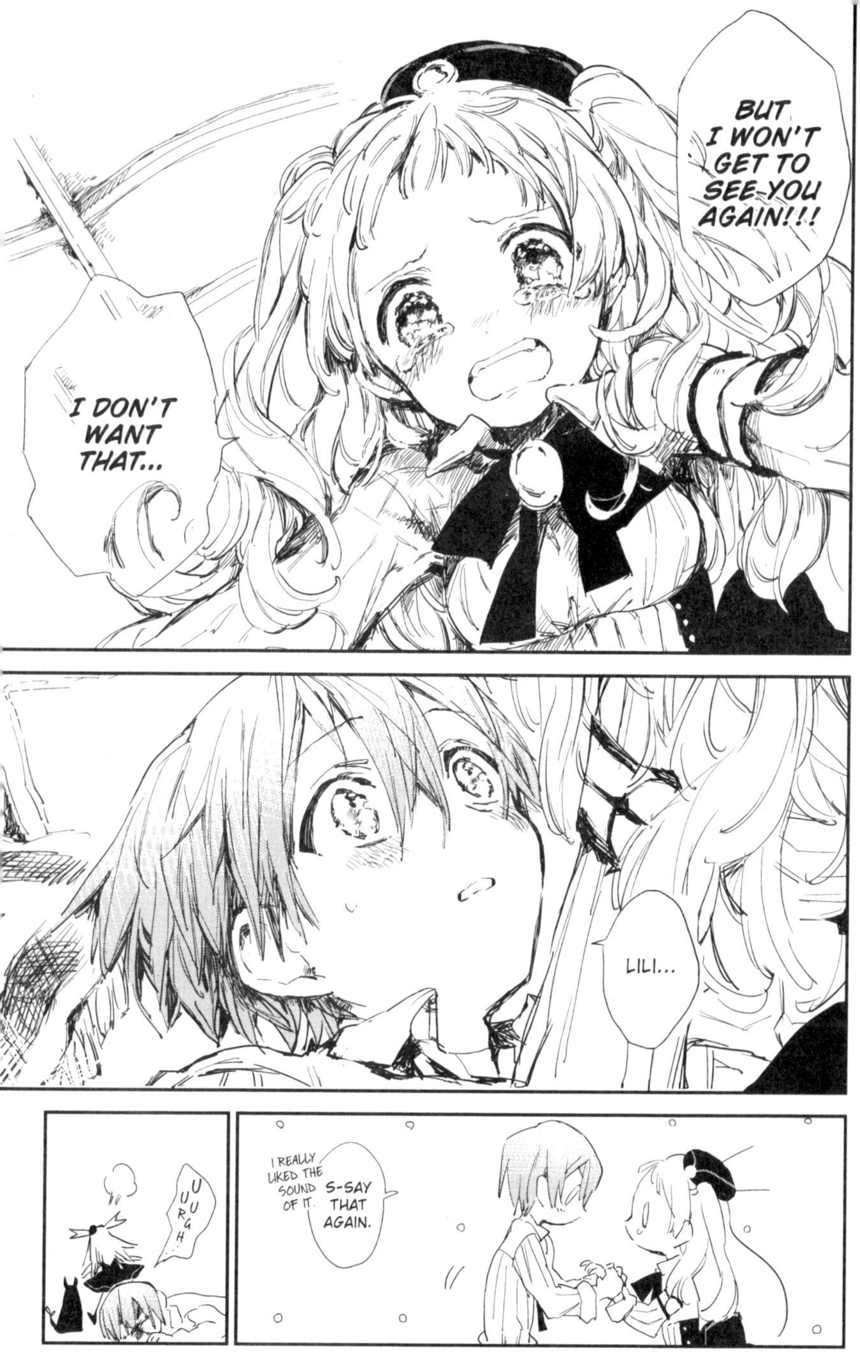
BUT I WON'T GET TO SEE YOU AGAIN!!!
I DON'T WANT THAT...
LILI...
S-SAY THAT AGAIN.
I REALLY LIKED THE SOUND OF IT.
UUURGH

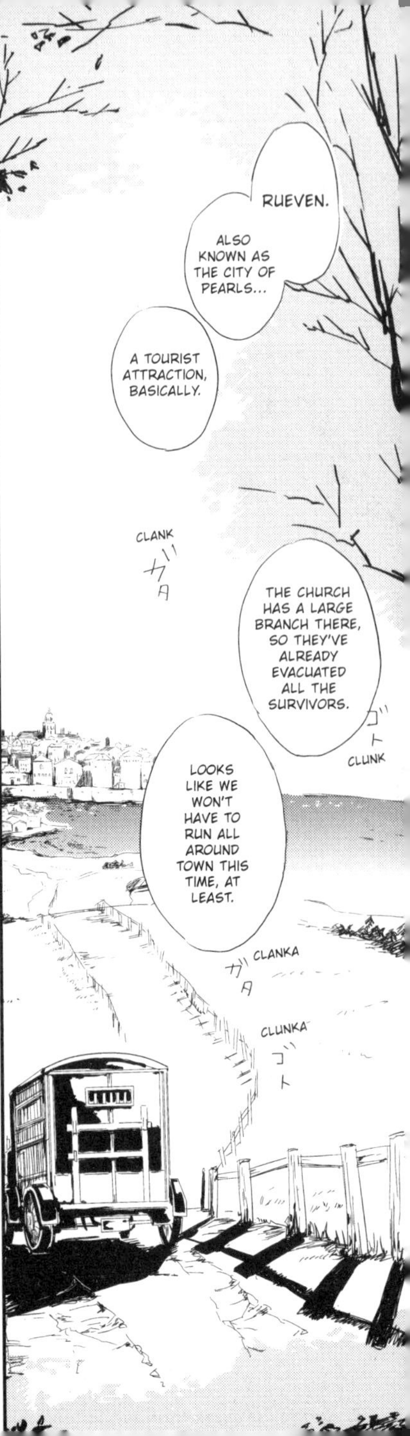
RUEVEN.
ALSO KNOWN AS THE CITY OF PEARLS...
A TOURIST ATTRACTION, BASICALLY.
CLANK
THE CHURCH HAS A LARGE BRANCH THERE, SO THEY'VE ALREADY EVACUATED ALL THE SURVIVORS.
CLUNK
LOOKS LIKE WE WON'T HAVE TO RUN ALL AROUND TOWN THIS TIME, AT LEAST.
CLANKA
CLUNKA

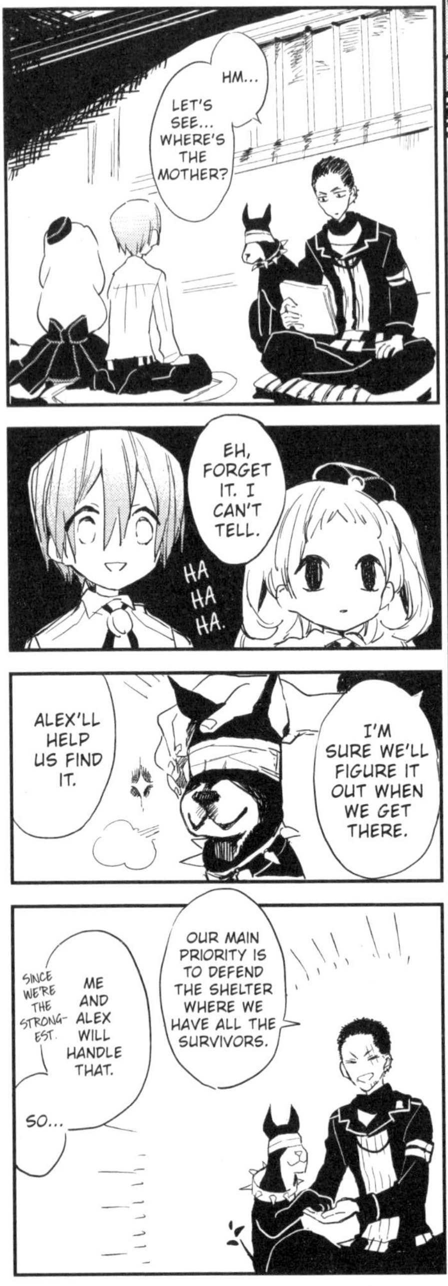
HM...
LET'S SEE... WHERE'S THE MOTHER?
EH, FORGET IT. I CAN'T TELL.
HA HA HA.
I'M SURE WE'LL FIGURE IT OUT WHEN WE GET THERE.
ALEX'LL HELP US FIND IT.
OUR MAIN PRIORITY IS TO DEFEND THE SHELTER WHERE WE HAVE ALL THE SURVIVORS.
ME AND ALEX WILL HANDLE THAT.
SINCE WE'RE THE STRONGEST.
SO...

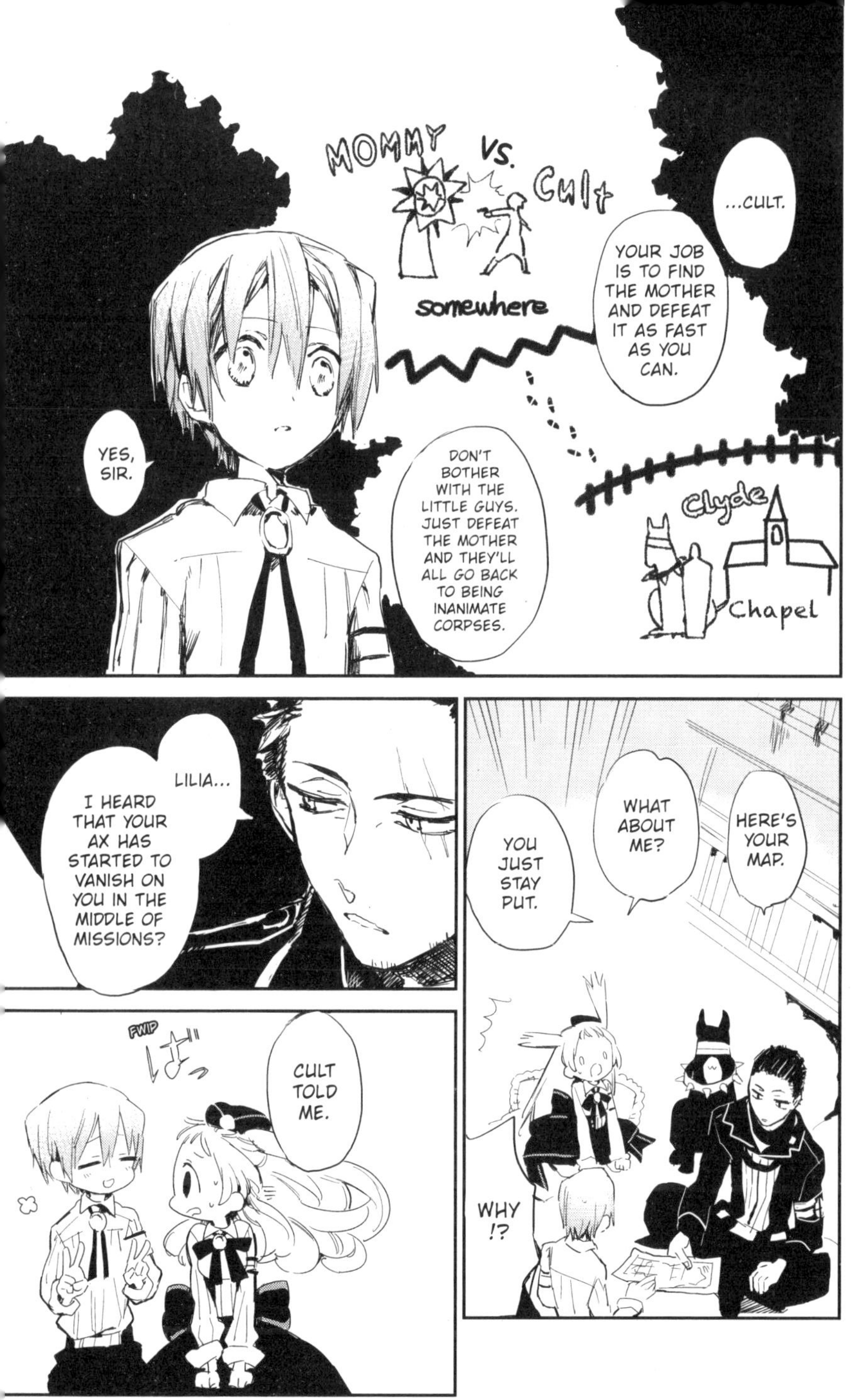
...CULT.
YOUR JOB IS TO FIND THE MOTHER AND DEFEAT IT AS FAST AS YOU CAN.
MOMMY VS. Cult
somewhere
Clyde
Chapel
DON'T BOTHER WITH THE LITTLE GUYS. JUST DEFEAT THE MOTHER AND THEY'LL ALL GO BACK TO BEING INANIMATE CORPSES.
YES, SIR.
HERE'S YOUR MAP.
WHAT ABOUT ME?
YOU JUST STAY PUT.
WHY !?
LILIA... I HEARD THAT YOUR AX HAS STARTED TO VANISH ON YOU IN THE MIDDLE OF MISSIONS?
CULT TOLD ME.
FWIP ばっ

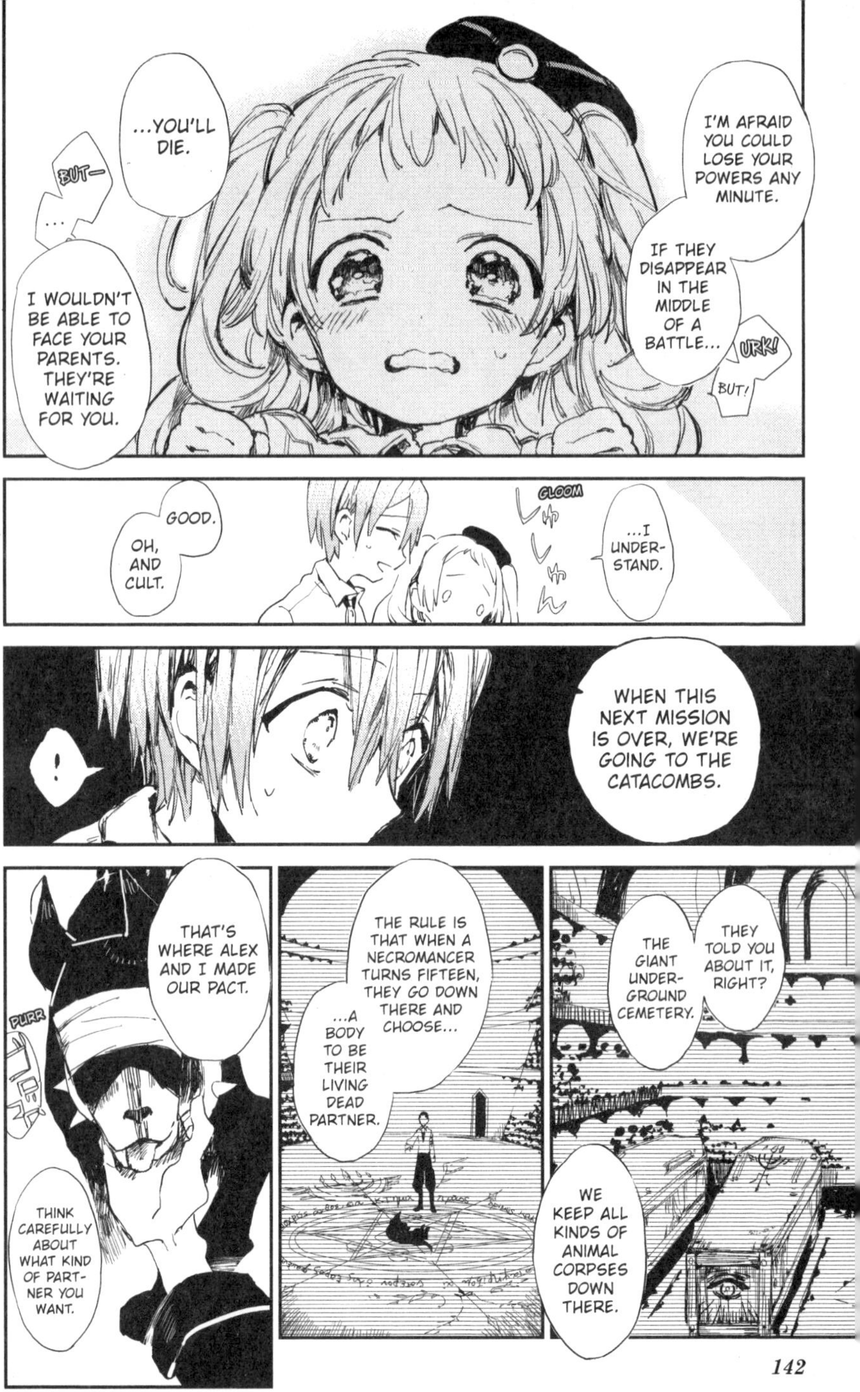
I'M AFRAID YOU COULD LOSE YOUR POWERS ANY MINUTE.
IF THEY DISAPPEAR IN THE MIDDLE OF A BATTLE...
URK!
BUT!
...YOU'LL DIE.
BUT—
...
I WOULDN'T BE ABLE TO FACE YOUR PARENTS. THEY'RE WAITING FOR YOU.
...I UNDER-STAND.
GLOOM
GOOD.
OH, AND CULT.
WHEN THIS NEXT MISSION IS OVER, WE'RE GOING TO THE CATACOMBS.
!
THEY TOLD YOU ABOUT IT, RIGHT?
THE GIANT UNDER-GROUND CEMETERY.
WE KEEP ALL KINDS OF ANIMAL CORPSES DOWN THERE.
THE RULE IS THAT WHEN A NECROMANCER TURNS FIFTEEN, THEY GO DOWN THERE AND CHOOSE...
...A BODY TO BE THEIR LIVING DEAD PARTNER.
THAT'S WHERE ALEX AND I MADE OUR PACT.
PURR
THINK CAREFULLY ABOUT WHAT KIND OF PART-NER YOU WANT.

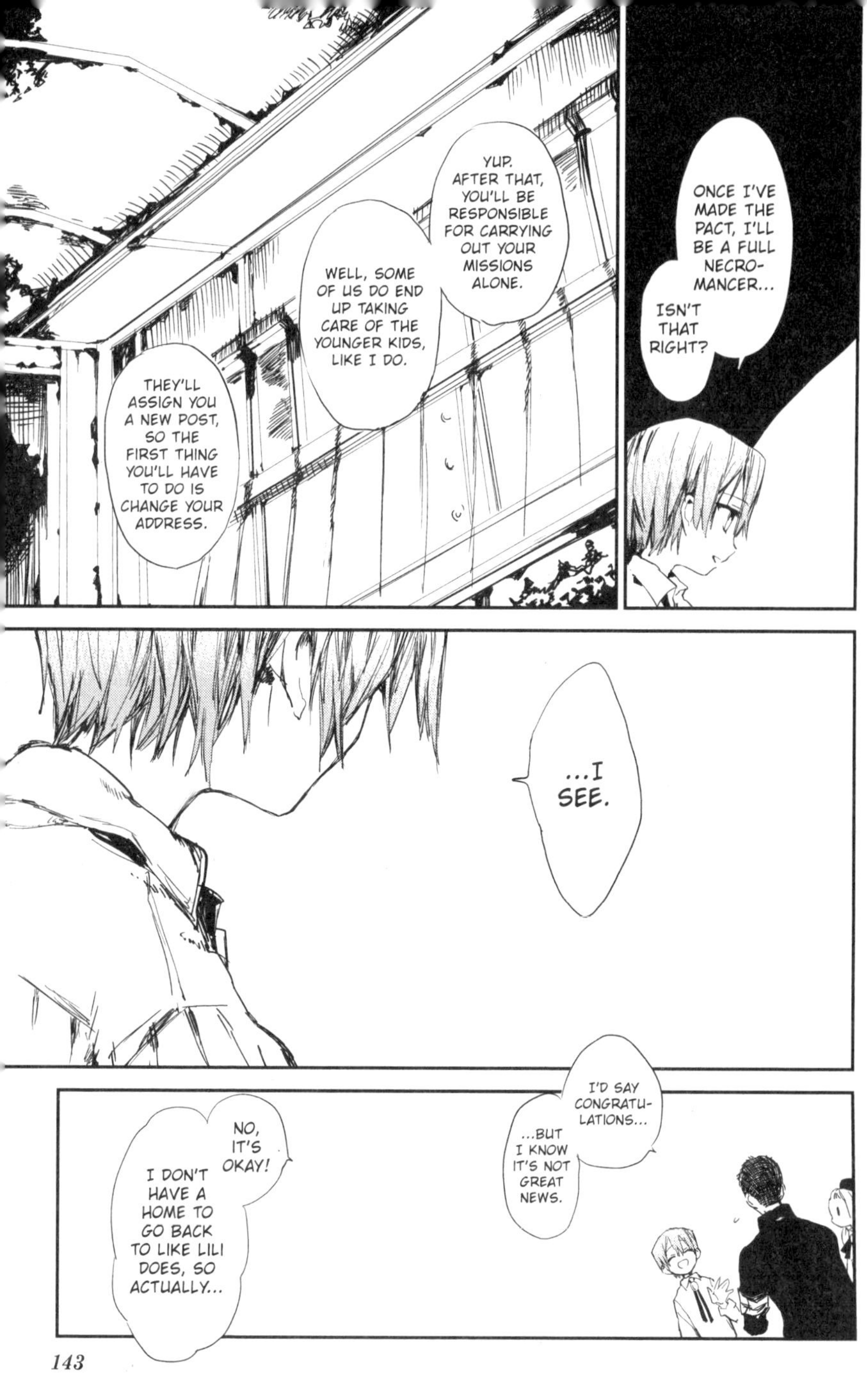
ONCE I'VE MADE THE PACT, I'LL BE A FULL NECRO-MANCER...
ISN'T THAT RIGHT?
YUP. AFTER THAT, YOU'LL BE RESPONSIBLE FOR CARRYING OUT YOUR MISSIONS ALONE.
WELL, SOME OF US DO END UP TAKING CARE OF THE YOUNGER KIDS, LIKE I DO.
THEY'LL ASSIGN YOU A NEW POST, SO THE FIRST THING YOU'LL HAVE TO DO IS CHANGE YOUR ADDRESS.
...I SEE.
I'D SAY CONGRATU-LATIONS...
...BUT I KNOW IT'S NOT GREAT NEWS.
NO, IT'S OKAY!
I DON'T HAVE A HOME TO GO BACK TO LIKE LILI DOES, SO ACTUALLY...

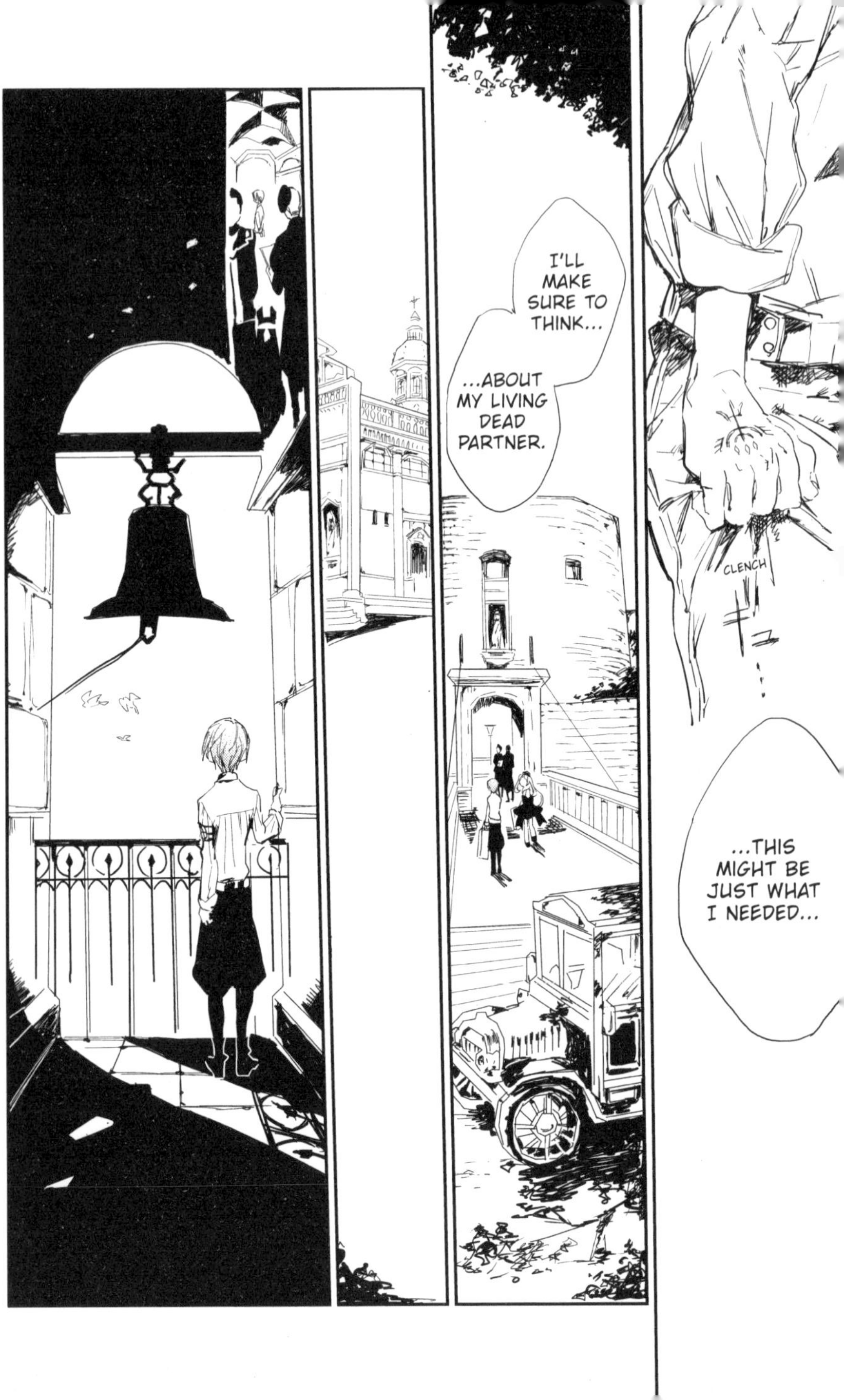
CLENCH
...THIS MIGHT BE JUST WHAT I NEEDED...
I'LL MAKE SURE TO THINK...
...ABOUT MY LIVING DEAD PARTNER.

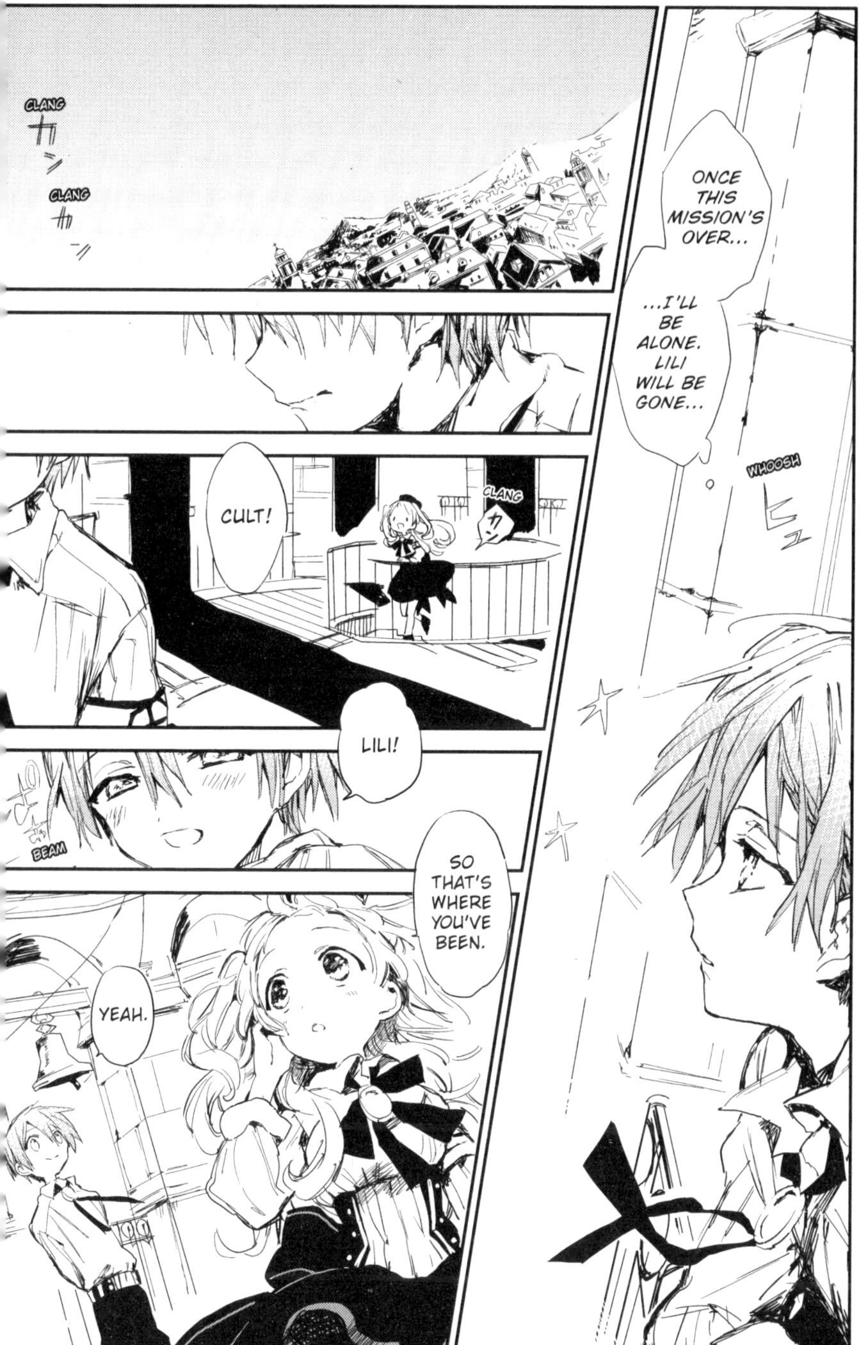
ONCE THIS MISSION'S OVER...
...I'LL BE ALONE. LILI WILL BE GONE...
WHOOSH
CLANG
CLANG
CLANG
CULT!
LILI!
BEAM
SO THAT'S WHERE YOU'VE BEEN.
YEAH.

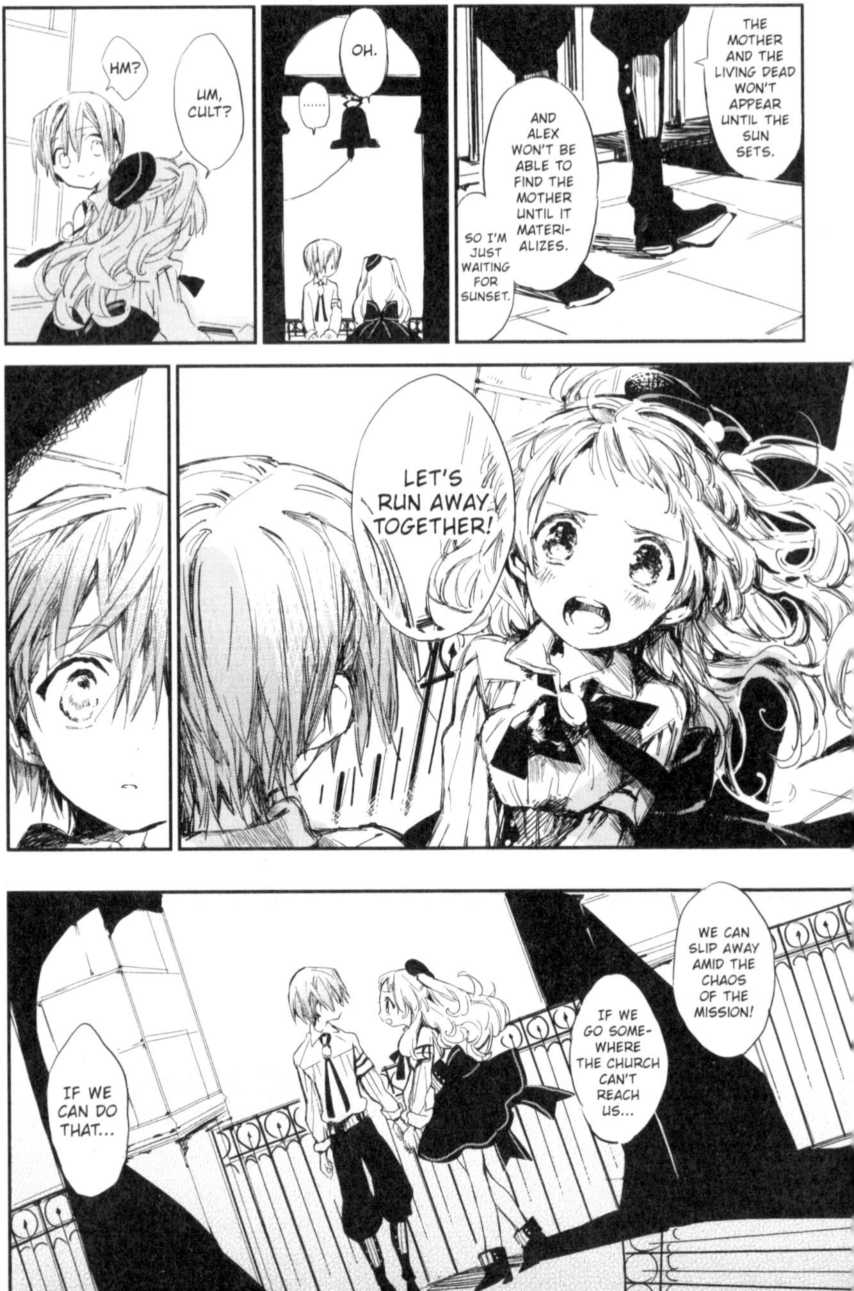
THE MOTHER AND THE LIVING DEAD WON'T APPEAR UNTIL THE SUN SETS.
AND ALEX WON'T BE ABLE TO FIND THE MOTHER UNTIL IT MATERIALIZES.
SO I'M JUST WAITING FOR SUNSET.
OH.
......
UM, CULT?
HM?
LET'S RUN AWAY TOGETHER!
WE CAN SLIP AWAY AMID THE CHAOS OF THE MISSION!
IF WE GO SOMEWHERE THE CHURCH CAN'T REACH US...
IF WE CAN DO THAT...

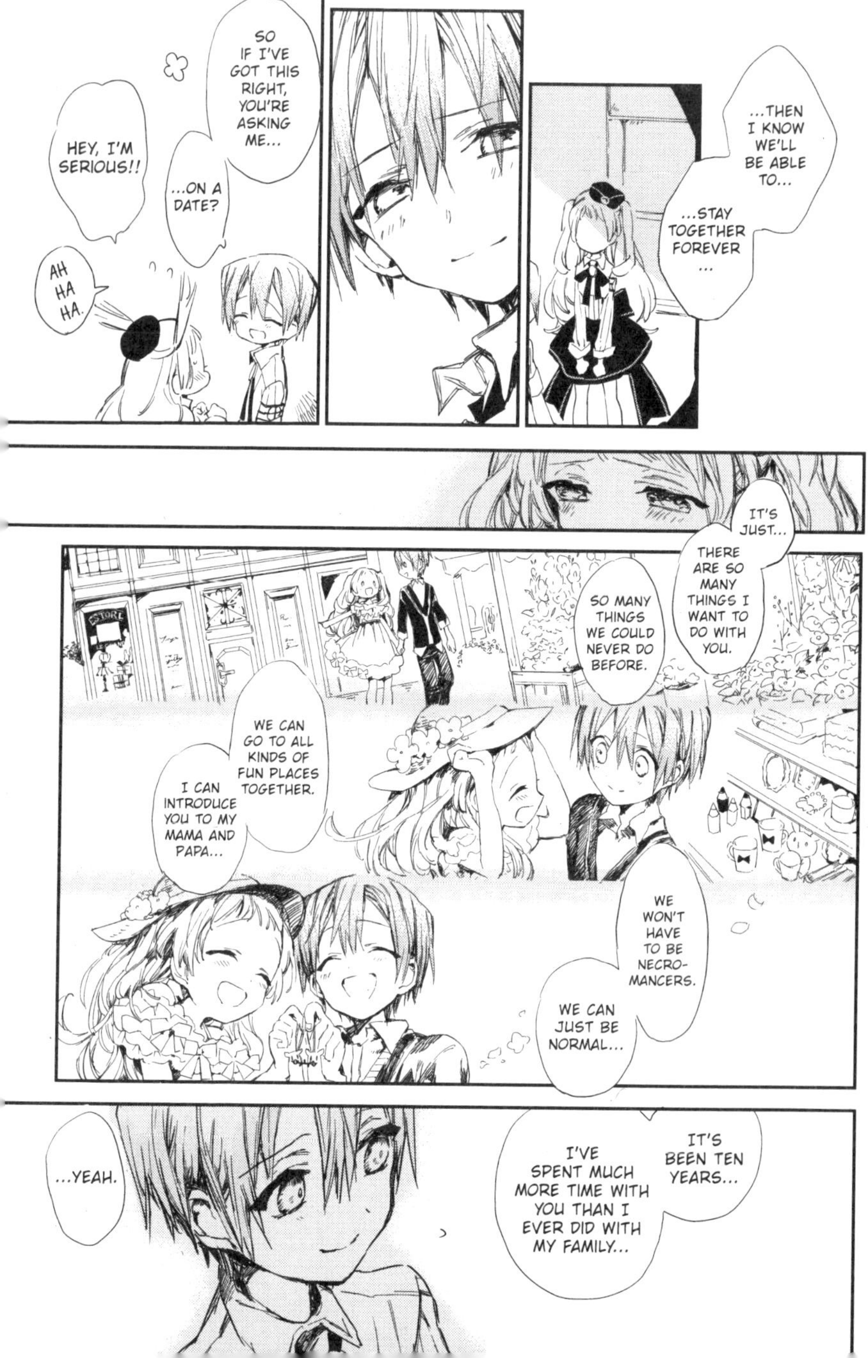
...THEN I KNOW WE'LL BE ABLE TO...
...STAY TOGETHER FOREVER...
SO IF I'VE GOT THIS RIGHT, YOU'RE ASKING ME...
...ON A DATE?
HEY, I'M SERIOUS!!
AH HA HA.
IT'S JUST...
THERE ARE SO MANY THINGS I WANT TO DO WITH YOU.
SO MANY THINGS WE COULD NEVER DO BEFORE.
WE CAN GO TO ALL KINDS OF FUN PLACES TOGETHER.
I CAN INTRODUCE YOU TO MY MAMA AND PAPA...
WE WON'T HAVE TO BE NECRO-MANCERS.
WE CAN JUST BE NORMAL...
IT'S BEEN TEN YEARS...
I'VE SPENT MUCH MORE TIME WITH YOU THAN I EVER DID WITH MY FAMILY...
...YEAH.

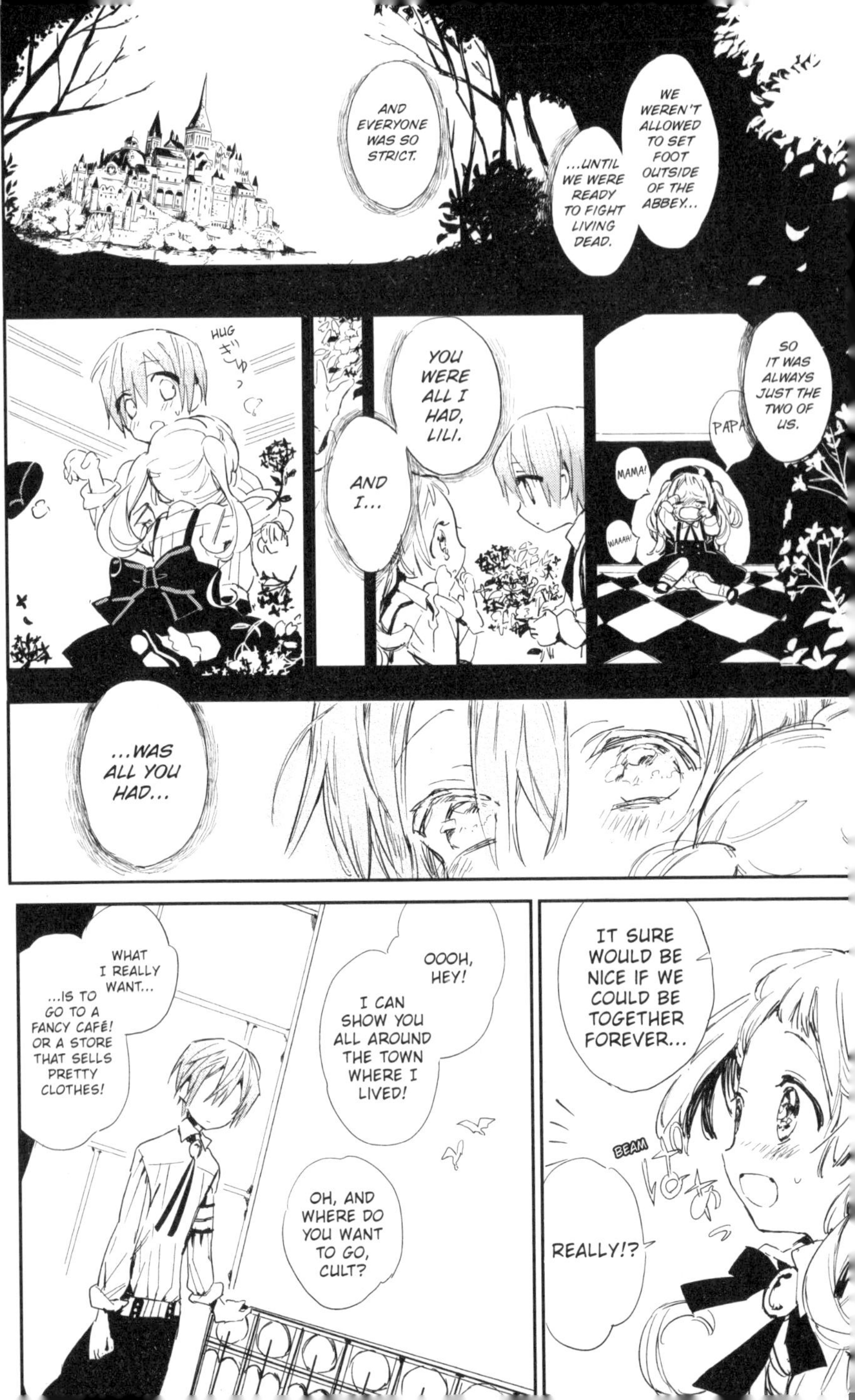
WE WEREN'T ALLOWED TO SET FOOT OUTSIDE OF THE ABBEY...
...UNTIL WE WERE READY TO FIGHT LIVING DEAD.
AND EVERYONE WAS SO STRICT.
SO IT WAS ALWAYS JUST THE TWO OF US.
PAPA
MAMA!
WAAAH!
YOU WERE ALL I HAD, LILI.
AND I...
HUG
...WAS ALL YOU HAD...
IT SURE WOULD BE NICE IF WE COULD BE TOGETHER FOREVER...
BEAM
REALLY!?
OOOH, HEY!
I CAN SHOW YOU ALL AROUND THE TOWN WHERE I LIVED!
OH, AND WHERE DO YOU WANT TO GO, CULT?
WHAT I REALLY WANT...
...IS TO GO TO A FANCY CAFÉ! OR A STORE THAT SELLS PRETTY CLOTHES!

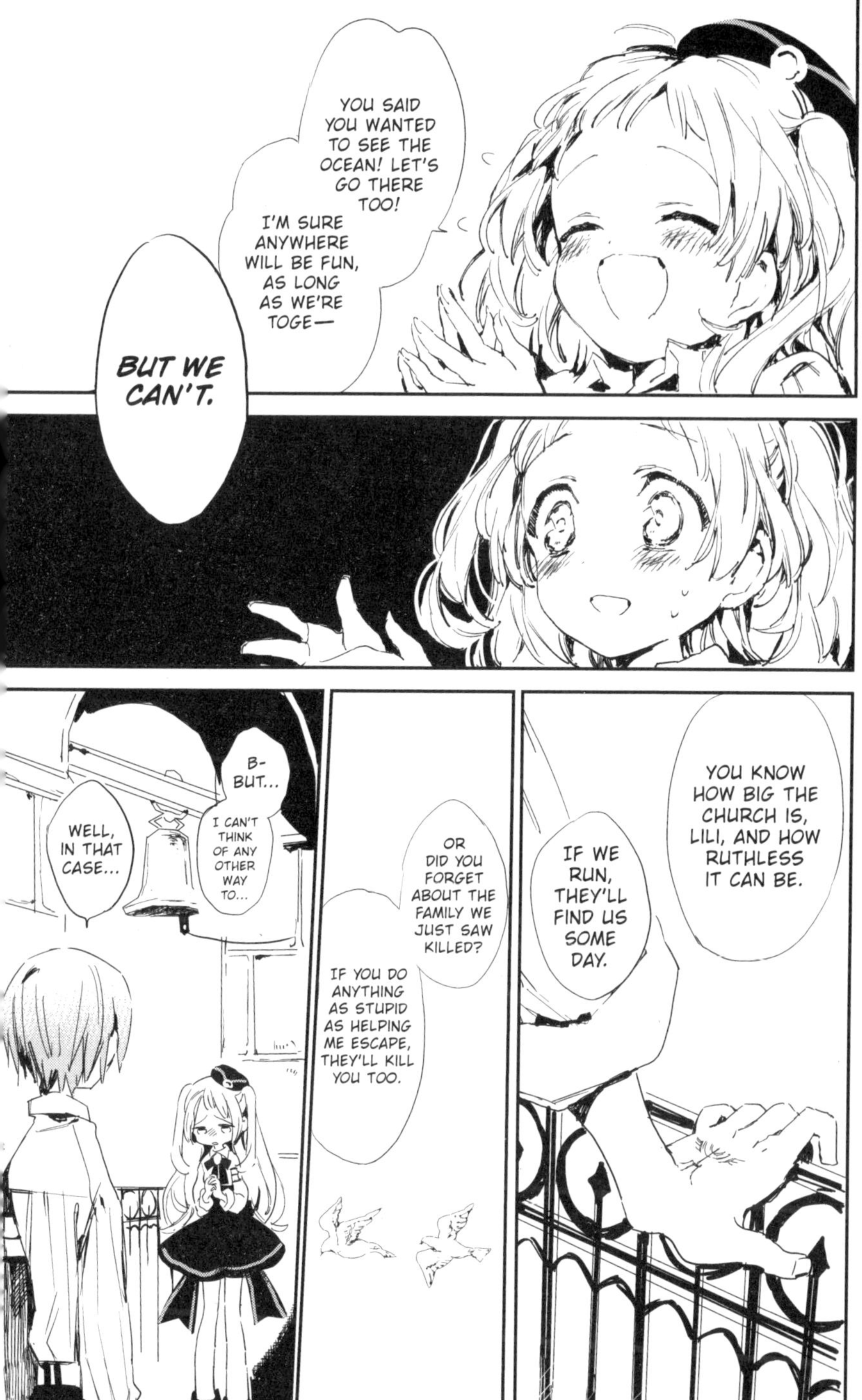
YOU SAID YOU WANTED TO SEE THE OCEAN! LET'S GO THERE TOO!
I'M SURE ANYWHERE WILL BE FUN, AS LONG AS WE'RE TOGE—
BUT WE CAN'T.
YOU KNOW HOW BIG THE CHURCH IS, LILI, AND HOW RUTHLESS IT CAN BE.
IF WE RUN, THEY'LL FIND US SOME DAY.
OR DID YOU FORGET ABOUT THE FAMILY WE JUST SAW KILLED?
IF YOU DO ANYTHING AS STUPID AS HELPING ME ESCAPE, THEY'LL KILL YOU TOO.
B-BUT...
I CAN'T THINK OF ANY OTHER WAY TO...
WELL, IN THAT CASE...

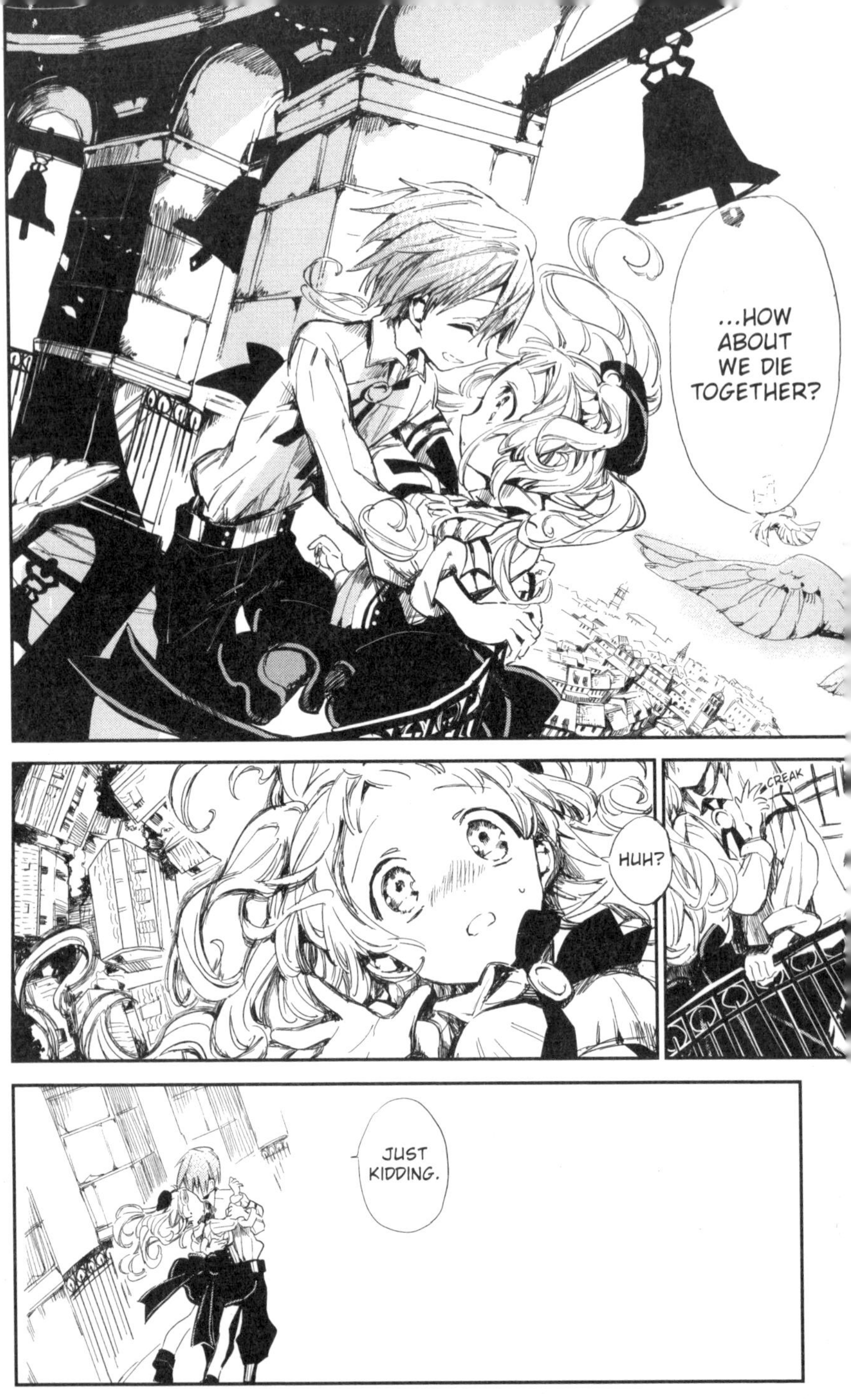
...HOW ABOUT WE DIE TOGETHER?
CREAK
HUH?
JUST KIDDING.

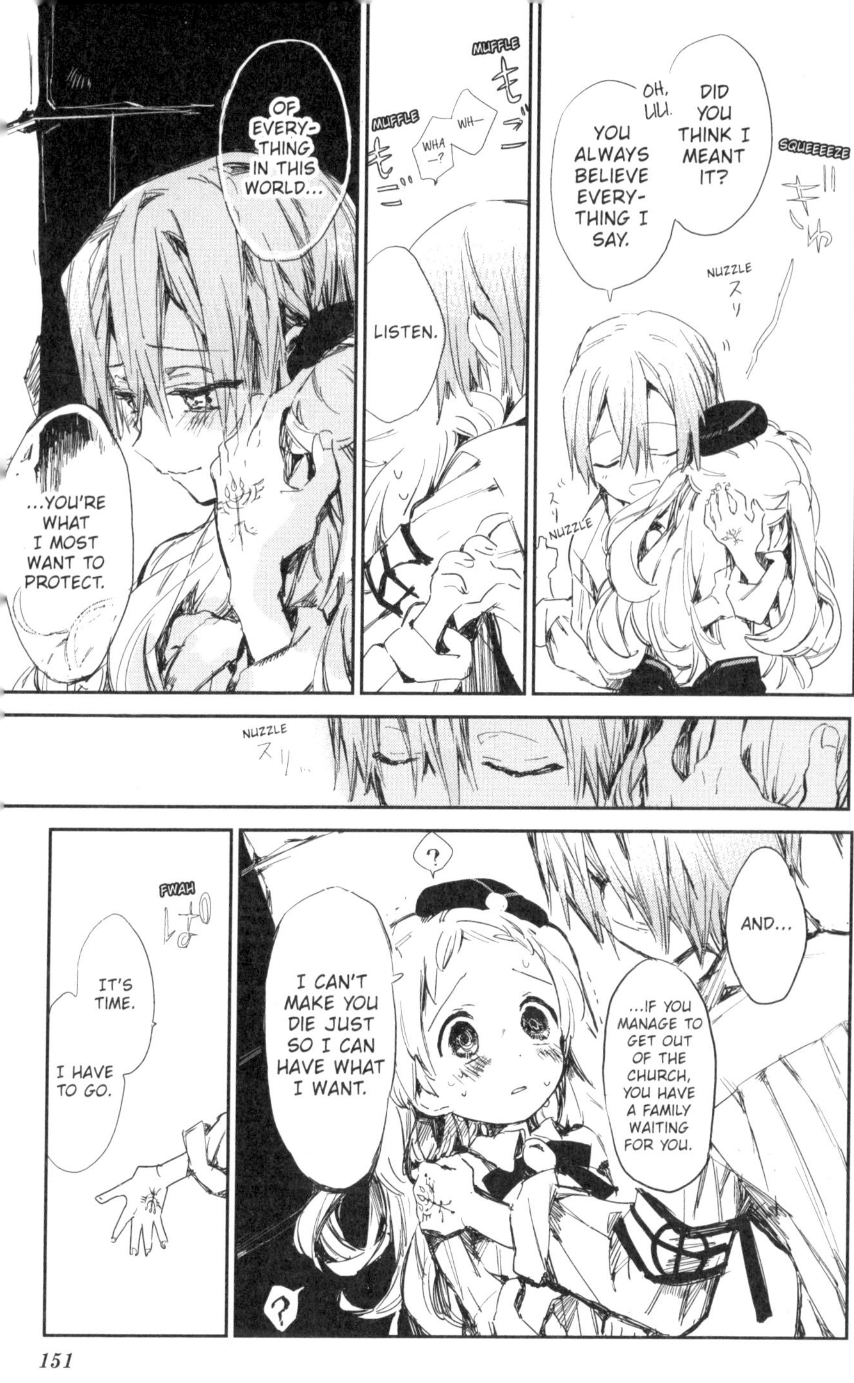
SQUEEEEEZE
DID YOU THINK I MEANT IT?
OH, UU. YOU ALWAYS BELIEVE EVERY-THING I SAY.
NUZZLE
NUZZLE
MUFFLE
WH—
WHA—?
MUFFLE
LISTEN.
OF EVERY-THING IN THIS WORLD...
...YOU'RE WHAT I MOST WANT TO PROTECT.
NUZZLE
AND...
...IF YOU MANAGE TO GET OUT OF THE CHURCH, YOU HAVE A FAMILY WAITING FOR YOU.
I CAN'T MAKE YOU DIE JUST SO I CAN HAVE WHAT I WANT.
FWAH
IT'S TIME.
I HAVE TO GO.

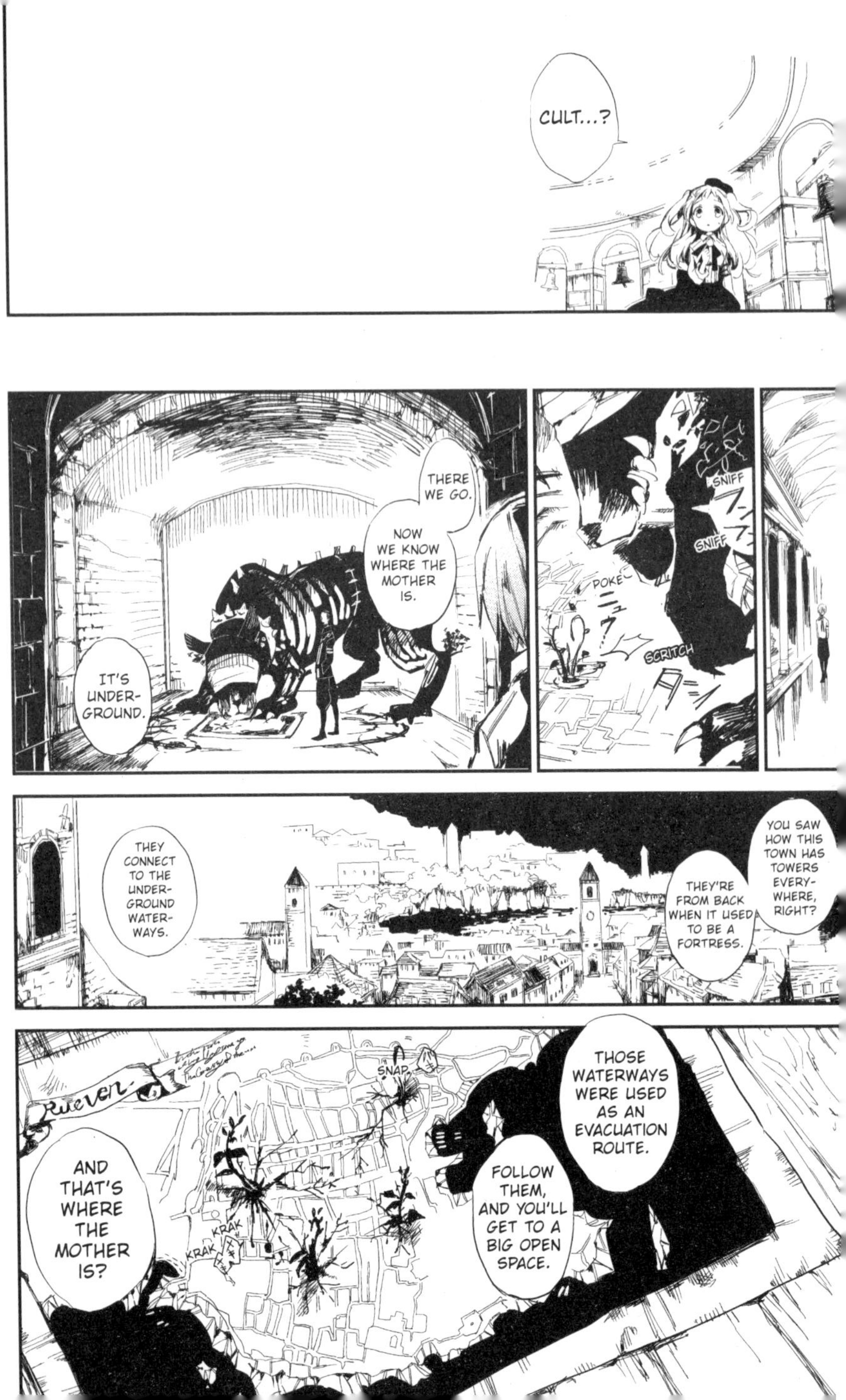
CULT...?
SNIFF
SNIFF
POKE
SCRITCH
THERE WE GO.
NOW WE KNOW WHERE THE MOTHER IS.
IT'S UNDERGROUND.
YOU SAW HOW THIS TOWN HAS TOWERS EVERYWHERE, RIGHT?
THEY'RE FROM BACK WHEN IT USED TO BE A FORTRESS.
THEY CONNECT TO THE UNDERGROUND WATERWAYS.
THOSE WATERWAYS WERE USED AS AN EVACUATION ROUTE.
FOLLOW THEM, AND YOU'LL GET TO A BIG OPEN SPACE.
SNAP
AND THAT'S WHERE THE MOTHER IS?
KRAK
KRAK

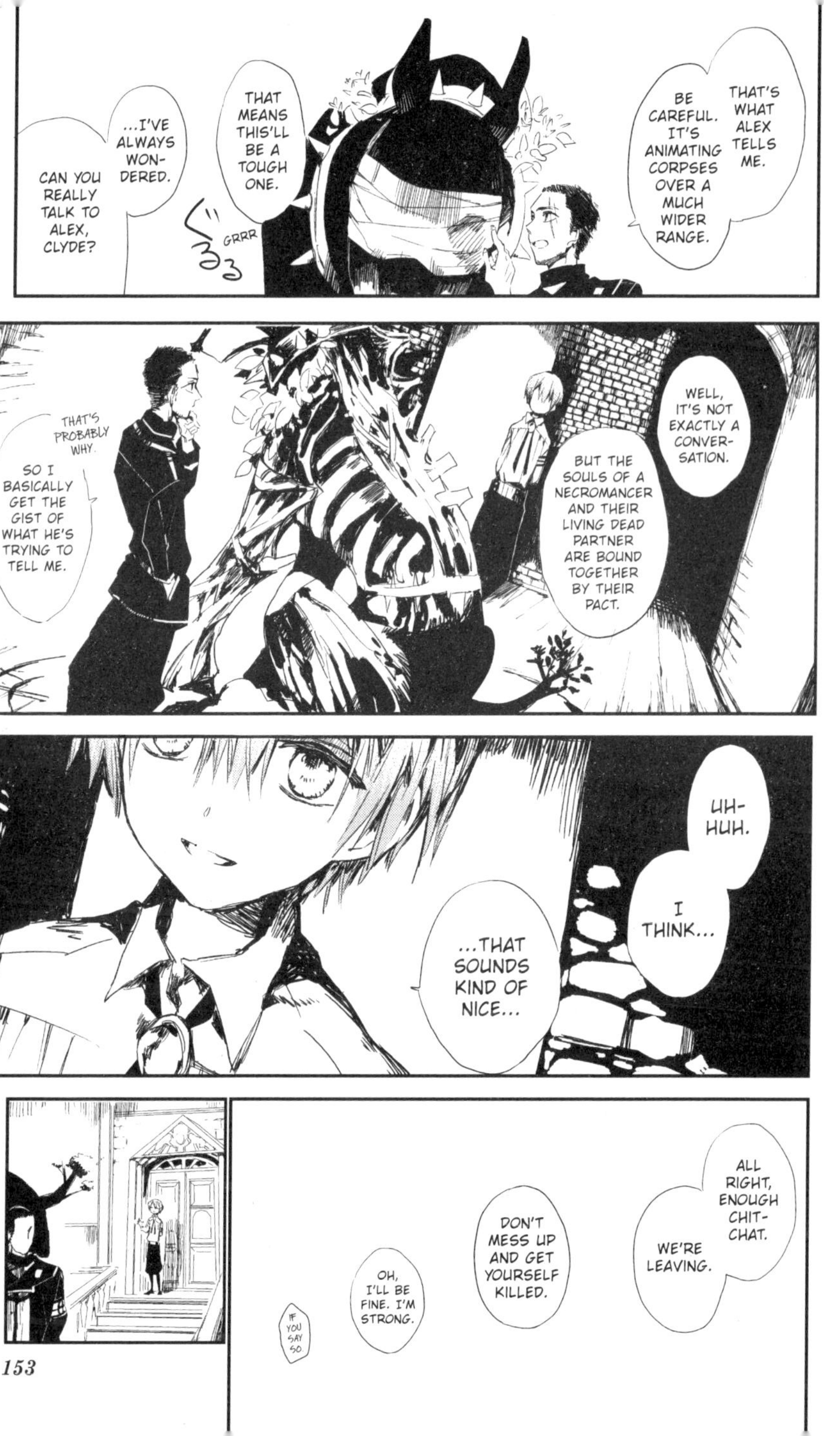
THAT'S WHAT ALEX TELLS ME.
BE CAREFUL. IT'S ANIMATING CORPSES OVER A MUCH WIDER RANGE.
THAT MEANS THIS'LL BE A TOUGH ONE.
GRRR
...I'VE ALWAYS WON-DERED.
CAN YOU REALLY TALK TO ALEX, CLYDE?
WELL, IT'S NOT EXACTLY A CONVER-SATION.
BUT THE SOULS OF A NECROMANCER AND THEIR LIVING DEAD PARTNER ARE BOUND TOGETHER BY THEIR PACT.
THAT'S PROBABLY WHY.
SO I BASICALLY GET THE GIST OF WHAT HE'S TRYING TO TELL ME.
UH-HUH.
I THINK...
...THAT SOUNDS KIND OF NICE...
ALL RIGHT, ENOUGH CHIT-CHAT.
WE'RE LEAVING.
DON'T MESS UP AND GET YOURSELF KILLED.
OH, I'LL BE FINE. I'M STRONG.
IF YOU SAY SO.

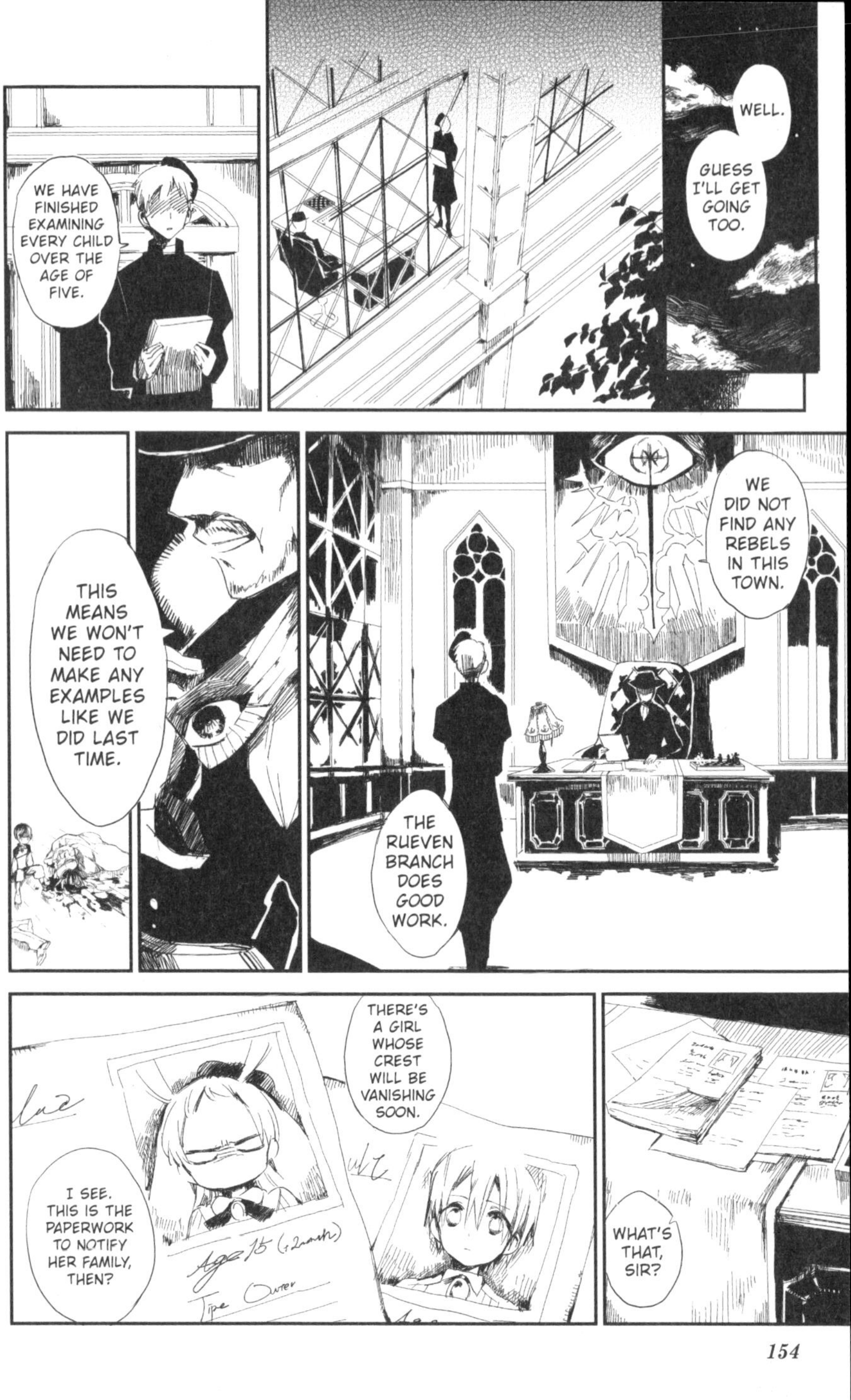
WELL.
GUESS I'LL GET GOING TOO.
WE HAVE FINISHED EXAMINING EVERY CHILD OVER THE AGE OF FIVE.
WE DID NOT FIND ANY REBELS IN THIS TOWN.
THE RUEVEN BRANCH DOES GOOD WORK.
THIS MEANS WE WON'T NEED TO MAKE ANY EXAMPLES LIKE WE DID LAST TIME.
WHAT'S THAT, SIR?
THERE'S A GIRL WHOSE CREST WILL BE VANISHING SOON.
I SEE. THIS IS THE PAPERWORK TO NOTIFY HER FAMILY, THEN?

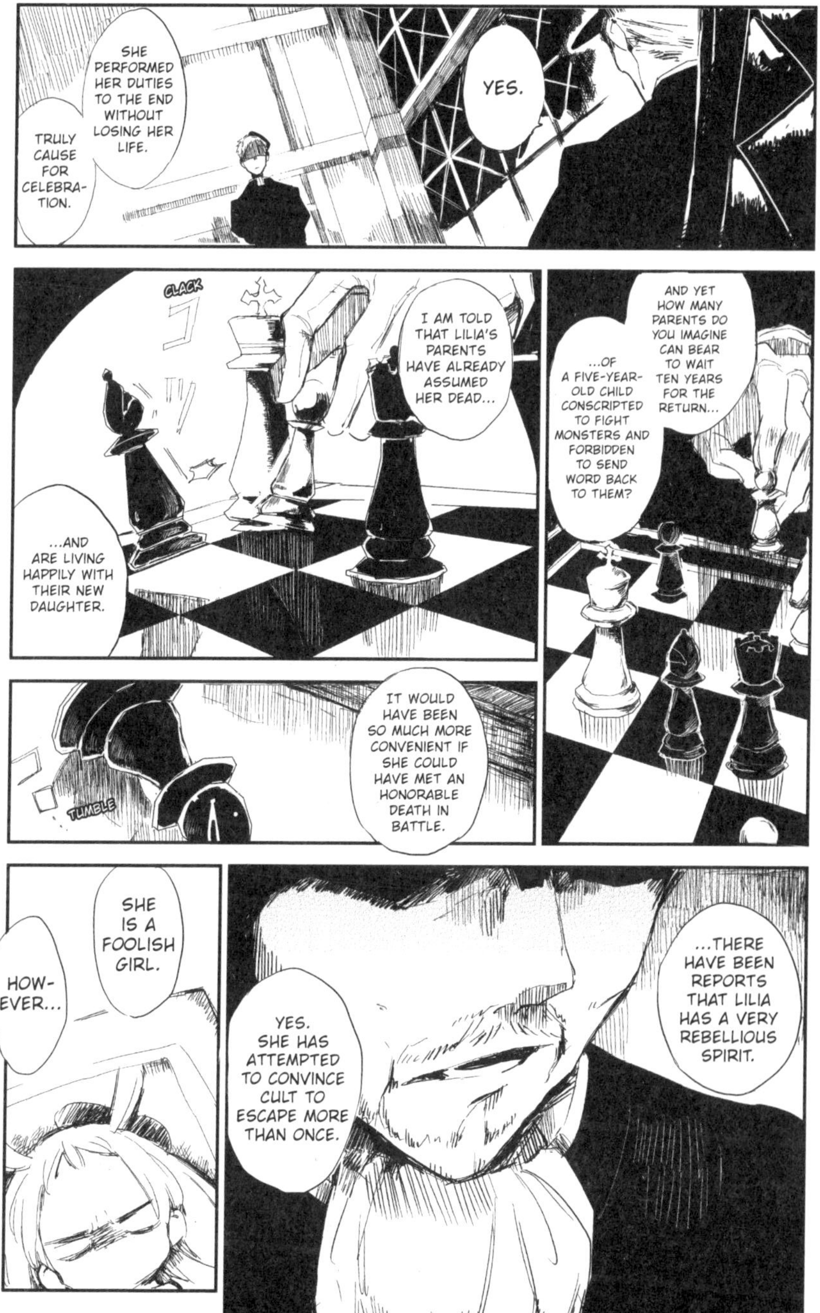
YES.
SHE PERFORMED HER DUTIES TO THE END WITHOUT LOSING HER LIFE.
TRULY CAUSE FOR CELEBRATION.
AND YET HOW MANY PARENTS DO YOU IMAGINE CAN BEAR TO WAIT TEN YEARS FOR THE RETURN...
...OF A FIVE-YEAR-OLD CHILD CONSCRIPTED TO FIGHT MONSTERS AND FORBIDDEN TO SEND WORD BACK TO THEM?
CLACK
I AM TOLD THAT LILIA'S PARENTS HAVE ALREADY ASSUMED HER DEAD...
...AND ARE LIVING HAPPILY WITH THEIR NEW DAUGHTER.
IT WOULD HAVE BEEN SO MUCH MORE CONVENIENT IF SHE COULD HAVE MET AN HONORABLE DEATH IN BATTLE.
TUMBLE
...THERE HAVE BEEN REPORTS THAT LILIA HAS A VERY REBELLIOUS SPIRIT.
YES. SHE HAS ATTEMPTED TO CONVINCE CULT TO ESCAPE MORE THAN ONCE.
SHE IS A FOOLISH GIRL.
HOW-EVER...

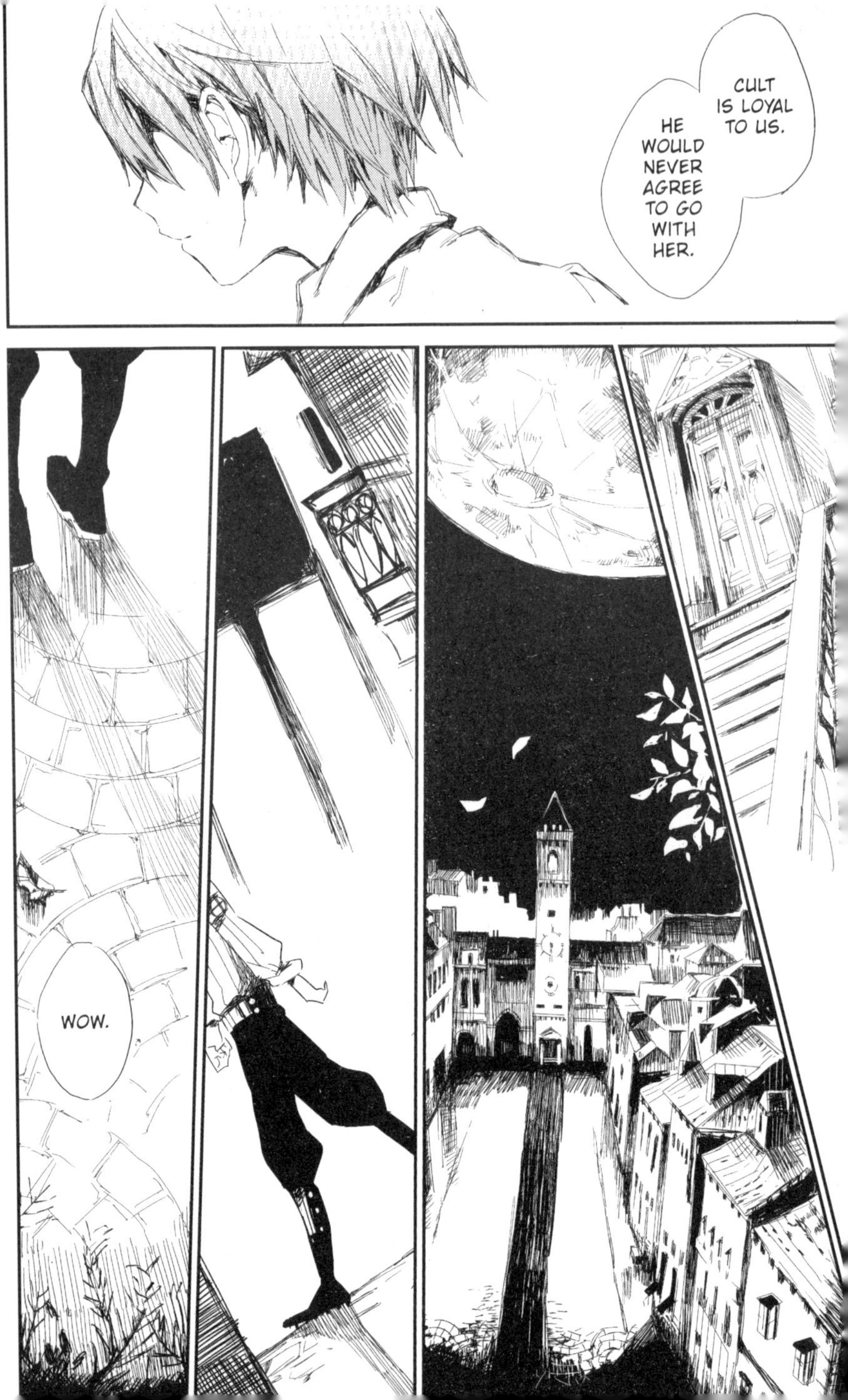
CULT IS LOYAL TO US.
HE WOULD NEVER AGREE TO GO WITH HER.
WOW.

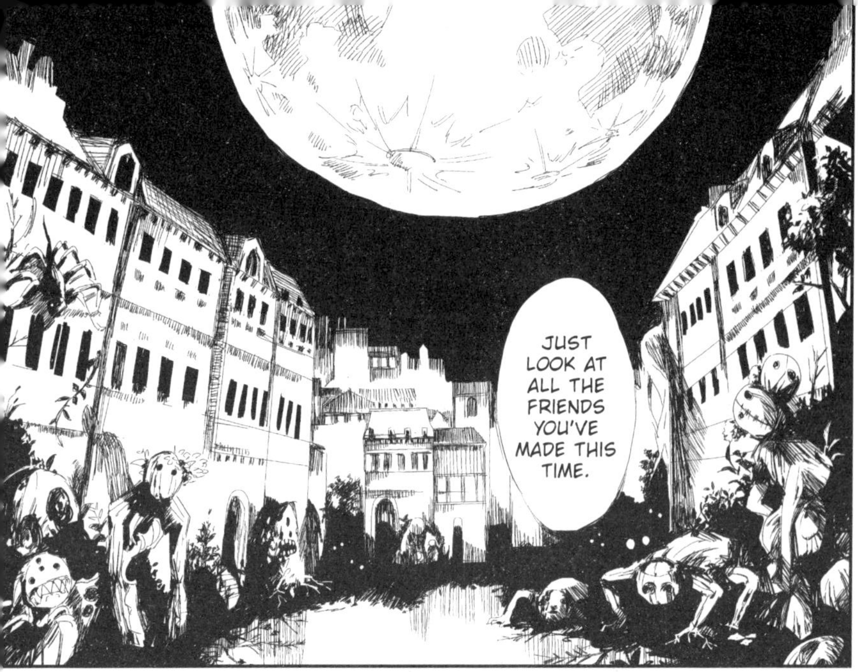
JUST LOOK AT ALL THE FRIENDS YOU'VE MADE THIS TIME.

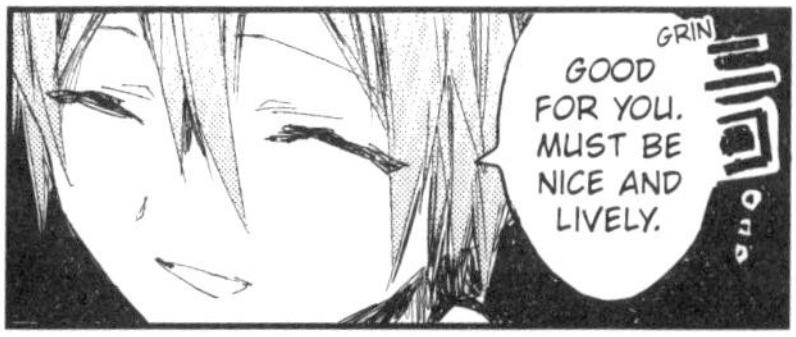
GRIN
GOOD FOR YOU. MUST BE NICE AND LIVELY.

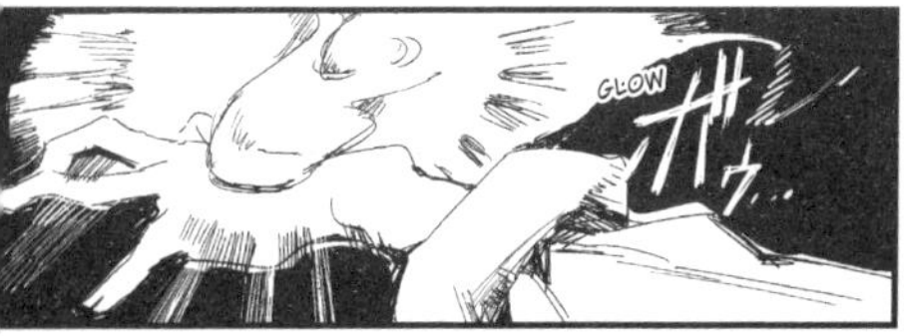
GLOW

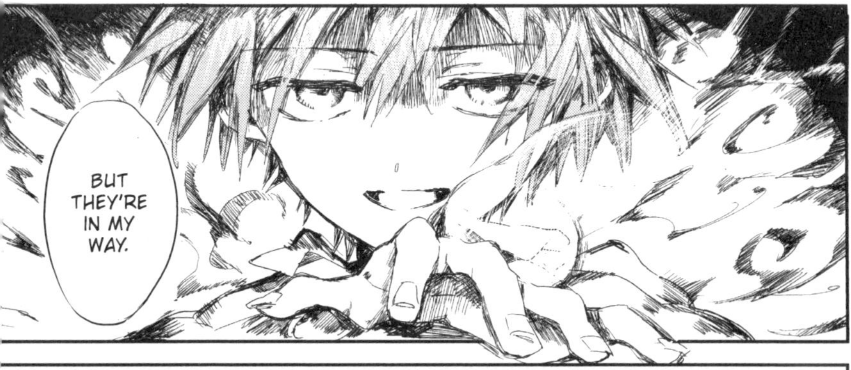
BUT THEY'RE IN MY WAY.

ALL MY LIFE...

...THERE'S ONE PERSON I'VE HATED WITH EVERY FIBER OF MY BEING.

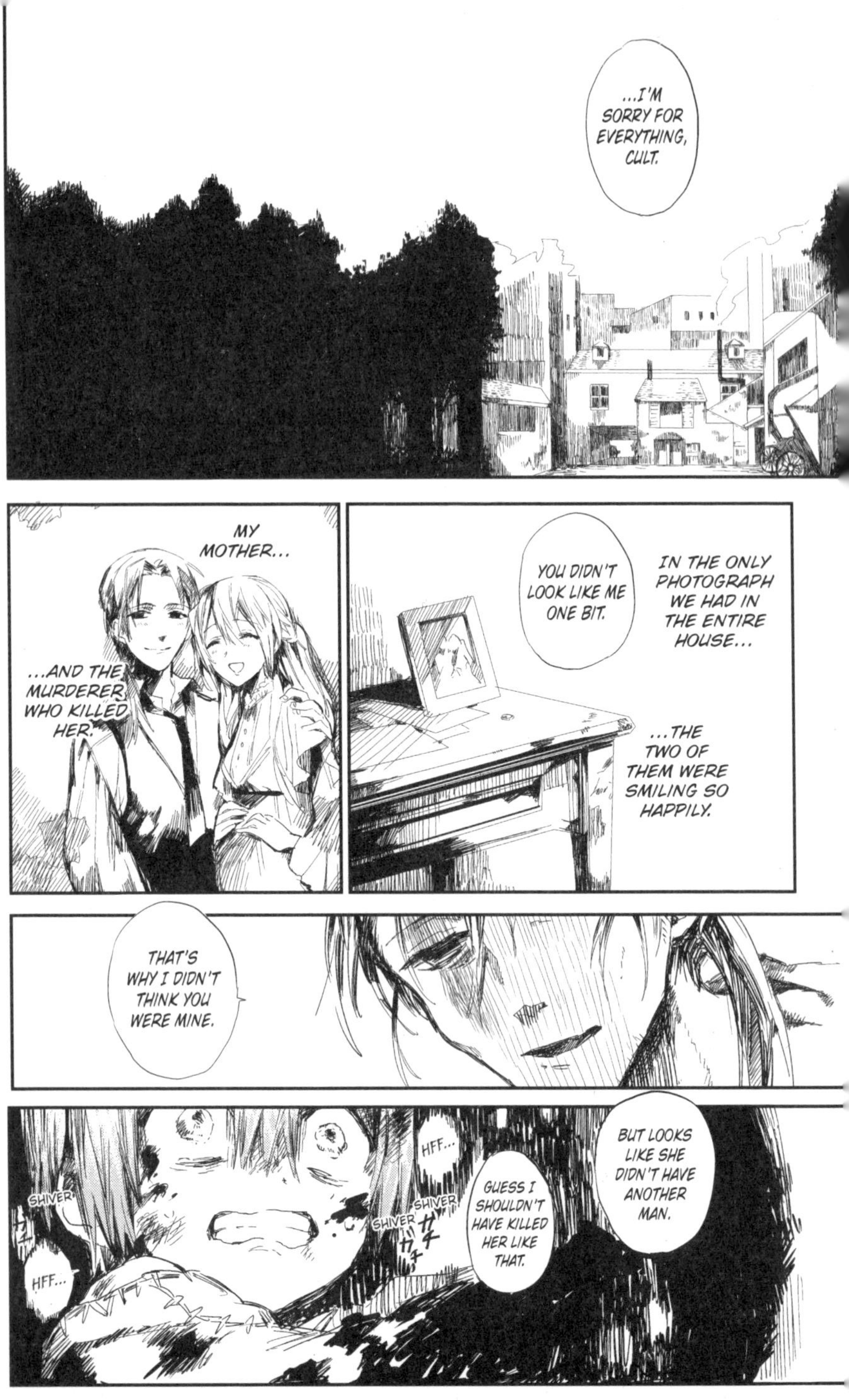
...I'M SORRY FOR EVERYTHING, CULT.
IN THE ONLY PHOTOGRAPH WE HAD IN THE ENTIRE HOUSE...
YOU DIDN'T LOOK LIKE ME ONE BIT.
...THE TWO OF THEM WERE SMILING SO HAPPILY.
MY MOTHER...
...AND THE MURDERER WHO KILLED HER.
THAT'S WHY I DIDN'T THINK YOU WERE MINE.
BUT LOOKS LIKE SHE DIDN'T HAVE ANOTHER MAN.
GUESS I SHOULDN'T HAVE KILLED HER LIKE THAT.
HFF...
SHIVER
ガチ
SHIVER
ガチ
SHIVER
ガチ
HFF...

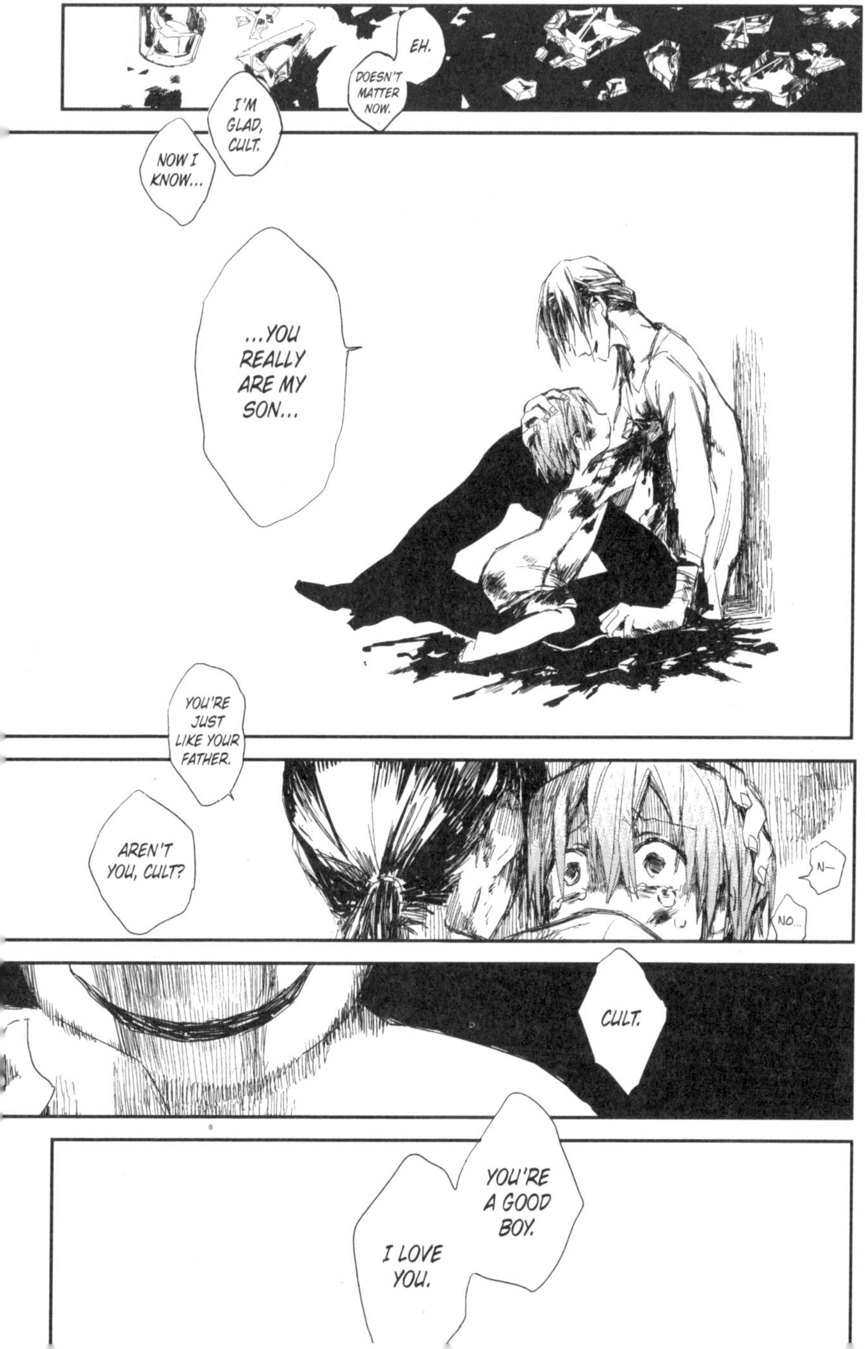
EH.
DOESN'T MATTER NOW.
I'M GLAD, CULT.
NOW I KNOW...
...YOU REALLY ARE MY SON...
YOU'RE JUST LIKE YOUR FATHER.
AREN'T YOU, CULT?
N—
NO...
CULT.
YOU'RE A GOOD BOY.
I LOVE YOU.

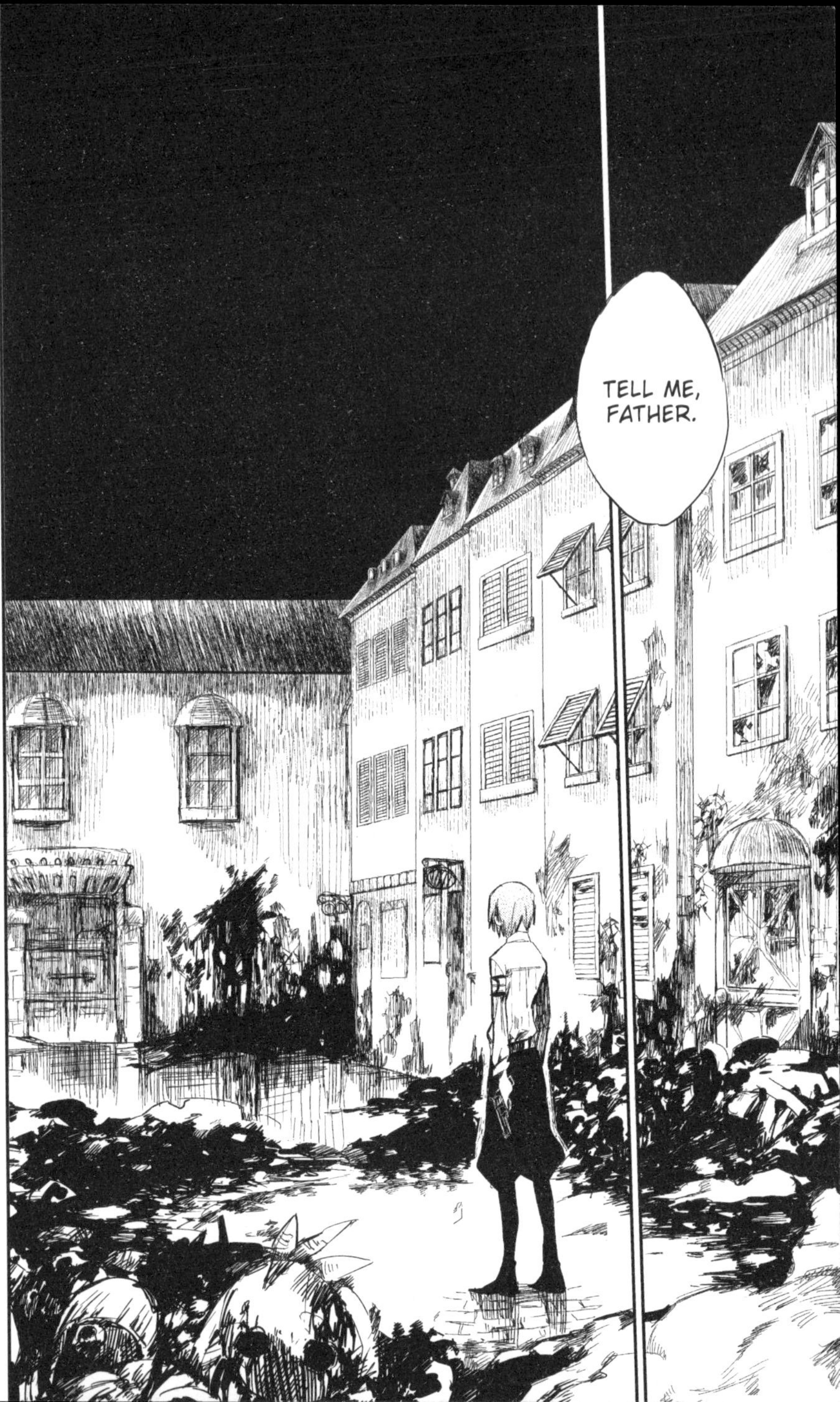
TELL ME, FATHER.

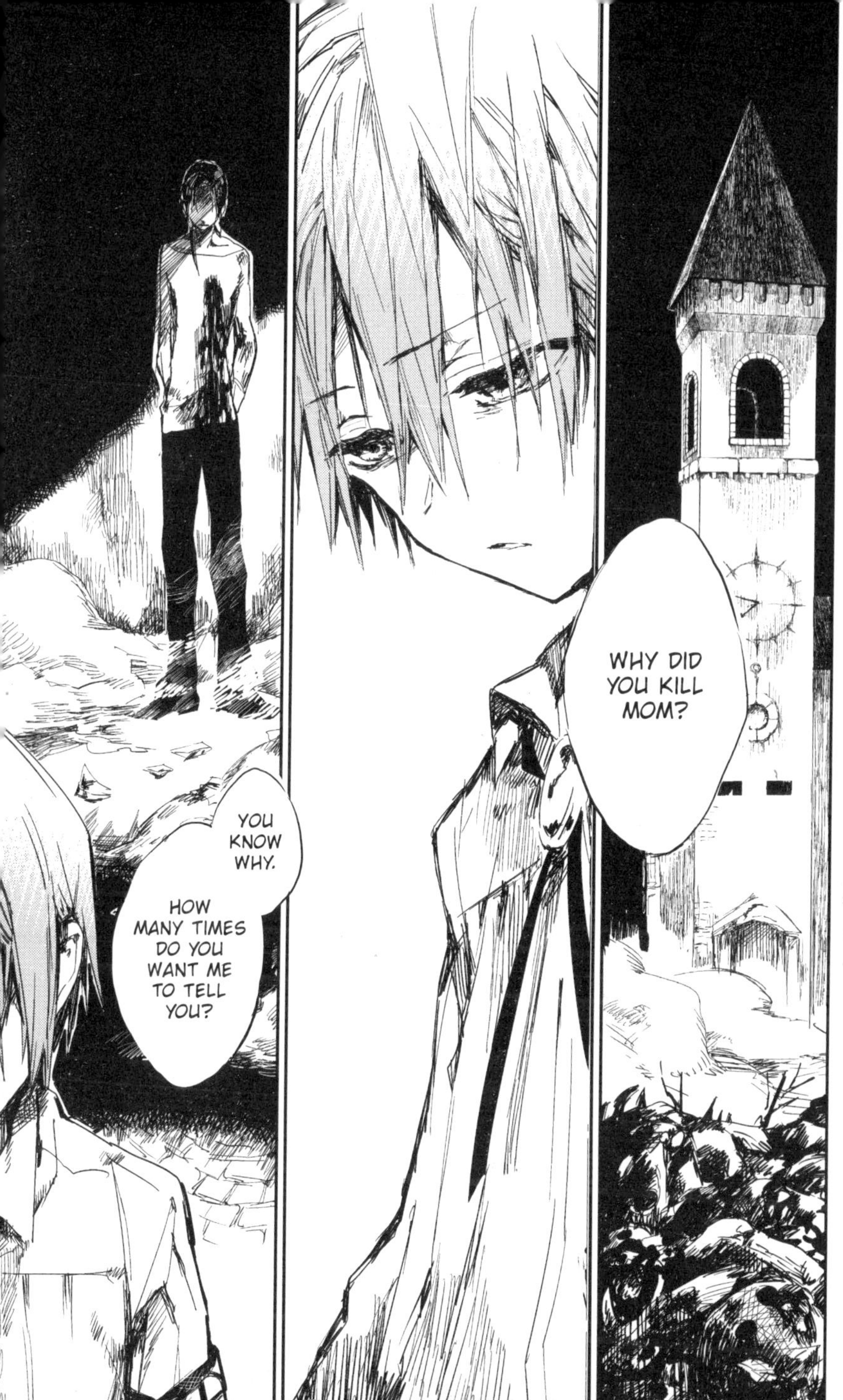
WHY DID YOU KILL MOM?
YOU KNOW WHY.
HOW MANY TIMES DO YOU WANT ME TO TELL YOU?

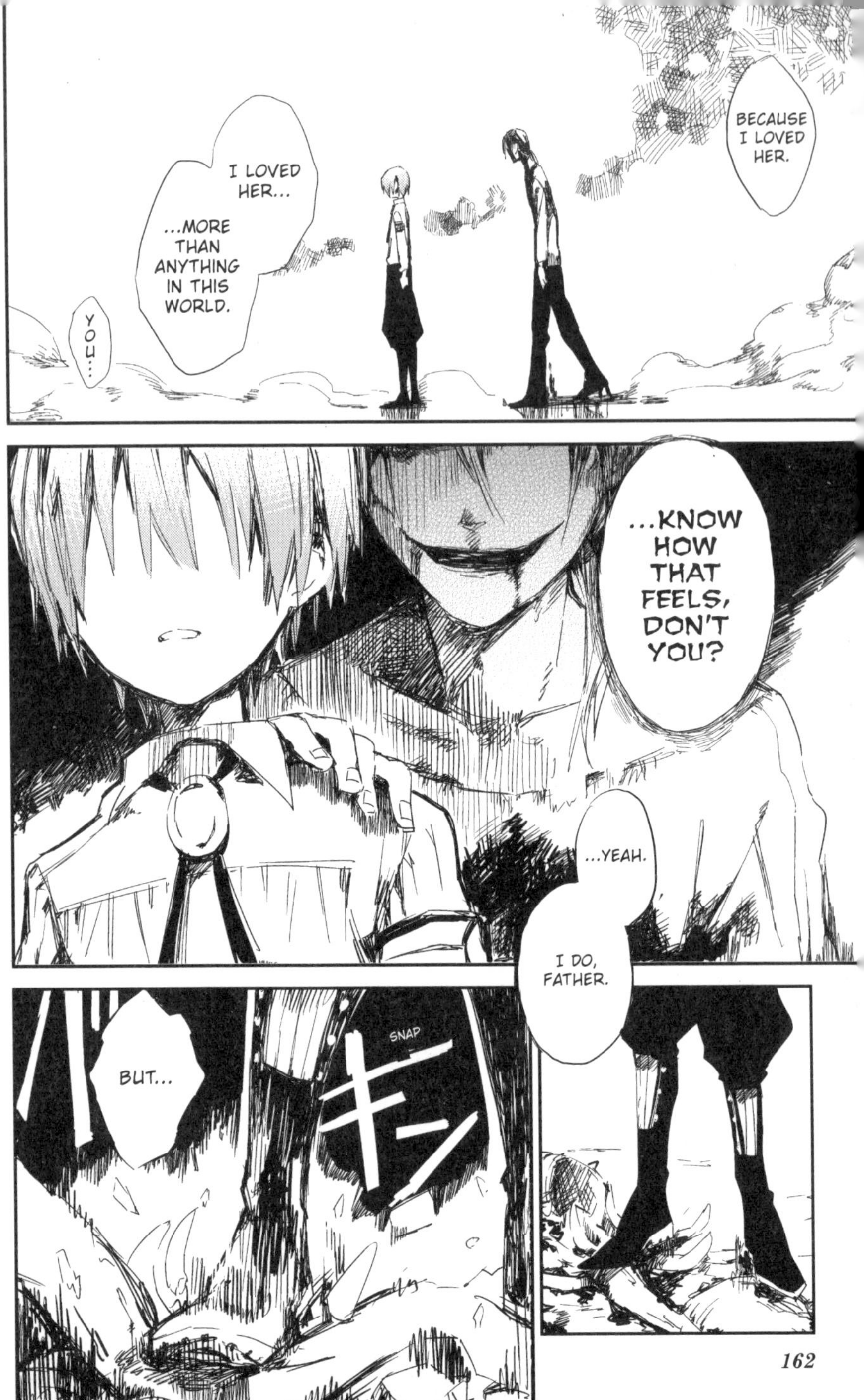
BECAUSE I LOVED HER.
I LOVED HER...
...MORE THAN ANYTHING IN THIS WORLD.
YOU...
...KNOW HOW THAT FEELS, DON'T YOU?
...YEAH.
I DO, FATHER.
SNAP
BUT...

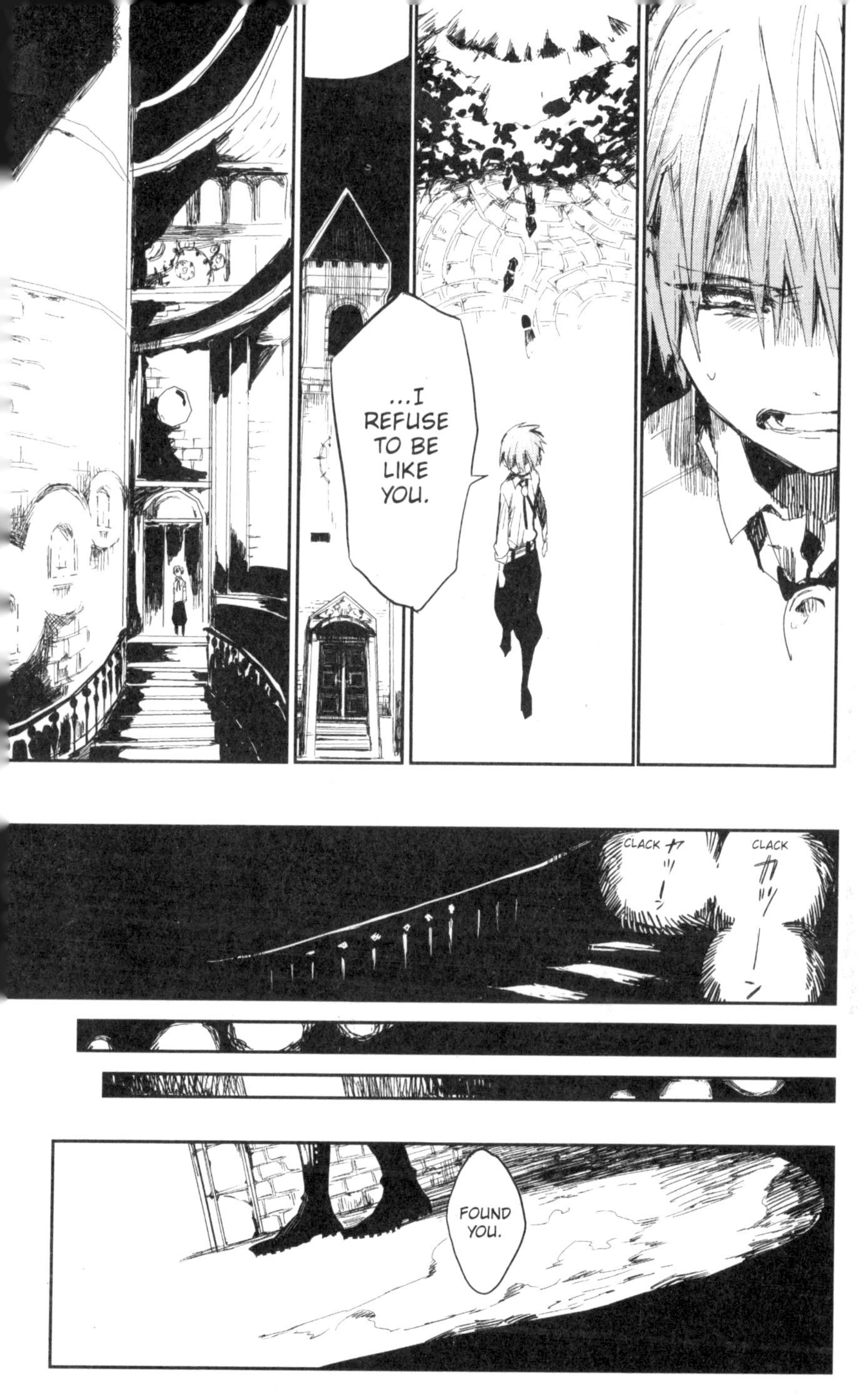
...I REFUSE TO BE LIKE YOU.
CLACK
CLACK
FOUND YOU.

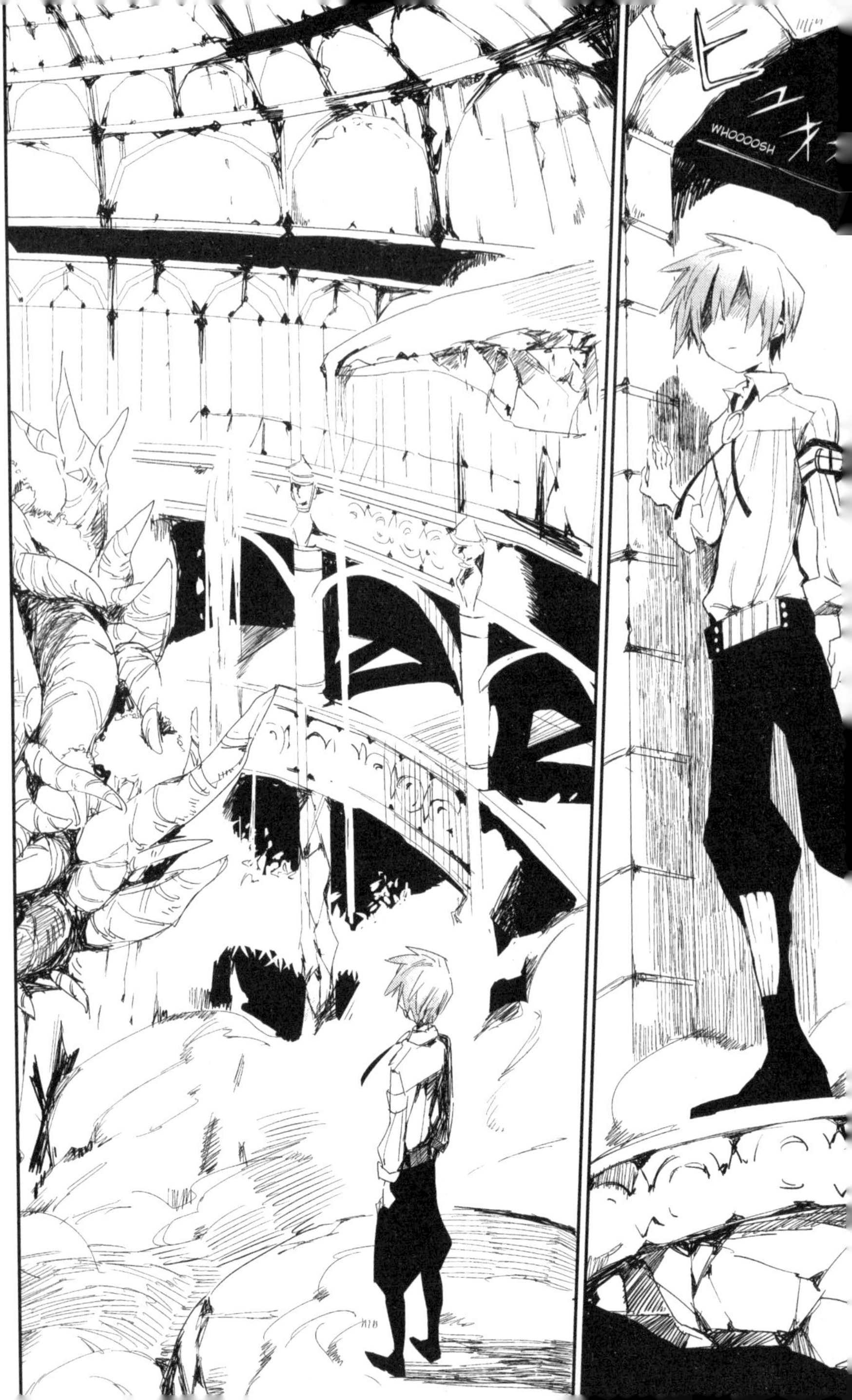
WHOOOOSH

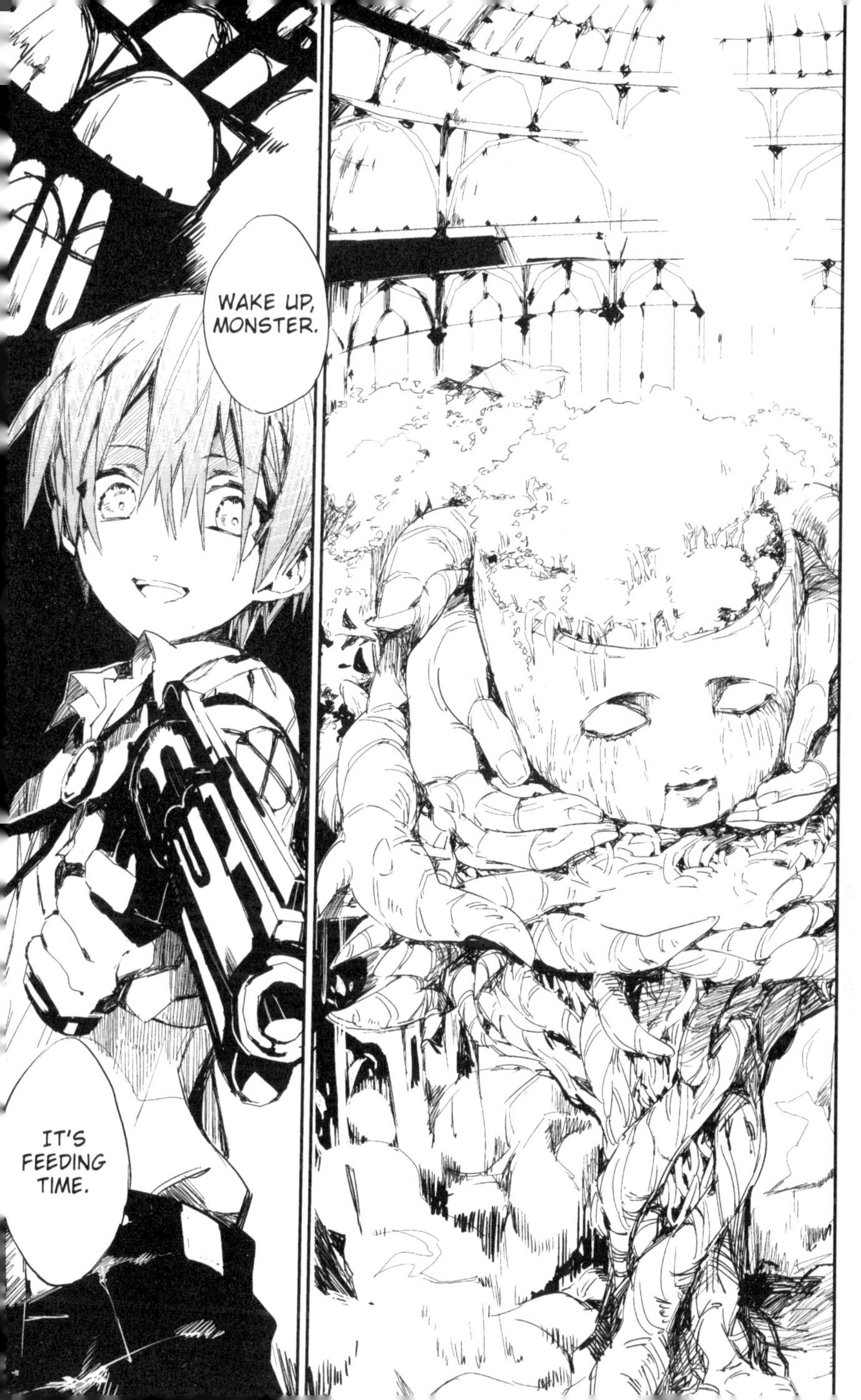
WAKE UP, MONSTER.
IT'S FEEDING TIME.

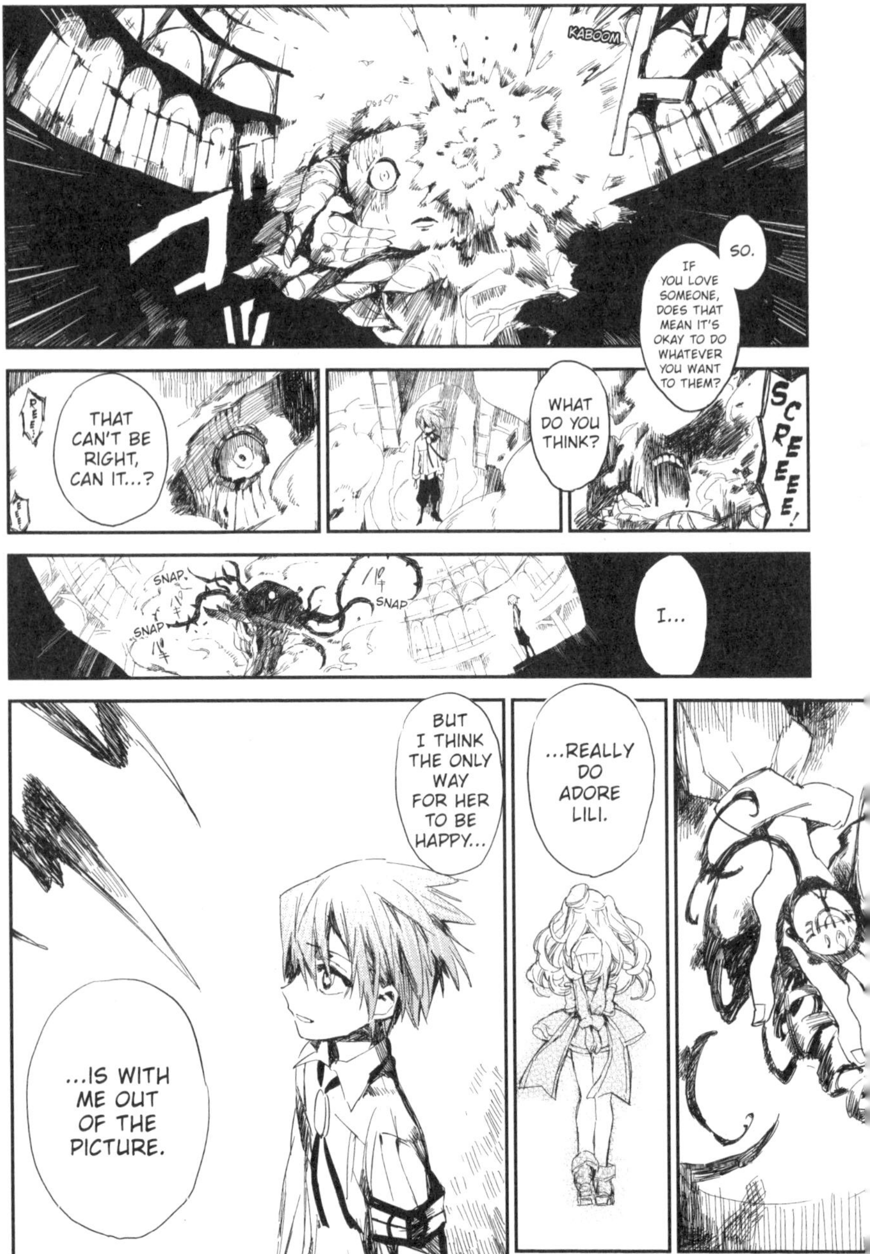
KABOOM
SO.
IF YOU LOVE SOMEONE, DOES THAT MEAN IT'S OKAY TO DO WHATEVER YOU WANT TO THEM?
SCREEEE!
WHAT DO YOU THINK?
THAT CAN'T BE RIGHT, CAN IT...?
PEE...
I...
SNAP
SNAP
SNAP
...REALLY DO ADORE LILI.
BUT I THINK THE ONLY WAY FOR HER TO BE HAPPY...
...IS WITH ME OUT OF THE PICTURE.

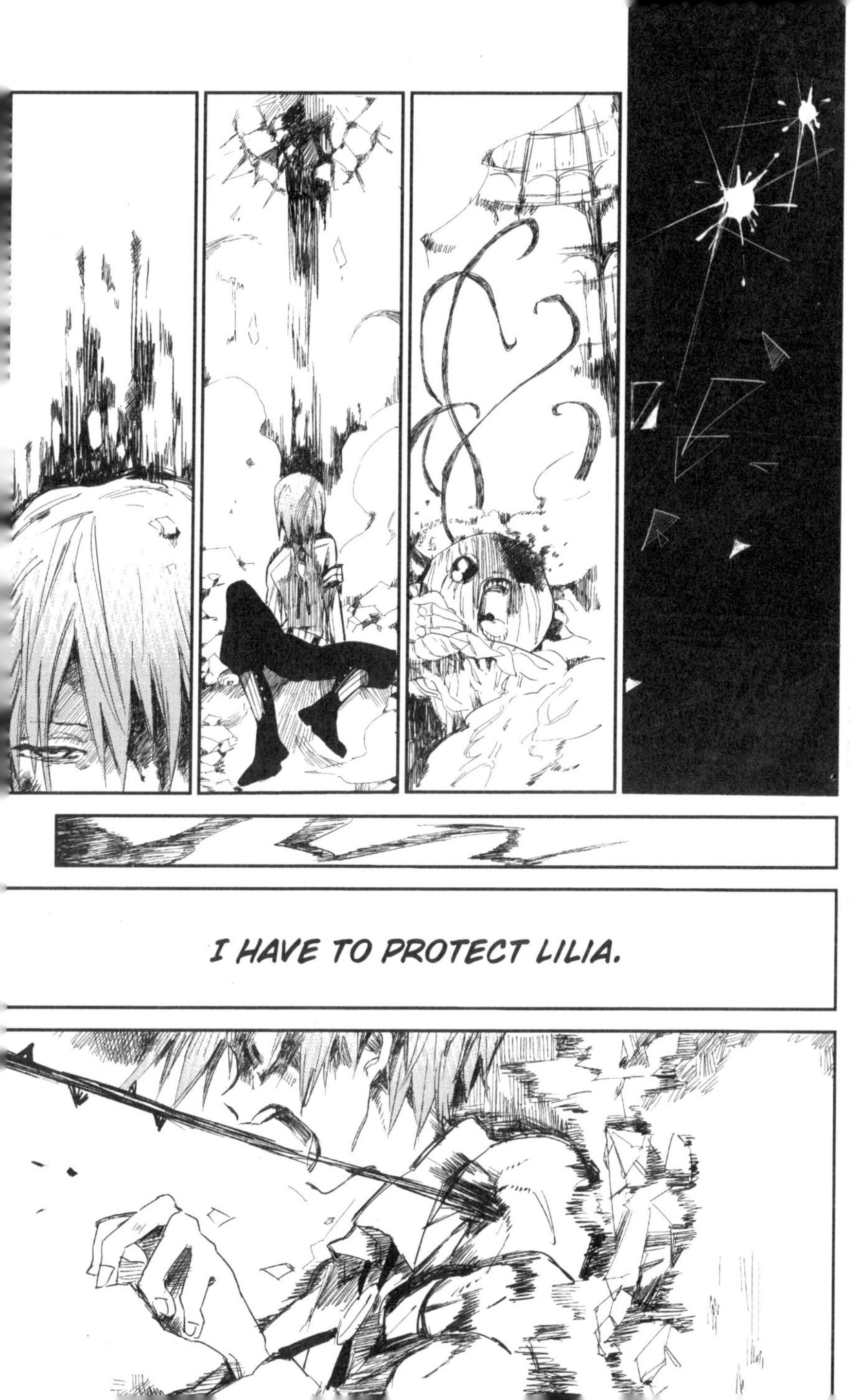
I HAVE TO PROTECT LILIA.

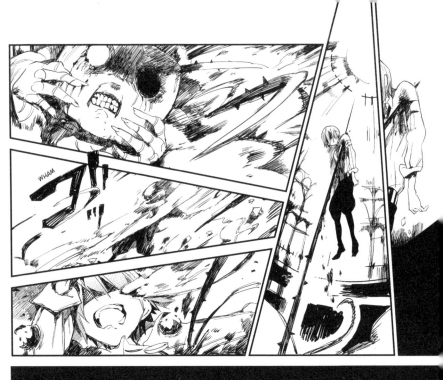

WHAM

I HAVE TO SAVE HER
FROM MY INSANITY.

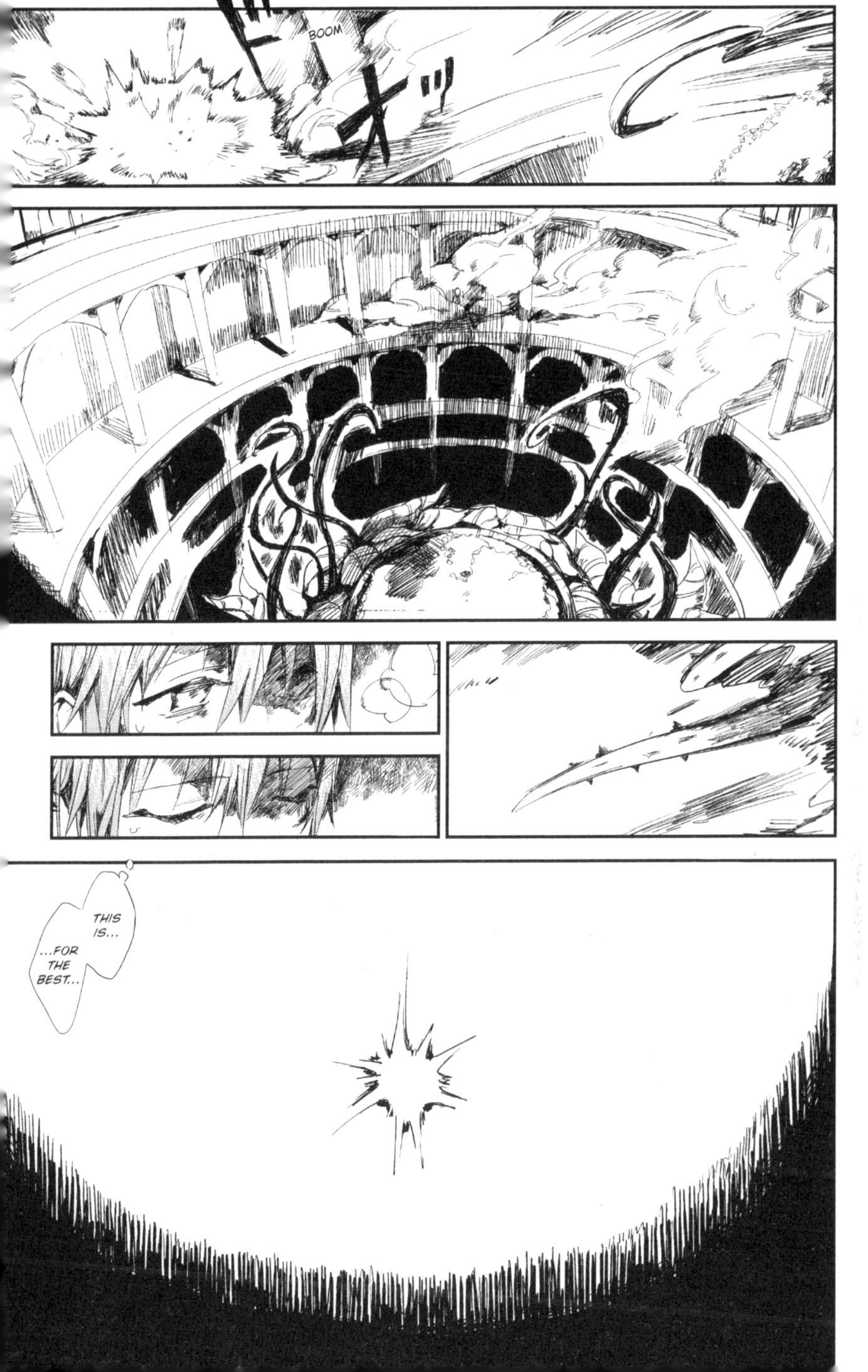
BOOM
THIS IS...
...FOR THE BEST...

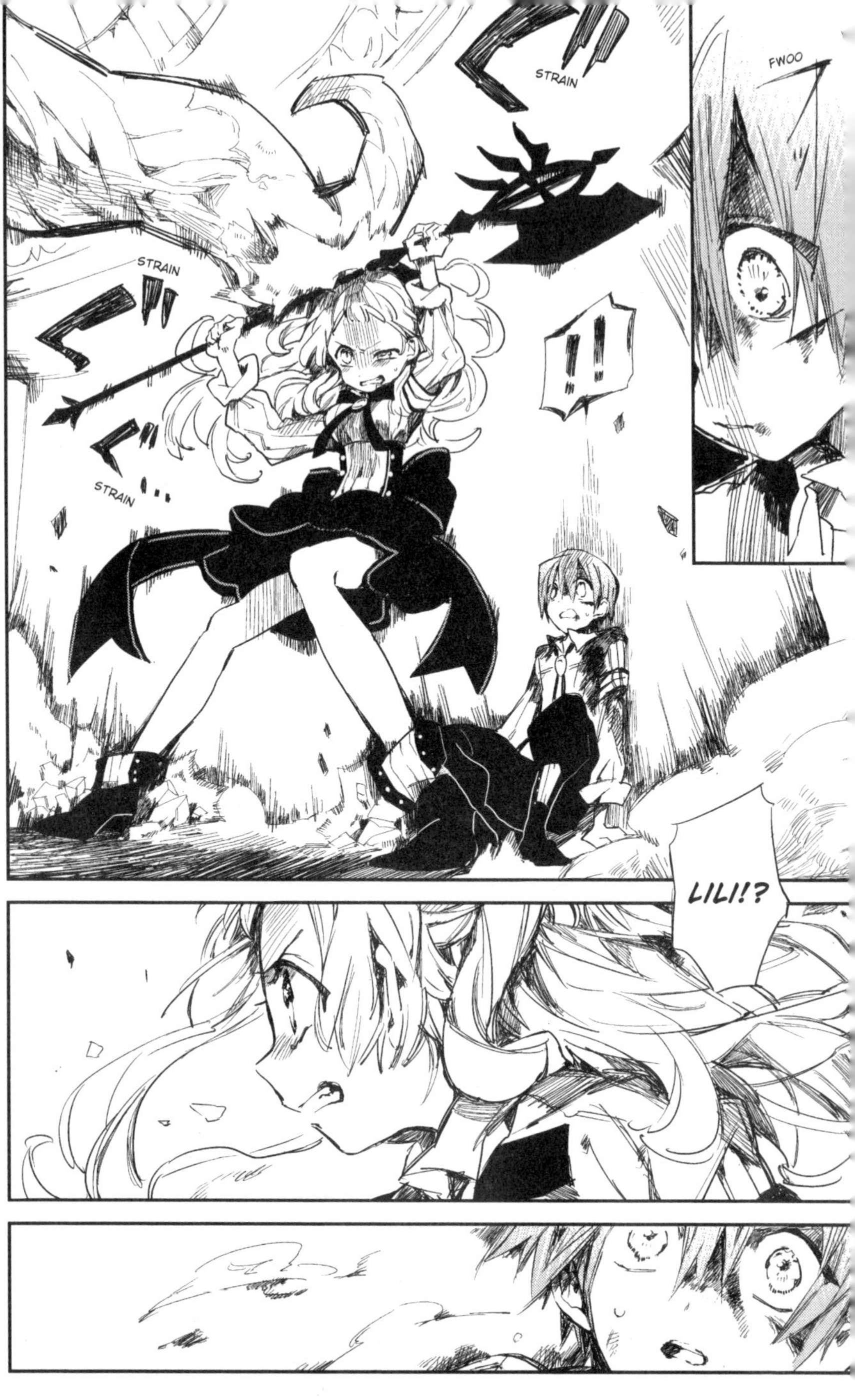
FWOO
STRAIN
!!
STRAIN
STRAIN
LILI!?

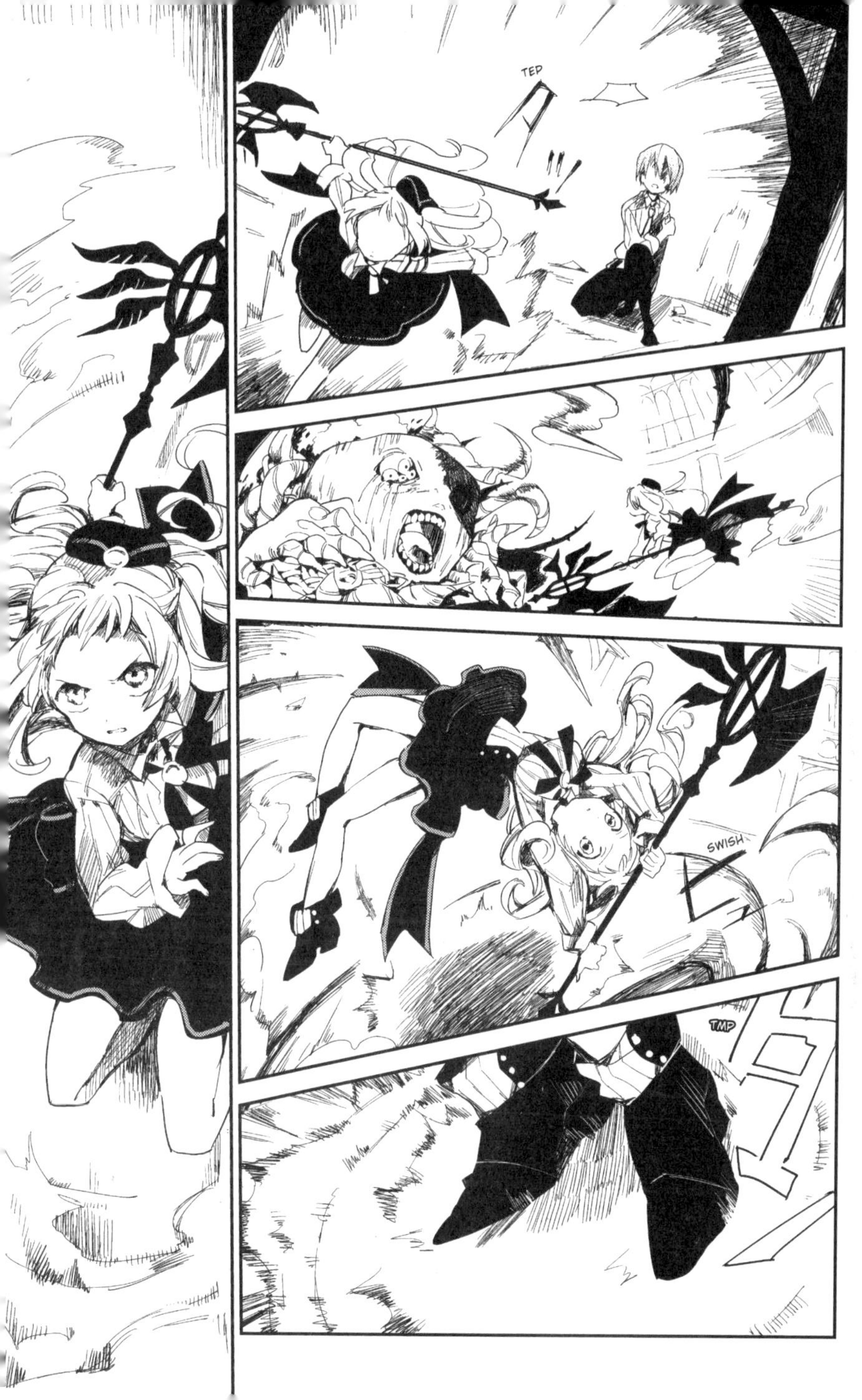
TEP
SWISH
TMP

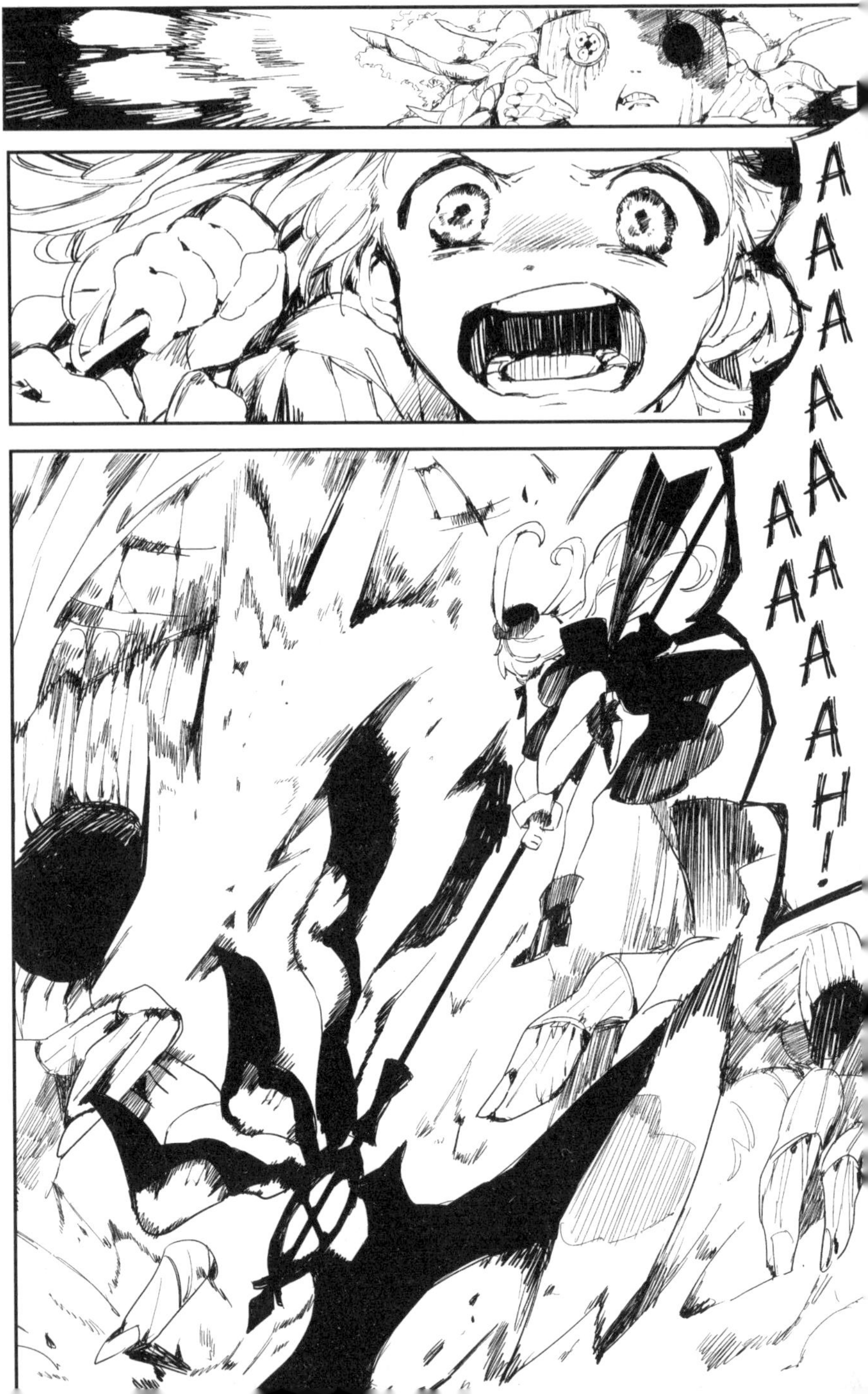
AAAAAAAAAAAAAAH!

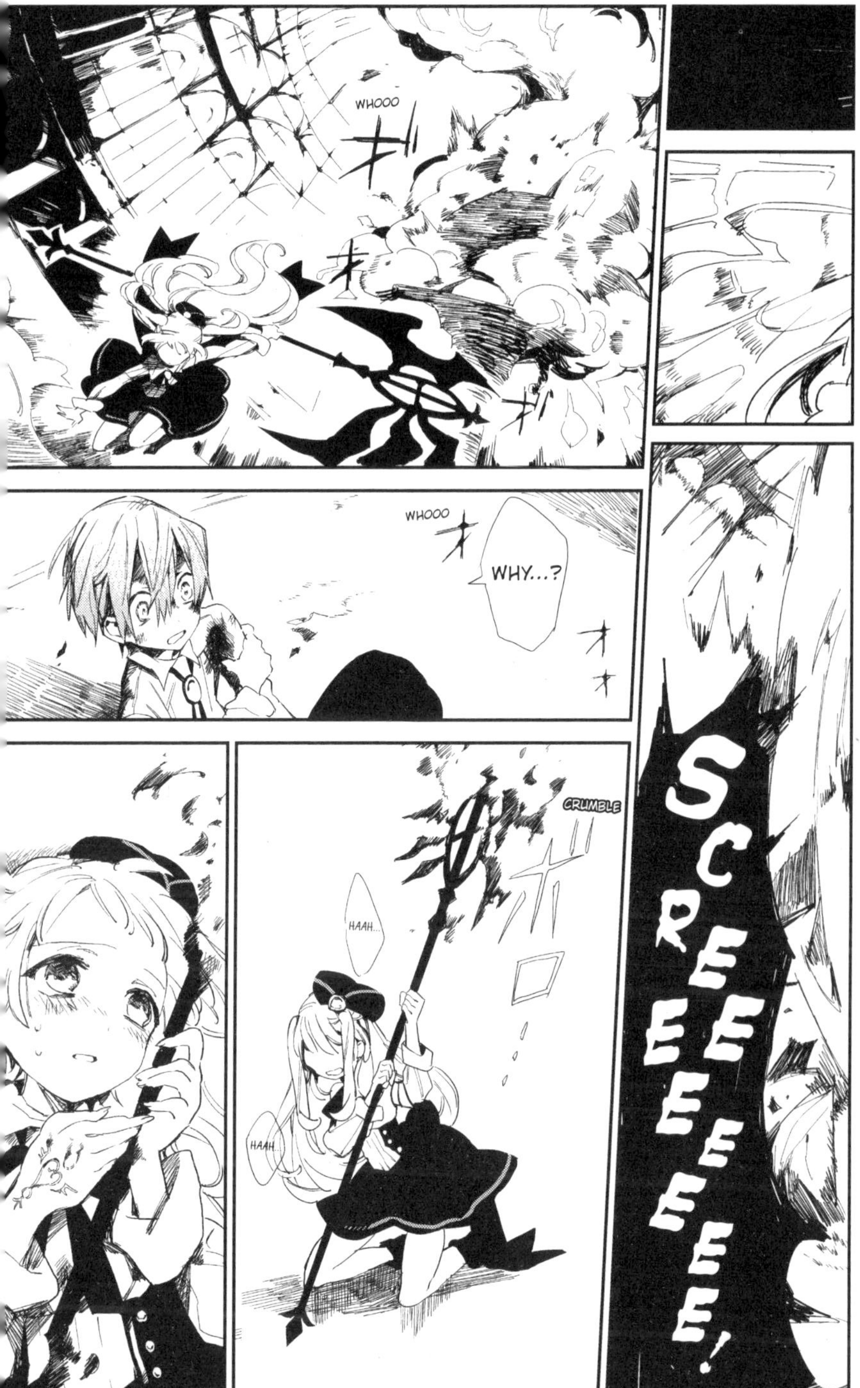
WHOOO
SCREEEEEEEEE!
WHOOO
WHY...?
CRUMBLE
HAAH...
HAAH...

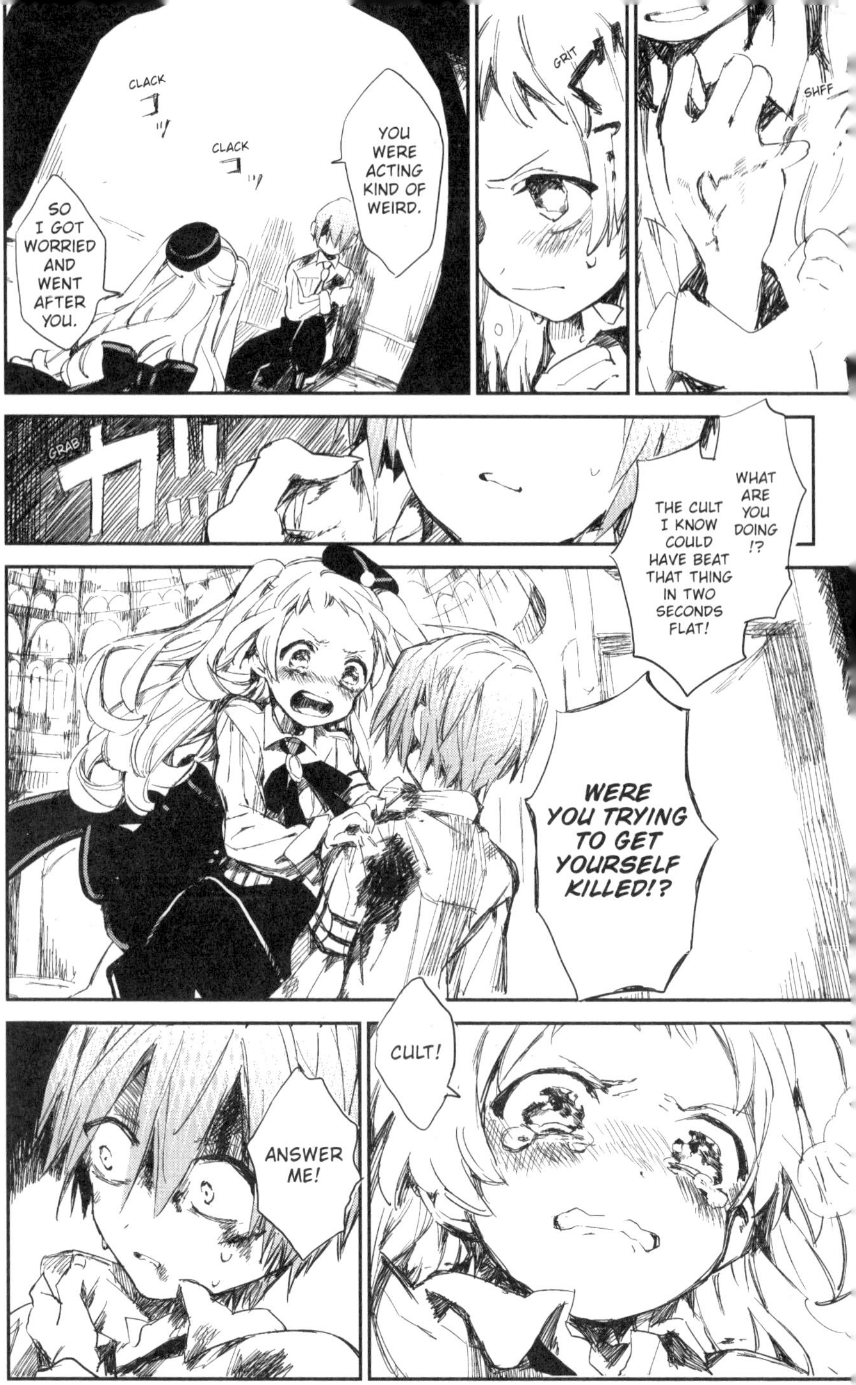
SHFF
GRIT
YOU WERE ACTING KIND OF WEIRD.
CLACK
CLACK
SO I GOT WORRIED AND WENT AFTER YOU.
GRAB
WHAT ARE YOU DOING!?
THE CULT I KNOW COULD HAVE BEAT THAT THING IN TWO SECONDS FLAT!
WERE YOU TRYING TO GET YOURSELF KILLED!?
CULT!
ANSWER ME!

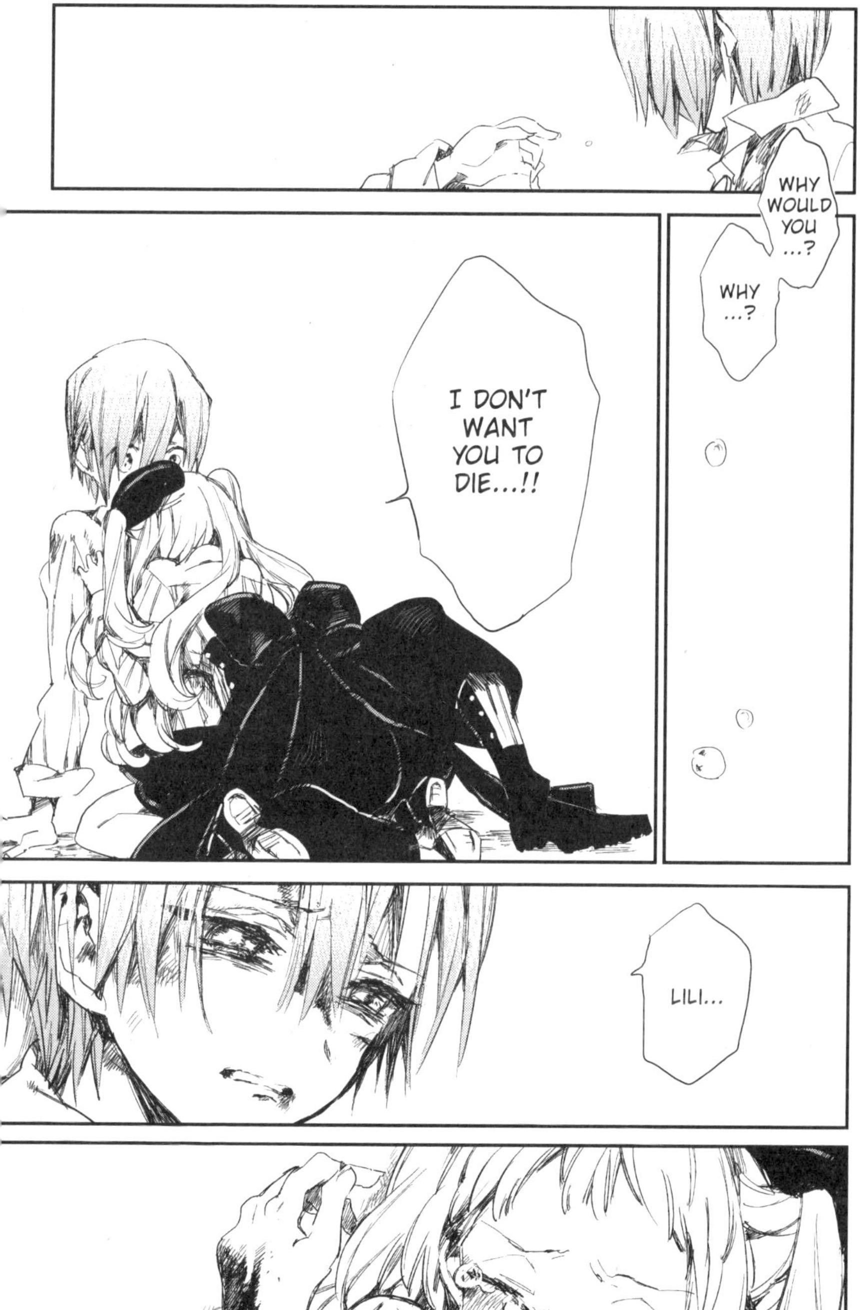
WHY WOULD YOU ...?
WHY ...?
I DON'T WANT YOU TO DIE...!!
LILI...

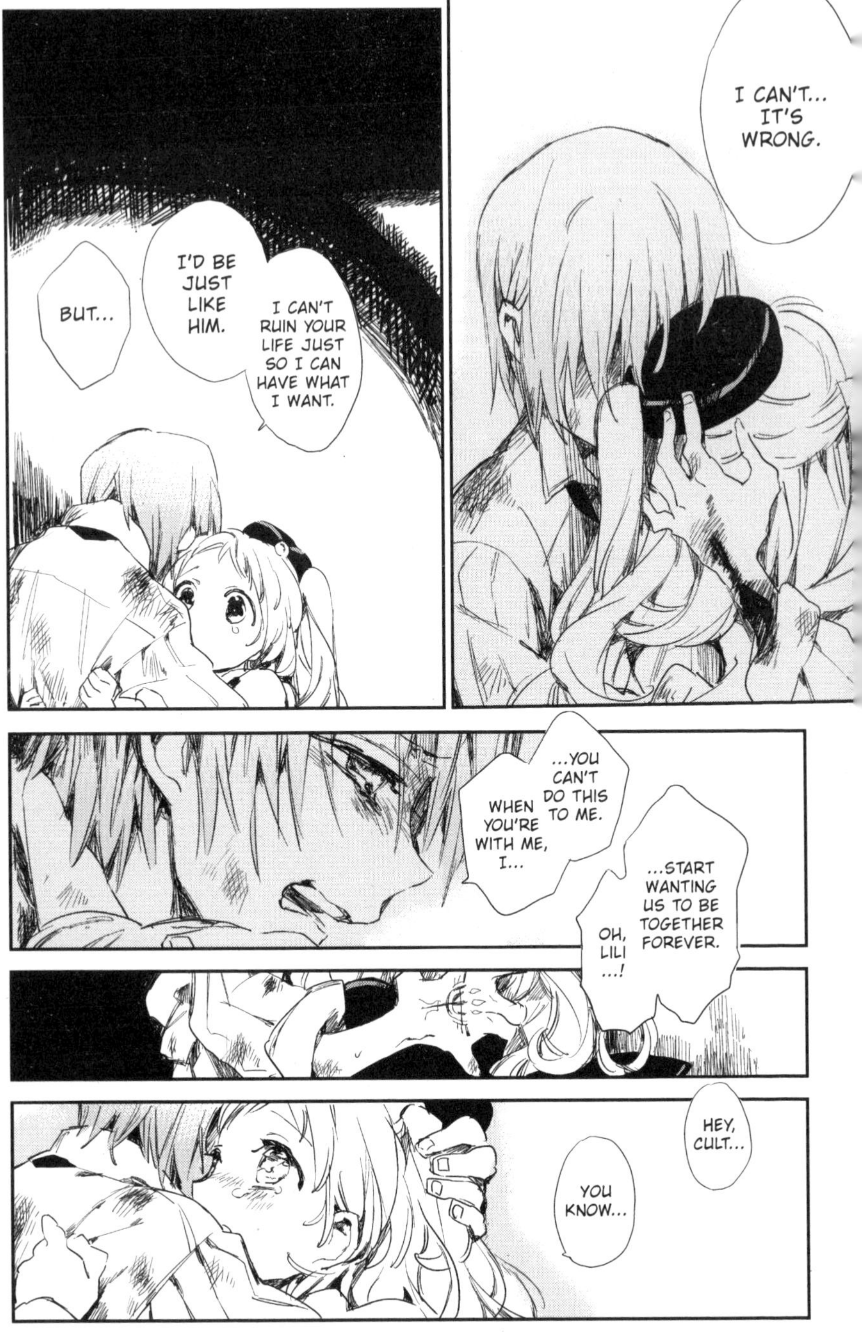
I CAN'T... IT'S WRONG.
I CAN'T RUIN YOUR LIFE JUST SO I CAN HAVE WHAT I WANT.
I'D BE JUST LIKE HIM.
BUT...
...YOU CAN'T DO THIS TO ME.
WHEN YOU'RE WITH ME, I...
...START WANTING US TO BE TOGETHER FOREVER.
OH, LILI ...!
HEY, CULT...
YOU KNOW...

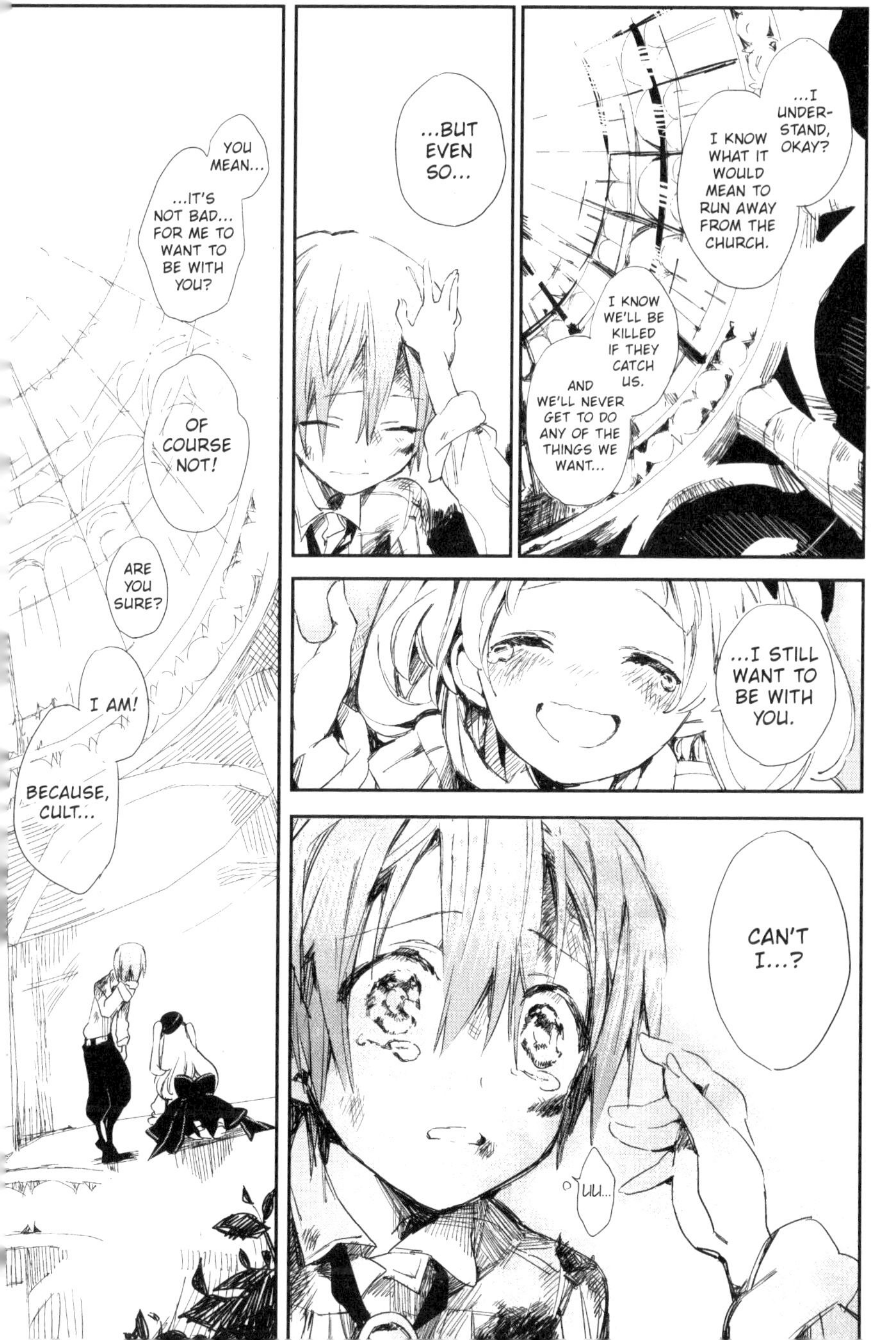
...I UNDER-STAND, OKAY?
I KNOW WHAT IT WOULD MEAN TO RUN AWAY FROM THE CHURCH.
I KNOW WE'LL BE KILLED IF THEY CATCH US.
AND WE'LL NEVER GET TO DO ANY OF THE THINGS WE WANT...
...BUT EVEN SO...
...I STILL WANT TO BE WITH YOU.
CAN'T I...?
UU...
YOU MEAN...
...IT'S NOT BAD... FOR ME TO WANT TO BE WITH YOU?
OF COURSE NOT!
ARE YOU SURE?
I AM!
BECAUSE, CULT...

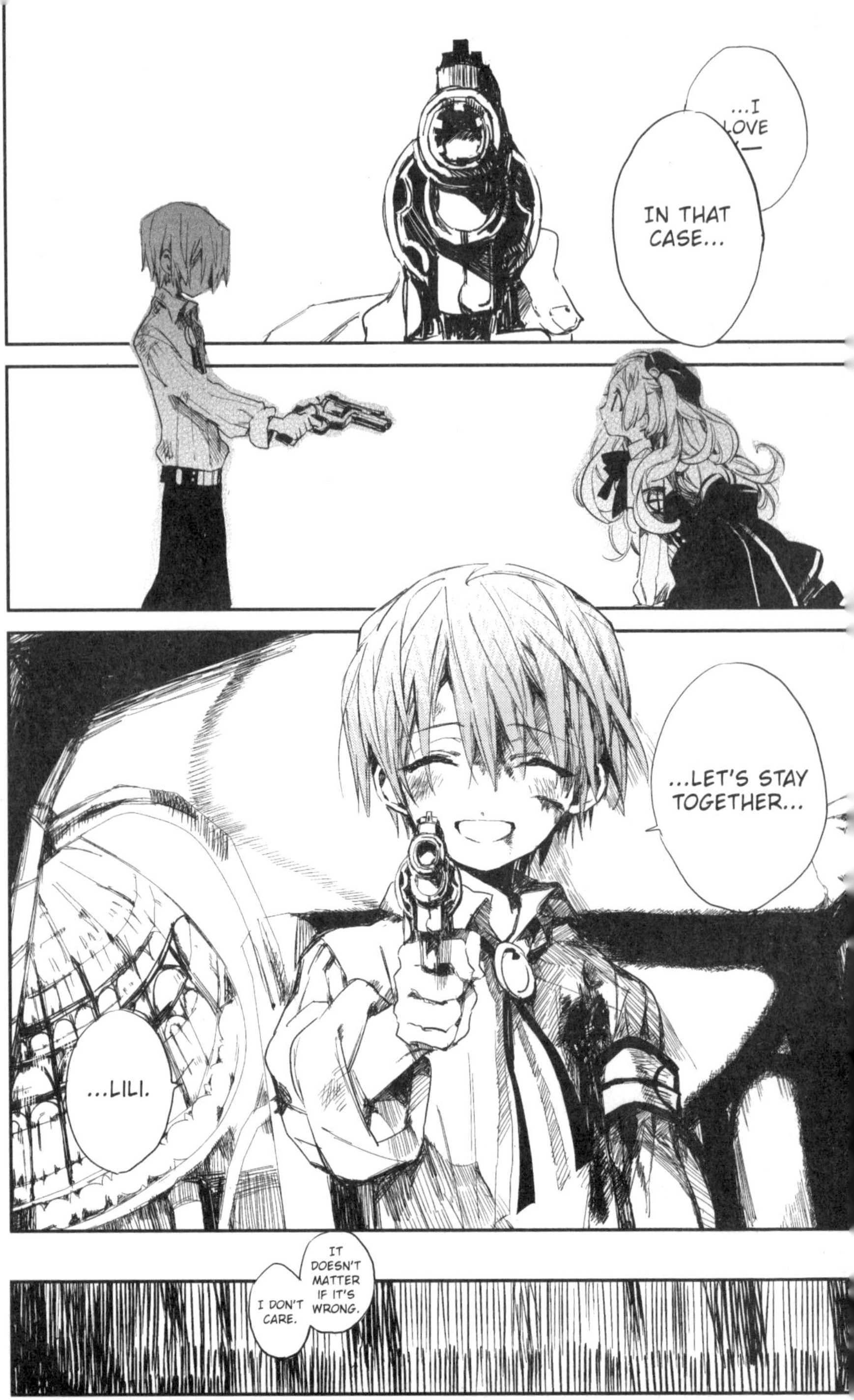
...I LOVE —
IN THAT CASE...
...LET'S STAY TOGETHER...
...LILI.
IT DOESN'T MATTER IF IT'S WRONG.
I DON'T CARE.

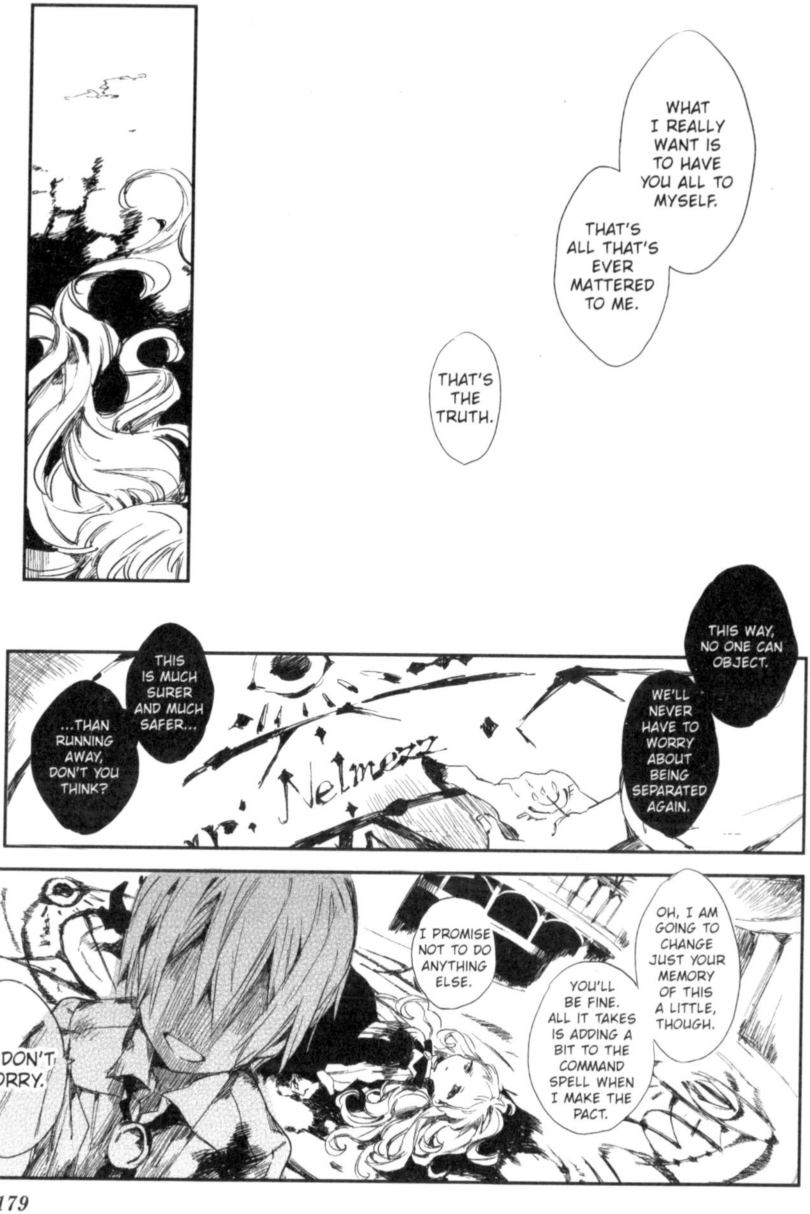
WHAT I REALLY WANT IS TO HAVE YOU ALL TO MYSELF.
THAT'S ALL THAT'S EVER MATTERED TO ME.
THAT'S THE TRUTH.
THIS WAY, NO ONE CAN OBJECT.
WE'LL NEVER HAVE TO WORRY ABOUT BEING SEPARATED AGAIN.
THIS IS MUCH SURER AND MUCH SAFER...
...THAN RUNNING AWAY, DON'T YOU THINK?
OH, I AM GOING TO CHANGE JUST YOUR MEMORY OF THIS A LITTLE, THOUGH.
YOU'LL BE FINE. ALL IT TAKES IS ADDING A BIT TO THE COMMAND SPELL WHEN I MAKE THE PACT.
I PROMISE NOT TO DO ANYTHING ELSE.
SO DON'T WORRY.

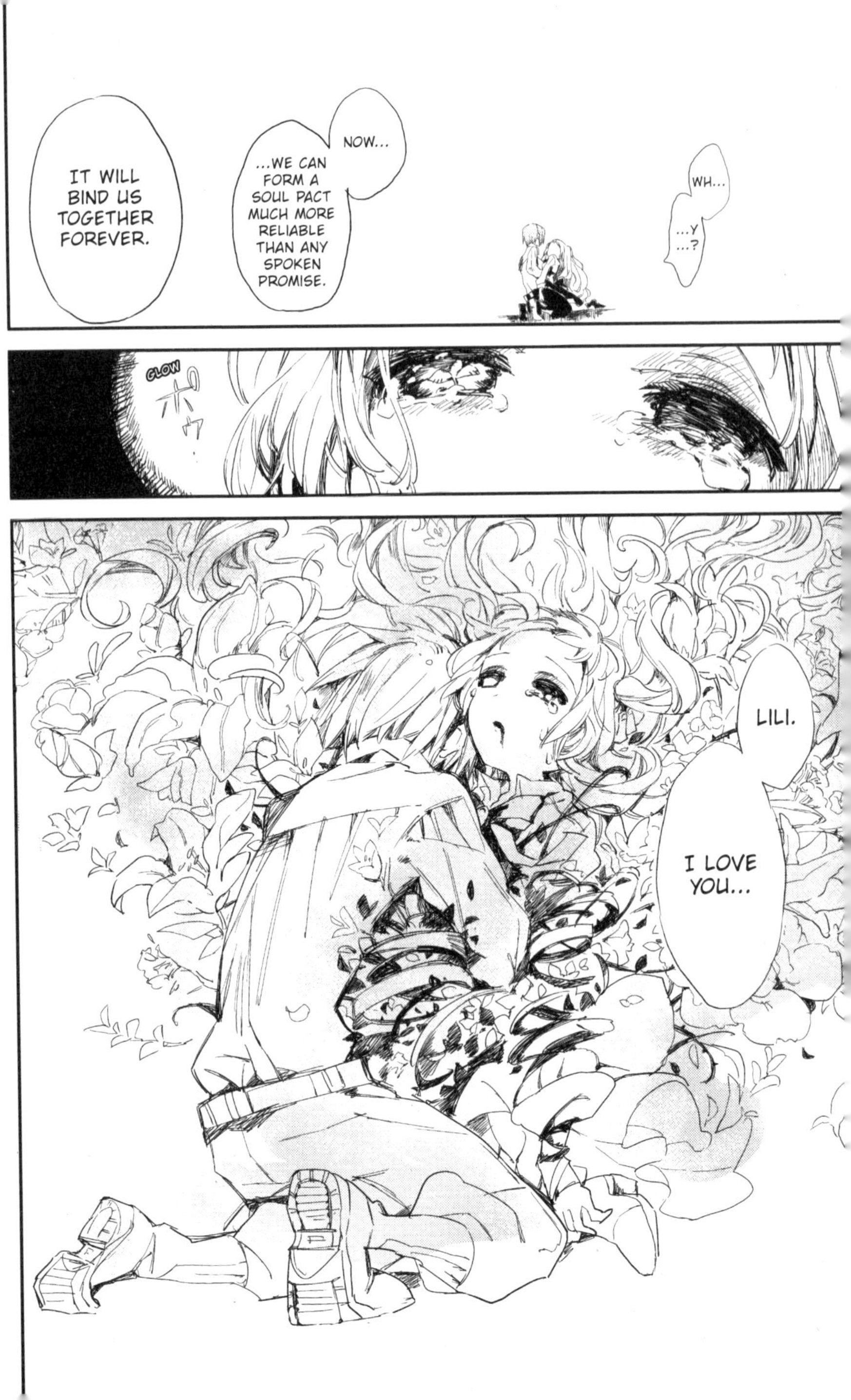
WH...
...Y
...?
NOW...
...WE CAN FORM A SOUL PACT MUCH MORE RELIABLE THAN ANY SPOKEN PROMISE.
IT WILL BIND US TOGETHER FOREVER.
GLOW
LILI.
I LOVE YOU...

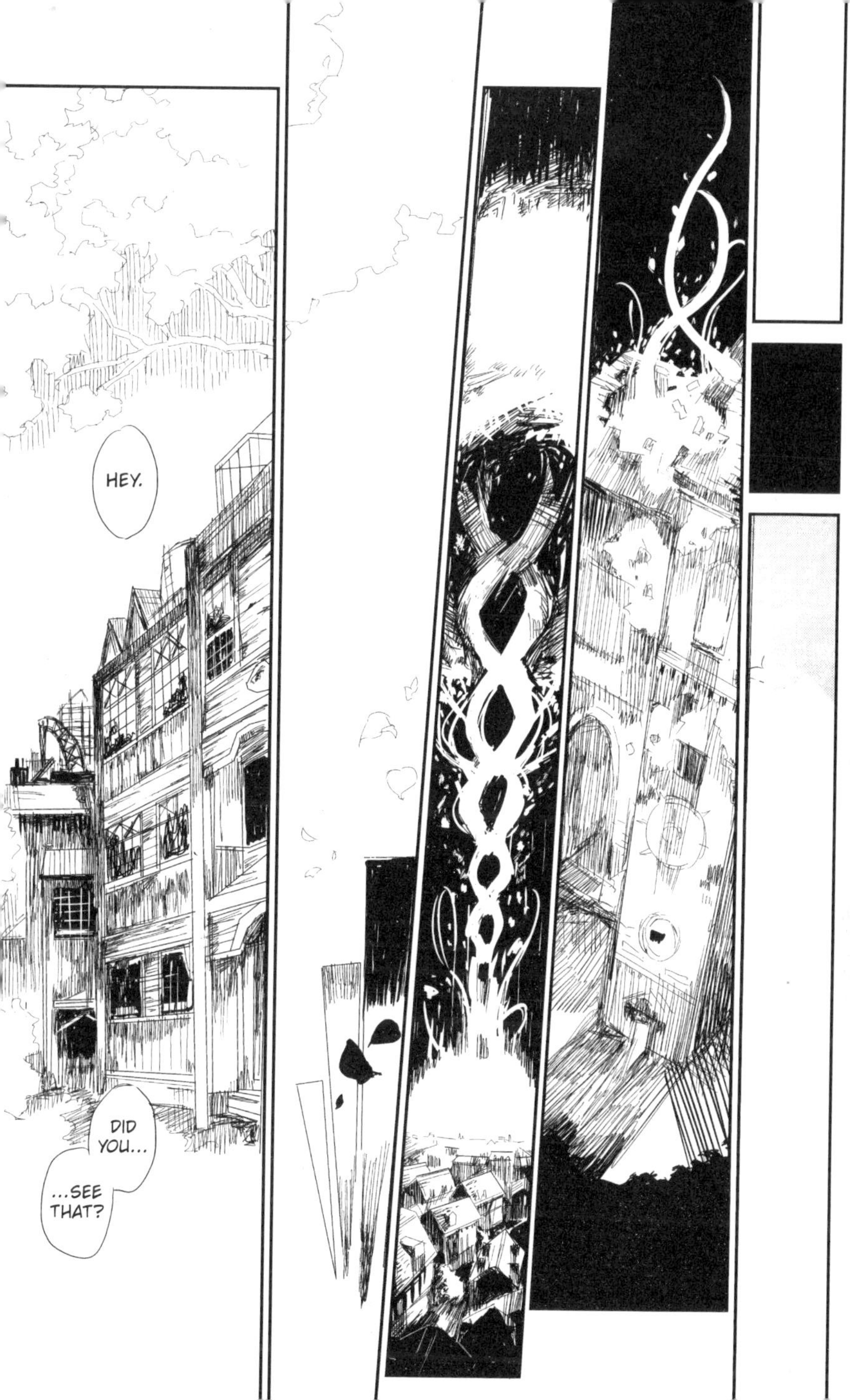
HEY.
DID YOU...
...SEE THAT?

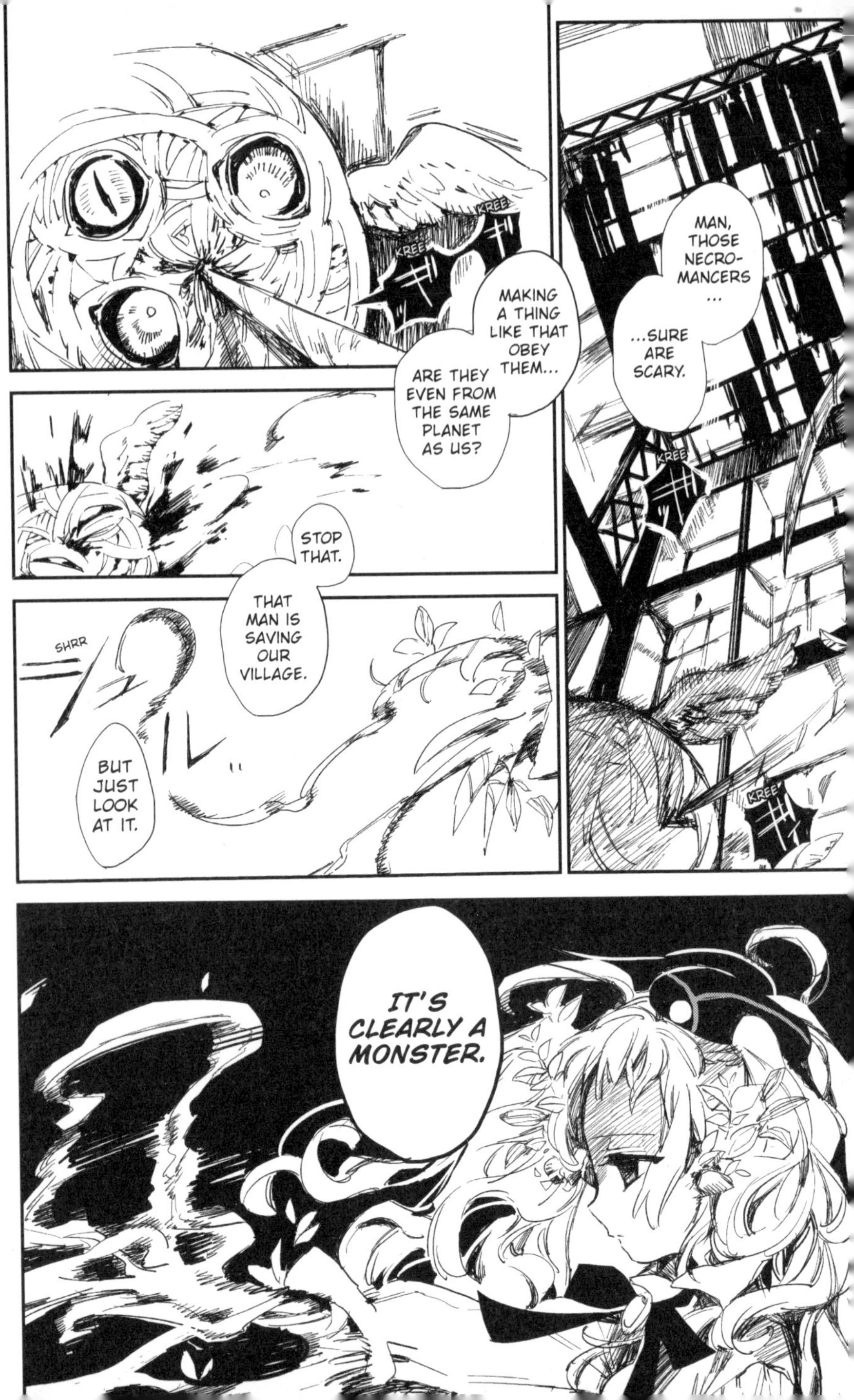
MAN, THOSE NECRO-MANCERS...
...SURE ARE SCARY.
KREE
KREE
KREE
KREE
MAKING A THING LIKE THAT OBEY THEM...
ARE THEY EVEN FROM THE SAME PLANET AS US?
STOP THAT.
THAT MAN IS SAVING OUR VILLAGE.
SHRR
BUT JUST LOOK AT IT.
IT'S CLEARLY A MONSTER.

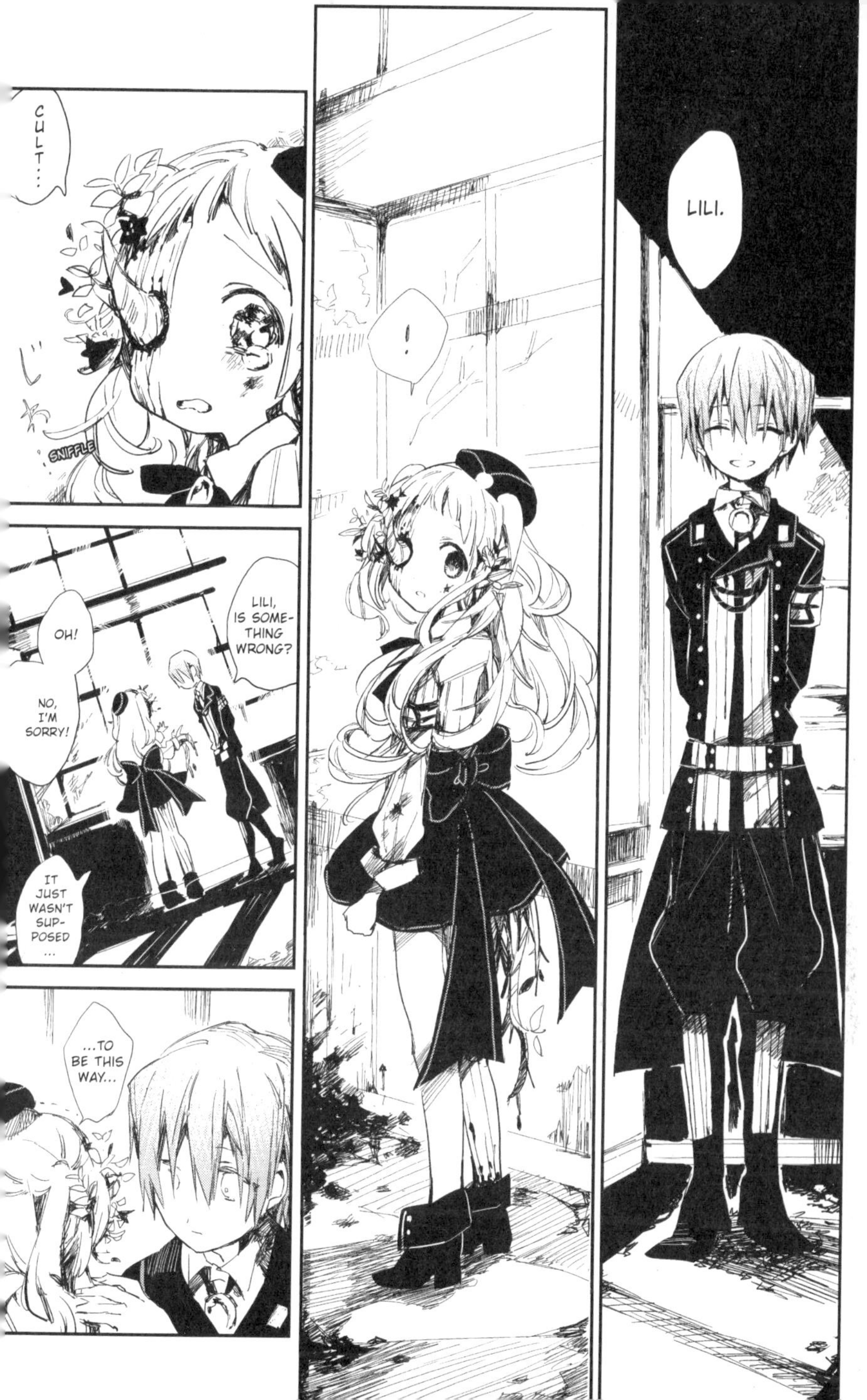
LILI.
!
CULT...
SNIFFLE
LILI, IS SOMETHING WRONG?
OH!
NO, I'M SORRY!
IT JUST WASN'T SUPPOSED...
...TO BE THIS WAY...

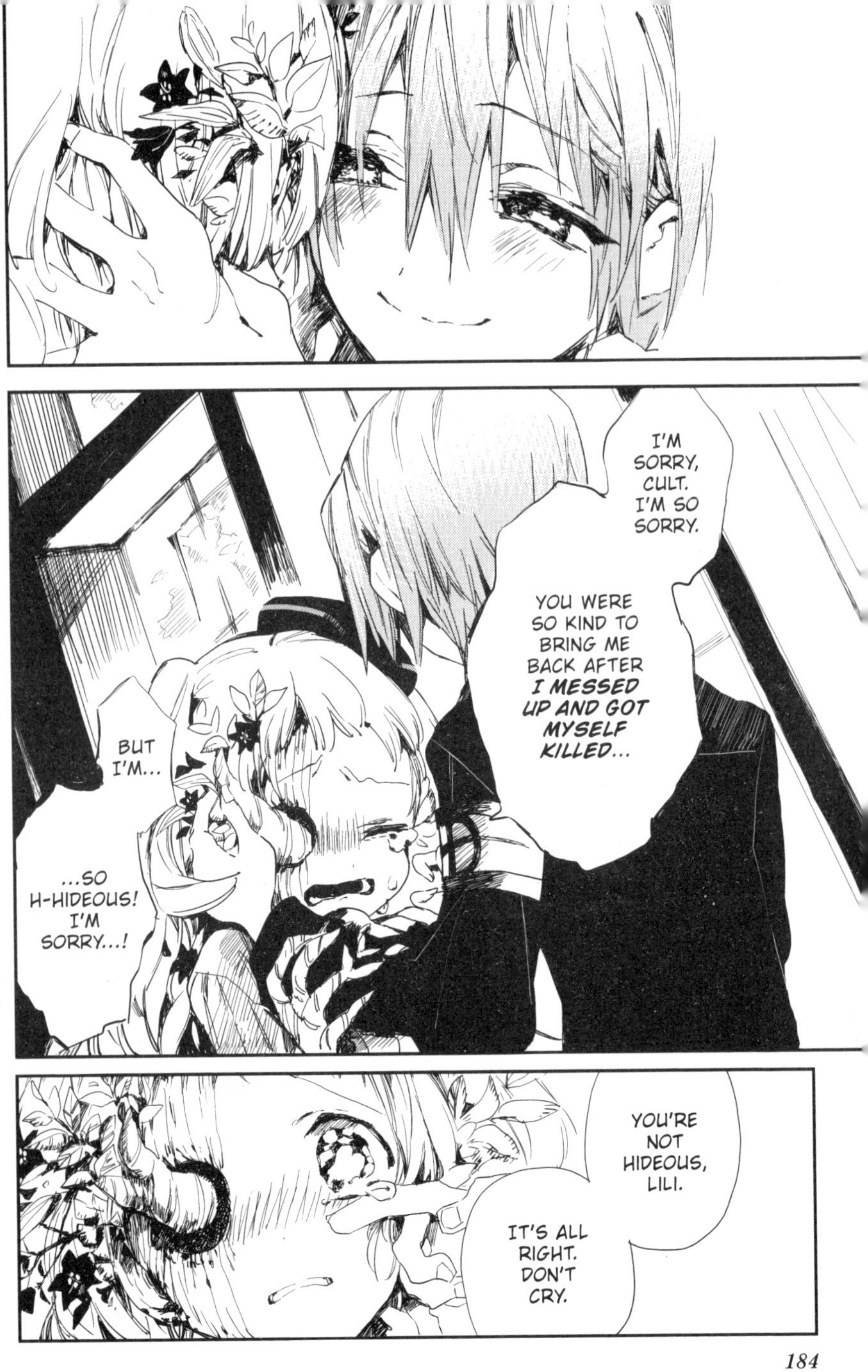
I'M SORRY, CULT. I'M SO SORRY.
YOU WERE SO KIND TO BRING ME BACK AFTER *I MESSED UP AND GOT MYSELF KILLED...*
BUT I'M...
...SO H-HIDEOUS! I'M SORRY...!
YOU'RE NOT HIDEOUS, LILI.
IT'S ALL RIGHT. DON'T CRY.

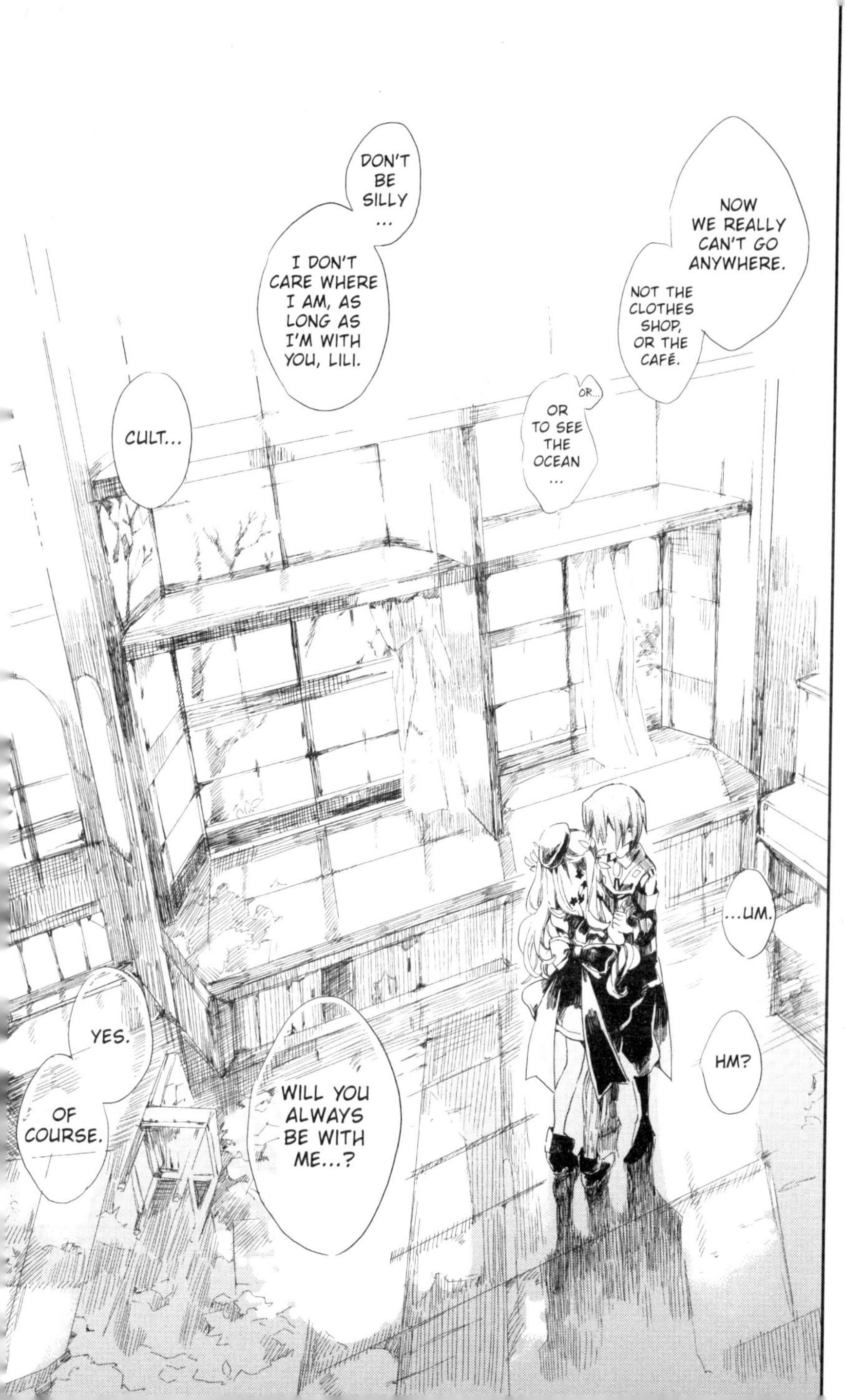
NOW WE REALLY CAN'T GO ANYWHERE.
NOT THE CLOTHES SHOP, OR THE CAFÉ.
OR...
OR TO SEE THE OCEAN...
DON'T BE SILLY...
I DON'T CARE WHERE I AM, AS LONG AS I'M WITH YOU, LILI.
CULT...
...UM.
HM?
WILL YOU ALWAYS BE WITH ME...?
YES.
OF COURSE.

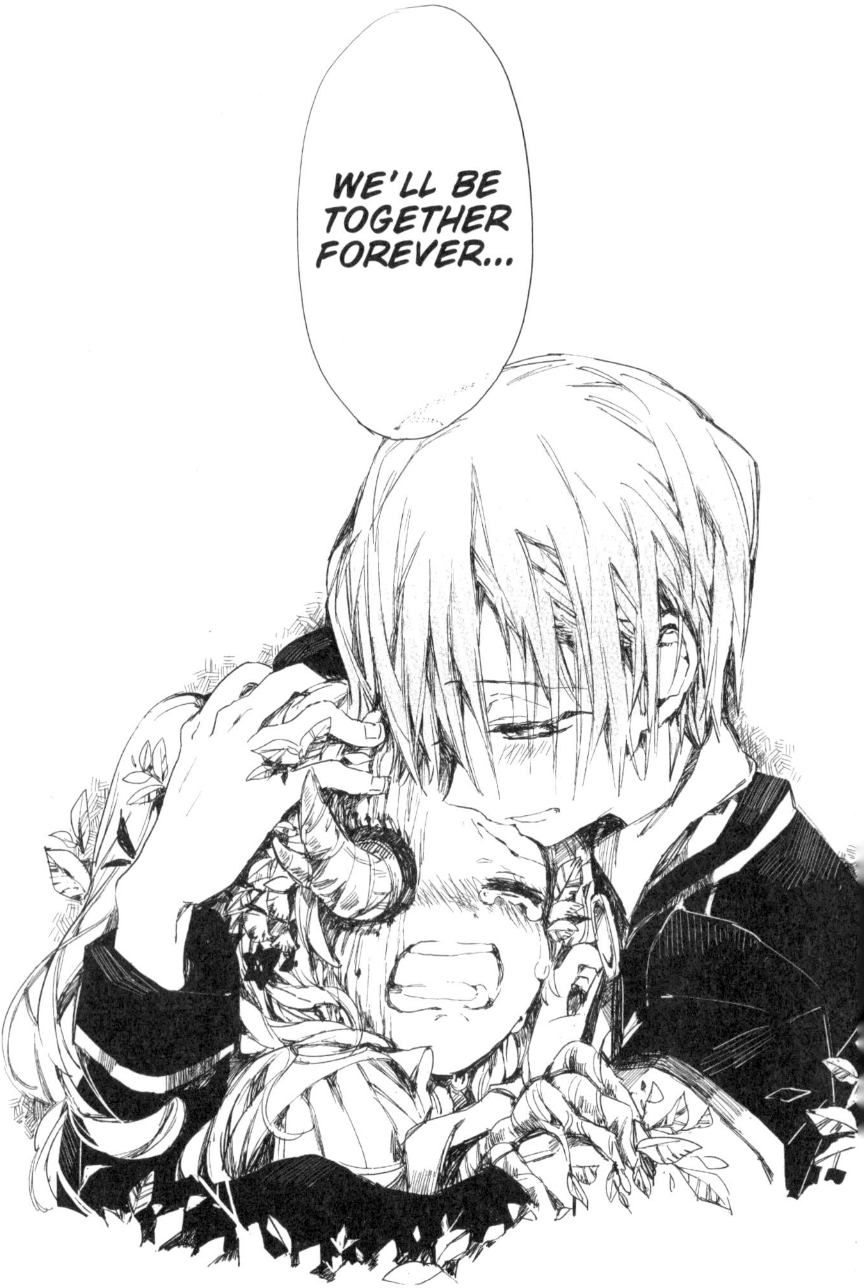
WE'LL BE TOGETHER FOREVER...

TOILET-BOUND HANAKO-KUN VOLUME 0 END

TRANSLATION NOTES

Common Honorifics
no honorific: Indicates familiarity or closeness; if used without permission or reason, addressing someone in this manner would constitute an insult.
-san: The Japanese equivalent of Mr./Mrs./Miss. If a situation calls for politeness, this is the fail-safe honorific.
-sama: Conveys great respect; may also indicate that the social status of the speaker is lower than that of the addressee.
-kun: Used most often when referring to boys, this indicates affection or familiarity. Occasionally used by older men among their peers, but it may also be used by anyone referring to a person of lower standing.
-chan: An affectionate honorific indicating familiarity used mostly in reference to girls; also used in reference to cute persons or animals of either gender.
-senpai: A suffix used to address upperclassmen or more experienced coworkers.
-sensei: A respectful term for teachers, artists, or high-level professionals.

Page 7
Throughout the main *Toilet-bound Hanako-kun* series, the term *kaii* (translated as "supernaturals") is used to refer to the vast majority of the supernatural beings that appear in it, from ghosts and spirits to more fantastical creatures. However, in this stand-alone version of *Hanako-kun*, a much wider variety of terms are used to refer to different categories of entities in the original Japanese, which have been translated here and on other pages as their English equivalents to reflect this difference.

Page 32
The Heian era in Japanese history lasted from 794 to 1185, beginning when the imperial capital was moved to Heian-kyo (modern Kyoto) and ending with the establishment of the Kamakura shogunate.

Page 33
Hanako-kun's line about not being a bad ghost is a reference to the *Dragon Quest* games, where the phrase "I'm not a bad slime" has been a running joke since the first installment.

Page 65
The kanji shown on this page (and later on Hanako-kun's arm), meaning "correct" or "just," is used for drawing tally marks in Japanese culture. The actual meaning of the kanji is largely irrelevant: it's just the only one you can write with exactly five horizontal and vertical lines, which allows it to function as a visually clear way to group tally marks, similar to the "four vertical lines with a diagonal line through them" method commonly used in the West. If you count the lines on Hanako-kun's arm on page 102, you can see that he has broken seven total rules up to this point.

Page 76
Youkai is a sort of catchall term for Japanese spirits, many of whom have more specific names and ascribed behaviors.

Page 103
Sunekosuri are indeed a type of *youkai* believed to be doglike in form that love to nuzzle peoples' legs and trip them up.

LILIA AND CULT READ *HANAKO-KUN*

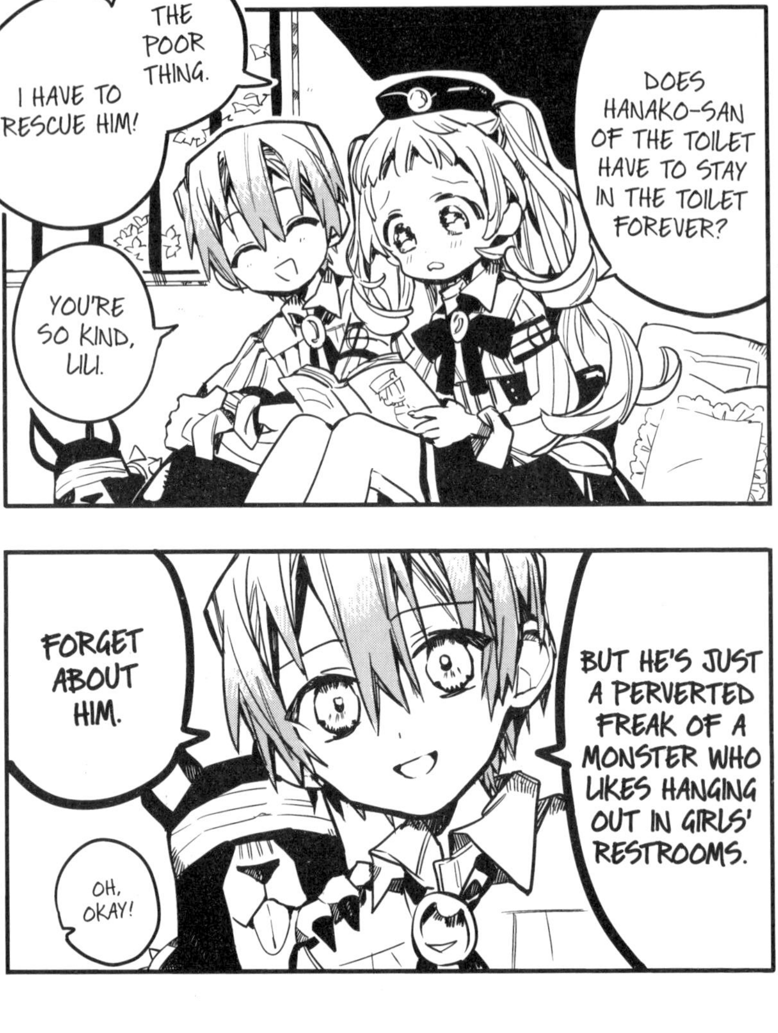
DOES HANAKO-SAN OF THE TOILET HAVE TO STAY IN THE TOILET FOREVER?
THE POOR THING.
I HAVE TO RESCUE HIM!
YOU'RE SO KIND, LILI.
BUT HE'S JUST A PERVERTED FREAK OF A MONSTER WHO LIKES HANGING OUT IN GIRLS' RESTROOMS.
FORGET ABOUT HIM.
OH, OKAY!

NENE AND HANAKO-KUN READ *LIVING DEAD*

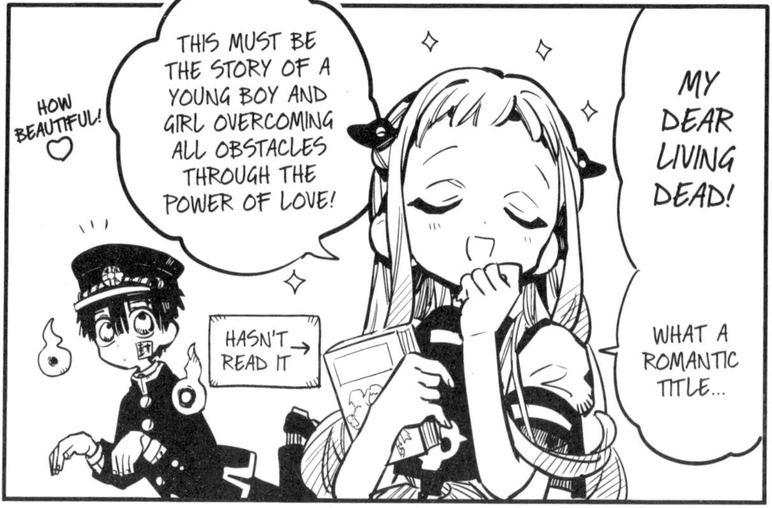
MY DEAR LIVING DEAD!
WHAT A ROMANTIC TITLE...
THIS MUST BE THE STORY OF A YOUNG BOY AND GIRL OVERCOMING ALL OBSTACLES THROUGH THE POWER OF LOVE!
HOW BEAUTIFUL! ♡
HASN'T READ IT →

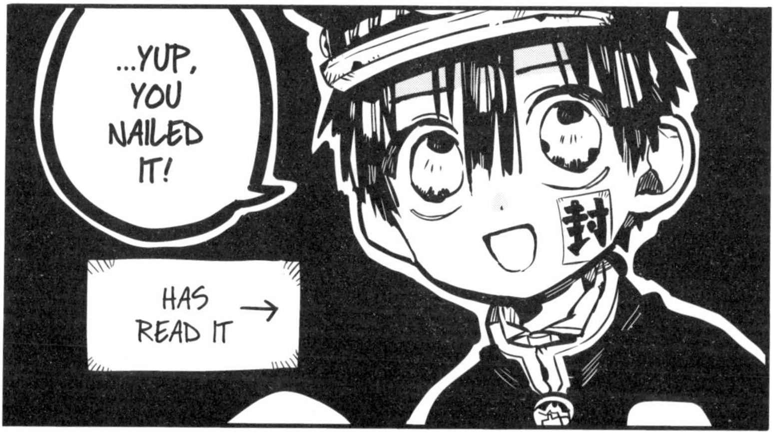
...YUP, YOU NAILED IT!
HAS READ IT →

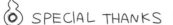

SPECIAL THANKS

YUUKI OMAYU-TAN WAKO-CHAN

MY EDITORS
IMANITY, MOCHIZUKI-SAN

COVER DESIGN
NAKAMURA-SAMA

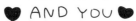

AND YOU

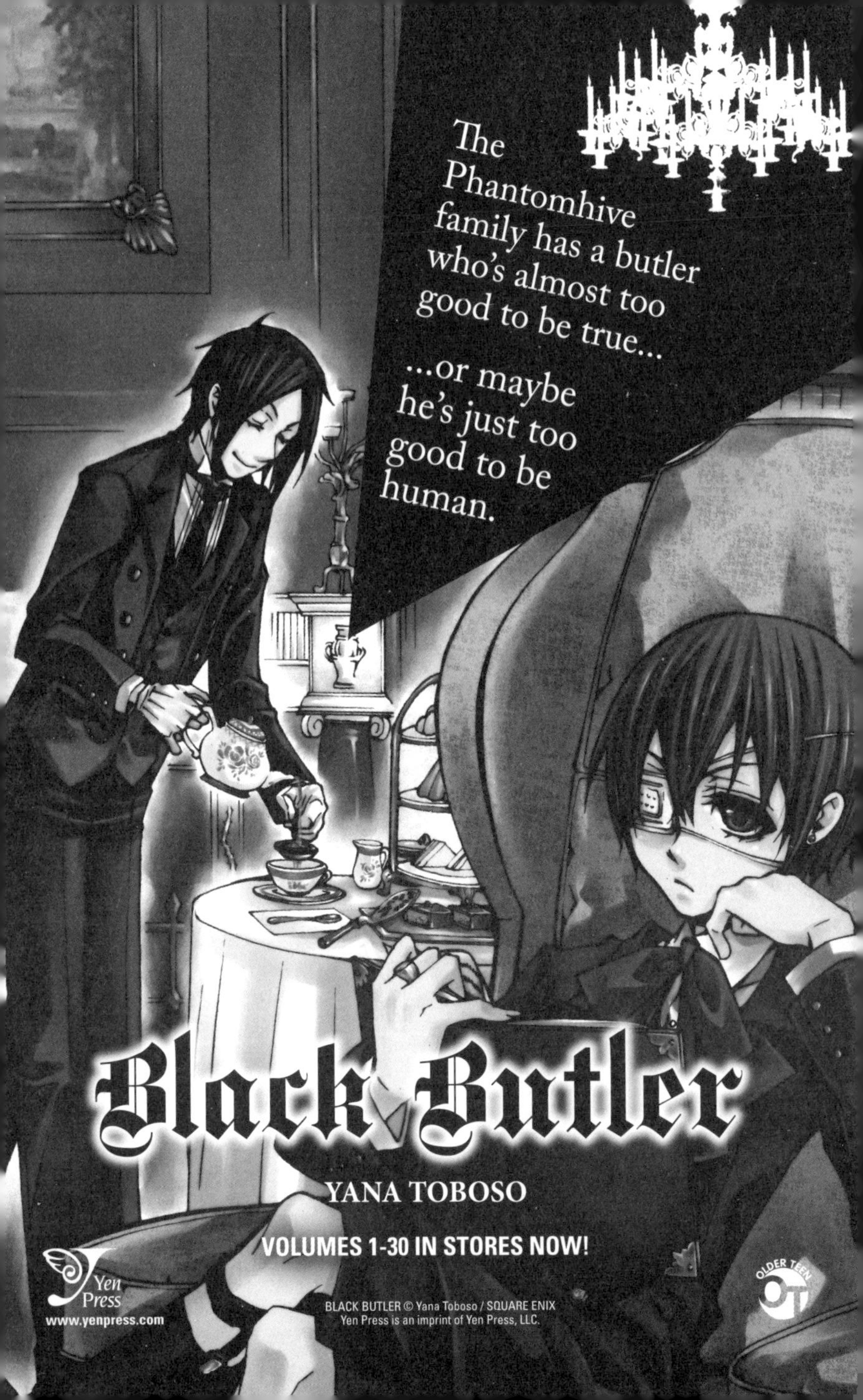
The Phantomhive family has a butler who's almost too good to be true...
...or maybe he's just too good to be human.
Black Butler
YANA TOBOSO
VOLUMES 1-30 IN STORES NOW!
Yen Press
www.yenpress.com
BLACK BUTLER © Yana Toboso / SQUARE ENIX
Yen Press is an imprint of Yen Press, LLC.
OLDER TEEN
OT

It's hard work taking it slow...

After living a painful life as an office worker, Azusa ended her short life by dying from overwork. So when she finds herself reincarnated as an undying, unaging witch in a new world, she vows to spend her days stress-free and as pleasantly as possible. She ekes out a living by hunting down the easiest targets—the slimes! But after centuries of doing this simple job, she's ended up with insane powers... how will she maintain her low-key life now?!

IN STORES NOW!

Light Novel Volumes 1–11

SLIME TAOSHITE SANBYAKUNEN,
SHIRANAIUCHINI LEVEL MAX
NI NATTEMASHITA
© 2017 Kisetsu Morita
© 2017 Benio / SB Creative Corp.

Manga Volumes 1–7

SLIME TAOSHITE SANBYAKUNEN,
SHIRANAIUCHINI LEVEL MAX
NI NATTEMASHITA
©Kisetsu Morita/SB Creative Corp.
Original Character Designs:
©Benio/SB Creative Corp.
©2018 Yusuke Shiba
/SQUARE ENIX CO., LTD.

For more information, visit www.yenpress.com

Toilet-bound Hanako-Kun 0

AidaIro

Translation: Alethea Nibley and Athena Nibley
Lettering: Phil Christie

JIBAKU SHONEN HANAKO-KUN Volume 0 ©2019 Aidalro / SQUARE ENIX CO., LTD.
First published in Japan in 2018 by SQUARE ENIX CO., LTD. English translation rights arranged with SQUARE ENIX CO., LTD. and Yen Press, LLC through Tuttle-Mori Agency, Inc.

English translation © 2022 by SQUARE ENIX CO., LTD.

Yen Press
150 West 30th Street, 19th Floor
New York, NY 10001

Visit us at yenpress.com • facebook.com/yenpress • twitter.com/yenpress • yenpress.tumblr.com • instagram.com/yenpress

First Yen Press Edition: February 2022

Yen Press is an imprint of Yen Press, LLC.
The Yen Press name and logo are trademarks of Yen Press, LLC.

The publisher is not responsible for websites (or their content) that are not owned by the publisher.

Library of Congress Control Number: 2019953610

ISBNs: 978-1-9753-2481-0 (paperback)
978-1-9753-2482-7 (ebook)

10 9 8 7 6 5 4 3 2 1

TPA

Printed in South Korea